T0330275

·

EUROPEAN WHITE-COLLAR CRIME

Exploring the Nature of European Realities

Edited by
Nicholas Lord, Éva Inzelt, Wim Huisman
and Rita Faria

BRISTOL
UNIVERSITY
PRESS

First published in Great Britain in 2021 by

Bristol University Press
1-9 Old Park Hill
Bristol
BS2 8BB
UK
t: +44 (0)117 954 5940
www.bristoluniversitypress.co.uk

British Library Cataloguing in Publication Data
A catalogue record for this book is available from the British Library

ISBN 978-1-5292-1232-7 hardcover
ISBN 978-1-5292-1234-1 ePub
ISBN 978-1-5292-1235-8 ePdf

Cover design: blu inc, Bristol
Front cover: Stocksy/Juan Moyano
Printed and bound in Great Britain by CPI Group (UK) Ltd,
Croydon, CR0 4YY
Bristol University Press uses environmentally responsible
print partners

Contents

List of Tables   vi

Notes on Contributors   vii

1   Introduction: In Pursuit of a European Dialogue on   1
White-Collar and Corporate Crimes
Nicholas Lord, Éva Inzelt, Wim Huisman and Rita Faria

PART I: Researching White-Collar and Corporate Crimes in Europe

2   Using Grid-Group Cultural Theory to Assess   17
Approaches to the Prevention of Corporate and
Occupational Crime: The EU as a Natural Experiment
Jeroen Maesschalck

3   How to Prioritize White-Collar Crime Research in the   39
European Union in Relation to Internal and External
Security
Sunčana Roksandić

4   Corruption and Comparative Analyses across   55
Europe: Developing New Research Traditions
Nicholas Lord, Karin van Wingerde and Michael Levi

PART II: Financial Crimes and Illicit Financial Flows

5   Identifying 'Europeanness' in European White-Collar   75
Crime: The Case Study of Criminal Responses to
'Market Abuse'
Sarah Wilson

6   Anti-Money Laundering and the Legal Profession in   89
Europe: Between Global and Local
Katie Benson

7   Responding to Money Laundering across Europe: What   103
We Know and What We Risk
Karin van Wingerde and Anna Merz

PART III: White-Collar Crime: European Case Studies

8   Food Production Harms in the European Context: 125
The EU as an Enabler or a Solution?
Ekaterina Gladkova

9   Understanding the Dynamics of White-Collar   143
Criminality in Ukraine
Anna Markovska and Iryna Soldatenko

10   Labour Exploitation and Posted Workers in the   163
European Construction Industry
Jon Davies

11   Struggles in Cooperation: Public–Private Relations in   175
the Investigation of Internal Financial Crime in the
Netherlands
Clarissa Meerts

12   Cartel Cases: From State Negligence to Direct Political   187
Interest in Hungary
Éva Inzelt and Tamás Bezsenyi

PART IV: Responding to White-Collar Crimes in Europe

13   Silencing Those Who Speak Up against Corporate   207
Power: Strategic Lawsuits against Public Participation
(SLAPPs) in Europe
Judith van Erp and Tess van der Linden

14   Same Difference? Reflections on the Comparative   221
Method in White-Collar Crime Research in Ireland
and the United States
Joe McGrath and Deirdre Healy

15   Settling with Corporations in Europe: A Sign of Legal   237
Convergence?
Liz Campbell

PART V: Observations from Outside of Europe

16   Observations on European White-Collar Crime   255
Scholarship from the United States
Melissa Rorie

17   What Is 'European' about White-Collar Crime in   271
Europe? Perspectives from the Global South
Diego Zysman-Quirós

18   Learning (Multiple) Lessons from Europe: 285
      Criminological Scholarship on White-Collar Crime
      Fiona Haines

Index   303

List of Tables

2.1	Four approaches to corporate and occupational crime prevention	20
4.1	Search criteria of the literature review	56
7.1	Overview of AML cases against banks across Europe	106
7.2	Sanctions levied on banks by European authorities, 2015–2020	112
14.1	Definitions of white-collar crime	225
16.1	Focus of articles from European and North American white-collar crime scholars	259

Notes on Contributors

Katie Benson is Lecturer in Criminology at Lancaster University. Her primary research focus is the role of legal (and other regulated) professionals in the facilitation of money laundering, and the regulatory and criminal justice responses to this. Her wider research interests cut across the fields of (anti-)money laundering and organized, white-collar and financial crimes. Recent publications include *Lawyers and the Proceeds of Crime: The Facilitation of Money Laundering and Its Control* (Routledge, 2020) and *Assets, Crimes and the State: Innovation in 21st Century Legal Responses* (Routledge, 2020).

Tamás Bezsenyi is a PhD candidate in the Department of Criminology at Eötvös Loránd University, researching the rise and fall of organized criminal groups that evolved as a result of regime change. He is also a research assistant on a two-year study funded by Hungary's National Office for Research, Development and Innovation (NFKIH) that seeks to understand the characteristics of corporate crime, based on theoretical considerations and empirical research. He is currently teaching in the Department of Criminal Sciences of Széchenyi University in Győr.

Liz Campbell is the inaugural Francine V. McNiff Chair in Criminal Jurisprudence at Monash University. Her research focuses on how the law responds to profit-driven crime, both by otherwise legitimate corporate entities as well as networks of organized crime. Another strand of her research looks at the use of biometrics in investigation and prosecution, and she is a member of the UK Home Office Biometrics and Forensics Ethics Group. She was a Fulbright Scholar in 2011, and her research has been funded by Research Councils UK, the Law Foundation of New Zealand, *The Modern Law Review* and the Carnegie Trust.

Jon Davies is Research Fellow at Tel Aviv University. His research interests include corporate crime, labour exploitation, food fraud and regulation. He is currently working on a series of projects funded by the European Research Council with colleagues from Tel Aviv University, University of Turku and the European Institute for Crime Prevention and Control (HEUNI) on criminogenic structures and corporate transparency of construction industries.

Rita Faria is currently Assistant Professor of Criminology and Vice-Director of the School of Criminology in the Faculty of Law of the University of Porto, as well as Director and founding member of the Interdisciplinary Research Center on Crime, Justice and Security (CJS). She holds a PhD in Criminology, a Masters in Sociology and an undergraduate degree in Law. She has been teaching undergraduate and masters students in the School of Criminology, as well in doctoral schools and research seminars in other European universities. Her research interests include white-collar, financial, corporate and environmental crime.

Ekaterina Gladkova is a PhD candidate in Criminology at Northumbria University. The PhD project focuses on the political economy of pig farming intensification in Northern Ireland, analyzing how it leads to environmental injustice. Ekaterina's research interests include green criminology, environmental justice and food crime and harm, and her research has been published in *Critical Criminology* and *Polar Research*.

Fiona Haines is Professor of Criminology in the School of Social and Political Sciences at the University of Melbourne, Adjunct Professor in the School of Regulation and Global Governance (RegNet) at the Australian National University and Fellow of the Academy of Social Sciences in Australia. Her research, which encompasses work on industrial disasters, grievances and multinational enterprises, centres on white-collar and corporate crime, globalization and regulation. Her books include *The Paradox of Regulation: What Regulation Can Achieve and What It Cannot* (Edward Elgar, 2011) and *Regulatory Transformations: Rethinking Economy–Society Interactions* (Hart Publishing, 2015), co-edited with Bettina Lange and Dania Thomas.

Deirdre Healy is Director of the UCD Institute of Criminology and Criminal Justice and Associate Professor at the Sutherland School of

Law, University College Dublin. Her teaching and research interests include desistance from crime, community sanctions, white-collar crime, victimology and criminological theory. Recent publications include *The Routledge Handbook of Irish Criminology* (Routledge, 2015), co-edited with Claire Hamilton, Yvonne Daly and Michelle Butler.

Wim Huisman is Professor of Criminology at Vrije Universiteit Amsterdam where he is also Head of the School of Criminology. Huisman is a founder and board member of the European Working Group on Organisational Crime (EUROC) of the European Society of Criminology. Currently, Huisman is Chair of the Netherlands Society of Criminology and Co-Editor-in-Chief of *Crime, Law & Social Change*. His research focus is on the field of white-collar crime, corporate crime and organized crime.

Éva Inzelt is Assistant Professor in the Faculty of Law of Eötvös Loránd University in Budapest. She has a PhD in Law and has been carrying out several empirical studies funded by national and international research funds. Her research interests are corruption, corporate crime and organized crime. She used to be an expert at the Hungarian chapter of Transparency International and has been a Visiting Scholar at Vrije Universiteit Amsterdam, Tel Aviv University and the UN European Institute for Crime Prevention and Control (HEUNI).

Michael Levi has been Professor of Criminology at Cardiff University since 1991. His main work has been on understanding the linkages and differences between white-collar and organized crime and their public– and private–sector controls. His mapping out of the local and transnational aspects of financial crimes and their control has won him major awards from the British and American societies of criminology. His current projects include the impact of technologies on criminal markets, cyber-enabled fraud and money laundering projects. He is the co-author of books on the organization of white-collar crimes, corporate and individual shaming and white-collar crimes and their victims.

Nicholas Lord is Professor of Criminology at the University of Manchester. He has research interests in white-collar and corporate crimes of a financial and economic nature, such as fraud, corruption and bribery, as well as the organization of serious crimes for financial gain, such as 'organized crime' and food fraud. Recent books include *Negotiated Justice and Corporate Crime: The Legitimacy of Civil Recovery Orders and Deferred Prosecution Agreements* (Palgrave Macmillan, 2018), co-authored with Colin King, and *Corruption in Commercial Enterprise: Law, Theory and Practice* (Routledge, 2018), co-edited with Liz Campbell.

Jeroen Maesschalck studied Public Administration and Philosophy at the University of Ghent in Belgium and at the London School of Economics and Political Science. He holds a PhD in Social Sciences from the University of Leuven. He is Professor in the Leuven Institute of Criminology at the University of Leuven. His research and teaching focuses on ethics in the public sector and on management and policy making in the criminal justice system, with a particular interest in policing. His publications include contributions to *Policing*, the *Journal of Business Ethics*, *Administration and Society*, *Public Administration* and *Public Integrity*.

Anna Markovska is Principal Lecturer in Criminology at the School of Humanities and Social Sciences at Anglia Ruskin University. Her research focuses on corruption, illegal markets and organized crime in Ukraine, policing reforms and issues of legitimacy.

Joe McGrath is Assistant Professor at the Sutherland School of Law, University College Dublin. He is the author of *Corporate and White-Collar Crime in Ireland: A New Architecture of Regulatory Enforcement* (Manchester University Press, 2015) and the editor of *White-Collar Crime in Ireland: Law and Policy* (Clarus Press, 2019). His recently published work appears in *Crime, Law and Social Change*, the *European Journal of Criminology*, *Justice Quarterly* and *Punishment and Society*.

Clarissa Meerts is Assistant Professor at the Department of Criminology in the Faculty of Law of Vrije Universiteit Amsterdam. Her research is at the nexus of corporate, employee and organized crime as well as being focused on the security industry and public–private relations within this field. Her work is widely published, with ongoing work focusing on corporate investigations, corporate settlements, public–private relations and financial crime. Her latest book is *Corporate Investigations, Corporate Justice and Public–Private Relations: Towards a New Conceptualisation* (Palgrave Macmillan, 2019).

Anna Merz is a PhD candidate at the Department of Criminology of the Erasmus School of Law, Erasmus University Rotterdam. Her research focuses on peer reactions to rule- and norm-violations in the financial sector.

Sunčana Roksandić is Assistant Professor at the Department of Criminal Law, Faculty of Law, University of Zagreb. She teaches criminal law, economic criminal law, transitional justice, bioethics and human rights. She obtained a PhD in the Department of Criminology at Max Planck Institute of Foreign and International Criminal Law in Freiburg. Her book, based on her doctoral research, *Prosecuting Serious Economic Crimes as International Crimes: A New Mandate for The ICC?* (Duncker & Humblot), was published in 2018. She is the Head of the Croatian Unit of the UNESCO Chair in Bioethics and member of UNODC Anti-Corruption Academic Initiative. She was the Head of the Jean Monnet Project Advanced Seminar in EU Criminal Law and Policy (2016–2019).

Melissa Rorie is Associate Professor of Criminal Justice at the University of Nevada-Las Vegas. Her research predominantly examines the impact of formal and informal controls on corporate and white-collar offending. She is currently involved in a variety of projects that examine regulation and corporate compliance, theoretical explanations for elite white-collar and corporate crime and quantitative research methodology. She was the Editor of *The Handbook of White-Collar Crime* (Wiley, 2019), and her research has been published in a variety of peer-reviewed journals, including *Criminology & Public Policy*, *Law & Policy* and the *Journal of Quantitative Criminology*, among others.

Iryna Soldatenko is Assistant Professor at the Department of Applied Sociology and Social Communications at Karazin Kharkiv National University. Iryna has worked as a United Nations consultant developing and implementing anti-corruption strategies in local governments in Luhansk and Donetsk regions. She has coordinated the USAID programme on education for judicial administrators, and developed communication technologies for The Fair Justice Initiative. Her research interests include public communications, state administration and anti-corruption policy and practice.

Tess van der Linden is a PhD candidate at the Radboud Business Law Institute of Radboud University in Nijmegen. She holds a LL.M. in

Legal Research from Utrecht University (2017). Her research interests include the tortious liability of companies, strategic litigation and collective redress mechanisms.

Judith van Erp is Professor of Regulatory Governance at Utrecht School of Governance, Utrecht University. She studies the regulation and governance of organizational crimes and deviancy, with a special interest on informal social control through media and social media publicity. Transparency and disclosure are important elements here. She co-edited the first edition of *The Routledge Handbook on White-Collar and Corporate Crime in Europe* (Routledge, 2015) and two special issues on corporate crime in the journals *Administrative Sciences* (2018) and the *European Journal of Criminology* (2020, with Nicholas Lord). She is currently working on a book on naming and shaming.

Karin van Wingerde is Associate Professor of Criminology at the Erasmus School of Law of Erasmus University. Her research focuses on the interplay between regulation and enforcement and behaviour of and within business firms. Recent research topics include risk-based regulation in occupational health and safety, the misuse of corporate vehicles for gain and effective means of combating organized crime.

Sarah Wilson is Senior Lecturer in Law at York Law School, University of York. After reading Law at Cardiff Law School she commenced studies in Modern British History, gaining an MA (History) and a PhD (History). Sarah has published widely in the sphere of financial crime and wider financial/banking law and regulation; her monograph, *The Origins of Modern Financial Crime: Historical Foundations and Current Problems in Britain* (Routledge, 2014), looks to encourage greater utilization of history and historical methodology for legal research and teaching. Sarah is a long-standing contributor to Lloyds Law Reports: Financial Crime and has helped to shape its emerging International section. In addition to her strongly European focus, Sarah's international work on financial crime and securities and financial regulation focuses on the APAC region and also the US.

Diego Zysman-Quirós is Associate Professor of Criminal Law and Criminology in the Faculty of Law of Universidad de Buenos Aires and Adjunct Professor of Queensland University of Technology. He has a Masters and PhD from Universidad de Barcelona and is currently a criminal law attorney. He has served as a Judge and High Law Clerk of the Criminal Court in Penal Economic Matters, Buenos Aires. He has authored two books, edited two books and written numerous chapters and journal articles.

Introduction: In Pursuit of a European Dialogue on White-Collar and Corporate Crimes

Nicholas Lord, Éva Inzelt, Wim Huisman and Rita Faria

This collection of chapters is about analyzing what is distinctly European about the nature of white-collar and corporate crimes in Europe. The chapters in the book put forward European perspectives on white-collar and corporate crimes, exploring the dynamics and tensions related to white-collar crimes that exist within and between the nation-states of Europe, and with the institutions of the European region. By speaking to the common theme of what is 'European' about the realities of white-collar crimes in Europe, the chapters encourage and engage in cross-European dialogue and collaboration as they seek to put forward key provocations about how we can better understand and examine the intricacies of associated offending and its control.

While having been coined in North American criminology, the origins of the concepts of white-collar and corporate crime lie in European criminology, in the work of Willem Bonger (1905; see also Hebberecht, 2015). These concepts are themselves contested and ambiguous, and this collection reflects the diversity of framings that exist in the academic literature, though more often than not the chapters foreground the duplicitous behaviours of business and political 'elites', including individuals and organizations, who often operate at the transnational level and in some way abuse their occupational and organizational positions while presenting an ostensibly legitimate exterior to society more widely. And, even without academic definition and conceptualization, in modern history, white-collar crime is a European 'invention', intrinsically linked to the introduction of the modern corporation, such as the Dutch East India Company and the British East India Company (Huisman et al, 2015).[1]

But what is meant by 'Europe', or 'European'? As a specified geographical region, is Europe in itself an appropriate unit of analysis for white-collar and corporate crime research? Borders change over time of course, but the continent of Europe represents a culturally rich and diverse set of nation-states that present a fertile ground for comparative empirical investigation and theory building over time. Often associated with Europe are the institutions of the European Union (EU) (that is, the European Parliament, the European Council, the European Commission and so on) and its conventions, directives, legal frameworks and policies that permeate from the supranational level down to individual member states. But is the EU an appropriate unit of analysis? Is this political and economic union representative of European perspectives? Or should we extend this institutional focus to the Council of Europe (CoE), which also includes 20 non-EU member states and aims at upholding human rights and the rule of law, the very things that are under threat by serious white-collar and corporate crime, and which has divisions targeting the typical white-collar crimes of corruption and money laundering? Or do we look to the social scientific or criminological perspectives, discourses and narratives of white-collar crimes originating in European universities and scientific societies such as the European Society of Criminology?

Whether we define Europe in geographical, political-legal-institutional or social scientific terms is semantics; the key issue is that within Europe, citizens and states continue to be confronted with a broad range of serious corporate and white-collar crimes: the Rolls-Royce international bribery case in the UK, the ING and Danske Bank money laundering cases, and of course emissions fraud at various car manufacturers such as Volkswagen, among others. These forms of deliberate dishonesty by businesses, in order to deceive the public, the state and investors, cause enormous financial damage and harm to individuals, markets and economies of European states. In addition to financial, physical and environmental damage, corporate crime undermines citizens' trust in (European) institutions. These major white-collar crime cases, but also many more 'mundane' cases that reflect the socially embedded and routine nature of occupational and organizational crimes (for example, petty corruption and bribery or tax evasion), are now a priority focus for social scientific research and are also emerging as policy concerns for individual nation-states and supranational organizations, such as the EU.

But white-collar and corporate crimes are not themselves necessarily limited to particular geographical and domestic boundaries, and can be organized internationally, multinationally, transnationally and globally, with offending potentially emanating in Europe but also being organized globally, via the financial system for example, or with harms and impacts occurring outside of the region through digital channels (see Lord et al, 2020). This might reflect the organization of criminality across borders (for example, exploiting legal loopholes for tax avoidance/evasion), or the creation of contrived financial arrangements for the movement of illicit finances (for example, creating UK companies with bank accounts in Latvia to conceal the proceeds of fraud and corruption in the Ukraine), among other issues. In these terms, white-collar and corporate crimes do not have sharp, physical boundaries, but the key issue is that European actors, organizations and institutions can be central to white-collar crimes, or their contexts can be facilitative of crimes taking place primarily outside of the region.

While having European roots, such transnational white-collar and corporate crimes are not only a European phenomenon, and neither are the attempts at regulation to prevent such crimes, which by their nature also need to be transnational. Theorizing and conceptualizing white-collar crimes in Europe is inevitably, in some way, informed by dominant approaches from elsewhere – the United States in particular – but Europe presents a diverse geo-historical and cultural context within and across which much can be learned, and where Europe-specific theories and concepts are generated and developed. For instance, with such a dense concentration of national jurisdictions as well as a multinational institutional regulatory framework (EU and CoE), Europe provides fertile ground for the study of the relationships between crime, control and place. While this book begins to think through the interactions between concepts and theories that are derived internally, or externally, to the European region, it is clear that the dynamics of associated mechanisms needs further comparative and collaborative research.

Criminological research on corporate and white-collar crime from across European jurisdictions has provided extensive insight into how opportunities for crime arise within organizational and industry contexts, how individuals are able to realize such opportunities and rationalize their behaviours in line with organizational cultures and formal and informal attempts to change or control corporate behaviour to reduce associated harmful behaviours and situations, among other areas. However, while these various national- and local-level studies have generated rich insights into corporate crimes in different European countries, there has been much less dialogue aiming to generate a rich, cohesive and distinctive European criminological discourse on white-collar and corporate crime. It is this latter point that provides the focus of this collection, as we seek to craft a dialogue on the following thematic question: what is 'European' about white-collar and corporate crimes in Europe? In addressing this question, this book presents an original series of chapters that seek to locate their focus of inquiry within a distinctively European framing, making connections between the local and the regional (or supranational), moving beyond the predilection for local or national case studies and in turn challenging mainstream white-collar crime theories and concepts that emanate primarily from the US context. Such a European voice is currently lacking in the academic discourse on white-collar crime. By engaging in this dialogue, the book also addresses the tensions that exist between different nation-states and between nation-states and supranational organizations such as the EU.

A European perspective on white-collar and corporate crime is imperative. Not only to balance North American dominance in the field, but even more to understand the contemporary society in which we study European white-collar and corporate crime. The question 'what is European?' has never been so topical. The rise of nationalism and anti-EU sentiments in many countries, the sharpening of differences due to Brexit, impacts arising from the US-China trade war, mass migration and the COVID-19 crisis are all major challenges for the common European ideal of previous decades. This ideal being that of having a single European market for the benefit of all, with free movement of capital, goods, services and labour, and with an appropriate distribution of power between state, commercial and civil society actors such that societal equalities and freedoms are protected. This European ideal and its threats are in various ways related to the prevalence of and responses to white-collar and corporate crimes. White-collar and corporate crimes are a threat to the European ideal as they undermine a fair and free market and impact individual liberties and civic rights. However, driven by economic interests, EU regulation can also incite corporate harm doing, as will be elaborated on in this book. The principle of national enforcement of European law, and national differences in such enforcement, further provide opportunities for white-collar and corporate crime. Yet, much EU regulation is a response to and seeks to prevent corporate crimes, such as market abuse, food fraud, environmental pollution and money laundering. It is then that nationalistic or protectionistic attempts to limit the regulatory power of 'Brussels' amplify opportunities for such crimes. Anti-EU sentiments can bring business and governments together for the defence of national economic interests, giving rise to forms of state-corporate crime, of which this book will also provide examples. Yet at the same time, nationalistic and anti-EU governments may still be perceived to be the true defenders of European ideals and values. They may claim inheritance of the Judeo-Christian and humanistic traditions that are seen as the common denominators of European culture. Defending this inheritance may serve as a justification for eroding the division of power and the rule of law, which may very well be the most important achievements of European civilization. This leads to the slippery slope towards state crime; the ultimate form of white-collar crime that is unfortunately also deeply rooted in European history. It is therefore not a surprise that in the closing chapter of this volume, Haines observes from an outside perspective that there are clear tensions in the European project as it aims at economic viability, respect for human rights and ecological sustainability.

Book genesis

The collection of chapters in this volume is a product of an initiative by the European Working Group on Organisational and White-Collar Crime (EUROC). EUROC is one of the largest working groups within the European Society of Criminology, with over 130 members from across Europe and also from other regions of the world, such as the US, South America and Australia. The membership converges around a common research interest in, and focus on, organizational and white-collar crimes, but the members approach associated social issues with a divergent set of social scientific philosophies and methodologies, making a vibrant environment within which to increase rigour and robustness in our individual and collaborative projects. Since the formation of the group in 2010, we have met annually at the European Society of Criminology (ESC) Annual Conference and in recent years EUROC introduced standalone workshops focused on specific aspects of white-collar and corporate crime research and scholarship. It is here that this collection originates.

In June 2019, EUROC organized its 2nd Biennial Workshop in Manchester, UK, outside of the ESC Annual Conference, to which EUROC members contributed short, provocative essays addressing the question and theme outlined earlier. A call for papers had been disseminated to the EUROC group in September 2018. Intentions to contribute, including provisional titles and abstracts, were submitted by January 2019. The abstracts were reviewed by the EUROC board prior to acceptance. Participants were required to submit their essays ahead of the workshop. Each paper was allocated two academics as discussants, who provided oral and written feedback at the workshop. In addition, other participants were able to offer feedback during the workshop itself. Thus, each chapter has been through a rigorous scrutiny process. Final submissions following revisions were also reviewed by the editors. The chapters in this collection contribute state-of-the-art knowledge from across Europe (and beyond) to inform the social scientific discourse on white-collar and corporate crimes. The volume's contributors come from nine different European countries, and they have brought together examples from and insights into a broad spectrum of European nations. Also included are three invited chapters from Argentina, Australia and the US that provide observations and commentary on the chapters and the collection as a whole from outside of Europe. There is a wide representation of female and of early career researchers. This composition of contributors speaks loudly not only to the innovative and pressing topics covered, but also to the richness brought by the inclusion of varied perspectives and backgrounds, which may well be a signpost for the future of European white-collar and corporate crime scholarship.

The 2019 workshop provided the motivation for producing this collection. Colleagues from across Europe were keen to put together a narrative around the value of social scientific, criminological research in Europe on white-collar crime in a format that would be accessible to many different groups, such as academics, students, practitioners and policy makers. As major corporate and white-collar crime scandals continue to come to light, it is important that we develop an independent narrative to provide commentary on and analysis of these developments. The contributions in the collection draw upon an array of (funded) empirical research projects from across Europe and/or present emerging key issues from the contributors' research programmes in this area over recent years and over their careers. The chapters present new and original knowledge and insights. The book builds on earlier EUROC outputs, including a special issue on 'The Organisational Dynamics of Corporate Crime in Europe' in the *European Journal of Criminology* that was published in 2020 (see van Erp and Lord, 2020) and *The Routledge Handbook of Corporate and White Collar Crime in Europe*, edited by van Erp et al (2015).

This book explores what is it about the European region that is unique, innovative or different (or not so different) in terms of the nature of white-collar and corporate crimes that are strongly connected to Europe. In this globalized world, academic research that retains a focus on local, national cases studies, while valuable, is also limited in relation to white-collar and corporate crimes, as these cases are often multi-jurisdictional in nature and scope. In these terms, the subjects analyzed in this collection have both local and regional significance and have common relevance in terms of the tensions and interconnections that exist between individual nation-states and localities, and supranational policies that originate from the institutions of the EU. The contributors in the collection seek to foreground 'European realities', which inevitably requires an analytical approach beyond the nation-state. By doing this, it is possible to craft a more European dialogue on white-collar and corporate crimes rather than a series of separate descriptions of what happens in different places; but as Haines (Chapter 18) notes in her observation on the collection, it is also important for a focus on similarities and shared experiences to not to lead to important differences and distinctions being glossed over. Moreover, as Zysman-Quirós (Chapter 17) puts it, it empowers European scholars to come to terms with historic European innovations in criminal law, business regulation and scholarship in early modernity (18th–19th centuries), that clearly influenced other parts of the globe to recognize and begin preventing harms and crimes of an economic and financial nature. This discursive process started with our deliberations in the Manchester workshop and continues in written form in the chapters submitted for this collection.

In addition, it is reality in the area of current white-collar and corporate crime scholarship that much theorizing and conceptualization on related issues emanates from the US context, where there is a strong tradition of scholarship in this area. This body of literature is undoubtedly useful, but in this collection we seek to foreground what European scholars can offer in terms of building theory and concepts, and methodological approaches, to global debates on white-collar and corporate crime. As stated earlier, the European region offers a rich, diverse geographical location that can provide insights relevant beyond any individual nation-state. By doing so, we address a major gap in the academic literature in an accessible but provocative form. Furthermore, the contributions not only offer state-of-the-art accounts of the dynamics of white-collar crimes in Europe, but also suggest a series of future paths for research, and for innovative perspectives and methods in the study of white-collar and corporate crime, its harms and regulation.

It is the opinion of the editors and contributors that there is much scope for us to better understand the multiplicity (or lack thereof) of European white-collar and corporate crime and its control, including processes of divergence and convergence within and across Europe, through dialogue and collaboration. The realist accounts of white-collar and corporate crimes seen in the chapters of this book constructively seek to inform the narrative around the multi-faceted nature of the conditions that shape their occurrence, and make concrete connections between particular instances of white-collar crimes and their embeddedness in the political-economic frameworks of Europe. The diversity of the European region and its rich geo-historical context offers an ideal region for the generation of ideas, theories and concepts, and for establishing common referents across varied cultures about what white-collar and corporate crime means in Europe.

Book structure

The book has been separated into five parts. These are, Part I: Researching White-Collar and Corporate Crimes in Europe; Part II: Financial Crimes and Illicit Financial Flows; Part III: White-Collar Crime: European Case Studies; Part IV: Responding to White-Collar Crimes in Europe; and Part V: Observations from Outside of Europe. We briefly outline the contributions in each part in what follows.

Part I focuses on research on white-collar and corporate crimes in Europe. In the first chapter, Jeroen Maesschalck considers the extent to which the EU, and its constituent member states, can be used as a natural experiment for mapping and assessing approaches to the prevention of corporate and occupational crimes. He foregrounds the potential of research designs that incorporate multiple case studies across the region, time series analyses and cross-sectional quantitative studies for understanding 'what works', 'for whom' and 'in what circumstances' in corporate and occupational crime prevention. This realist account of researching white-collar and corporate crimes in Europe reflects an appreciation of the multi-faceted factors that contribute to the emergence of these crimes, and in doing so, presents a robust framework for undertaking empirical analysis and building theory within the European region. Following on from this, Sunčana Roksandić explores the important question of how white-collar crime research should be prioritized in the EU in relation to the EU's internal and external security. More specifically, by foregrounding the

EU as a key unit of analysis within the European region, she argues in favour of integrating the 'human security' component of white-collar and corporate crimes, particularly those implicating political elites, in order to address corruption within broader social issues such as healthcare and migration. The third chapter in Part I, from Nicholas Lord, Karin van Wingerde and Michael Levi, analyzes corruption and comparative analyses across Europe. Given the cultural and legal diversity across the European region, the authors pose the question of 'how and what do we know about "corruption", domestically and transnationally, across Europe?' They identify four main research traditions in criminological research into corruption in Europe (surveys and experiments, qualitative studies, national case studies and analyses of specific cases of corruption) and foreground the use of deliberative methods to better understand what is European about corruption in Europe, with a focus on new concepts and tools of producing knowledge and theory cross-culturally.

Part II focuses its attention on financial crimes and illicit financial flows in Europe. Sarah Wilson analyzes market abuse within the EU, taking the UK as a case study and exploring the tensions and interactions that exist in legal discourse over time. More specifically, Wilson analyzes what can be gained by identifying the 'Europeanness' in understandings of white-collar crimes through reference to key European policies on market-related violations. She argues that behaviours such as insider dealing and market manipulation, termed 'market abuse' by European discourse, demonstrate a European commitment to the use of criminal responses to behaviour which is considered unacceptable. Karin van Wingerde and Anna Merz analyze varieties of responses to money laundering across Europe. They undertake an analysis of 47 anti-money laundering (AML) cases against banks across Europe and map the similarities and differences in responses to establish what is particularly 'European' about how AML violations are dealt with across the nation-states of Europe. They argue that a stringent and aggressive enforcement paradigm exists in Europe, but highlight the implications of this for the legitimacy of the AML regime as a whole, as those banks and compliance actors that are 'criminalized' may become less willing to take on AML responsibilities. Illicit finance and AML not only relate to financial institutions, but also other professions and industries. Katie Benson drills down into the role of legal professionals, such as lawyers, in the response to money laundering, and considers the policy connections and interplay between local-, EU- and global-level expectations. She argues that how AML is experienced by legal professionals in particular situations and settings is a product of these multi-level interconnections. While there are some aspects of the EU AML agenda that are distinct, she explores how AML interactions at the global, regional and local level play out in the UK specifically.

In Part III, five case studies of white-collar crimes in Europe are presented. These cases not only provide insight into the specific dynamics of the harms and crimes under study, but also into the broader context and criminogenics of the (de)regulation of markets and the inherent tensions of balancing economic interests and preventing such harms. Ekaterina Gladkova analyzes food production harms in the European context, scrutinizing how the EU may be an enabler or a solution. She empirically investigates Northern Ireland as a case study of farming industrialization to demonstrate how the EU's regulated market model can create asymmetries, biased interests and opportunities or conditions for harm. Anna Markovska and Iryna Soldatenko examine the dynamics of white-collar criminality in Ukraine, with particular focus on what they refer to as the concept of politically driven white-collar criminality. These white-collar crimes, they argue, harm otherwise legal entrepreneurship in the Ukrainian context and generate overtly illegal activities, such as those related to labour violations in certain industries. Such dynamics reflect the role of the legacy of the Soviet Union in creating and sustaining destructive and politically motivated entrepreneurship that leads to criminality that reaches beyond the borders of Ukraine, particularly as law enforcement has not been sufficiently enforced in Ukraine and its trading partners. Jon Davies looks at labour exploitation and 'posted workers' within the European construction industry. He uses a lens of 'corporate criminology' to identify how businesses are able to exploit posted workers in the context of free movement and the ways in which this is made possible due to regulatory gaps and insufficient accountability mechanisms. According to Davies, the phenomenon of posted workers is distinct to the EU and the associated exploitation raises questions over the functionality of a 'one-size-fits-all' policy approach to such harmful activities. Clarissa Meerts analyzes public–private relations in the investigation of 'internal financial crimes' in the Netherlands. She interrogates the role of corporate investigators in the context of what is typically termed 'cooperation', arguing instead that public–private 'separation' is a more accurate conceptualization of the nature of these relationships, due to the operational autonomy that private actors possess. Eva Inzelt and Tamas Bezsenyi focus on the characteristics of cartels as a type of corporate crime in Hungary and consider the implications of such corporate crimes for the European region. Their core intention is to examine what the role of the state is in responding to cartel cases and in ensuring freedom of competition in the market. Their analysis reveals that the state has different approaches to dealing with corporate criminal actors like cartels. In some cases, the state itself 'initiates' (that is, tacit approves of) the criminal activity of cartels, in others, the state 'facilitates' the process, in line with the concept of 'state-corporate crime'.

Part IV focuses on the responses to white-collar crimes in Europe. Judith van Erp and Tess van der Linden analyze so-called strategic lawsuits against public participation (SLAPPs) in Europe. Their chapter examines the issue of strategic libel and defamation suits by corporate actors against non-governmental organizations and journalists in Europe in relation to corporate environmental crime and corruption. They conclude with insights into the consequences of SLAPPs in Europe, and consider the connections to free speech and public-interest litigation. Joe McGrath and Dierdre Healy reflect on the comparative method in criminal justice research with a focus on white-collar crime enforcement data and official crime statistics in Ireland and the US. While doing this, they simultaneously provide valuable insight about the differentiated working methods of both jurisdictions regarding, for instance, crime nomenclatures, as well as identifying several issues with using such data and conclude that much can be gained through comparative, qualitative and mixed-methods case study approaches. They conclude by arguing in favour of the value of comparative methods for developing shared understandings, common obstacles and good practice, while also recognizing the difficulties of doing such research. Liz Campbell analyzes the growing number of jurisdictions, in Europe and elsewhere, turning to Deferred Prosecution Agreements (DPAs) and negotiated settlements more generally in response to corporate offending, questioning whether legal convergence is taking place. She analyzes how DPAs have been 'defined, developed and deployed' in different European jurisdictions and how this has varied across common law and civil law countries, before going on to scrutinize key procedural issues.

In Part V, the book concludes with three observations on white-collar crime in Europe from North America, South America and Australia. Melissa Rorie seeks to examine what is European about white-collar and corporate crime scholarship in Europe, as opposed to manifestations of white-collar crimes specifically. She has undertaken a content analysis of academic articles on white-collar crime and related issues appearing in 21 different journals, in order to gain empirical insight into where white-collar crime research is generated, which topics European scholars tend to research and the methods and strategies implemented and theories used when compared with their counterparts in North America. Rorie concludes that European white-collar crime scholarship is thriving, with European studies overrepresented in major criminology journals and a wide array of methods and theories being utilized. However, as a word of caution, Rorie suggests that care needs to be taken by US scholars not to omit this 'deeper, thorough and effortful' body of (often qualitative) research that may fall outside of the scope of quantitative-oriented systematic reviews of the subject. Diego Zysman-Quirós contributes with a view from the Global South, aiming to help rethink the idea of the Europeanization of white-collar and corporate crime scholarship. Pinpointing how European scholarship uses the US as a single referent, the author stresses European variations in economic and political systems, as well as national histories, cultures and languages, despite common concerns driven by the EU project. Using the concept of 'situated knowledge', the author offers a critique of a universal and timeless model of science and of the risk of generalization about phenomena which are not universal. He concludes by suggesting that European white-collar and corporate crime scholarship should unleash its multiplicity and diversity, in the manner of a music concert with multiple instruments. In the final chapter, Fiona Haines argues that the contributions to this collection 'shed considerable light on the contribution of a European perspective on a literature often dominated by US perspectives and Anglo perspectives more broadly' and considers which lessons can be learnt from Europe. To do this, she interrogates the chapters in relation to four key issues: the units of analysis, the challenges in comparative work, orientation towards the study of white-collar crime and the different ways to collaborate. Haines offers useful insights into each of these fundamental dimensions, and concludes by exploring the value that might be gained through a 'field of struggle orientation' that encourages an integrated appreciation of place, a supra-problem perspective and collaboration within and beyond criminology. This presents an analytical framework that can, for instance, guide us towards understanding how 'changing the rules around business behaviour might be achieved'.

This collection could not have been brought together were it not for the support of others in the EUROC network. As editors, our thanks go to those colleagues who participated at the Manchester workshop and went on to contribute the rich chapters in this book, but also to those who did not attend the workshop but joined the project later as co-authors or invited sole authors of chapters. In addition, some colleagues attended the Manchester workshop but did not contribute to the collection, yet we are grateful for their contributions to the critical discussion of the project rationale and to the final volume. We would also like to thank our former EUROC board member, Judith van Erp, for helping with the organizing of the Manchester event. It is also important to acknowledge that the Manchester workshop was funded by the University of Manchester's School of Law, Utrecht University's Strategic Theme Institutions for Open Societies and the Vrije Universiteit Amsterdam School of Criminology. Finally, we would like to thank the publisher for giving us the opportunity to share these contributions with a wider audience and for their continued support throughout the production process.

Note
[1] Notwithstanding historical evidence of elite fraud and corruption in ancient societies in Europe (for example, Greek and Roman) and not even touching upon the crimes of European colonial states and their business partners (Johnstone, 1999; Ward, 2005).

References

Bonger, W.A. (1905) *Criminalité et Conditions Économiques*, Amsterdam: G.P. Tierie.

Hebberecht, P. (2015) 'Willem Bonger: the unrecognized European pioneer of the study of white-collar crime', in J. van Erp, W. Huisman and G. Vande Walle (eds) *The Routledge Handbook of White-Collar and Corporate Crime in Europe*, Abingdon: Routledge, pp 125–32.

Huisman, W., van Baar, A. and Gorsira, M. (2015) 'Corporations and transnational crime', in G.J.N. Bruinsma (ed) *Histories of Transnational Crime*, New York: Springer, pp 147-170.

Johnstone, P. (1999) 'Serious white collar fraud: historical and contemporary perspectives', *Crime, Law & Social Change*, 30: 107–30.

Lord, N., Zeng, Y. and Jordanoska, A. (2020) 'White-collar crimes beyond the nation-state', *Oxford Research Encyclopedias: Criminology and Criminal Justice*. doi:10.1093/acrefore/9780190264079.013.575

van Erp, J., Huisman, W. and Vande Walle, G. (eds) (2015) *The Routledge Handbook of White-Collar and Corporate Crime in Europe*, Abingdon: Routledge.

van Erp, J. and Lord, N. (2020) 'Is there a "European" corporate criminology? Introduction to the Special Issue on European Corporate Crime', *European Journal of Criminology*, 17(1): 3–8.

Ward, T. (2005) 'State crime in the heart of darkness', *British Journal of Criminology*, 45: 434–45.

PART I

Researching White-Collar and Corporate Crimes in Europe

2

Using Grid-Group Cultural Theory to Assess Approaches to the Prevention of Corporate and Occupational Crime: The EU as a Natural Experiment

Jeroen Maesschalck

Introduction

In their 2015 volume on white-collar and corporate crime in Europe, Lord and Levi (2015) argue that much work remains to be done if we want to really understand white-collar crime prevention. We not only need to understand more about the phenomenon of white-collar crime itself, for example, by combining quantitative data with qualitative information (Lord and Levi, 2015), but also about the efforts to prevent it. This implies that researchers should move beyond 'crude indicators of levels of enforcement' such as prosecution data (Lord and Levi, 2015: 41) and look at descriptors of a broad range of types of regulation, of which criminal prosecution is just one. It is to that latter research agenda, using mixed methods research to understand white-collar crime prevention, that this chapter intends to contribute.

Specifically, this chapter will propose a number of building blocks for a theoretical framework to address the question of 'what works in the prevention of corporate and occupational crime?'; moreover, it will argue that Europe provides a promising environment to test and further develop such a framework. An important advantage of the

European, and particularly the European Union (EU), context is that a number of relevant environmental characteristics (for example, EU law and policies) are shared, while there is still important and theoretically useful variation across countries, industries and organizations.

These reflections will be formulated in three steps. First, the chapter will present a number of classifications by which to map variation in corporate and occupational crime-prevention approaches in Europe. After the presentation of a classification used within ethics management at the organizational level and a classification used within regulation at the industry level, it will argue for a more generic classification drawn from grid-group cultural theory. Second, against the background of those classifications, this chapter will identify the building blocks of a theoretical framework that could guide research on the impact of efforts to prevent corporate and occupational crime. Third, some designs for empirical research within the EU to test and further develop the proposed theoretical framework will be briefly discussed.

Mapping variation in the prevention of corporate and occupational crime

Before addressing approaches to prevention, it is useful to first delineate what it is that is to be prevented. This is a common challenge in the field of white-collar crime research, notorious for its conceptual and terminological debates. Essentially, this chapter focuses on a particular category of white-collar crime: crime within and by organizations. There is no generic term to describe this phenomenon. Most authors refer to it by using two labels (Clinard and Quinney, 1973; Coleman, 1987: 407; Gerber and Jensen, 2007: xiii–xiv; Huisman, 2016). The first label, occupational crime, refers to crimes committed by employees for their own benefit. The second label, corporate (or, more generally, organizational) crime, refers to crimes committed by employees or organizations for the benefit of the organization. The distinction between both is not always clear-cut, as crime is sometimes committed both for individual and organizational benefit (Gerber and Jensen, 2007: xiv), nor is it really important for this chapter. That is why this chapter will refer to 'corporate and occupational crime', 'crime within and by organizations' and sometimes the more generic label 'white-collar crime'.

Research in various academic fields generated assorted classifications and typologies to conceptualize variation in approaches to the prevention of corporate and occupational crime. The growing field of regulation is an obvious source of classifications and we will indeed draw from it. However, as Almond and van Erp (2018) observe, most studies in the field of regulation largely overlook individual-level motivations and mechanisms within the regulated organization. That is why, we would argue, insights from the literature on regulation can be usefully complemented with insights from organizational ethics and particularly ethics management. Starting from the lower level of analysis, this paragraph will first present a classification from organizational ethics and then discuss a number of classifications from research on regulation. It will conclude with a third, more generic classification that helps to encompass the previous classifications.

The first classification of white-collar crime-prevention approaches focuses on the organizational level. As Huisman (2016) describes, an important strand within the white-collar crime research tradition focuses on the organization itself as criminogenic. This has delivered very useful explanations of crime within organizations, but it does not really offer typologies of strategies for its prevention. For that, it is useful to turn to the growing field of business ethics or organizational ethics and to look at the prevention of crime within organizations as an aspect of 'ethics management'. The most classic distinction of approaches in this field is between the rules-based (or compliance-based) and values-based approaches to ethics management (Paine, 1994). The rules-based approach emphasizes extensive formal controls that reduce individual employees' discretion (for example, rules, monitoring and stringent enforcement). The values-based approach, on the other hand, accepts employees' discretion and offers support for using that discretion (for example, frequent deliberation about ethical dilemmas, coaching, aspirational codes of ethics) (see, for example, Paine, 1994; Maesschalck, 2004a; Cooper, 2006).

The second classification, or rather group of classifications, focuses on prevention at a higher level: the approaches that can be used by regulators to prevent crime by and within the organizations they regulate. The classifications of those approaches are remarkably similar to those used within organizations in the ethics management literature. Gunningham (2010, 2016), for example, distinguishes between the 'rules and deterrence' approach and the 'advice and persuasion' approach.[1] The former emphasizes the sanctioning of rule-breaking behaviour and expects that sufficiently frequent detection and sufficiently severe punishment will deter from future violations. The latter emphasizes cooperation over confrontation, using bargaining and negotiation instead of deterrence (Gunningham, 2010: 121–2).

The third classification is more ambitious as it claims to be more comprehensive and generic. It is inspired by grid-group cultural theory (also called the theory of 'sociocultural viability') (Thompson et al, 1990), which was originally developed by the anthropologist Mary Douglas (1970) and later applied at various levels of analysis (international and national regulatory regimes, organizational policies) and in various academic fields relevant to the study of white-collar crime, including criminology (Vaughan, 2002, 2004; Mars, 2006), regulation (Lodge and Hood, 2010) and organizational ethics (Maesschalck, 2004a). Table 2.1 draws from Maesschalck (2004a) and Lodge and Hood (2010: 599) to present the four approaches to the prevention of corporate and occupational crime that can be derived from grid-group cultural theory. The typology is defined by two dimensions. 'Grid' refers to the extent to which life is circumscribed by externally imposed conventions and rules, and 'group' refers to the extent to which individuals are bound in a collective unit (Thompson et al, 1990: 5; Hood, 1998: 8). Together, they define four approaches to corporate and occupational crime prevention that can be presented in a two-by-two matrix (see Table 2.1).

The two high-group types at the right-hand side of the matrix in Table 2.1 are very close to the distinctions in the previous two typologies. The hierarchy and oversight approach is very close to the rules-based approach to ethics management and to the deterrence approach to regulation. The egalitarianism and mutuality approach largely coincides with the values-based approach to ethics management

Table 2.1: Four approaches to corporate and occupational crime prevention

		Group	
		Low	High
Grid	High	Fatalism and contrived randomness *Ensure a considerable degree of randomness and unpredictability in the standard setting as well as the interactions*	Hierarchy and oversight *Provide rules and regulations (usually on the basis of expert advice) and enforce these strictly*
	Low	Individualism and rivalry *Ensure as much competition as possible so as to avoid, for example, unethical monopoly rents or nepotism at organizational level or excessive power concentration, shirking or unhealthy loyalties at the level of individual employees*	Egalitarianism and mutuality *Allow organizations or individuals a considerable degree of discretion and support them in dealing with it. If there are any rules and standards, they are set through a participatory process and applied by persuasion*

and the advice and persuasion approach to regulation. The two remaining low-group approaches on the left-hand side of the table feature much less in typologies of ethics management or regulation, but can nevertheless be found in the practice of corporate and occupational crime prevention. Rivalry and competition have become popular approaches to regulation. In the wake of the success of the 'new public management' rhetoric, they are seen as ways to avoid corrupt monopolies (Klitgaard, 1988). They have also been suggested as solutions to avoiding occupational crime within organizations. In the public sector, for example, pay-for-performance schemes and other forms of competition among employees were introduced to reduce the risk of shirking. Competition among (senior) employees is also expected to ensure that they keep one another honest. It might help to avoid dangerous concentration of power within individual employees as well as to avoid unhealthy loyalties that might lead to cover-ups (Hood, 1998: 55–60). Likewise, the unpredictability typical to fatalism and contrived randomness can also been found in both regulation and ethics management within organizations. Surprise inspections, for example, are a common feature of most regulatory regimes. Contrived randomness is also common within organizations, for example, in the form of random internal audits or unpredictable posting of employees to avoid 'over-familiarity with clients or colleagues' (Hood, 1998: 65). In sum, this typology is more generic than the typologies in regulation and ethics management and as a fourfold typology it is broader than the two-way distinctions in regulation and ethics management. It is also embedded in a much broader literature, which allows the linking of the four different approaches presented here with different worldviews (including different views on risk, for example, Sparks, 2001) and different ways of organizing. That broader grid-group typology has been used, for example, to describe and compare national cultures (for example, Caulkins, 1999; Hood et al, 2004; Maleki and Hendriks, 2015), making it particularly useful for the aims of this chapter.

Understanding what works in the prevention of corporate and occupational crime

Combining approaches

Having distinguished between different approaches to corporate and occupational crime prevention, the obvious next question is what their respective impact is. That is, to what extent do they 'work'? The conclusion for all three classifications in the previous paragraph seems to be largely the same: all the respective approaches have their advantages but also their disadvantages, and, in practice, it will often be a mixture of several approaches that will be most effective. We briefly develop this argument for each of the three classifications.

First, each of the two approaches to ethics management has its own 'dark side'.[2] If an organization only went for the rules-based approach, then this might weaken the moral competence (and particularly the moral imagination) of its staff, undermine employee morale, generate increasingly complex layers of rules and exceptions, lead to fear-induced paralysis and so on. However, if an organization allowed the values-based approach to develop unabatedly, this might lead to indecisiveness because of endless discussions, individual employees abusing their discretion and so on. Thus, each of the separate approaches will generate its own excesses if the approach is allowed to grow relentlessly. To avoid that, organizations should ensure a sufficient degree of each of the approaches, which would allow those approaches to compensate for each other's weaknesses and blind spots. Thus, the rules fetishism and rigidity of the rules-based approach will be alleviated by the discretion and strengthened moral imagination that follow from the values-based approach. Likewise, cunning employees' abuse of a naïve form of the values-based approach can be prevented by having at least a minimum of the rules, monitoring and enforcement that are typical for the rules-based approach. Thus, the recommendation is to ensure some kind of balance between the two approaches. In that sense they are rather to be seen as extremes on a continuum, with real organizations usually taking a position somewhere in-between (Maesschalck, 2004a).

Second, a very similar argument can be found in the regulation literature. Gunningham (2010: 122) also describes 'rules and deterrence' and 'advice and persuasion' as 'two polar extremes' and observes that most regulatory specialists now recommend a judicious mix of both approaches (Gunningham, 2010: 125). Focusing on the individual enforcement officer, May and Winter (2011: 229) describe punitive or strict enforcement on the one hand and an accommodative or conciliatory regulatory style on the other as the ends of a continuum with more moderate, adaptive styles in the middle. Probably the best-known representation of the various approaches to regulation is the enforcement pyramid, proposed by Ayres and Braithwaite (1992) as part of their broader theory on 'responsive regulation'. At the bottom, the pyramid presents the most cooperative strategies (guidance, persuasion) and at the top the most deterrent ones (nondiscretionary punishment, incapacitation) (Ayres and Braithwaite, 1992: 35–40). With this pyramid comes a sophisticated theory about how the approaches relate to one another. At the core of this theory is a strong normative recommendation that regulators should only escalate towards deterrence and then incapacitation when repeated interaction has shown that the regulated actor is not able and/or willing to comply (Braithwaite, 2011: 30–4). More recent models have further expanded on these ideas by taking on board the complexities of polycentric regulatory regimes in which regulation occurs through a web of not only state actors but also private and third-sector actors at regional, national and transnational level. Proponents of 'smart regulation', for example, argue that in many cases the use of multiple regulatory instruments and a broad range of actors will be most effective (Gunningham et al, 1998; Gunningham, 2010: 131). In fact, as Almond and van Erp (2018: 10) observe, 'the interaction between deterrence and compliance, and the ways in which state sanctions and social pressures reinforced each other's effectiveness' was 'a defining feature of the emergent research of the 1990s and 2000s at the intersection of corporate criminology and regulatory governance'.

The regulation literature also has its own versions of the argument that we also saw in the ethics management literature: complementary approaches can compensate for their respective weaknesses. For example, in explaining responsive regulation, Braithwaite (2002: 32) observes that the different theories underlying the various approaches that are represented in the layers of the regulatory pyramid 'are all limited and flawed theories of compliance'. Hence, 'what the pyramid does is cover the weakness of one theory with the strength of another'. If escalation to deterrence and eventually incapacitation is a real threat, then it is rational for regulated actors to comply even without any coercion being exercised (Braithwaite, 2011: 475). Gunningham offers another reason why the advice and persuasion approach is not sufficient. If that approach leads the regulator to allow wrongdoers to go unpunished, then this might discourage well-intentioned organizations from complying, as their investment in compliance would lead to a competitive disadvantage (Gunningham, 2010: 125). Hence, if the advice and persuasion approach is to be effective, it has to do so 'in the shadow of deterrence' (Gunningham, 2016: 515). Finally, Lord and Levi (2015: 41) formulate a similar argument in the area of corporate crime by describing a 'spectrum of regulatory mechanisms'. At one end would be various levels of self-regulation within industries and organizations and at the other end would be various enforcement practices (for example, criminal prosecution, disruption strategies, licensing mechanisms) that are mainly performed by state actors. As such, the lines between regulation and criminal procedure become increasingly blurred. Again, the argument is that contradictory approaches can reinforce each other, for example when regulatory techniques enable prosecution (Lord and Levi, 2015: 41).

Third, it is again grid-group cultural theory that offers the most ambitious approach. Because it hypothesizes a fourfold typology defined by two dimensions instead of a continuum defined by a single dimension, it allows for more complex and nuanced thinking. It does not look for a middle position between the extremes of a continuum, nor does it propose a normative argument about the escalation of approaches along one dimension (as is done with the regulatory pyramid). Instead, it allows for a more complex dynamic between the four types along two dimensions. For example, while the traditional continua in ethics management suggest that, say, less hierarchy (that is, a rules-based approach) implies more egalitarianism (that is, a values-based approach), the fourfold typology allows to see that less hierarchy might also lead to two other outcomes: more individualism or even more fatalism (Maesschalck, 2004a). This is a very important addition that might help to avoid blind spots. As with the discussed continua in ethics management and regulation, grid-group cultural theory predicts that each of the approaches has its own built-in weaknesses that will inevitably occur if the approach is not compensated for by the other three approaches. This basic insight is developed into a theory that predicts that, particularly for problems such as white-collar crime, 'clumsy' or 'polyrational' policies that combine elements of all four types will be more viable (Verweij et al, 2006; Ney and Verweij, 2015). That theory has generated a series of studies in various policy fields further testing and developing this basic idea (Verweij and Thompson, 2006; Lodge, 2009). In sum, grid-group cultural theory not only helps to bring together typologies commonly used in the ethics management and regulation literatures in one typology, it also generates hypotheses about the expected impact of the types. Applied to the topic, this would imply that those countries, industries or organizations that do not offer a corporate and occupational crime-prevention policy that is sufficiently diverse across the four types will exhibit more corporate and occupational crime than others.

Looking for the 'right' combination

The prediction that crime-prevention approaches will be more effective when they are sufficiently diverse is just the start of a theory, of course. It certainly does not mean that all policies that combine elements of various approaches will be desirable. Simply piling up instruments and approaches will not do. Braithwaite et al (2007: 312) warn against a 'kitchen sink' approach to regulation, referring to Gunningham et al's (1998) warning against 'smorgasbordism', that is, 'wrongly assuming that all complementary instruments should be used rather than the minimum number necessary to achieve the desired result' (Gunningham and Sinclair, 2017: 134). One would hope, though, that some combinations are more fruitful than others and that a theory would help us understand why that is the case. I now propose three roads towards developing a more sophisticated theory.

The first road is the most developed one in the ethics management and regulation literatures. It is a contingency approach, focusing on conditions: depending on the circumstances, the appropriate mix between the approaches (or the position on the continuum) will differ. The typologies and continua used in the regulation literature often come with specifications of the conditions under which particular types should be used. The regulatory pyramid for responsive regulation, for example, prescribes that regulators adapt their strategy to the compliance motives they ascribe to those they regulate (Mascini, 2016). In a further development of the regulatory pyramid, Braithwaite et al (2007: 305–23) propose to adapt the regulatory strategy to levels of complexity. Risk-based regulation expects regulators to adapt their strategy to the risks that non-compliance by the regulated might pose to their mission (Black and Baldwin, 2010: 181; Mascini, 2016). Similar arguments, specifying which approach (or rather combination of approaches) should be used under which circumstances, exist in the ethics management literature (for example, Maesschalck, 2004a).

The second road resembles the first one, but it particularly focuses on the different ways in which the approaches can be combined, the types of 'settlements' between the contradictory approaches. It theorizes different ways of combining approaches and hypothesizes what the likely impact of such combinations will be under various circumstances. Thacher and Rein (2004), for example, show that balancing values or striking trade-offs between values is just one strategy of dealing with contradictory approaches (and, therefore, values). They propose three alternative ways of managing conflict between values (and, therefore, also between grid-group cultural theory's four perspectives). The first alternative approach they propose is to cycle between values by first emphasizing one value and then the other. A case in point is the pendulum dynamic that can be seen in ethics management in organizations between the rules-based and values-based approaches, with scandals often playing a role in changing the direction of the pendulum. In responsive regulation, this sequence is deliberately designed. It prescribes that regulators should escalate or de-escalate on the pyramid depending on the degree of cooperation by the regulated actor 'so that, in sequence, the strengths of one tool be given a chance to cover the weaknesses of another tool' (Braithwaite, 2011: 505). The second alternative to balancing proposed by Thacher and Rein (2004) is to organize a structural separation between values by assigning the responsibility for those values to different institutional actors. In ethics management, these could take the form of 'firewalls' within organizations, for example, separating the investigative unit on the one hand from an ethics unit that provides support and training on the other. An example of structural separation in a regulatory context is provided by Braithwaite's (2002: 35) restorative justice approach to responsive regulation (as opposed to the 'tit-for-tat' approach to responsive regulation; see Nielsen and Parker, 2009). This restorative justice approach prescribes that individual regulatory staff members always focus on cooperation and take a positive attitude towards the regulated actor. They never have to sanction or even threaten to sanction. This is possible because there are other actors in a broader system of escalating sanctions for non-compliance who will take up the punitive role if necessary (Nielsen and Parker, 2009: 395–6). As such, the structural separation between cooperation on the one hand and punitive actions on the other helps to combine both contradictory approaches in a functioning overall system. The third alternative to balancing values proposed by Thacher and Rein (2004) is that of 'casuistry': trying to transcend value conflicts from case to case, relying on one's experience with previous cases. Both the ethics management and regulatory literature offer examples of this gradual, pragmatic approach. In conclusion, Thacher and Rein (2004) argue that, depending on the context, all four approaches to managing value conflicts (balancing, cycling, structural separation, casuistry) could be 'rational', and they offer some hypotheses about the conditions under which each approach is most promising. Others have built on Thacher and Rein's work by using empirical research to add more approaches to managing value conflicts (for example, Stewart, 2006; de Graaf et al, 2014). This road could generate hypotheses about the impact of particular combinations of approaches on the prevention of corporate and occupational crime. Such hypotheses would be more sophisticated than the simple hypotheses about the impact of one approach that were formulated earlier but they would also be less complicated and more parsimonious than a virtually endless list of hypotheses about the impact of all imaginable combinations between approaches.

A third road to further develop the idea of combining approaches is suggested by grid-group cultural theory literature itself. This road particularly focuses on the dynamics between the approaches to understand their impact. Drawing from social systems theory, Perri 6 (2003) proposes two mechanisms to explain those dynamics: positive and negative feedback. Positive feedback is a process by which an approach reinforces itself through a dynamic of self-radicalization. This can be benign at the start, but as the ethics management and regulation literatures described previously would predict, at some stage it will become vicious and self-destructive. Negative feedback occurs when the approaches clash. This could be the correcting 'homeostatic' processes described previously where, for example, the values-based approach to ethics management is checked by the rules-based approach. Yet, not all negative feedback leads to these correcting dynamics. Sometimes, the negative feedback can lead to gridlock or extreme forms of polarization. Using these two fundamental forces, Perri 6 (2003) proposes a theory on 'institutional viability', distinguishing between different forms of settlements between the four types of grid-group cultural theory.

What works for whom in what circumstances, and how?

Inspired by realist evaluation (Pawson and Tilley, 1997), our original 'what works in corporate and occupational crime prevention?' question can be reformulated as the more nuanced 'what works for whom in what circumstances?' This section attempts to offer the building blocks for a theoretical framework that guides the answer to this question.

First, and most obviously, as for the 'what' in 'what works?', we argued that the grid-group typology provides a language that can be used to conceptualize a broad range of corporate and occupational crime-prevention approaches. It claims that the effectiveness of a specific crime-prevention strategy in a specific regulatory regime or organization will depend on an appropriate mix between the four grid-group types. A hypothetical example in the area of ethics management can help to make this more concrete: the prevention of theft by employees. A policy that emphasizes the two high-grid quadrants in Table 2.1 comes easily to mind. Such a policy would combine elements of the hierarchist type, such as clear rules that include well-defined procedures for sanctioning those who break those rules, with some fatalist elements such as random inspections or unpredictable staffing. While less obvious, the low-grid quadrants of Table 2.1 could also generate interesting ideas. From an egalitarian perspective, an employee theft-prevention policy would emphasize fair treatment of staff members, relying on a long tradition of research showing the impact of fairness on unethical behaviour such as stealing (for example, Greenberg, 1990). It would also emphasize group loyalty and solidarity within the organization, expecting that this would reduce the likelihood that people would want to damage the organization through stealing. An individualist employee theft-prevention policy could contain incentive schemes. These might reward individuals who report on stealing by their colleagues or might offer free products to members of units where no stealing has been reported. More generally, one might expect that an individualist, entrepreneurial culture with fair rewards for performance might reduce the temptation to steal. Grid-group cultural theory would predict that each of these approaches not only has its desirable effects, but also its built-in risks and excesses. For example, if allowed to develop unabated, hierarchy and fatalism can lead to a rigid, rules-obsessed attitude among staff that weakens creativity and innovation. They can also demotivate staff and provoke reactance, thus ironically increasing the risk of employee theft. Their emphasis on respecting authority can also lead to staff members not speaking out against managers who are engaged in theft themselves. Of course, egalitarianism also carries its risks. Strong ties among employees increases the risk of collusion to steal. Likewise, individualism's emphasis on self-interest and individual performance can lead to a 'greed is good' culture that actually increases the risk of stealing. With all four types having their advantages as well as disadvantages, it is important to develop an appropriate mix that allows the types to compensate for one another's excesses. For example, an egalitarian-style emphasis on group solidarity and an individualist emphasis on an entrepreneurial attitude might help to compensate for the suffocating rigidity and paranoia that might come from fatalism. Egalitarianism can also help to mitigate the risks of an individualist-style emphasis on performance. Egalitarianism's own risk of unhealthy loyalties can in turn be mitigated by a mix of individualism, unpredictability (and, therefore, fatalism) and clear rules and sanctions (and, therefore, hierarchy). This employee theft example helps to show the power of the framework in developing the 'what' in 'what works?'. It supports creativity in the design of prevention strategies by offering four perspectives; it recognizes that each of the four perspectives has its own risks and it proposes to prevent those risk by designing an appropriate mix of the four perspectives.

Second, the 'works for whom?', part in our central research question might be the most contested one.[3] There are many different stakeholders in corporate and occupational crime prevention who all might have their own view on what it means for crime prevention to work. From a regulatory perspective, one might argue that the real indicator for success in, say, environmental crime prevention is less pollution (Braithwaite, 2016). Hence, if a conciliatory approach would reduce pollution it would be considered successful, even if that would mean perpetrators from the past getting away unpunished. Those reflecting from a more critical corporate crime perspective, on the other hand, might emphasize the importance of the punishment itself. From this perspective, criminalization is about satisfying public demands for justice, and more conciliatory approaches might undermine that goal (Almond and van Erp, 2018: 8). The fourfold grid-group typology might offer a fresh way of looking at these debates. Underlying each of the four approaches is a worldview that generates different views of risks and, therefore, different definitions of what is to be counted as success. Earlier work by Vaughan (2002, 2004) to use the typology to describe various approaches to punishment and social control might be helpful here.

Third, as for the 'in what circumstances?' part of the central research question, the contingency approaches to ethics management and regulation provide many conditions that might help to explain the success or failure of particular approaches to the prevention of corporate and occupational crime. The grid-group typology might help to reduce the complexity of those factors. For that, it might look for inspiration in earlier studies that used grid-group cultural theory to describe national cultures in the EU (Grendstad, 1999; Mamadouh, 1999) or across the world (Akbar and Vujić, 2014), bearing mind that using 'national culture' to explain corporate and occupational crime is not without its problems (Jou et al, 2016). The typology has also been used to describe organizational culture (Maesschalck, 2004b; Wouters and Maesschalck, 2014), an important contextual factor for crime prevention within organizations.

Europe as a laboratory to test what works in the prevention of corporate and occupational crime

This section proposes some ideas for a research agenda to test and further develop in a European context the theoretical framework of which some building blocks were presented earlier. Before turning to some examples of research designs, it is useful to point out that strategies to prevent corporate and occupational crime could work at different levels of analysis: teams or units within an organization, organizations, networks of organizations, industries, cities, regions, countries and the various transnational levels. Research designs could focus on all these levels separately, but could also aim to combine multiple levels, as will often be necessary to really understand corporate and occupational crime and how it can be prevented. Punch's (2008: 108–11) account of Nick Leeson's fraudulent behaviour that led to the collapse of the Barings Bank is a useful illustration. It shows failures in the Singapore office where he was working, in the bank's head office in London, at the level of the regulators and at the level of the banking industry as a whole.

The three research designs proposed here are intended to address the basic research question introduced previously: What works in corporate and occupational crime prevention? Against the background of the earlier discussion, that very general question can be specified in many more specific research questions. For example: is the grid-group typology of four approaches to corporate and occupational crime prevention empirically meaningful and analytically useful? Does empirical research show that a mix of the four types is more effective than strategies that are less polyrational? Are some combinations more effective than others in a particular context? If so, what are those combinations (for example, using Thacher and Rein's [2004] classification) and which elements in the context make a difference? Do mechanisms like positive and negative feedback help to explain the evolution of prevention strategies and their impact over time?

A first possible design to address those questions would consist of multiple case studies to assess the impact of a particular prevention strategy, that is, a particular mix of approaches in a particular context. To do that kind of analysis one would hope to find cases that are largely similar in context, but different in their prevention strategies. That would allow for conclusions where variation in the outcome can be explained by variation in the prevention strategies. To some extent, the EU provides such an environment. Member states share the EU's overall legal and regulatory framework and, to varying degrees, some characteristics of their political and cultural environment. At the same time, countries or even regions still differ significantly in their specific mix of approaches to the prevention of corporate and occupational crime. One could, for example, compare different prevention strategies in different countries within the same industry. A particularly interesting design would be to investigate a multinational company operating in several European countries and to compare how the same company responds to different prevention approaches within an overall shared framework and market. This is not to say, of course, that the EU provides a perfect natural experiment. There will be variations in the context (for example, national political culture, related policies) and differences in crime-prevention approaches will be confounded with those variations. In practice, it will be difficult to know whether differences in outcomes should be ascribed to the crime-prevention approach, to those contextual factors or to an interaction between both. While the experimental logic might help in the sampling of the cases (only vary on the intervention and keep the context as constant as possible), the actual research would benefit more from other, more flexible approaches such as realist evaluation (Pawson and Tilley, 1997; Pawson, 2006). The latter takes variation in context as a given and focuses on how, in a particular context, the intervention (for example, a particular corporate and occupational crime-prevention strategy) triggers particular mechanisms that lead to a particular outcome.

A second interesting design to address the research questions listed previously would be case studies centred around time series. In a critique of a systematic review on corporate crime deterrence (Schell-Busey et al, 2016), Braithwaite (2016) argues for such designs. He particularly invites criminologists to focus on big changes over time. Those changes can be beneficial, such as with the dramatic reduction in fatalities in mining in the UK and France in the 20th century, but they can also be problematic as with indicators of growing crime in the pharmaceutical industry (Braithwaite, 2016). While such studies would start from a quantitative time series, they should become real case studies, combining all types of quantitative and qualitative data to develop an explanation for those evolutions (Braithwaite, 2016). It would be very interesting to develop such time series for a particular phenomenon (for example, types of environmental pollution or types of crime in the pharmaceutical industry) for several European countries. Comparative case studies would then investigate whether changes in the corporate and occupational crime-prevention policy (and particularly positive and negative feedback dynamics between the approaches and the resulting mixes of approaches) help to explain between-country variations in the time series.

Third, cross-sectional quantitative studies could also help to test the theoretical framework introduced earlier in an EU context. At the organizational level, standardized measurement instruments could be developed to map the specific prevention strategies (as a combination of the four approaches) used within these organizations. This would then allow one to see whether those strategies and the way they are combined correlate with incidence of corporate and occupational crime or other related indicators. Similar studies could be imagined to compare national approaches in a particular industry across countries. Mixed-method designs are also possible, of course. One could, for example, apply nested analysis (Lieberman, 2005; Swedlow et al, 2009) by using the results of cross-sectional large-N research as a basis for the sampling of more in-depth case studies.

None of these designs will be easy to develop and many issues will have to be addressed. Some of those are specific to the theoretical framework. For example, how is it possible to measure a mixture of four approaches in a systematic way? Others are well known in the study of white-collar crime.

Conclusion

In her afterword to *The Routledge Handbook of White-Collar and Corporate Crime in Europe*, Croall (2015: 544) concludes: 'Even if asking a "what works question" is hampered by measurement and evidential difficulties, exploring alternative forms of law, different levels of state and self-regulation, compliance policies and different forms of sanction through comparative work and case studies is of great importance.'

While acknowledging these many difficulties, this chapter has nevertheless attempted to address the 'what works?' question by proposing the building blocks of a theoretical framework and suggesting three research designs to further test and develop that theoretical framework in a European context.

The advantage of reducing research on the prevention of corporate and occupational crime to an answer to the 'what works?' question is that it provides focus. In doing so, it increases the chance of cumulative research that progressively generates more sophisticated insights that are actually useful for practice. The disadvantage of such a focus, and particularly the focus on 'what works?', is the risk of developing blind spots, particularly for normative issues behind the question. To some extent, the suggestions formulated in this chapter do address those normative concerns. Expanding 'what works?' to 'what works for whom in what circumstances?' takes on board an awareness of the many different interests and perspectives that are at play in the prevention of corporate and occupational crime. Likewise, the proposed fourfold typology not only presents four approaches to the prevention of corporate and occupational crime, it also refers to four more fundamental worldviews. Hence, the recommendation that real-life prevention strategies should combine elements of all four approaches is actually also an argument for ideological pluralism. Sufficient sensitivity to these normative issues will remain important, however. The ambiguity that will result from polyrational combinations of all four types can also have its own price. Nelken (2012), for example, shows the risks of moral ambiguity around corporate crime and how this could lead to more permissive environments.

Notes

[1] The literature on regulation often refers to the latter strategy as 'compliance' (for example, Gunningham, 2010: 121), thus referring to voluntary compliance, as opposed to enforced compliance as a consequence of deterrence. Likewise, referring to debates in the 1980s and 1990s on how to react to white-collar crime, Lord and Levi (2015: 40) also refer to the 'compliance' and 'deterrence' approaches. Interestingly, and confusingly, ethics management literature at the organizational level often uses 'compliance' as a label for what we described as the 'rules-based' approach (for example, Paine, 1994), referring to the fact that employees are expected to comply with rules and regulations rather than use ethical decision making in which those rules are just one source. Thus, while there are significant similarities between the dichotomies in both areas, the label 'compliance' is used in opposite sides of the dichotomy.

[2] This paragraph is almost entirely taken from Maesschalck (2019).

[3] While in realist evaluation research 'works for whom' usually refers to the differential impact of an intervention on different groups of people, it might also refer to different perspectives on the intervention.

Acknowledgements

The author wishes to thank the participants in the seminar of the European Working Group on Organisational Crime in Manchester in June 2019 and particularly the discussants Judith van Erp and Aleksandra Jordanoska for their suggestions. He also thanks Rita Faria, Nicholas Lord, Milou Van Dijk and Marco Verweij for their very helpful comments on a later draft of this chapter.

References

6, P. (2003) 'Institutional viability: a neo-Durkheimian theory', *Innovation: The European Journal of Social Science Research*, 16(4): 395–416.

Akbar, Y. and Vujić, V. (2014) 'Explaining corruption: the role of national culture and its implications for international management', *Cross Cultural Management*, 21(2): 191–218. doi:10.1108/CCM-03-2013-0050

Almond, P. and van Erp, J. (2018) 'Regulation and governance versus criminology: disciplinary divides, intersections, and opportunities', *Regulation & Governance*, 14(2): 167–83. doi:10.1111/rego.12202

Ayres, I. and Braithwaite, J. (1992) *Responsive Regulation: Transcending the Deregulation Debate*, Oxford: Oxford University Press.

Black, J. and Baldwin, R. (2010) 'Really responsive risk-based regulation', *Law & Policy*, 32(2): 181–213.

Braithwaite, J. (2002) *Restorative Justice and Responsive Regulation*, Oxford: Oxford University Press.

Braithwaite, J. (2011) 'The essence of responsive regulation', *University of British Columbia Law Review*, 44: 475–520.

Braithwaite, J. (2016) 'In search of Donald Campbell', *Criminology & Public Policy*, 15(2): 41–37. doi:10.1111/1745-9133.12198

Braithwaite, J., Makkai, T. and Braithwaite, V.A. (2007) *Regulating Aged Care: Ritualism and the New Pyramid*, Cheltenham: Edward Elgar Publishing.

Caulkins, D.D. (1999) 'Is Mary Douglas's grid/group analysis useful for cross-cultural research?', *Cross-Cultural Research*, 33(1), 108–28.

Clinard, M.B. and Quinney, R. (1973) *Criminal Behavior Systems. A Typology* (2nd edn), New York: Holt, Rinehart and Winston.

Coleman, J.W. (1987) 'Toward an integrated theory of white-collar crime', *The American Journal of Sociology*, 93(2): 406–39.

Cooper, T. (2006) *The Responsible Administrator: An Approach to Ethics for the Administrative Role* (5th edn), San Francisco: Jossey-Bass.

Croall, H. (2015) 'White collar crime in Europe: afterword', in J. van Erp, W. Huisman and G. Vande Walle (eds) *The Routledge Handbook of White-Collar and Corporate Crime in Europe*, Abingdon: Routledge, pp 533–47.

de Graaf, G., Huberts, L. and Smulders, R. (2014) 'Coping with public value conflicts', *Administration & Society*, 48(9): 1101–27. doi:10.1177/0095399714532273

Douglas, M. (1970) *Natural Symbols: Explorations in Cosmology*. New York: Random House.

Gerber, J. and Jensen, E.L. (eds) (2007) *Encyclopedia of White-Collar Crime*, Westport: Greenwood Press.

Greenberg, J. (1990) 'Employee theft as a reaction to underpayment inequity: the hidden cost of pay cuts', *Journal of Applied Psychology*, 75(5): 561–8.

Grendstad, G. (1999) 'A political cultural map of Europe: a survey approach', *GeoJournal*, 47: 463–75.

Gunningham, N. (2010) 'Enforcement and compliance strategies', in R. Baldwin, M. Cave and M. Lodge (eds) *The Oxford Handbook of Regulation*, Oxford: Oxford University Press, pp 120–45.

Gunningham, N. (2016) 'Regulation: from traditional to cooperative', in S.R. Van Slyke, M.L. Benson and F.T. Cullen (eds) *The Oxford Handbook of White-Collar Crime*, Oxford: Oxford University Press, pp 503–20.

Gunningham, N., Grabosky, P. and Sinclair, D. (1998) *Smart Regulation: Designing Environmental Policy*, Oxford: Oxford University Press.

Gunningham, N. and Sinclair, D. (2017) 'Smart regulation', in P. Drahos (ed) *Regulatory Theory: Foundations and Applications*, Acton: Australian National University Press, pp 133–48.

Hood, C. (1998) *The Art of the State. Culture, Rhetoric, and Public Management*, Oxford: Clarendon Press.

Hood, C., James, O., Peters, G.B. and Scott, C. (2004) *Controlling Modern Government: Variety, Commonality and Change*, Cheltenham: Edward Elgar Press.

Huisman, W. (2016) 'Criminogenic organizational properties and dynamics', in S.R. Van Slyke, M.L. Benson and F.T. Cullen (eds) *The Oxford Handbook of White-Collar Crime*, Oxford: Oxford University Press, pp 435–62.

Jou, S., Hebenton, B. and Chang, L. (2016) 'Cultural variation', in S.R. Van Slyke, M.L. Benson, and F.T. Cullen (eds) *The Oxford Handbook of White-Collar Crime*, Oxford: Oxford University Press, pp 345–66.

Klitgaard, R. (1988) *Controlling Corruption*, Los Angeles: University of California Press.

Lieberman, E.S. (2005) 'Nested analysis as a mixed-method strategy for comparative research', *American Political Science Review*, 99(3): 435–52.

Lodge, M. (2009) 'The public management of risk: the case for deliberating among worldviews', *Review of Policy Research*, 26(4): 395–408. doi:10.1111/j.1541-1338.2009.00391.x

Lodge, M. and Hood, C. (2010) 'Regulation inside government: retro-theory vindicated or outdated?', in R. Baldwin, M. Cave and M. Lodge (eds) *The Oxford Handbook of Regulation*, Oxford: Oxford University Press, pp 590–609.

Lord, N. and Levi, M. (2015) 'Determining the adequate enforcement of white-collar and corporate crimes in Europe', in J. van Erp, W. Huisman and G. Vande Walle (eds) *The Routledge Handbook of White-Collar and Corporate Crime in Europe*, Abingdon: Routledge, pp 39–56.

Maesschalck, J. (2004a) 'Approaches to ethics management in the public sector: a proposed extension of the compliance-integrity continuum', *Public Integrity*, 7(1): 21–41. doi:10.1080/10999922.2004.11051267

Maesschalck, J. (2004b) 'Research note: a method for applying cultural theory in the study of organizations', *Innovation: The European Journal of Social Sciences*, 17(4): 377–86.

Maesschalck, J. (2019) 'Facing the dark side: on the unintended, unanticipated and unwelcome consequence of ethics management', in C.L. Jurkiewicz (ed) *Global Corruption and Ethics Management: Translating Theory into Action*, New York: Roman & Littlefield, pp 159–66.

Maleki, A. and Hendriks, F. (2015) 'Grid, group, and grade: challenges in operationalizing cultural theory for cross-national research', *Cross-Cultural Research*, 49(3): 250–80. doi:10.1177/1069397114555843

Mamadouh, V. (1999) 'National political cultures in the European Union', in M. Thompson, G. Grendstad and P. Selle (eds) *Cultural Theory as Political Science*, London: Routledge, pp 138–53.

Mars, G. (2006) 'Changes in occupational deviance: scams, fiddles and sabotage in the twenty-first century', *Crime, Law and Social Change*, 45: 285–96.

Mascini, P. (2016) 'Comparing assumptions underlying regulatory inspection strategies: implications for oversight policy', in S.R. Van Slyke, M.L. Benson and F.T. Cullen (eds) *The Oxford Handbook of White-Collar Crime*, Oxford: Oxford University Press, pp 521–39.

May, P.J. and Winter, S.C. (2011) 'Regulatory enforcement styles and compliance', in C. Parker and V.L. Nielsen (eds) *Explaining Compliance: Business Responses to Regulation*, Cheltenham: Edward Elgar, pp 222–44.

Nelken, D. (2012) 'White-collar and corporate crime', in M. Maguire, R. Morgan and R. Reiner (eds) *The Oxford Handbook of Criminology* (5th edn), Oxford: Oxford University Press, pp 623–59.

Ney, S. and Verweij, M. (2015) 'Messy institutions for wicked problems: how to generate clumsy solutions?' *Environment and Planning C: Government and Policy*, 33(6): 1679–96.

Nielsen, V.L. and Parker, C. (2009) 'Testing responsive regulation in regulatory enforcement', *Regulation & Governance*, 3(4): 376–99.

Paine, L.S. (1994) 'Managing for organizational integrity', *Harvard Business Review*, 72(2): 106–17.

Pawson, R. (2006) *Evidence-Based Policy: A Realist Perspective*, London: Sage.

Pawson, R. and Tilley, N. (1997) *Realistic Evaluation,* London: Sage.

Punch, M. (2008) 'The organization did it: individuals, corporations and crime', in J. Minkes and L. Minkes (eds) *Corporate and White-Collar Crime*, London: Sage, pp 102–21.

Schell-Busey, N., Simpson, S.S., Rorie, M. and Alper, M. (2016) 'What works? A systematic review of corporate crime deterrence', *Criminology & Public Policy*, 15(2): 387–416. doi:10.1111/1745-9133.12195

Sparks, R. (2001) 'Degrees of estrangement: the cultural theory of risk and comparative penology', *Theoretical Criminology*, 5(2): 159–76. doi:10.1177/1362480601005002002

Stewart, J. (2006) 'Value conflict and policy change', *Review of Policy Research*, 23(1): 183–95. doi:10.1111/j.1541-1338.2006.00192.x

Swedlow, B., Kall, D., Zhou, Z., Hammitt, J.K. and Wiener, J.B. (2009) 'Theorizing and generalizing about risk assessment and regulation through comparative nested analysis of representative cases', *Law & Policy*, 31(2): 236–69.

Thacher, D. and Rein, M. (2004) 'Managing value conflict in public policy', *Governance*, 17(4): 457–86. doi:10.1111/j.0952-1895.2004.00254.x

Thompson, M., Ellis, R. and Wildavsky, A. (1990) *Cultural Theory*, Boulder: Westview Press.

Vaughan, B. (2002) 'Cultured punishments: the promise of grid-group theory', *Theoretical Criminology*, 6(4): 411–31.

Vaughan, B. (2004) 'The greening and governance of crime control', *Criminal Justice*, 4(1): 5–28. doi:10.1177/1466802504042221

Verweij, M., Douglas, M., Ellis, R., Engel, C., Hendriks, F., Lohmann, S. and Thompson, M. (2006) 'Clumsy solutions for a complex world: the case of climate change', *Public Administration*, 84(4): 817–43.

Verweij, M. and Thompson, M. (2006) *Clumsy Solutions for a Complex World: Governance, Politics and Plural Perceptions*, Basingstoke: Palgrave Macmillan.

Wouters, K. and Maesschalck, J. (2014) 'Surveying organizational culture to explore grid-group cultural theory: instrument design and preliminary empirical results', *International Journal of Organizational Analysis*, 22(2): 224–46.

3

How to Prioritize White-Collar Crime Research in the European Union in Relation to Internal and External Security

Sunčana Roksandić

Introduction

As has been underlined by the European Union (EU), many of today's security concerns originate from instability in the EU's immediate neighbourhood and changing forms of radicalization, violence and terrorism. Threats are becoming more varied and more international, as well as increasingly cross-border and cross-sectorial in nature. These threats require an effective and coordinated response at the European level. The European Agenda on Security (European Commission, 2015b) from 2015 prioritizes terrorism, organized crime and cybercrime as interlinked areas with a strong cross-border dimension, where 'EU action can make a real difference' (European Commission, 2015b: 2). On the other hand, in September 2018, a historic meeting of the United Nations (UN) Security Council occurred, focusing for the very first time on corruption and conflict and emphasizing the role of anti-corruption policies in maintaining international peace and security. After the COVID-19 pandemic, it is expected that health-related questions and access to healthcare will become key security issues. In the healthcare sector, close links to corruption and fraud are found as well. Given these diverse security concerns within the EU region, this chapter deals with questions about which areas could be considered as the key priority areas for European white-collar and corporate crime scholarship when taking into consideration the European Agenda on Security, especially if the EU maintains its role as a global leader. This chapter argues that white-collar crime research should prioritize violations of human security in the context of the EU's internal and external security.

How security should be understood today

When discussing not only security agendas and policies but also research in Europe, the idea of security should be understood within the concept of 'human security'. This refers to protecting 'vital freedoms' which are fundamental to human existence and development. Human security is therefore a means of 'protecting people from severe and pervasive threats, both natural and societal, and empowering individuals and communities to develop the capabilities for making informed choices and acting on their own behalf', while 'vital freedoms' refers to the 'inalienable fundamental rights and freedoms that are laid down in the Universal Declaration of Human Rights and other human rights instruments' (Ogata and Cels, 2003: 274). The concept of human security partly emerged from the United Nations Development Programme (UNDP) Human Development Report 1994 (United Nations Development Programme, 1994), which lists seven types of security: economic, food, health, environment, personal, community and political. The Commission on Human Security, an independent group not affiliated with the UN Commission on Human Security mentioned later, defines human security as 'protecting the vital core of all human lives in ways that enhance human freedoms and human fulfilment' and 'protecting people from critical (severe) and pervasive (widespread) threats and situations' (Commission on Human Security, 2003: 4). The goals mentioned in the Commission on Human Security's (2003) report are often summarized as the 'freedom from fear and want' and they include: protecting people in violent conflict; supporting the security of people on the move, establishing a human security transition fund for post-conflict situations; encouraging fair trade and markets to benefit the extreme poor; working to provide minimum living standards everywhere; according a higher priority to ensure universal access to basic healthcare; developing an efficient and equitable global system for patent rights; empowering all people with universal basic education; and clarifying the need for a global human identity while respecting the freedom of individuals to have diverse identities and affiliations.

Here, the 'four freedoms' set out by US President Franklin Roosevelt during his State of the Union address on 6 January 1941 should be remembered. These are freedom of speech, freedom of worship, freedom from want and freedom from fear: freedoms people ought to enjoy everywhere in the world. By expressing these freedoms, Roosevelt endorsed what would later become known as human security. As emphasized by Louise Arbour, then United Nations high commissioner for human rights, in January 2005, the importance of economic, social and cultural rights cannot be overstated in the protection of security and should have an impact in the creating and researching of EU security policy:

> The importance of economic, social and cultural rights cannot be overstated. Poverty and exclusion lie behind many of the security threats that we continue to face both within and across borders and can thus place at risk the promotion and protection of all human rights. Even in the most prosperous economies, poverty and gross inequalities persist and many individuals and groups live under conditions that amount to a denial of economic, social, civil, political and cultural human rights. Social and economic inequalities affect access to public life and to justice. Globalization has generated higher rates of economic growth, but too many of its benefits have been enjoyed unequally, within and across different societies. Such fundamental challenges to human security require action at home as well as international cooperation. (Cited in United Nations Office of the High Commissioner for Human Rights, 2008: 5)

Human security can be understood as an emerging normative framework in international relations (Oberleitner, 2005: 188). With the adoption of the Sustainable Development Goals (SDGs), the United Nations General Assembly has reaffirmed the notion of human security. Therefore, the notion of human security provides an even more integrated approach relevant to governments and societies affected by extreme poverty, underdevelopment, recurring violent conflicts, systemic violence and human rights violations. In addition, corruption and bribery in all their forms are one of the targeted areas of Sustainable Development Goal 16 (SDG 16), which addresses 'peace, justice and strong institutions'. Beyond SDG 16, corruption is also considered an impediment to the attainment of all other SDGs.[1]

White-collar crime and corruption

The 'mess' invoked by definitional issues relating to white-collar and corporate crimes has long been recognized (see Friedrichs, 2015: 552; who is invoking Geis, 1974: 283; see also Roksandić, 2017b: 51–65). In this chapter, I use the term in the widest possible sense, including economic crimes and 'hybrid types' (Friedrichs, 2015: 553) such as political white-collar crimes (including political-corporate crimes), state-corporate crimes and crimes of the powerful. White-collar crimes lead not only to monetary loss but also to corporate and/or economic violence. Economic violence includes, but is not limited to, violations of economic and social rights, corruption and plunder of natural resources (Sharp, 2014: 2). A holistic approach to the narrative of security is becoming more visible in recent security policies (see, for example, European Commission, 2015a; European Commission, 2015b; European Union Global Strategy, 2016) that also emphasize the relevance of the fight against corruption. Also, several North Atlantic Treaty Organization (NATO) Summit Declarations (for example, those from the Chicago, Brussels and Warsaw summits) contain references to corruption and its relationship to security challenges. At the Warsaw Summit, the new NATO Building Integrity policy was introduced which reaffirmed NATO's conviction that transparent and accountable defence institutions under democratic control are fundamental to stability in the Euro-Atlantic area and essential for international security cooperation (see Paragraph 130 of the Warsaw Declaration, NATO, 2016). It is well known today that large-scale corruption in Afghanistan is one of the main security threats to long-term stability and security in the country (see North Atlantic Treaty Organization, 2014; Special Inspector General for Afghanistan Reconstruction, 2016). Similar conclusions could be stated for the Western Balkans (WB) countries. As emphasized in an EU communication from 2018 regarding WB countries (European Commission, 2018a), WB countries show clear elements of state capture, including links with organized crime (see also Kemp et al, 2013) and corruption at all levels of government and administration, as well as a strong entanglement of public and private interests. A concrete and sustained track record in tackling corruption, money laundering and organized crime should be established as a matter of urgency. In addition, for all WB states it was underlined that trial monitoring in the field of serious corruption and organized crime should be introduced and indicators of reform implementation should be developed. Progress in judicial reform needs to be measured by the effectiveness of justice that the system is able to provide to its citizens and businesses (European Commission, 2018a: 10).

Tackling organized crime and corruption are identified among the most important preconditions for EU integration and this is a priority security question. Especially for such corruption cases that belong to political white-collar crimes or state-corporate crimes, it would be of great importance for policy makers (including regulatory bodies) to have available criminological research that compares different types of perpetrators of such crimes and their culpability with, for example, perpetrators of classical international crimes (see Smeulers and Hola, 2010: 179–88).

Corruption as understood through the prism of human security is not just the abuse of entrusted power by public officials in their interactions with citizens, it is a serious crime that poses a threat to the stability and security of societies. It can cause conflict and undermine peace-building initiatives, jeopardizing good governance, economic development and the rule of law (Rose-Ackerman, 2008; Shelley, 2014).[2] Corrupt and unaccountable security institutions are a cause for human insecurity and state failure (Oberleitner, 2005: 196).

It is surprising that it took the international community a while to achieve a global consensus on how corruption is detrimental to long-term stability and global prosperity (Roksandić, 2017a, 2017b). In 2015, the Ramos-Horta Report that reviewed United Nations peace operations, underlined how corruption and ostentation are causes of inequality and tension: the more a country is free from corruption, the more leaders show humility and integrity, the more they are respected and are followed, the better the chances for peace to gain roots (Ramos-Horta, 2015: 27). At the inaugural United Nations Security Council Briefing on Corruption in 2018, UN Secretary-General António Manuel de Oliveira Guterres emphasized that 'corruption breeds disillusion with government and governance and is often at the root of political dysfunction and social disunity' (UN Security Council Briefing, 2018). He also noted that corruption is closely intertwined with other forms of instability, such as illicit trafficking in arms, drugs and people, terrorism and violent extremism.[3]

White-collar crime and healthcare after COVID-19

Health is among the most profitable and corrupt sectors (see United Nations General Assembly, 2015). Health-sector corruption, including, for example, the bribing of health officials and unofficial payments to healthcare providers, obstructs the ability of states to fulfil their right to health obligations and to guarantee available, accessible, acceptable and good-quality health services, goods and facilities. Corruption affecting health also occurs in other sectors and industries, such as water, food and beverages and tobacco. Moreover, corruption has significant implications for equality and non-discrimination since it has a particularly marked impact on the health of populations in situations of vulnerability and social exclusion, in particular those living in poverty and children (United Nations General Assembly, 2015: 3, para 3). Furthermore, in the report, it was emphasized that there is a need to apply a human rights-based approach to health and related policies and avoid selective approaches to human rights (United Nations General Assembly, 2015: 20, para 86; Roksandić, 2020: 145). By underlying that, the European Agenda on Security, with regards to both internal and external security, should be amended to include biosecurity and access to healthcare as well as all seven types of security (for food security, see Johnson and Walters, 2014). After the COVID-19 pandemic it is to be expected that public procurement of necessary equipment will be linked to corruption and therefore is of interest for white-collar criminology.

A strong healthcare system is a security issue. Slovenia has already started a criminal investigation, in June 2020, in relation to the abuse of procurement procedures in purchasing medical equipment during COVID-19's first wave (Trkanjec, 2020), which resulted in the resignation of two ministers and scrutiny of the whole government. The victims are the most vulnerable, patients in general, and the threat exists that access to COVID-19 treatment will be halted or unavailable due to white-collar crimes. It seems that this new security threat needs new research. As Sutherland (1983) researched war profiteering, contemporary white-collar criminologists should do the same with COVID-19 profiteers. It is as much as a security threat even if not yet defined as such in security policies. In June 2020, the United States bought up the entire global supply of the key COVID-19 drug Remdesivir for the following three months, leaving none for the UK, Europe or most of the rest of the world, putting the right to healthcare and the adequate response to the deprivation of access to essential medicine and medical care to the test (see Boseley, 2020).

Given the above, and as Quinney (1973) has emphasized, criminologists should study the mechanisms that prevent socially harmful business behaviour from being criminalized by law. For this reason, most criminologists do not limit the definition of corporate crime to behaviour that is punishable by criminal law, but also include the violations of administrative and civil regulation of business (Huisman, 2008: 185). This perspective is embedded within the very core of the white-collar crime concept: researching perpetrators who are of high social status and respectability and their motivations, forms of involvement and denial. The same is valid for corporations (for example, motivation, opportunity and lack of control).

White-collar crime and migration

Another relevant area for the EU's internal and external security is migration. For migration, it is worth citing A European Agenda on Migration (European Commission, 2015c):

> Every person's migration tells its own story. Misguided and stereotyped narratives often tend to focus only on certain types of flows, overlooking the inherent complexity of this phenomenon, which impacts society in many different ways and calls for a variety of responses. To try to halt the human misery created by those who exploit migrants, we need to use the EU's global role and wide range of tools to address the root causes of migration. Some of these are deep-seated but must be addressed. Globalisation and the communication revolution have created opportunities and raised expectations. Others are the consequence of wars and crises from Ukraine to the Middle East, Asia and North Africa. The impact of global poverty and conflict do not end at national frontiers. Europe should continue to be a safe haven for those fleeing persecution as well as an attractive destination for the talent and entrepreneurship of students, researchers and workers. Upholding our international commitments and values while securing our borders and at the same time creating the right conditions for Europe's economic prosperity and societal cohesion is a difficult balancing act that requires coordinated action at the European level.

This adds another argument to the statement that it is quite clear that European white-collar criminologists could engage more in research that is oriented towards political white-collar crimes that are fuelling conflicts outside of Europe due to large-scale profiteering and financing of corrupt leaders to get access to much-needed natural resources (see, for example, Congo and Sierra Leone; for further examples see

Huisman, 2014; Huisman and van Sliedregt, 2014; Roksandić, 2017a). Those crimes are not only the issue of external but also internal EU security. In this vein, more research of the abuse of migrant workers and workers coming from countries in the south-east of Europe that work in, for example, meat factories in Western European states is needed to be among the priorities. These revelations (see, for example, Lee, 2020), due to their severe consequences for human dignity and the destiny of many individuals, should have an impact in prioritizing white-collar crime research during the currently ongoing COVID-19 pandemic. According to Levi (2014: 256–7), it has become hard for business actors to justify their behaviour by invoking willful blindness as an excuse for the consequences of their actions, especially when dealing with state officials or companies located in conflict or transitional areas. The same could be stated for factories within the EU if large-scale human rights violations occur. For instance, although serving as a catalyst for conflicts, and as a consequence of and an incentive for migration, natural resource-related crimes still constitute an under-explored field within criminology (for example, the illicit activity and looting of natural resources in West Africa.

Here, criminologists are bound by incomplete data (see Barak, 2008: 68). However, there are many reports by non-governmental organizations (NGOs) available, including those by The Sentry on profiteering from conflict areas that could be of value (see, for example, The Sentry, 2020). In addition, as can be seen by the recent report by the UN Independent International Fact-Finding Mission on Myanmar (Business and Human Rights Resource Centre, 2019) concerning the persecution of the Rohingya people, military business ties are exposed that deserve the attention of white-collar crime scholars.

In any case, identification of what a security threat is must be done in accordance with the human security concept and must be re-evaluated to correspond to today's realities. Due to globalization and the current economic system, much of the threats are linked to (political) white-collar and organized crime. In the European Security Strategy 2003, key threats were identified as terrorism, proliferation of weapons of mass destruction, regional conflicts, state failure and organized crime. In 2010, the European Internal Security Strategy identified the following key threats: terrorism, serious and organized crime, cybercrime, cross-border crime, violent crimes, natural and man-made disasters, and a number of other common phenomena such as traffic accidents. In the European Agenda on Security, priority areas for response were identified, including: a stronger response to domestic and international terrorism and related activities, serious and organized cross-border crime, trafficking in human beings, trafficking in firearms, economic crimes and crimes against the environment. It is underlined that human, social and economic costs feed terrorism and cybercrime. Of course, we must be aware of possible breaches of human rights while trying to enhance human security: security from terrorism being an excellent example (Ramakrishna, 2014: 159–81).

How to proceed

Today, it cannot not be overlooked how serious and widespread economic and environmental offences and serious violations of the right to health, threaten peace, security and the wellbeing not only of nation-states, but of Europe and of the world. If security threats and criminological research as well as law should follow the pace of society, the question is why there is a discrepancy between defined security threats in the EU (both internal and external), actual human security threats, scientific research and policy making and legal regulations that follow those policies.

It seems that ignoring the aforementioned crimes and violations, human security threats and violations that often are among root causes of conflicts, create new cycles of armed conflict and/or physical violence as well as internal and external insecurity. In addition, it seems that contemporary security threats, as defined in national policies and in the European Agenda on Security, alongside today's internationally recognized human rights, require a substantial development of new definitions and/or interpretations of existing legal provisions. In any case, the European and global understanding of what security threats are today and whether to prioritize white-collar crime research in the EU should be re-examined. The opposite holds true as well. Security policies must follow research findings of white-collar crime research in Europe in relation to creating comprehensive internal and external security policy for the EU. In that sense, all EU member states and white-collar crime experts should have an equal say. Only synergy can paint the whole story on the consequences of white-collar crimes on human security, both internal and external.

The fear of 'governing through crime' and enhancing 'security over justice' cannot be taken as an argument to easily dismiss the need to connect white-collar and organized crime research with researching priority security areas. As Hudson emphasized (2012: 6), recent criminological and socio-legal literature has tended to dichotomize justice and security: the pursuit of one being at the expense of the other. Rather than looking at security and justice as both being valued social goods – interrelated and complementary even if sometimes conflicting – criminological attention, in particular, has tended to see the relationship as somewhat zero-sum, such that increasing emphasis on one is almost inevitably at the expense of the other. Furthermore, when discussing the nexus of internal and external security question, one can agree with Hudson (2012: 13):

> There is no evidence to suggest that the inhabitants of the more dangerous places on the earth do not have the same desire for security than the inhabitants of affluent, well-governed places do. Neither is there any evidence that they do not also desire justice in the sense of being treated fairly, being able to defend themselves against accusations, being free from torture if they are suspected or convicted of offences, and receiving assistance and compensation if they suffer losses. The distribution problem is entailed in the fact that we want security and justice for ourselves and for those with whom we share a sense of community, and we want security from others and have little concern for justice toward others if we feel they threaten our own safety and well-being.

In addition, research is needed to see whether European white-collar crime research is following defined security threats, and/or to what extent human security threats are defined based on the findings of European white-collar and organized crime scholars. More research is needed as well in the area that connects biosecurity, health and food security and white-collar and organized crime.

Conclusion

As witnesses of the need to implement the Paris Agreement, we need to achieve the 'targets' of reducing global emissions by 40 per cent by 2030. The European Agenda on Security explicitly enumerates criminal offences against the environment and emphasizes that the European Commission itself will consider the need for strengthening regulatory and prosecutorial bodies. For business and economic actors, this concept often entails significant savings due to non-compliance with the legal framework for the protection of environment. This does not only have a clear effect on fair market competition, but also on the certainty of implementing the Paris Agreement. It seems that an extra tool is needed in the fight against non-compliance of businesses with the environmental legal framework in today's globalized world. White-collar criminology could be of great help here in order to achieve environmental security.

Finding the answer on how to prioritize white-collar crime research in the EU in relation to the EU's internal and external security has the potential to have a strong impact on the wider society as well. At the European level, many of today's human security concerns originate from the instability in the EU's immediate neighbourhood and the changing forms of radicalization, violent terrorism and organized corruption that are occurring both within and outside of the EU's external borders (for example, the WB countries and the Caucasus). European internal and global security is mutually interdependent and interlinked. The European response to security threats must therefore be comprehensive and based on a coherent set of actions combining internal and external dimensions. For groups involved in transnational organized crime, like trafficking in drugs, arms or persons, countries emerging from conflict often present the perfect conditions for their activities. Weak state institutions, including the judiciary, widespread availability of weapons, large numbers of unemployed former fighters and well-established smuggling networks used during conflict, among other factors, could easily turn post-conflict environments into areas prone to organized crime.[4] In any case, threats are becoming more varied and more international, as well as increasingly cross-border and cross-sectorial in nature (European Commission, 2015b). Such complex threats require not only a unified, practical response from member states of the EU, but also the tracking down of the root causes and following them up with adequate legal responses. For example, Recommendations 46–7 from the Oslo Outcome Statement on Corruption involving Vast Quantities of Assets (VQA) (United Nations Office on Drugs and Crime, 2019) stressed the need to explore more new, innovative ideas concerning addressing the problem of serious corruption cases, such as the establishment of an international special rapporteur for anti-corruption, the development of a protocol to the UN Convention Against Corruption on corruption involving VQA, exploring the possibility of extending the jurisdiction of the International Criminal Court to include corruption involving VQA, creating international commissions against corruption and impunity, as well as elevating the Jakarta Statement on Principles for Anti-Corruption Agencies to a more binding instrument, as well as the promotion of the three zero principles as enshrined in the Beijing Initiative for the Clean Silk Road. To make a parallel comparison, at the African Union level, more and more emphasis in research and policy making is being given to state capture due to large scale corruption and denial of basic rights.

Notwithstanding the large number of opportunities for white-collar crimes scholars for testing theories and typologies, a clear emphasis on understanding the root causes of conflicts or threats in the EU Security Agenda could be one of the ways to priorities white-collar crime research in the EU in conjunction with the EU's internal and external security. The other way to prioritize research could be by identifying harm and economic violence that are greatly violating human dignity and universally recognized human rights. According to the EU Security Agenda, tackling security threats while upholding European values is underlined. To maximize the benefits of existing EU measures and, where necessary, deliver new and complementary actions, all actors involved have to work together based on five key principles: ensuring full compliance with fundamental rights; guaranteeing more transparency, accountability and democratic control; ensuring better application and implementation of existing EU legal instruments; providing a more cohesive inter-agency and a cross-sectorial approach; and bringing together all internal and external dimensions of security.

If clear discrepancies exist between the notion of human security, security policy agendas, the criminological research of white-collar crime experts and legal responses, the reason as to why those discrepancies exist should be further researched as well. In these terms, white-collar criminologists should also study the mechanisms that prevent harmful business behaviour from being criminalized by law (Quinney, 1973). It also could include why the concept of human security is not entirely embraced by EU security agendas (both internal and external).

Notes

[1] See Module 11: Access to Justice for Victims, of the United Nations Office on Drugs and Crime (UNODC) Education for Justice (E4J) University Module Series on Anti-Corruption, Available at: www.unodc.org/e4j/en/crime-prevention-criminal-justice/module-11/index.html

[2] See also Module 2: Crime Prevention, of the UNODC E4J University Module Series on Anti-Corruption, Available at: www.unodc.org/e4j/en/crime-prevention-criminal-justice/module-2/index.html

[3] See the UNODC E4J Modules on Anti-Corruption for more details and cases.

[4] See the UNODC E4J Modules on Anti-Corruption.

References

Barak, G. (2008) 'Towards an integrative study of international crimes and state-corporate gross criminality: a reciprocal approach to human rights violations', in A. Smeulers and R. Haveman (eds) *Supranational Criminology: Towards a Criminology of International Crimes*, Antwerp, Oxford, Portland: Intersentia, pp 51–76.

Boseley, S. (2020) 'US buys up world stock of key Covid-19 drug Remdesivir', *The Guardian*, [online] 30 June, Available at: www.theguardian.com/us-news/2020/jun/30/us-buys-up-world-stock-of-key-covid-19-drug

Business and Human Rights Resource Centre (2019) 'UN Fact-Finding Mission on Myanmar exposes military business ties, calls for targeted sanctions and arms embargoes', 5 August, Available at: www.business-humanrights.org/en/un-fact-finding-mission-on-myanmar-exposes-military-business-ties-calls-for-targeted-sanctions-arms-embargoes

Commission on Human Security (2003) 'Human security now: protecting and empowering people', 1 May, Available at: https://reliefweb.int/report/world/human-security-now-protecting-and-empowering-people

European Commission (2015a) 'A European agenda on migration', 13 May, Available at: https://ec.europa.eu/home-affairs/sites/homeaffairs/files/what-we-do/policies/european-agenda-migration/background-information/docs/communication_on_the_european_agenda_on_migration_en.pdf

European Commission (2015b) 'The European agenda on security,' 28 April, Available at: www.cepol.europa.eu/sites/default/files/european-agenda-security.pdf

European Commission (2015c) 'A European agenda on migration', 13 May, Available at: https://eur-lex.europa.eu/legal-content/EN/TXT/HTML/?uri=CELEX:52015DC0240&from=EL

European Commission (2018) 'A credible enlargement perspective for and [sic] enhanced EU engagement with the Western Balkans', 6 February, Available at: https://op.europa.eu/en/publication-detail/-/publication/e3f0797b-28cb-11e8-b5fe-01aa75ed71a1

European Union (2016), 'Delivering on the European Agenda on Security to fight against terrorism and pave the way towards an effective and genuine Security Union', 20 April, Available at: https://eur-lex.europa.eu/resource.html?uri=cellar:9aeae420-0797-11e6-b713-01aa75ed71a1.0022.02/DOC_1&format=PDF

European Union Global Strategy (2016) 'Shared vision, common action: a stronger Europe', June, Available at: http://eeas.europa.eu/archives/docs/top_stories/pdf/eugs_review_web.pdf

Friedrichs, D.O. (2015) 'White-collar crime in Europe: American reflections', in J. van Erp, W. Huisman and G. Vande Walle (eds) *The Routledge Handbook of White-Collar and Corporate Crime in Europe*, London and New York: Routledge, pp 548–60.

Geis, G. (1974) 'Avocational crime', in D. Glazer (ed) *Handbook of Criminology*, New York: Rand McNally, pp 273–98.

Hudson, B. (2012) 'Who needs justice? Who needs security?', in B. Hudson and S. Ugelvik (eds) *Justice and Security in the 21st Century: Risks, Rights and the Rule of Law*, Abingdon, New York: Routledge, pp 6–24.

Huisman, W. (2008) 'Corporations and international crimes', in A. Smeulers and R. Haverman (eds) *Supranational Criminology: Towards a Criminology of International Crimes*, Mortsel: Intersentia, pp 181–213.

Huisman, W. (2014) 'Compliance and corporate crime control', in D. Weisburd and G.J.N. Bruinsma (eds) *The Encyclopedia of Criminology and Criminal Justice*, New York: Springer, pp 489–96.

Huisman, W. and van Sliedregt, E. (2010) 'Rogue traders, Dutch businessmen, international crimes and corporate complicity', *Journal of International Criminal Justice*, 8: 803–28.

Johnson, H. and Walters, R. (2014) 'Food security', in M. Gill (ed) *The Handbook of Security* (2nd edn), Basingstoke: Palgrave, pp 404–26.

Kemp, W., Shaw, M. and Boutellis, A. (2013) 'The elephant in the room: how can peace operations deal with organized crime?', International Peace Institute, Available at: www.ipinst.org/wp-content/uploads/2013/06/elephant_in_the_room.pdf

Lee, G. (2020) 'Coronavirus: what went wrong at Germany's Gütersloh meat factory?', *BBC News*, [online] 25 June, Available at: www.bbc.com/news/world-europe-53177628

Levi, M. (2014) 'Fighting organized crime and the threats to business', in M. Gill (ed) *The Handbook of Security* (2nd edn), Basingstoke: Palgrave, pp 256–78.

North Atlantic Treaty Organization (NATO) (2013) 'Building integrity and reducing corruption in defence', Available at: www.nato.int/cps/en/natohq/topics_104893.htm

NATO (2014) 'Building integrity and reducing corruption in defence, a compendium for best practices' (vol 2), Available at: www.nato.int/nato_static_fl2014/assets/pdf/pdf_2016_12/20161209_1612-Anti-corruption-Effort-Afghanistan.pdf

NATO (2016) 'Warsaw Summit Communiqué', Available at: www.nato.int/cps/en/natohq/official_texts_133169.htm

Oberleitner, G. (2005) 'Human security: a challenge to international law?', *Global Governance*, 11: 185–203.

Ogata, S. and Cels, J. (2003) 'Human security: protecting and empowering the people', *Global Governance,* 9(3): 273–82.

Quinney, R. (1973) *Critique of Legal Order: Crime Control in Capitalist Society*, Boston: Little Brown & Company.

Ramakrishna, K. (2014) 'From "old" to "new" terrorism: history, current trends and future prospectives', in M. Gill (ed) *The Handbook of Security* (2nd edn), Basingstoke: Palgrave, pp 159–81.

Ramos-Horta, J. (2015) 'Report of the High-level Independent Panel on Peace Operations on uniting our strengths for peace: politics, partnership and people', S/2015/446, Available at: https://digitallibrary.un.org/record/795940?ln=en

Roksandić, S. (2017a) 'Filling the void: the case for international economic criminal law', *Zeitschrift für die gesamte Strafrechtswissenschaft*, 129: 581–884.

Roksandić, S. (2017b) *Prosecuting Serious Economic Crimes as International Crimes: A New Mandate for the ICC?* Berlin: Duckner & Humblot.

Roksandić, S. (2020) 'Systemic deprivation of access to essential medicine and medical care: a crime against humanity?', in C. Fournet and A. Matwijkiw (eds) *Bio Law and International Criminal Law, Towards Interdisciplinary Synergies*, Leiden, Boston: Brill, pp 141–68.

Rose-Ackerman, S. (2008) 'Corruption and post-conflict peace building', *Yale Law School Faculty Scholarship Series*, 593, Available at: https://digitalcommons.law.yale.edu/fss_papers/593

Sharp, D.N. (2014) 'Introduction: addressing economic violence in times of transition', in D.N. Sharp (ed) *Justice and Economic Violence in Transition*, New York: Springer, pp 1–26.

Shelley, L.I. (2014) *Dirty Entanglements: Corruption, Crime, and Terrorism*, Cambridge: Cambridge University Press.

Smeulers, A. and Hola, B. (2010) 'ICTY and the culpability of different types of perpetrators of international crimes', in A. Smeulers (ed) *Collective Violence and International Criminal Justice: An Interdisciplinary Approach*, Antwerp, Oxford, Portland: Intersentia, pp 175–206.

Special Inspector General for Afghanistan Reconstruction (SIGAR) (2016) 'Corruption in conflict: lessons from the U.S. experience in Afghanistan', September, Available at: www.sigar.mil/pdf/lessonslearned/SIGAR-16-58-LL.pdf

Sutherland, E. (1983) *White-Collar Crime: The Uncut Version*, New Haven: Yale University Press.

The Sentry (2020) 'Making a killing: South Sudanese military leaders' wealth, explained', 27 May, Available at: https://thesentry.org/reports/making-a-killing/

Trkanjec, Ž. (2020) 'Potpuni kaos u Sloveniji: uhićen ministar gospodarstva, U Janšinoj Vladi nižu se ostavke! Potpredsjednik vlade Počivalšek sumnjiči se za kazneno djelo nanošenja štete javnim sredstvima pri nabavi respiratora', *Jutarnji list*, [online] 30 June, Available at: www.jutarnji.hr/vijesti/svijet/potpuni-kaos-u-sloveniji-uhicen-ministra-gospodarstva-u-jansinoj-vladi-nizu-se-ostavke-15005445

United Nations Development Programme (UNDP) (1994) 'Human development report 1994', 16 March, Available at: http://hdr.undp.org/sites/default/files/reports/255/hdr_1994_en_complete_nostats.pdf

United Nations General Assembly (2015) 'Report of the Special Rapporteur on the right of everyone to the enjoyment of the highest attainable standard of physical and mental health', 2 April, Available at: www.ohchr.org/EN/HRBodies/HRC/RegularSessions/Session29/Documents/A_HRC_29_33_ENG.DOCX

United Nations Office on Drugs and Crime (UNODC) (2019) 'Oslo outcome statement on corruption involving vast quantities of assets', 14 June, Available at: www.unodc.org/documents/corruption/meetings/OsloEGM2019/Oslo_Outcome_Statement_on_Corruption_involving_Vast_Quantities_of_Assets_-_FINAL_VERSION.pdf

United Nations Office of the High Commissioner for Human Rights (OHCHR) (2008) 'Fact sheet no. 33, frequently asked questions on economic, social and cultural rights', [online] December, Available at: www.refworld.org/docid/499176e62.html

United Nations Secretary-General (2018) 'Secretary-General's remarks to the Security Council on corruption in conflict', UN Security Council Briefing, Available at: www.un.org/sg/en/content/sg/statement/2018-09-10/secretary-generals-remarks-security-council-corruption-conflict

4

Corruption and Comparative Analyses across Europe: Developing New Research Traditions

Nicholas Lord, Karin van Wingerde and Michael Levi

Introduction

The significance of 'corruption' in Europe has arisen both through the work of established scientific studies and scholarship seeking to understand its nature, scope, extent and control, and as a priority of state and non-state organizations seeking to reshape anti-corruption policy and practice within individual nation-states and the European Union (EU) more generally. Corruption is variously defined in social science and policy, but the European Commission (EC), in line with the international anti-corruption agenda, defines the concept as 'the abuse of power for private gain' (European Commission, nd). The EC suggests corruption takes many forms, including bribery, trading in influence, abuse of functions alongside nepotism, conflicts of interest and revolving doors between the public and the private sectors. However, the EC is not in a position to impose a common legal definition on what (other than fraud against the EU) remains a national issue for each member and non-member state. Given the cultural and legal diversity across the European region, this chapter poses the question: how and what do we know about 'corruption', domestically and transnationally, across Europe? This question inevitably encourages thinking about theory, methodology and evidence in social scientific inquiry and more specifically the nature of the comparative method to gain insight into corruption at universal, idiographic and integrated levels. To inform this debate, we outline in brief what we see as the four main research traditions in criminological research in Europe (surveys, experiments and modelling studies; qualitative studies; national case studies; and analyses of specific cases of corruption) that have sought to empirically investigate, and contribute to knowledge on, corruption. Following an evaluation of what can be learnt, methodologically and substantively, we see a predominance of national and subnational level analyses which raise implications for what a European perspective on corruption looks like. For this reason, we then go on to argue for the need to cultivate theoretically driven comparative methods of research that can stimulate interactive dialogue, deliberation and argument across European countries, regions and localities with a view to establishing robust empirical and theoretical insights. This chapter explores ways of doing this, foregrounding the use of deliberative methods to better understand what is European about corruption in Europe, with focus on new concepts and tools of producing knowledge and theory cross-culturally.

What we know about corruption in Europe: mapping the major research traditions

To inform our understanding of how and what we know about corruption across Europe, we undertook a review of the available academic literature using three databases: ProQuest, Scopus and Web of Science. Table 4.1 provides an overview of the criteria used to search these databases.

Table 4.1: Search criteria of the literature review

Time period	June 2009–May 2019
Geographical scope	Global (English-language publications)
Primary concept	'corruption' (in the abstract)
Secondary concepts	'Europe', 'European' (document text)
Tertiary concepts	'white collar crime', 'white-collar crime', 'corporate crime', 'organizational crime' (document text)

This search resulted in a total of 422 possibly relevant academic publications. A further round of manual sifting, identifying only those publications based on empirical research and removing duplicates and pay-walled or otherwise inaccessible articles, resulted in 157 articles with an empirical underpinning of relevance for our research question.

We focus here on research into corruption in Europe specifically. Our interest is in understanding how European social scientists interested in European white-collar crimes have built knowledge, theory and concepts, and the methodologies they have used to do so, rather than looking at other jurisdictions. Similarly, we are concerned with empirical insights rather than theoretical, abstract thinking alone. In these terms, we suggest that research into corruption in Europe can be understood in terms of four broad methodological traditions:

- surveys, experiments and modelling evaluations;
- qualitative studies;
- national case studies;
- analyses of specific cases of corruption (but not limited to the nation-state).

Of course, there may be overlap between these traditions in practice. For example, national case studies may employ a variety of qualitative and quantitative methodologies. Moreover, the analysis of specific cases of corruption may often focus on a specific country, but is not necessarily limited to the nation-state, as the analysis of the FIFA (Federation Internationale de Football Association) corruption scandal by Bayle and Rayner (2018) illustrates. We could also point to the Luanda Leaks and the case of Isabel Dos Santos, because although the crime originated, and the harm primarily was felt, in Angola, the case extends to various other countries, including the United Kingdom, the Netherlands, Portugal and other European countries. For analytical purposes, however, we have categorized a study as a national case study if the analysis was limited to a culture or organization of corruption within a specific country. In the discussion that follows, we draw upon particular empirical studies as indicative of the wider methodological tradition and so make no attempt to represent the full body of literature within each tradition.

Surveys and experiments

This research tradition includes large-scale, quantitative studies aimed at testing hypotheses and producing generalizable results. Within this tradition we can distinguish two types of methodologies that fall within the scope of criminological inquiry: experiments and large-scale quantitative surveys.

Experiments (and quasi-experiments) in criminological inquiry are rare due to ethical considerations, but they do nonetheless exist. For instance, such approaches in criminology are often used for policy/programme evaluation (that is, pre-/post-evaluation of crime prevention) and, notwithstanding ethical concerns, may use cities, neighbourhoods, places, services, institutions and agencies as control and experimental groups, instead of laboratory experimentation with human participants as we see in the natural sciences. To give an example, in her study on intrinsic motivations for corruption, Burdea (2013) draws on a laboratory experiment to analyze correlations between individual performance and bribery. The experiment, run with 72 students from Amsterdam, involved playing the 'bribery game' in groups of three players. Two players competed for a specific prize by solving a task, the third player decided the winner. During the game, the competing players could bribe the referee. The study revealed a significant correlation between low-performing individuals and their propensity to engage in bribery. (Though perhaps they realized this was their only way to win.) In a similar laboratory experiment, Christöfl et al (2017) tested whether a) detection probabilities and b) leniency policies affect the propensity to bribery. Using a sample of 180 undergraduate, graduate and postgraduate students in Austria, they found that increased risks of detection can impact the propensity to bribery (passive and active), but this is more likely in the absence of lenient policies.

A frequently heard criticism of experimental studies, specifically laboratory experiments, is that they do not resemble real-life settings. Most researchers in this tradition, therefore, tend to implement large-scale surveys to study corruption. These often include self-reports about past or potential offending behaviour or perceptions about corruption (for example, Dormaels, 2015). These studies often analyze individual characteristics of offenders or motives for engaging in corruption. Using a vignette survey collected from 148 entrepreneurs, Dickel and Graeff (2018) analyzed whether cost-benefit considerations influence the likelihood of engaging in corruption in Germany. They found that while the probability of detection did not impact the propensity of engaging in corruption, the expected benefits and the belief that the corruption would be effective did impact the likelihood of engaging in corruption. Gorsira et al designed three studies using surveys in the Netherlands to understand why individuals engage in corruption (Gorsira et al, 2018a), how ethical organizational cultures interact with individual motives in shaping corruption (Gorsira et al, 2018b) and the relationship between ethical climate, corruption and personal norms

(Gorsira et al, 2018c). Their first study (Gorsira et al, 2018a) included a sample of 202 public officials and 200 business employees and showed that social norms, personal norms and the perceived opportunity to comply significantly correspond to decisions to engage in corruption. Their second study (Gorsira et al, 2018b), using a slightly larger sample, suggested that employees who perceive their organizational culture to be more egoistic are more prone to corruption. The third study (Gorsira et al, 2018c), a multi-layered survey and experiment, suggested that there is a causal relationship between how employees perceive the ethical climate of their organizations and corrupt behaviours.

In sum, with surveys and experiments, and the quantitative tradition more generally, there is a tendency to privilege generalization above context and specificity, making such approaches vulnerable to a 'false universalism' (Edwards and Hughes, 2005). Within this tradition, there is an absence of contextualized and 'deep' data on particular manifestations of corruption at local levels, which generates obstacles to developing comprehensive explanatory accounts.

Qualitative studies

The qualitative tradition involves in-depth, 'thick' analyses of particular cases, people, institutions or organizations and their everyday settings. Within this tradition, we find interviews and content analysis of media or secondary sources, such as criminal case files, as the main methodologies. For example, in their study on anti-bribery compliance in the pharmaceutical industry, David-Barrett et al (2017) conducted 14 in-depth, semi-structured, face-to-face interviews with (senior) managers of pharmaceutical firms and a focus group of compliance professionals covering the UK primarily, but also other regions. The in-depth approach allowed the authors to identify two tensions that inhibit organizations' implementation of anti-corruption policies in practice: mismatches between local and global norms and between commercial and compliance functions within firms. Studies employing similar methods include, for instance, research on Estonian law enforcement (Sööt, 2012), a study on the motives for corruption among a sample of convicted 'delinquents' in various penitentiaries in Germany (Cleff et al, 2013), a study on match fixing in professional football which showed that older players near the end of their careers are at risk of becoming involved in match fixing (Hill, 2015) and a study into the regulation of corporate bribery in the UK and Germany (Lord, 2014).

Besides interviews and focus groups, a second qualitative methodology involves analyzing secondary data, like media content, court or other judicial documents and so on. For example, in a study examining how corporate vehicles are used for corruption by government officials in Hungary, Jancsics (2017) used 225 newspaper articles containing information about the use of shell corporations. These articles were collected from K-Monitor, a Hungarian watchdog organization that gathers, stores and classifies articles concerning corruption, public financing and the transparency of public life in Hungary. Gorsira et al (2018d) qualitatively analyzed confidential criminal case files of bribery investigations undertaken by two Dutch enforcement authorities to better understand the interplay between individual, organizational and interactional factors in the onset and/or continuance of corrupt collaborations.

While providing key insights into the real, deep causal mechanisms of corrupt activities, this qualitative tradition also runs the risk of creating 'falsely particular' (see Edwards and Hughes, 2005: 349) accounts of corruption, as insights gained can be entirely idiographic with a tendency towards relativism, or showing no desire to inform or learn from debate and insights in other localities.

National case studies

Another main tradition in corruption research in Europe is the predilection for focusing on the national level as the primary unit of analysis. While transnational and comparative studies come closest to developing transnational/supranational narratives on corruption, most studies on corruption entail national case studies (or rather case studies taken from events within nation-states, sometimes taking for granted national homogeneity). These case studies provide us with key information about national circumstances or developments that explain why and how corruption may take place under varying conditions over time.[1] Some nations have attracted more scholarly attention than others, reflecting the combination of a concentration of academics and political/social/sociological fascination with organized crime. For instance, there are many studies focusing on Italy as a case study, analyzing issues such as corruption in football (Di Ronco and Lavorgna, 2015) and the solid waste industry (Abrate et al, 2014).

The focus on the nation-state as the primary unit of analysis in such studies inhibits true comparative, cross-cultural research, as researchers remain embedded in their particular socio-legal environments. This may reflect the reality that comparative work is intellectually problematic and difficult to be embedded in different contexts (Nelken, 2010).

Analyzing specific cases of corruption in Europe

The final main tradition involves the analysis of specific cases of corruption in Europe. These include local case studies and ethnographies of specific cases. Case studies offer rich, detailed insights into specific contexts or practices in which corruption takes place and the antecedent factors that contributed to the unfolding of the corrupt behaviours. Methodologically, these studies often make use of a combination of qualitative methods, including observational fieldwork, interviews, and documentary analysis of texts (Edwards et al, 2013). One such case study example is that of Bayle and Rayner (2018), who analyze how the corrupt practices at FIFA suddenly turned into a scandal. The authors claim that in order to understand this it is vital to look at scandals as social processes that may develop in several directions. Using all sorts of secondary data, they use the FIFA case study to present a new model to analyze corruption scandals. In another study, Slingerland (2018) analyzed three case studies – FIFA, the scandal surrounding *The News of the World* in the UK and the Roermond scandal in the Netherlands – using a conceptual analysis to understand the network components of the cases, and present 'network corruption' as a new concept.

In a very rich ethnography based on interviews, analysis of secondary sources, and participant observations, De Rosa and Trabalzi (2016) explain how illegality and corruption are constructed among water buffalo mozzarella producers in the southern Italian region of Campania. Only through such detailed case studies can one understand that the practices of mozzarella producers are shaped by the presence of organized crime, and inefficient and corrupt state officials. Within such a context, producers did not perceive legal and illegal acts as mutually exclusive opposites. However, this study is the exception, as more generally there is a notable absence of methodological approaches such as ethnography and participant-observation, particularly in relation to organizational deviance. This likely reflects issues of access and the length of time taken for ethnographic accounts.

What can we learn from these main traditions of corruption research in Europe?

Delineating the main research traditions described previously is not just a futile exercise of description but also provides important insights into the commonalities and differences that exist across and between these approaches, in addition to any research gaps that ought to be further scrutinized. In these terms, much can be learnt, methodologically and substantively, from these existing traditions. For instance, we see a predominance of national- and subnational-level analyses, which raises questions for how we can create a European dialogue on corruption. If academic research has a predilection for national-level or even more local insights, how can we generate common references about the European region? That said, where the nature, prevalence or causes of corruption are related to country-specific characteristics, this still makes for an interesting point of comparison. The question is, can we establish common conceptual referents across these diverse occurrences of corruption?

While in this short chapter we do not have scope to analyze in depth all of the related issues, we instead focus on two main contributions to how corruption has been conceptualized across these research traditions and, where, in terms of research gaps, we see promising lines of enquiry for future research on corruption that can inform a European and empirically informed dialogue on corruption.

Conceptualizing corruption in Europe: content vs analysis

In the research traditions we have identified, and the corresponding empirical research, we were able to identify two main approaches to conceptualizing the specific focus of the research that are common across the traditions:

- *Content definitions*: conceptualization informed by normative policy/ enforcement agendas and categorizations of specific offences that constitute corruption.
- *Analytical definitions*: conceptualization informed by key features, processes and behaviours considered 'corrupt'; often empirically derived and/or operationalized for empirical research (usually, but not exclusively, quantitative).

First, we can see that social scientific research into corruption in Europe conceptualizes the research focus in terms of specific offence types relevant to corruption, such as bribery, embezzlement, misconduct in public office, nepotism/cronyism and so on; that is, defining the focus in terms of the content. Such conceptualization falls in line with state definitions of crime as seen in policy documentation and/or legislative frameworks. In terms of operation and strategy, this offence-based focus is undoubtedly beneficial for practitioners, in that that they can easily digest empirical materials associated with the offences they prioritize. Second, we also see that some social scientific research into corruption in Europe conceptualizes the research focus in terms of the analytical features of the behaviours of interest, such as an abuse of a 'normal' relationship in the course of public duties or illicit relationships of exchange or transfers of wealth to induce desired behaviours. Analytical definitions are generally informed by and built on empirical research through inductive-deductive-adaptive reasoning to inform the nature of corrupt behaviour. Corruption can, therefore, be a method for achieving other economic and sometimes political goals.

It is clear that corruption is a contested concept, used to denote a diverse array of behaviours, human characteristics, states of being and conditions across varied social contexts, and sometimes is employed without sufficient care or reflection, particularly when framed in terms of morality and ethics in the international discourse (for example, Transparency International, United Nations) (Campbell and Lord, 2018). The conventional, predominant interpretation tends to individualize and decontextualize associated behaviours, losing sight of the cultural conditions that shape their situated production (Campbell and Lord, 2018). What is clear is that opportunities for corrupt behaviours and the pursuit of self-interest are, in varying ways, routine and embedded within, across and between all forms of political economy, particularly in government (Rose-Ackermann and Palifka, 2016). For instance, procurement practices that lack transparency, the financing of political campaigning and organizational funding from hidden benefactors and tight connections between business and political elites generate opportunities for corrupt activities.

In general terms, the concept of corruption refers to a variety of illicit behaviours and transactions that necessarily involve actors within government (for example, politicians) and/or its decentralized units (for example, public officials, such as procurement officers within the police, military, transport and transit, education, healthcare and so on) and that undermine the use of public funds during the provision of services. Corruption is conceptualized in mainstream European discourse as 'the abuse of (entrusted) power for private gain' (European Commission, 2020; Transparency International, nd), but such narratives are ill-defined as they incorporate an overly broad number of behaviours that are qualitatively different (for example, including bribery and embezzlement alongside nepotism, patronage and conflicts of interest) and do not appreciate the complex 'situated production' of corrupt practices (that is, individualizing these behaviours shifts attention away from organizational, structural and cultural influences or the nature of the illicit relations between cooperating legitimate and illegitimate actors, and/or the interdependencies of licit and illicit markets and systems). Legislation differs from country to country in terms of which of these behaviours is criminalized, though bribery is a common factor.

Academics have also sought to frame the narrative even more broadly to include a diverse array of public and private behaviours (see Whyte, 2015) with corruption being defined as 'the distortion and subversion of the public realm in the service of private interests' (Beetham, 2015: 41). These wider definitions reflect the immersion of the concept of corruption within ideological tensions driven by 'informed morality', for example, serving the perspectives of 'moral entrepreneurs' such as Transparency International, who promote general 'integrity' values, as well as those seeking to link illicit and unethical 'corrupt' behaviours with neoliberal politico-economic structures. Such corruption can be found at the 'petty' level, that is, where low and mid-level public officials abuse their entrusted power to undertake acts or omissions that contravene their public duties for personal financial gain and/or relations with powerful others; at the 'grand' level, that is, acts or omissions at a high level of government; and at the 'political' level, that is, the manipulation of policies, institutions and rules of procedure by political decision-makers to sustain their power, status and wealth (for a breakdown of such classifications see Transparency International, nd). Like 'corporate crime', the corruption label can be a form of 'virtue signalling'.

The key issue is that in order to establish a dialogue on corruption at the European level, there need to be common referents across cultures that correspond with behaviours that exist in those localities but that also make sense for broader narratives. We explore these issues in what follows.

Promising lines of inquiry: a European dialogue on corruption?

Two core questions that interest us relate to a) how (or indeed whether) we can establish consensus among key stakeholders on the nature, extent and scope of corruption within and across Europe, and b) how the diverse European region can be used to generate cross-cultural theory and concepts on corruption. However, as with much national and comparative cross-national research, there may not be common conceptual or technical translations in relation to the nature/organization of, and appropriate responses to, corruption, but it is important that different audiences understand the concepts as we intend them. This can be seen in the diversity of research traditions discussed earlier, and the varying conceptualizations of corruption. For example, it is plausible that differences may exist over what ought to be perceived as the priority corruption 'threats' in a specific locality, or the primary actors that ought to be responsible for dealing with such risks (for example, state bodies, commercial enterprises, advocacy groups and so on). In other words, it cannot be presumed that such concepts are commonly understood across or even within different countries, and that even if there are common understandings that there is, by extension, consensus about how to move forward, considering differences in jurisdictions, social values and historical experiences, and the divergent political economies of European states.

The earlier analysis demonstrates that there are notable inadequacies in existing research traditions on understanding corruption, as the focus on experiments and large surveys sacrifices specificity in favour of false universality (that is, 'one model fits all'), while the preponderance of national and local case studies (both qualitative and quantitative), do little to talk to a cross-cultural audience, sacrificing the possibility of cross-cultural debate to specificity. To this end, representation is required from across the European region to inform what we know about corruption at the subnational, national and supranational levels, with a view to developing fuller accounts of related phenomena, including appropriate regulatory and prevention strategies.

With the previous questions in mind, and given the necessity for policy development at the supranational level (that is, the EU) in the context of competing interests at the national/local levels, it is our view that 'deliberative methods' for researching informed judgements are emerging as a way of inventing or discovering satisfactory cross-cultural policy responses. This is particularly the case where there is a lack of agreement or an incomplete state of knowledge concerning either the nature of the phenomenon or the components which must be included in a successful solution. One methodological approach, but not the only approach, to addressing this complex issue may be to implement deliberative methods, such as the Delphi method (see below), to enable specialist academics from different jurisdictions to have more equal input into the development of regional policies.

In brief, deliberative methodology, and the Delphi method specifically, is a 'method for structuring a group communication process allowing a group of individuals, as a whole, to deal with a complex problem' (Linstone and Turoff, 2002: 3). Deliberative methods attempt to identify consensus in agreement/disagreement in relation to public policy problems, such as corruption and its control, by translating the subjective insights of individual informed respondents into more objective group consensus over time. The Delphi method is one of the most mature, reliable methods of deliberative research design. Advocates also note its advantages for enabling communication among geographically dispersed informants, particularly where there are major restraints on the time and cost of bringing them together in face-to-face meetings.

In our view, this process of structured communication can inform a cross-cultural understanding of the nature of corruption with a view to informing social scientific discourse and policy agendas and interventions. We cannot presume to know the nature of corruption across European contexts where we have little knowledge or assume that dominant Anglo–American literatures and data on corruption are also applicable in all cultures. It is important that we investigate corruption cross-culturally to ensure that a fuller theoretical account can be developed. What is more, in the light of methodological difficulties in undertaking extensive data collection in each European jurisdiction, we require a more efficient, rigorous and robust method to generate empirical insights that can account for the specificity of different European localities alongside the generality of Europe-wide issues. Deliberative methodologies such as the Delphi method enable such social scientific research. Absent multi-site, embedded case-study analyses, we believe structured deliberation offers an informed 'voice' to discrete regions and enables us to produce policy-relevant social scientific insights through iterative and deliberative dialogue between informed actors (from social science, policy and practice of varying types) in these regions. Efficiency and expediency are also notable strengths of the method.[2]

Deliberative methods and corruption in Europe

To give an example of how this might look, we might, for instance, seek to empirically analyze the perspectives and agendas of those operating within interacting local, national and global contexts and generate inclusive, deliberative and iterative dialogue between those key stakeholders to establish an evidence base for:

- the nature, and underlying 'root causes', of the corruption phenomenon and 'problems' created (that is, how is corruption understood?) in Europe;

- how best to effectively respond to the nature and 'problems' of corruption in Europe;
- lines of appropriate action and accountability for addressing corruption in Europe (that is, which authorities are or ought to be responsible?);
- the types of expertise and knowledge that responsible parties ought to possess (that is, skills and competencies for action and capacity building);
- the ways in which the results of this dialogue ought to be disseminated in order to maximize utilization in practice, given different cultural and legal contexts.

Through deliberative research as outlined above, consensus among key interacting stakeholders at the local, national and global level regarding the nature of, and policy and practice towards, corruption can be gained. The method offers the prospect of dialogue that is insulated from the more immediate, ad hominem pressures on the policy process and consequently a more defensible 'construct validation' of social, economic and political problems (for example, corruption). But for constructive dialogue to take place, the very terms of debate between different communities (for example, academics, policy makers, practitioners) need to be established, especially in the cross-cultural comparative context. The method enables respondents, and therefore recipient governments, to obtain co-ownership of the construction of the problem and appropriate policies – the more co-ownership there is between investor and recipient states around policy interventions, the more likely policy adherence will take place.

Conclusion

Corruption in Europe is a core area of social scientific research and public policy and has clear relevance to white-collar and corporate crime research. In our view, while there is no sharp geographical boundary for corruption, exploring it within the European region offers a rich and diverse arena for empirically derived theory and concept building, as much can be learned if we talk to, rather than past, one another. That is, current research traditions indicate a preponderance of both a) national and local level qualitative case studies that offer rich, idiographic and specific insights into corruption in particular contexts and b) cross-cultural and national-level quantitative analyses (usually survey-based) that offer more universal insights into multivariate relationships. However, integrating the specific with the universal is necessary for an international research programme into corruption, and selecting those who have chosen to be members of a legal entity like the EU is a productive basis (even if two of the authors of this chapter now belong to a country that has left the EU). However, whether Europe or the EU is a properly distinct analytical category is debatable. 'Europe' represents a varied set of places for some purposes, and the EU, EC or Council of Europe for others.

Dialogue between social scientists from different countries, as well as between different stakeholders from social science, policy and practice, needs to be deliberative and iterative to produce fuller theoretical accounts. It should avoid falling into the methodological trap of reproducing insights from very particular geo-historical contexts or from highly decontextualized universal accounts, instead of identifying common referents for producing scientific and policy consensus. Whether there will ever be a common policy discourse on corruption remains an open question, with fissures (currently in highly corrupt but populist countries like Hungary and Poland) driving policies and recommended controls apart. However, at least we may find greater scientific harmony in analyzing these trends in corruption and its control.

Notes

[1]   National evaluations by intergovernmental organizations such as the Council of Europe's GRECO also seek to do this, but our focus is on academic studies.

[2]   For an overview of how the Delphi method has been applied in social science, see de Loë et al (2016); and for its application to criminological issues relating to urban security specifically, see Edwards et al (2013).

References

Abrate, G., Erbetta, F., Fraquelli, G. and Vannoni, D. (2014) 'The cost of corruption in the Italian solid waste industry', *Industrial and Corporate Change*, 24(2): 439–65.

Bayle, E. and Rayner, H. (2018) 'Sociology of a scandal: the emergence of "FIFAgate"', *Soccer & Society*, 19(4): 593–611. doi: 10.1080/14660970.2016.1228591

Beetham, D. (2015) 'Moving beyond a narrow definition of corruption', in D. Whyte (ed) *How Corrupt is Britain?* London: Pluto Press, pp 41–6.

Burdea, V. (2013) 'Research note on an experimental approach to the intrinsic motivations of corruption', *The Journal of Philosophical Economics*, 7(1): 2–37.

Campbell, L. and Lord, N. (2018) *Corruption in Commercial Enterprise: Law, Theory and Practice*, Abingdon: Routledge.

Cleff, T., Naderer, G. and Volkert, J. (2013) 'Motives behind white-collar crime: results of a quantitative and qualitative study in Germany', *Society and Business Review*, 8(2): 145–59.

Christöfl, A., Leopold-Wildburger, U. and Rasmußen, A. (2017) 'An experimental study on bribes, detection probability and principal witness policy', *Journal of Business Economics*, 87: 1067–81. doi:10.1007/s11573-017-0846-8

David-Barrett, E., Basak, Y.-D., Moss-Cowan, A. and Nguyen, Y. (2017) 'Bitter pill? Institutional corruption and the challenge of antibribery compliance in the pharmaceutical sector', *Journal of Management Inquiry*, 26(3): 326–47.

de Loë, R.C., Melnychuk, N., Murray, D. and Plummer, R. (2016) 'Advancing the state of policy Delphi practice: a systematic review evaluating methodological evolution, innovation, and opportunities', *Technological Forecasting & Social Change*, 104: 78–88.

Dickel, P. and Graeff, P. (2018) 'Entrepreneurs' propensity for corruption: a vignette-based factorial survey', *Journal of Business Research*, 89: 77–86.

De Rosa, M. and Trabalzi, F. (2016) 'Everybody does it, or how illegality is socially constructed in a southern Italian food network', *Journal of Rural Studies*, 45: 303–11.

Di Ronco, A. and Lavorgna, A. (2015) 'Fair play? Not so much: corruption in the Italian football', *Trends in Organized Crime*, 18(3): 176–95.

Dormaels, A. (2015) 'Perceptions of corruption in Flanders: surveying citizens and police: a study on the influence of occupational differential association on perceptions of corruption', *Policing and Society*, 25(6): 596–621. doi:10.1080/10439463.2014.895351

Edwards, A. and Hughes, G. (2005) 'Comparing the governance of safety in Europe: a geo-historical approach', *Theoretical Criminology*, 9(3): 345–63.

Edwards, A., Hughes, G. and Lord, N. (2013) 'Crime prevention and public safety in Europe: challenges for comparative criminology', in S. Body-Gendrot, M. Hough, K. Kerezsi, R. Lévy and S. Snacken (eds) *The Routledge Handbook of European Criminology*, Abingdon: Routledge, pp 368–84.

Edwards, A., Hughes, G. and Lord, N. (2013) 'Urban security in Europe: translating a concept in public criminology', *European Journal of Criminology*, 10(3): 260–83.

European Commission (nd) 'Corruption', Available at: https://ec.europa.eu/home-affairs/what-we-do/policies/organized-crime-and-human-trafficking/corruption_en

Gorsira, M., Steg, L., Denkers, A. and Huisman, W. (2018a) 'Corruption in organizations: ethical climate and individual motives', *Administrative Sciences*, 8(1): 4–22.

Gorsira, M., Denkers, A. and Huisman, W. (2018b) 'Both sides of the coin: motives for corruption among public officials and business employees', *Journal of Business Ethics*, 151(1): 179–94.

Gorsira, M., Denkers, A., Steg, L. and Huisman, W. (2018c) 'Chapter 4: Effects of ethical climate on corruption: an experimental study', in M. Gorsira, 'Corruption: why two tango out of step', PhD dissertation, Vrije Universiteit Amsterdam, pp 73–88, Available at: https://research.vu.nl/en/publications/corruption-why-two-tango-out-of-step

Gorsira, M., Huisman, W., Denkers, A. and Steg, L. (2018d) 'Government up for sale: why Dutch officials take bribes', in M. Gorsira, 'Corruption: why two tango out of step', PhD dissertation, Vrije Universiteit Amsterdam, pp 91–121.

Hill, D. (2015) 'Jumping into fixing', *Trends in Organized Crime*, 18(3): 212–28.

Jancsics, D. (2017) 'Offshoring at home? Domestic use of shell companies for corruption', *Public Integrity*, 19(1): 4–21. doi:10.1080/10999922.2016.1200412

Linstone, H.A. and Turoff, M. (2002) 'Introduction', in H.A. Linstone and M. Turoff (eds) *The Delphi Method: Techniques and Applications*, Available at: https://web.njit.edu/~turoff/pubs/delphibook/delphibook.pdf

Lord, N. (2014) *Regulating Corporate Bribery in International Business*, Abingdon: Routledge.

Nelken, D. (2010) *Comparative Criminal Justice: Making Sense of Difference*, London: Sage.

Rose-Ackermann, S. and Palifka, B.J. (2016) *Corruption and Government: Causes, Consequences, and Reform* (2nd edn), Cambridge: Cambridge University Press.

Sööt, M.-L. (2012) 'The role of management in tackling corruption', *Baltic Journal of Management*, 7(3): 287–301.

Slingerland, W. (2018) 'Network corruption: when social capital becomes corrupted: Its meaning and significance in corruption and network theory and the consequences for (EU) policy and law', PhD dissertation, Vrije Universiteit Amsterdam, Available at: https://research.vu.nl/en/publications/network-corruption-when-social-capital-becomes-corrupted-its-mean

Transparency International (nd) 'Anti-corruption glossary: "corruption"', Available at: www.transparency.org/glossary/term/corruption

Whyte, D. (ed) (2015) *How Corrupt is Britain?* London: Pluto Press.

World Bank (1997) 'Helping countries combat corruption: the role of the World Bank', September, Available at: www1.worldbank.org/publicsector/anticorrupt/corruptn/corrptn.pdf

PART II

Financial Crimes and Illicit Financial Flows

Identifying 'Europeanness' in European White-Collar Crime: The Case Study of Criminal Responses to 'Market Abuse'

Sarah Wilson

Introduction

This chapter explores the value of identifying 'Europeanness' in understandings of white-collar crime through reference to key European policies relating to unlawful behaviours which are termed 'market abuse'. Most proximately, 'market abuse' is a term of European capital markets law, but the behaviours underpinning it – insider dealing and market manipulation – are commonly identified with the terminology of 'financial crime' and 'white-collar crime' and are analyzed across key discourses in academic scholarship, practitioner interest and policy making. The analysis considers how such ideas of substantive activity and rhetoric can be joined in different ways, and directed towards evaluating the feasibility of identifying Europeanness in conceptualizations of white-collar crime, and the benefits which might accrue from this. In doing so, utmost significance is attached to how behaviours termed 'market abuse' by European discourse demonstrate a European commitment to the use of criminal responses for behaviour which is considered unacceptable. In focusing on the policies of European Union (EU) institutions, particular attention is paid to the reflections of the European Commission (EC) on new market abuse legislation proposed in 2011. Indeed, it was in relation to market abuse specifically that in 2011 the EC presented the perceived superior value of criminal responses for connoting high levels of social disapproval for 'unacceptable' behaviours, in comparison with other possible enforcement pathways (European Commission, 2011).

This discussion of Europeanness in understandings of white-collar crime is strongly premised on intellectual and wider understandings of white-collar crime, and how these can be aligned with the closely associated rhetorical construct of 'financial crime'. 'Financial crime' terminology, like that of 'white-collar crime' is particularly widely used in the United States and United Kingdom, and the wider common law 'world', with both constructs found less in European discourse,[1] mirroring the very premise of challenging Anglo–American dominance that shapes the narrative on white-collar crime. While in European discourse references made to 'economic crime' or even the combination 'financial-economic crime' are much more common (for example, Ligeti and Franssen, 2017: 1) the 'financial crime' construct as it is found in Anglo–American analysis can nevertheless be useful for exploring European conceptualizations of white-collar crime. This is so on account of how a) behaviours which European discourse terms 'market abuse' are widely analyzed as 'financial crime' across key discourses, and b) how such analyses of 'financial crime' speak very persuasively to European understandings of the challenges presented by 'market abuse'.

Indeed, 'financial crime' analysis characteristically shows extensive engagement with how the activities it analyzes as such attract perceptions of being 'victimless' and lacking real harm and/or moral culpability (for example, Davies et al, 1999: 3) with European policy makers clearly of the view that market abuse behaviour presents considerable social and economic risks. Analyses of financial crime also commonly emphasize how these activities are appropriately regarded as being 'amongst the most difficult' for legal systems to deal with let alone respond to (Tomasic, 2011: 7) and with no jurisdiction being perceived to have achieved 'great . . . success [in using] the criminal law' with respect to them (Rider, 1995: 13). The latter position is, in turn, widely attributed to how 'standards and procedures of the traditional criminal justice system, which are necessary to ensure general civil and human liberties,' represent 'almost insurmountable barriers' to effective prosecution (Rider, 1995: 13). These perspectives are of utmost importance in the light of the 'minimum criminalization' policy at the heart of the Directive on Criminal Sanctions for Market Abuse (CSMAD),[2] implemented across EU member states in 2016 as part of a new suite of 'market abuse' legislations, which also included the Market Abuse Regulation 2014 (MAR).[3]

Identifying connections between the construct of 'white-collar crime' and the case study of 'market abuse'

In the first instance, these overarching themes are drawn together by illuminating the conceptual and intellectual links which can be made between what European discourses term 'market abuse' and 'white-collar crime'. The purpose of doing so lies in explaining why the former can be a case study for exploring what is, or might be, distinctively European about European thinking on 'white-collar crime'. As signposted, this entails examining the connections which can be made between conceptualizations of 'market abuse', 'white-collar crime' and what is commonly termed 'financial crime'. While 'financial crime' is not a term which is widely used in European discourses as a whole, and which is not commonly associated with 'market abuse' in European parlance (see endnote 1) academic literature on white-collar crime, together with practitioner interest and policy discourse does commonly situate the terms 'white-collar crime' and 'financial crime' closely together (see, for example, Wilson and Wilson, 2021).

Albeit this is with relatively little said about how these constructs can be connected intellectually through the work of Edwin Sutherland (see Wilson and Wilson, 2021), such links can be made from Sutherland's conceptualizations of 'white-collar crime' and 'fraud'. In elaborating on what kinds of behaviours he understood to be 'white-collar' crimes, Sutherland included activities which 'approximated with' fraud or swindling (Sutherland, 1940; 3). In turn the term 'financial crime' appears to be an outgrowth from Sutherland's original work, and has become adopted as such by those whose interests in white-collar crime have become oriented towards types of 'financial misconduct' which are identifiable as 'fraud' and 'swindling'. 'Financial crime' is in many ways itself a flawed construct in the light of the absence of an agreed international definition and that its potentially wide-ranging import has led to carelessness in its use, both factors being present in the critique of this terminology by the International Monetary Fund and contributing to its apparent preference for 'financial abuse' (International Monetary Fund, 2001: Paragraph 5, for example). Nevertheless, this analysis draws on how 'financial crime' is a term which is widely used. It also regards as significant that legal definition of 'financial crime' can be found in UK law.

A legal definition of 'financial crime' can be found within the UK's Financial Services and Markets Act (FSMA) 2000 (as amended by the Financial Services Act 2012). This location does perhaps limit the general utility value of this definition, given that as part of the framework of domestic financial services regulation in the UK, it is inextricably attached to statutory duties of the UK regulatory authorities (previously the Financial Services Authority and now the Financial Conduct Authority). And while it does provide some indication of what might, as a matter of law, be meant by 'financial crime', at the same time, the significance attached by this definition to offences of fraud or dishonesty does perhaps present a limited view on what might be regarded as 'financial crime'.[4] However, its reference to 'fraud' does reinforce how the intellectualization of white-collar crime has occurred through the work of Sutherland and those who have followed his lead. This statutory reference point also identifies 'misconduct in, or misuse of information relating to, a financial market' as a type of 'financial crime', which is helpful for how this analysis focuses on 'market abuse'. This reference made to 'misconduct in' or 'misuse of information' relating to financial markets reflects how behaviours which are termed 'insider dealing' and 'market manipulation' in UK domestic law and the wider legal culture both concern the importance of information which is available to financial market participants. These terminologies are applied respectively to situations where information is not fully accessible to market participants, or where the information which is available to them is inaccurate (see Wilson and Wilson, 2010). These are the behaviours which are collectively termed 'market abuse' in European discourse. In turn the reasons why 'market abuse' provides an excellent case study for exploring the complexities surrounding how financial crime is intellectualized, phenomenalized, perceived and enforced underpin why it can act as a useful reference point for exploring what might be considered particularly 'European' about 'European white-collar crime'.

What makes 'market abuse' a useful reference point for exploring European 'white-collar crime' and Europeanness in perceptions of and responses to it flows from how 'financial market misconduct' attracts a very broad spectrum of viewpoints as to its wrongfulness. Indeed, some legal traditions have been reluctant to even regard it as unlawful, let alone appropriately criminalized. Such viewpoints are strongly associated with the classic arguments of Henry G. Manne, made initially against the prohibition of insider dealing, and clustering around the perceived beneficial effects of these forms of 'market behaviour' for overall market buoyancy through encouraging trade, and for ascertaining market availability and assisting in price discovery (Manne, 1966). These views, bolstered by assertions that no long-term losses are experienced by markets on account of them (Manne, 1966) continue to persist (see Ashe and Counsell, 1993), even in some quarters of regimes with extensive prohibitions (Wilson, 2015), and can now be found expressed increasingly in relation to market manipulation (Wilson and Wilson, 2014). European prohibitions for market abuse are overall very extensive, and can be seen to contrast markedly with the US: the key reference point for UK in many respects, especially in respect of insider dealing. The attention which is paid by European law and policy making to 'market abuse' is interesting in the light of these perceived ambiguities in moral and even legal culpability.

The moral and even legal ambiguities which can be found in narratives of market abuse activity might be seen to contrast with the position of other high-profile 'financial crimes'. Money laundering does of course attract a great deal of attention within European discourse, as well as beyond it, and with the very premise of these activities being the fruits of criminal enterprise, it might well be that this encourages more 'fixed' views on 'wrongfulness', both moral and legal. In this vein, the attention being paid to 'market abuse' might be considered analogous with the current emphasis on the rhetoric of 'tax abuse',[5] where the latter could play an important part in eroding traditional domestic distinctions drawn between 'tax avoidance' and 'tax evasion'.[6] Again, it could be interesting to reflect on whether tax evasion might traditionally have been perceived as attracting greater opprobrium than 'misconduct' in, or 'misuse of information' relating to, financial markets. All these examples of 'financial crimes' can become part of the search for Europeanness in responding to financial crimes, and arguably they should.

The UK case study: what is European about the UK?

Although the UK has now formally departed from the EU, UK 'market abuse' prohibitions naturally show a predominance of European influences. The rhetoric of 'market abuse' is very much European terminology for activity that is widely identified elsewhere – and especially throughout the common-law world - as 'securities violations', and which is underpinned by a framework of 'securities law' (rather than the European moniker of 'capital markets law'). This was not always the case, and this strongly European orientation of laws governing 'misconduct in financial markets' has been persuasively analyzed as the migration of European capital markets law into UK corporate and securities law (Davies, 1991). UK provisions governing financial market/securities violations predating this 'migration' show a stronger US influence, particularly in respect to behaviour known as insider dealing/trading. In this vein, significance is attached to how the rhetoric of 'capital markets law' – in contrast with 'securities law' – manifests the European commitment to laws which are reasoned as necessary to protect the European Single Market, and single market aspirations. Alongside this it is also interesting that while UK law clearly is very strongly shaped by European thinking and law making processes, rhetorical adoption of the terminology of 'market abuse' itself has been less pronounced.

Market abuse and the search for Europeanness in understandings of white-collar crime: macro and micro complexity

In announcing the importance of 'minimum rules on criminal offences and on criminal sanctions for market abuse' in 2011, a premise which would become embodied in the CSMAD, the EC emphasis was clearly on the importance of harmonization for delivering EU policy on 'market integrity' (European Commission, 2011). This was contextually positioned as a response to the facilitation of market abuse by technological advances and also increasingly porous jurisdictional boundaries arising from this greater (virtual) connectivity (see Wilson, 2015). As the EC explained, in the European law and policy making sphere this context created an imperative for greater overall enforcement emphasis for unlawful behaviours termed 'market abuse' (European Commission, 2011). This was evident in the key directions and contents of MAR, which extended existing definitions of market abuse and locations for its perpetration, together with the powers available to competent authorities to investigate market abuse, with this supported by increased administrative sanctioning capacity and available penalties (European Commission, 2011; Wilson, 2015). The envisioned role for the CSMAD lay in how, in a setting where greater overall enforcement emphasis was required, there was a perceived important role for criminal enforcement specifically, reflecting that criminal sanctions were believed to 'demonstrate social disapproval of a qualitatively different nature compared with administrative sanctions' (European Commission, 2011). This is very significant for exploring what might be specifically European about European responses to white-collar crime. However, in doing so it is appropriate to ask just how distinctively 'European' this 'thinking' is.

It is important to question a distinctive Europeanness in the light of the view that reactions to the 2008–09 global financial crisis are likely to manifest demand for tough new bodies (Ryder, 2014) and for policies, trends and sanctions which might mark a retreat from the 'haphazard pursuit' of financial white-collar crimes (Tomasic, 2011: 7), and even that the crisis could be 'transformative' for directing responses towards financial misconduct which befit its criminal – or at least criminogenic – qualities (Friedrichs, 2013). While the evaluation of such predictions is proving to be complex in a post-crisis context, presenting both greater enforcement aggression and apparent high levels of tolerance of wrongdoing (such as in high-profile 'sweetheart' deals between regulators and key financial institutions), heightened enforcement aggression can be seen in the US where securities violations laws are quite differently configured. This can be seen in 'spoofing' enforcement – the US counterpart to market manipulation – (see, for example, United States v Coscia, No. 14-CR-551 [2015] United States District Court, N.D. Illinois, Eastern Division), and even in insider trading where insider trading laws are recognized as being very narrowly drawn and where there is an explicit lack of commitment to equality for market participants, in contrast with the 'market egalitarianism' cornerstone of European approaches (see United States v Newman, No. 13-1837 [2014] United States Court of Appeals 2d Cir.). Furthermore, European policy making can be situated persuasively alongside International Organization of Securities Commissioners (IOSCO) reflections in the supranational setting (see International Organization of Securities Commissioners, 2015).

Identifying Europeanness in enforcement trends for market abuse

Such global dimensions of 'interest' in using criminal enforcement for activities which can be considered white-collar crimes alone suggests that from a macro and global perspective it is right and proper to question just how distinctively 'European' the thinking on white-collar crime emanating from Europe actually is. The example of MAR also invites scrutiny of the Europeanness of current thinking on the purported benefits of criminal enforcement from a different angle – one provided by a micro emphasis on individual EU member states. Indeed prior to this legislation, European market abuse legislation, together with companion policy and thought, was very strongly rooted in the perceived superiority of administrative sanctions. Here, Article 14 of the Market Abuse Directive 2003 (MAD 2003) obliged member states to provide a regime of 'effective, proportionate, and dissuasive' administrative responses to market abuse, and in doing so rather reluctantly acknowledged that member states might also wish to have a regime for criminal enforcement alongside this. It was not until 2016 that member states were obliged to set out minimum criminalization.

In the era of MAD 2003, European regard for administrative sanctions reflected a wider general appeal for enforcement approaches which were considered capable of addressing a perceived enforcement gap. This was a gap arising from the difficulties associated with achieving criminal convictions, and which meant the criminal pathway was unlikely to provide an effective deterrent. MAD 2003 thus reflected how administrative actions, in contrast with the criminal enforcement pathway, were underpinned by fewer procedural protections for those subject to them, including a lower burden of proof for the state to satisfy, (see, for example, Hannam v The Financial Conduct Authority UKUT 0233 [2014] (TCC)). Administrative sanctions also embodied a different consciousness of wrongdoing – in the common law tradition expressed as moral culpability, and captured in so-called mens rea requirements – but where enforcement pursued by the state identified this misconduct as that which was nevertheless considered to be serious. Interestingly, at the time that this strongly administrative orientation held favour in European approaches and underpinning thinking, the then UK financial regulator (the FSA) was questioning the purported simplicity of administrative enforcement relative to criminal enforcement, doing so directly in relation to 'market abuse' activities (for example, Cole, 2007). Very significantly, and from 2009 certainly, the FSA was also critiquing the ability of administrative sanctions to deliver high standards of market conduct through 'credible deterrence' of wrongdoing (Cole, 2007); also directly in relation to market abuse – in ways which chime closely with current European thinking on framing appropriate responses to this type of financial misconduct (Wilson and Wilson, 2014).

The UK's pro-criminal enforcement position identified with the organizational philosophy of 'credible deterrence' – that whereby wherever there existed the possibility for both criminal and non-criminal action, that the former would be pursued in preference to the latter – does predate the formal publicity of a European stance in this regard. Nevertheless, configuring UK thinking and European thinking as being ad idem is appropriate. This is also notwithstanding the politicization of the UK's 'opt out' from the CSMAD and the introduction of criminal liability for benchmark manipulation courtesy of Section 91 of the Financial Services Act 2012. In respect of the former, elements within the UK Conservative Party government were keen to emphasize not simply the constitutional 'opt out' enjoyed by the UK, but also how UK criminalization already exceeded the minimum criminalization required under the CSMAD (see Ministerial Statement from Rt Hon Mark Hoban MP on the CSMAD, 20 February 2012); and similarly, in some quarters introduction of new criminal liability for benchmark manipulation was properly considered a domestic initiative, rather than one originating in a mandate from Europe (see Wilson and Wilson, 2021). Nonetheless, situating the position of the UK alongside the US shows just how marked the contrasts in philosophy and perception and articulation of enforcement policy can be, and from this perhaps just how identifiably *European* UK approaches might be considered.

European market abuse prohibitions are underpinned by the macro – or market-based – philosophy of 'market egalitarianism' that exists within European capital markets law (Moloney, 2014: 700–5). For market egalitarianism, market confidence is delivered through investor confidence that information relating to investment decisions can be accessed by all market participants, and that this information is also accurate.[7] This provides the basis for a wide conception of how market functionality can be interfered with, and configuring the ways in which this arises as being 'abusive' (for markets), and thus encouraging extensive prohibitions on 'interferences' with the availability of information and its quality (namely accuracy); with this itself underpinned by European single market aspirations, built on four freedoms of movement, including free movement of capital (European Commission, 2014). European approaches manifest thinking that social as well as economic consequences attach to interruptions in efficient capital flows between those who have capital and the sectors of the economy most in need of it (for example, European Social Watch, 2010).

Conclusion

Measured alongside European regard for the accuracy of information available to market participants, the contrasts in US approaches to insider trading are particularly stark. A micro – or relationships-based – philosophy, rather than market-based philosophy has ensured that prohibitions are drawn overall narrowly, by confining trading restrictions to a corporate fiduciary insider, and to those who have been 'tipped off' by such a corporate fiduciary insider in exchange for a benefit for that insider; or those who have stolen information from the issuing institution. Even following the Supreme Court decision in Salman v United States – 137 S. Ct. 420 [2016] United States Supreme Court these prohibitions manifest specific restrictions on the use of 'non-public' information which is the property of the issuing entity. And as Newman stated very clearly, there is no requirement of symmetry of information among investors under US law, and there is no 'general duty between all participants in market transactions to forgo actions based on material, nonpublic information' (United States v Newman, No. 13-1837 [2014] United States Court of Appeals 2d Cir.).

As Newman explains, the policy rationale for the prohibitions on insider trading which do subsist 'stops well short of prohibiting all trading on material nonpublic information'. This is because while the protection of an issuer's information was one component of efficient capital markets operation, equally so is the ability of those who acquire such information to be at liberty to act on this and profit from it. In the UK, market manipulation prohibitions have a much longer history than ones relating to insider dealing. The roots of criminalizing the dissemination of information or other actions designed to give a false or misleading impression of the price or availability of securities can be seen in legislation dating from 1857, some 130 years earlier than the Section 47 'conduct of business' prohibitions under the Financial Services Act 1986 (Wilson, 2015). The creation of the specific crime of insider dealing in the UK in 1980 (and 1985; respectively Companies Act 1980 and Company Securities [Insider Dealing Act 1985]) initially followed the US micro (fiduciary) relationships-based approach, and it was in the implementation of the 1989 Directive on Insider Dealing (Council Directive 89/592/EEC of 13 November 1989 coordinating regulations on insider dealing) that UK insider dealing law became very consciously European in a highly fundamental way. Similarly, much interesting discussion can be had about Europeanness through tracking the use of the construct of 'credible deterrence' by the UK from 2009, by the EU from (at least) 2011, and formally by IOSCO as of 2015.

While uncertainty over the precise nature and configuration of domestic law following Brexit continues, different possibilities for 'future law' and its underpinnings remain open. This could include a continuation of influences associated with existing European implementations, and this is a scenario which seems likely if access to the European single market continues. Given that there are other possible futures which can be envisioned, this spotlight on finding Europeanness in conceptualizations of white-collar crime could play an important part in embedding Europeanness in post–Brexit Britain. This analysis proposes that it is possible to identify Europeanness in white-collar crime through exploring 'market abuse' activities, and furthermore that exploring a distinctive European identity for white-collar crime is important. This is important for the UK, given that a clear vision for post-Brexit Britain has yet to transpire. It is also proposed that this exercise is also important for Europe, at a time when the very existence of the EU is at risk – legally and politically, socially and culturally. This is a time when threats abound for the European 'project' from Brexit itself, and its possible 'contagion' effects, and also continuing economic fragility throughout the Eurozone; and also from the rise of right wing populism throughout the bloc, and beyond in many western democracies.

Notes

[1]   The CSMAD *does* cite the reference to 'financial crime' in the de Larosière Group Report (High-Level Group on Financial Supervision in the EU) 2009, but reference to economic crime is overall more prominent and extensive; see, for example, the Council of Europe Economic Crime and Cooperation Division website, at: www.coe.int/en/web/corruption/home

[2]   Directive 2014/57/EU [2014] OJ L173/179. See, especially, Recitals 6 and 7, and Article 3. This is through requiring all member states to 'provide for harmonised criminal offences of insider dealing and market manipulation, and to impose maximum criminal penalties of not less than 4 and 2 years imprisonment for the most serious market abuse offences'. Under the CSMAD, member states must ensure that such behaviour is a criminal offence, punishable with effective sanctions everywhere in Europe. The most 'serious cases' are considered to be ones of insider dealing, market manipulation and unlawful disclosure of inside information which are committed intentionally, and attempts thereof on account that it is not only successful trades which adversely affect the 'integrity of the financial markets and on investor confidence in those markets'.

[3]   Regulation (EU) No 596/2014 [2014] OJ L173/1.

[4]   And where this would appear not to reach certain offences which might readily be brought within the rubric of 'financial crime'; for example, criminal liability for 'reckless banking' under Section 36 of the Financial Services (Banking Reform) Act 2013

[5]   As manifested in the General Anti-Abuse Rule (GAAR), set out in Part 5 of the Finance Act 2013 (together with Schedules 43–43C of the Act). See, for example, HM Revenue & Customs guidance designed to assist in the recognition of tax arrangements which are considered abusive, and the process for counteracting them, at: www.gov.uk/government/publications/tax-avoidance-general-anti-abuse-rules

[6]   For example, OECD reactions to 'aggressive tax planning'. These include initiatives from 2018 (developed in the context of the OECD and G20 action plan on base erosion and profit shifting) setting out actions to equip governments with domestic and international rules and instruments to address tax avoidance, ensuring that profits are taxed where economic activities generating the profits are performed and where value is created. See: www.oecd.org/tax/beps/beps-actions/

[7]   For a key statement of this see, for example, the introductory Recitals of the Market Abuse Regulation (MAR) 2014.

References

Ashe, T.M. and Counsell, L. (1993) *Insider Trading*, London: Tolley.

Cole, M. (2007) 'The FSA's approach to insider dealing', speech to the American Bar Association, 4 October, Available at: https://webarchive.nationalarchives.gov.uk/20090903073700/http://www.fsa.gov.uk/pages/Library/Communication/Speeches/2007/1004_mc.shtml

Davies, P. (1991) 'The European Community's Directive on Insider Dealing: from company law to securities market regulation', *Oxford Journal of Legal Studies* 11(1): 92–105.

Davies, P., Francis, P. and Jupp, V. (1999) 'The features of invisible crimes', in P. Davies, P. Francis and V. Jupp (eds) *Invisible Crimes: Their Victims and their Regulation*, Basingstoke: Palgrave, pp 3–28.

European Commission (2011) 'Proposals for a regulation on market abuse and for a directive on criminal sanctions for market abuse: frequently asked questions', 20 October, Available at: https://ec.europa.eu/commission/presscorner/detail/fr/MEMO_11_715

European Commission (2014) 'Single Market Forum 2014: snapshot of results', 8 December, Available at: http://ec.europa.eu/growth/single-market/forum/2014

European Social Watch Report (2010) 'Time for action: responding to poverty, social exclusion and inequality in Europe and beyond', Available at: www.socialwatch.org/sites/default/files/European_SW_Report_2010-eng.pdf

Friedrichs, D.O. (2013) 'Wall Street: crime never sleeps', in S. Will, S. Handelman and D. Brotherton (eds) *How They Got Away With It: White Collar Criminals and the Financial Meltdown*, New York: Columbia University Press, pp 3–25.

Hoban, M. (2012) 'Ministerial statement on the Criminal Sanctions Directive on Market Abuse', 20 February, Available at: https://publications.parliament.uk/pa/cm201212/cmhansrd/cm120220/wmstext/120220m0001.htm#1202202000003

International Organization of Securities Commissioners (2015) 'Credible deterrence in the enforcement of securities regulation', June, Available at: www.iosco.org/library/annual_conferences/pdf/40/Credible%20Deterrence%20Report.pdf

International Monetary Fund (2001) 'Financial system abuse, financial crime and money laundering: background paper', 12 February, Available at: www.imf.org/external/np/ml/2001/eng/021201.htm

Ligeti, K. and Franssen, V. (2017) 'Current challenges in economic and financial criminal law in Europe and the US', in K. Ligeti and V. Franssen (eds) *Challenges in the Field of Economic and Financial Criminal Law in Europe and the US*, Oxford: Hart, pp 1–15.

Manne, H.G. (1966) *Insider Trading and the Stock Market*, New York: Collier-Macmillan.

Moloney, N. (2014) *EU Securities and Financial Markets Regulation* (3rd edn), Oxford: Oxford University Press.

Rider, B. (1995) 'Civilising the law: the use of civil and administrative proceedings to enforce financial services law', *Journal of Financial Crime* 3(1): 11–33.

Ryder, N. (2014) *The Financial Crisis and White-Collar Crime: The Perfect Storm,* Cheltenham: Edward Elgar.

Tomasic, R. (2011) 'The financial crisis and the haphazard pursuit of financial crime', *Journal of Financial Crime*, 18(1): 7–31.

Sutherland, E.H. (1940) 'White-collar criminality', *American Sociological Review*, 5(1): 1–12.

Wilson, S. (2015) 'High frequency trading and criminal liability for "market abuse"', *Lloyd's Reports: Financial Crime*, 5: 380–85.

Wilson, S. (2015) 'The new market abuse regulation and directive on criminal sanctions for market abuse: European capital markets law and new global trends in financial crime enforcement', *ERA Forum (The Journal of the Academy of European Law)*, 16: 427–48.

Wilson, G. and Wilson, S. (2010) 'Market misconduct, the FSA and creating a system of "city grasses": blowing the whistle on whistle-blowing', *Company Lawyer*, 31(3): 67–80.

Wilson, G. and Wilson, S. (2013) 'Criminal responses and financial misconduct in 21st century Britain: tradition and points of departure, and the significance of the conscious past', *Law, Crime and History*, 3(3): 1–24.

Wilson, G. and Wilson, S. (2014) 'The FSA, "credible deterrence", and criminal enforcement: a "haphazard pursuit"?', *Journal of Financial Crime*, 21(1): 4–28.

Wilson, G. and Wilson, S. (2021, forthcoming) 'The interplay between criminal and quasi-criminal enforcement mechanisms in the UK context explored through the prism of "market abuse": current and historical perspectives', in V. Franssen and C. Harding (eds) *Quasi-Criminal Enforcement Mechanisms in Europe: Historical Origins, Contemporary Concepts and Future Perspectives*, Oxford: Hart.

6

Anti-Money Laundering and the Legal Profession in Europe: Between Global and Local

Katie Benson

Introduction

The role played by legal professionals in the laundering of criminal proceeds generated by others has remained a concern for policy makers since their identification (along with accountants and other financial services providers) as 'gatekeepers', able to block or allow the movement of 'dirty' money into the legitimate financial system. An array of control measures has been put in place at global, regional and national levels to prevent legal (and other) professionals from facilitating money laundering. This chapter will consider the 'Europeanness' of the anti-money laundering framework for legal professionals working within countries of the European Union (EU),[1] asking if there is a particularly European nature to this framework (that is, in comparison with the rest of the world) and whether it is experienced as such by those working in individual nation-states. The anti-money laundering framework within Europe is shaped primarily by the EU Anti-Money Laundering Directives, which are themselves shaped by global standards such as the Financial Action Task Force (FATF) Recommendations on money laundering and terrorism financing. The EU Anti-Money Laundering Directives, therefore, create a 'European' anti-money laundering environment, which has both consistencies and discrepancies with other parts of the world. However, anti-money laundering policies and processes in individual nation-states will be shaped not only by the EU Directives, but also by local contexts and priorities. Therefore, how anti-money laundering is experienced by legal professionals in particular settings will depend on an interaction between the 'global' and the 'local'.

The global context

The primary driver behind the global anti-money laundering (and counter-terrorism financing) regime is the FATF. The FATF was established at the 1989 G7 Summit in Paris as a one-year, 11-member taskforce with a mandate to

> assess the results of co-operation already undertaken in order to prevent the utilisation of the banking system for the purpose of money laundering, and to consider additional preventative efforts in this field, including the adaptation of the legal and regulatory systems so as to enhance multilateral judicial assistance.[2]

Its establishment followed two other significant moments in the development of the global anti-money laundering regime, which had occurred the previous year: the introduction of the United Nations Convention Against Illicit Traffic in Narcotic Drugs and Psychotropic Substances (the Vienna Convention) and the adoption of the Basel Committee on Banking Supervision Statement of Principles on the Prevention of Criminal Use of the Banking System for the Purpose of Money Laundering (the Basel Statement). The Vienna Convention obliged states to 'deprive persons engaged in illicit traffic of the proceeds of their criminal activities and thereby eliminate their main incentive for doing so',[3] and was the first international legal instrument to establish a specific offence of money laundering. It focused on the laundering of the proceeds of drug trafficking only, with subsequent international instruments widening the scope of predicate offences beyond those related to illicit drugs.[4] Similarly, the FATF's initial focus was on funds derived from the illicit drugs trade.

The Basel Statement highlighted concerns about the laundering of criminal proceeds through financial institutions and encouraged banks to implement a range of procedures to prevent or reduce money laundering. It reflected the recognition that financial institutions were instrumental to money laundering and, therefore, were also key to the prevention and detection of laundering activity. In 1990, the FATF issued 40 Recommendations for action, to be implemented by the governments of its member states, which focused on three key objectives: a) the improvement of national legal systems, particularly in the area of criminal law; b) the strengthening of international cooperation; and c) the enhancement of the role of financial institutions in combating money laundering. The third objective expanded the scope and content of the Basel Principles to suggest that financial institutions commit to implementing a range of policies and procedures to enhance customer due diligence, identification and record keeping.

The FATF's remit has extended far beyond its initial one-year mandate, and in the three decades since its establishment it has become 'the focal institution of a powerful financial governance regime' (Nance, 2018a: 131). There are now 37 full members with seats at the 'top table' (Benson et al, 2020: 4), nine regional groups acting as associate members and 28 observer bodies (Nance, 2018b).[5] There have been amendments to the FATF Recommendations in 1996 (extending the focus beyond the proceeds of drug trafficking) and in 2004 (when nine 'special recommendations' were added to address terrorist financing, following the 9/11 terrorist attacks and the subsequent 'War on Terror'). The Recommendations are not legally binding; they provide a 'blueprint' to guide member states' own policies, legislation and regulations. The FATF carries out an ongoing 'mutual evaluation' process to evaluate how individual states' anti-money laundering systems and processes align with the Recommendations. The Recommendations – and the FATF itself – have, therefore, been hugely influential in the development of international, regional and, ultimately, national initiatives and legislative changes – including in Europe.

The development of a 'European' anti-money laundering framework for legal professionals

In 1991, the first EU Anti-Money Laundering Directive[6] was introduced, bringing the FATF standards to the European sphere. The first Directive took a two-pronged approach, focusing on both the criminalization and the prevention of money laundering. Based on the original FATF Recommendations and using the definition of money laundering from the Vienna Convention, it prohibited the laundering of the proceeds of drug trafficking only, although it gave member states the discretion to extend criminalization to other offences. When the first Directive was updated in 2001,[7] the criminalization of the laundering of proceeds from offences other than drug trafficking was made mandatory, reflecting the revised FATF Recommendations published in 1996.

The preventative strand of the first Directive introduced a series of obligations for financial and credit institutions to implement adequate money laundering procedures, policies and training programmes; to carry out appropriate 'customer due diligence' measures, including verifying customers' identities and maintaining identification records; to refrain from transactions they knew or suspected were associated with money laundering; to report suspicious transactions to the relevant national authorities; and to not 'tip off' customers who were being investigated for money laundering. The Second Anti-Money Laundering Directive, introduced in 2001, extended the preventative obligations beyond the financial sector to include a range of non-financial businesses and professions considered to pose a money laundering risk, such as real estate agents, high-value dealers, auditors, external accountants and tax advisers, and legal professionals. This extension came in response to the growing concern that certain 'gatekeeper professionals' outside of the financial sector were being exploited by individuals wishing to launder criminal proceeds, acting as intermediaries in money laundering schemes or providing advice to criminals to assist them in the management of their illicit funds. The Second Directive was therefore a landmark moment in the development of a European anti-money laundering framework for legal professionals – it required members states to incorporate legal professionals into their own anti-money laundering frameworks and subject them to the 'know your customer' and reporting requirements that had previously only applied to financial institutions.

The inclusion of legal professionals in the preventative measures of the anti-money laundering regime proved contentious, with particular resistance to the reporting obligations of the regime. Concern was raised both by legal scholars (for example, Gentzik, 2000; Xanthaki, 2001; Mitsilegas, 2006; Gallant, 2013) and by legal professional associations (see Kirby, 2008; Terry, 2010) about the implications of reporting duties and other measures for the confidential nature of the lawyer–client relationship and the potential risk to lawyers who come into contact with 'dirty' money. In some countries, such as Canada,[8] these objections led to lawyers being exempted from the reporting obligations. But EU member states were required to adhere to them, establishing one characteristic of the 'European' anti-money laundering environment. This environment has been further shaped by four subsequent EU Anti-Money Laundering Directives, which have each had implications for the obligations and working practices of legal professionals.

The Third Directive[9] of 2005 extended the scope of the anti-money laundering regime to include activities related to terrorist financing (in line with the revised FATF Recommendations) and made trust and company providers subject to the its preventative obligations, among other changes. This was followed by the Fourth Directive,[10] which gave effect to the latest version of the FATF Recommendations, issued in February 2012. The Fourth Directive contained a number of new developments, with a greater emphasis on a risk-based approach to anti-money laundering, requirements for more transparency around beneficial ownership, and changes to customer due diligence measures. This was quickly amended by the Fifth Anti-Money Laundering Directive,[11] agreed in May 2018, which added some new provisions rather than making wholesale changes. These provisions focused on the regulation of virtual currencies, greater access to and sharing of information, and further increased transparency in relation to beneficial ownership of companies and trusts (primarily driven by the Panama Papers revelations). Only five months later, the Sixth Anti-Money Laundering Directive was adopted, aiming, among other things, to harmonize the definition of money laundering and predicate offences across member states, extend criminal liability to legal persons and impose minimum penalties for money laundering offences.[12]

The 'glocality' of anti-money laundering

There is, therefore, a 'European' anti-money laundering environment for legal professionals, influenced by the global context but created by the EU Anti-Money Laundering Directives, which aim for consistency and harmonization in the ways that member states enact anti-money laundering policy. However, the anti-money laundering regime that is experienced by legal professionals within particular locales will be shaped by local (that is, national-level) factors, as well as the global and regional (that is, EU-level) contexts outlined earlier. Such local factors include: the nature and structures of the legal profession, which vary between different countries;[13] the roles and responsibilities of the bodies that regulate or supervise members of the legal profession in relation to their anti-money laundering obligations; national legislative and regulatory frameworks; and the priorities and policy agenda set by national governments.

The concept of 'glocalization' captures this interaction between the global and the local, with its simultaneous characteristics of universality and particularity (Robertson, 1995; Roudometof, 2016, 2019). As global phenomena make their way to the local level, processes of both adoption and adaptation occur (Giulianotti and Robertson, 2007), as they are 'refracted' through the local lens (Van Hellemont and Densley, 2019: 174) and shaped by 'local contextualities' (Giddens, 1991: 22). As local practices develop, they may themselves reshape global frameworks in a reverse of this process. For example, the introduction of public registers of beneficial ownership in individual countries, driven by national policy agendas, is now reflected in requirements for increased transparency in relation to beneficial ownership of companies and trusts seen in the Fifth Anti-Money Laundering Directive. There is insufficient space in this chapter to explore all the factors that shape anti-money laundering environments at the local level. The production of 'glocality' in legal professionals' actual, material experience of anti-money laundering will be demonstrated through two examples, related to the UK context.

Criminal offences in the UK: beyond international standards

The EU Anti-Money Laundering Directives have been transposed to the UK through successive Money Laundering Regulations (1993, 2003, 2007 and 2017), which implement the main preventative measures of the Directives, and the Proceeds of Crime Act (POCA) 2002, which established the primary criminal money laundering offences in the UK.

The EU Directives define money laundering as conduct that is 'committed intentionally' and highlight the 'knowledge' of the individual involved. For example, in wording that echoes that of previous Directives, Article 1 of the Fourth Directive states:

1. This Directive aims to prevent the use of the Union's financial system for the purposes of money laundering and terrorist financing.
2. Member States shall ensure that money laundering and terrorist financing are prohibited.
3. For the purposes of this Directive, the following conduct, when committed intentionally, shall be regarded as money laundering:
   a. the conversion or transfer of property, knowing that such property is derived from criminal activity or from an act of participation in such activity, for the purpose of concealing or disguising the illicit origin of the property or of assisting any person who is involved in the commission of such an activity to evade the legal consequences of that person's action;

b. the concealment or disguise of the true nature, source, location, disposition, movement, rights with respect to, or ownership of property, knowing that such property is derived from criminal activity or from an act of participation in such activity;

c. the acquisition, possession or use of property, knowing, at the time of receipt, that such property was derived from criminal activity or from an act of participation in such activity;

d. participation in, association to commit, attempts to commit and aiding, abetting, facilitating and counselling the commission of any of the actions referred to in points (a), (b) and (c).[14]

The Sixth Anti-Money Laundering Directive, introduced in 2018, declares its aim 'to criminalise money laundering when it is committed intentionally and with the knowledge that the property was derived from criminal activity'.[15] Similarly, the Vienna Convention and the 2005 Council of Europe Convention on Laundering, Search, Seizure and Confiscation of the Proceeds from Crime and on the Financing of Terrorism (the Warsaw Convention) required states to create criminal offences related to money laundering in domestic law only 'when committed intentionally'.[16] International and regional frameworks therefore focus on intent and knowledge, and are directed towards those deliberately laundering criminal proceeds.

However, the offences contained within POCA 2002 have a mens rea at the level of 'suspicion', and so actual knowledge of money laundering is not required for conviction. Sections 327 and 329 of POCA 2002, which relate to concealing, disguising, converting, transferring, removing, acquiring, possessing or using criminal property, do not stipulate mens rea in themselves; that is taken from the definition of 'criminal property' in Section 340.[17] Under Section 328, there is a double mens rea requirement: this offence covers situations where a third party becomes involved in an arrangement they know or suspect facilitates the acquisition, retention, use or control of what they know or suspect to represent direct or indirect 'benefit' from criminal conduct.

For legal professionals, there is a further offence of relevance: the Section 330 offence, 'Failure to Disclose: Regulated Sector', which applies to those in sectors designated as being at risk for money laundering and subject to the Money Laundering Regulations. In this offence, which creates the obligation to inform the authorities of suspicions of money laundering, the mental element of knowledge and suspicion is extended. An offence is committed if an individual in the regulated sector knows or suspects, or has reasonable grounds to know or suspect, that another person is engaged in money laundering and does not make the required disclosure to the relevant authority (if the information comes to them in the course of their business in the regulated sector). This means that those working in the regulated sector can be found guilty of a 'failure to disclose' offence under Section 330 if they should have known or suspected another person was engaged in money laundering, even if they lacked actual knowledge of such conduct. Therefore, money laundering offences for which legal professionals could be prosecuted in the UK have a wider scope than that required by the regional and global standards from which they derived.

Regulatory/supervisory environment in the UK: complex and context-specific

The nature of the regulation and supervision of the legal profession in relation to money laundering in the UK is shaped by the Money Laundering Regulations (hereafter 'MLR 2017'),[18] which implement the main preventative measures of the EU Anti-Money Laundering Directives. MLR 2017 applies to certain groups, including 'independent legal professionals', and requires members of those groups to comply with a number of measures to 'know their clients' and monitor the use of their services, including risk assessment, customer due diligence and record-keeping measures and the implementation of adequate policies, systems and procedures. Regulated sectors are also required to be supervised for anti-money laundering purposes by a designated supervisory authority. The role of the supervisory authority is to effectively monitor the persons it is responsible for, take necessary measures to ensure their compliance with the requirements of the Regulations and report any suspicions or knowledge that a person it is responsible for is or has engaged in money laundering or terrorist financing to the NCA (see Regulation 46 of MLR 2017).

Within MLR 2017, the designated supervisory authorities for those that belong to regulated professions are their professional bodies. The legal profession in the UK comprises a range of different types of 'independent legal professional' and varies in structure between the constituent parts of the UK (that is, England and Wales, Scotland and Northern Ireland). This creates a number of professional bodies, resulting in their being nine named supervisory bodies for the profession.[19] Furthermore, developments in the regulation of parts of the profession in different areas of the UK have led to divergent anti-money laundering regulatory/supervisory contexts. For example, in 2007, the representative and regulatory roles of the Law Society (the professional body for solicitors in England and Wales) were split, and the Solicitors Regulation Authority (SRA) was established. This followed a review of the regulatory framework for legal services in England and Wales, which had raised concerns about the complexity of the existing self-regulatory regime and its lack of transparency and accountability (Clementi, 2004). While the Law Society retains the representative function, the SRA acts as the regulatory and disciplinary body for solicitors in England and Wales. Therefore, while the designated supervisory authority for solicitors in this part of the UK under MLR 2017 is the Law Society (due to the first iteration of the Regulations being enacted prior to the establishment of the SRA), this role is delegated in practice to the SRA. The Law Society's anti-money laundering role is focused on providing guidance and training for its members and making representations on their behalf in relation to new or amended policy.

However, the separation between representation and regulation did not take place in Scotland or Northern Ireland, and so in these areas the regulation – and anti-money laundering supervision – of solicitors remains the remit of the professional bodies (the Law Society of Scotland and the Law Society of Northern Ireland), alongside their representative functions. In 2018, a further dynamic was added to the anti-money laundering regulatory landscape for legal professionals in the UK with the establishment of the Office for Professional Body Anti-Money Laundering Supervision (OPBAS). OPBAS was introduced to oversee the range of bodies responsible for supervision in the legal and accountancy sectors, due to concern about the lack of consistency in their supervisory practices and weaknesses in collaboration and information sharing. A report produced by OPBAS in 2019 highlighted the competing priorities between supervisory bodies' anti-money laundering roles and their members' interests (Office for Professional Body Anti-Money Laundering Supervision, 2019: 7), finding a tendency for some professional bodies to 'focus more on representing their members rather than robustly supervising standards'.[20] Therefore, the separation of regulatory and representative functions which has occurred in England and Wales but not Scotland or Northern Ireland may have created supervisory asymmetries between different parts of the UK (the existence and effects of such asymmetries require empirical examination).

Conclusion

There is undoubtedly a 'European' anti-money laundering environment for legal professionals. This has been produced by the fundamental role of the EU Anti-Money Laundering Directives in creating a regional framework for anti-money laundering in its member states. Though based on global standards, these standards are not enacted uniformly across the world, and so disparities can be noted between EU member states and other jurisdictions (such as the exemption of legal professionals within Canada from reporting requirements). However, the way in which anti-money laundering policies and processes are experienced by individual legal professionals – and the potential implications of these policies – is shaped by their specific local context. The 'glocality' of this experience is produced by the interaction between global, regional, national and local factors, creating both universal and particular characteristics through processes of adoption and adaptation. Therefore, while there is clearly value in considering the 'Europeanness' of anti-money laundering frameworks due to the relevance of the EU in shaping legislation and policy, the importance of the national context in shaping experience at the local level must also be taken into account. There are also questions about what we mean by 'Europe' in this context and whether, in relation to (anti-)money laundering, 'the EU' is a more useful and relevant unit of analysis. The imminent departure of the UK from the EU, while being likely to continue mirroring EU policy in this area, at least in the short term, creates further questions about this distinction.

This chapter suggests a number of areas for further research and analysis. A project comparing the potential role of lawyers in facilitating money laundering, the various structures of the legal profession and its regulatory frameworks, in France, Italy, the Netherlands and the UK remains the only comparative work in this area (see Chevrier, 2004; Di Nicola and Zoffi, 2004; Lankhorst and Nelen, 2004; Levi et al, 2004; Middleton and Levi, 2004). Analysis of the nature and structures of the legal profession, roles and responsibilities of regulatory/supervisory bodies and national priorities, policies, legislation and regulations, in various countries within Europe, would enhance understanding of the factors that shape the anti-money laundering experience at the local level. Their relationship to EU frameworks and comparisons between anti-money laundering in the EU and other parts of the world would provide insights into the nature and influence of the 'European' anti-money laundering environment.

Notes

[1] When we talk about Europe or the European context in relation to anti-money laundering, we are primarily referring to the EU as it is at this level that anti-money laundering policy is made. Using the UK as an example for analysis, therefore, raises questions about its future position in the 'European' anti-money laundering sphere with its withdrawal from the EU.

[2] Paragraph 53 of G7, Economic Declaration, Paris Summit (16 July 1989). Available at: www.g8.utoronto.ca/summit/1989paris/communique/index.html

[3] See page 1 of the United Nations Convention Against Illicit Traffic in Narcotic Drugs and Psychotropic Substances 1988.

[4] For example, the Council of Europe Convention on Laundering, Search, Seizure and Confiscation of the Proceeds from Crime 1990 (the Strasbourg Convention); United Nations International Convention for the Suppression of the Financing of Terrorism 1999; United Nations Convention against Transnational Organized Crime 2000 (the Palermo Convention).

[5] For an overview and critical analysis of the role, functions and development of the FATF see the special issue on the subject in Volume 69, Issue 2 of *Crime, Law and Social Change*, published in March 2018.

[6] Council Directive 91/308/EEC of 10 June 1991 on prevention of the use of the financial system for the purpose of money laundering, 1991 (First Money Laundering Directive).

[7] Directive 2001/97/EC of the European Parliament and of the Council of 4 December 2001 amending Council Directive 91/308/EEC on prevention of the use of the financial system for the purpose of money laundering, 2001 (Second Money Laundering Directive).

[8] In 2015, the Supreme Court of Canada found that the reporting requirements were a breach of the constitutional right to attorney-client privilege. The exemption of legal professionals within Canada from the reporting requirements is considered by the FATF to be 'a serious impediment to Canada's efforts to fight money laundering' (Financial Action Task Force, 2016: Paragraph 27).

[9] Directive 2005/60/EC of the European Parliament and of the Council of 26 October 2005 on the prevention of the use of the financial system for the purpose of money laundering and terrorist financing, 2005 (Third Anti-Money Laundering Directive).

[10] Directive (EU) 2015/849 of the European Parliament and of the Council of 20 May 2015 on the prevention of the use of the financial system for the purposes of money laundering or terrorist financing, 2015 (Fourth Anti-Money Laundering Directive).

[11] Directive (EU) 2018/843 of the European Parliament and of the Council of 30 May 2018 amending Directive (EU) 2015/849 on the prevention of the use of the financial system for the purposes of money laundering or terrorist financing, 2018; and amending Directives 2009/138/EC and 2013/36/EU, 2018 (Fifth Anti-Money Laundering Directive).

[12] Directive (EU) 2018/1673 of the European Parliament and of the Council of 23 October 2018 on combating money laundering by criminal law [2018] (Sixth Anti-Money Laundering Directive). EU member states are expected to transpose this Directive into national law by December 2020. At the time of writing, the Sixth Anti-Money Laundering Directive has not yet been transposed into UK law.

13 For example, in the UK, there are two main categories of lawyer: solicitors and barristers (in Scotland, barristers are known as advocates). Solicitors provide expert legal advice and assistance on a range of matters, and usually have direct contact with clients. Barristers are legal advisers and courtroom advocates, representing clients in court. While barristers fall under the scope of anti-money laundering regulations, the risk of money laundering and focus of anti-money laundering policies are more relevant for solicitors, as they handle clients' money and participate in certain transactions and services. Other categories of legal professional in the UK include licensed conveyancers (also found in other countries such as Australia and New Zealand), whose work focuses on property transactions. The UK, however, does not have the civil law notaries that are found in other countries of Europe, such as France, Italy and the Netherlands.

14 Directive 2015/849/EU of the European Parliament and of the Council of 20 May 2015 on the prevention of the use of the financial system for the purposes of money laundering or terrorist financing, 2015 (Fourth Anti-Money Laundering Directive), emphases added.

15 Paragraph 13 of Directive (EU) 2018/1673 of the European Parliament and of the Council of 23 October 2018 on combating money laundering by criminal law, emphasis added.

16 See Article 3, Paragraph 1 of the United Nations Convention Against Illicit Traffic in Narcotic Drugs and Psychotropic Substances 1998 and Article 9, Paragraph 1 of the Council of Europe Convention on Laundering, Search, Seizure and Confiscation of the Proceeds from Crime and on the Financing of Terrorism (CETS 198) 2005.

17 Criminal property is defined as property that 'constitutes a person's benefit from criminal conduct or it represents such a benefit (in whole or part or whether directly or indirectly), and the alleged offender *knows or suspects* that it constitutes or represents such benefit' (POCA, 2002: Section 340, emphasis added).

18 The full name being the Money Laundering, Terrorist Financing and the Transfer of Funds (Information on the Payer) Regulations 2017.

19 These are: the Chartered Institute of Legal Executives, the Council for Licensed Conveyancers, the Faculty of Advocates, the Faculty Office of the Archbishop of Canterbury, the General Council of the Bar, the General Council of the Bar of Northern Ireland, the Law Society, the Law Society of Northern Ireland, the Law Society of Scotland. See Regulation 7 of the Money Laundering, Terrorist Financing and Transfer of Funds (Information on the Payer) Regulations 2017.

20 Speech by Alison Barker, Director of Specialist Supervision (OPBAS), RUSI 12/03/2019.

References

Barker, A. (2019) 'Money laundering and supervising trusted professionals', speech by Alison Barker, Director of Specialist Supervision, on the role of OPBAS at the RUSI, Available at: www.fca.org.uk/news/speeches/alison-barker-speech-on-opbas-at-rusi

Benson, K., King, C. and Walker, C. (2020) 'Dirty money and the new responses of the 21st century', in K. Benson, C. King and C. Walker (eds) *Assets, Crimes and the State: Innovation in 21st Century Legal Responses*, Abingdon: Routledge, pp 1–19.

Chevrier, E. (2004) 'The French government's will to fight organized crime and clean up the legal professions: the awkward compromise between professional secrecy and mandatory reporting', *Crime, Law and Social Change*, 42(2/3): 189–200.

Clementi, D. (2004) 'Review of the regulatory framework for legal services in England and Wales: final report', December, Available at: webarchive.nationalarchives.gov.uk/+/http://www.legal-services-review.org.uk/content/report/index.htm

Di Nicola, A. and Zoffi, P. (2004) 'Italian lawyers and criminal clients: risks and countermeasures', *Crime, Law and Social Change*, 42(2/3): 201–25.

Financial Action Task Force (FATF) (2016) 'Anti-money laundering and counter-terrorist financing measures: Canada: mutual evaluation report', September, Available at: www.fatf-gafi.org/media/fatf/documents/reports/mer4/MER-Canada-2016.pdf

Gallant, M. (2013) 'Lawyers and money laundering regulation: testing the limits of secrecy in Canada', 4 October, Available at: https://papers.ssrn.com/sol3/papers.cfm?abstract_id=2336219

Gentzik, D. (2000) 'Laundering and lawyers: the payment of legal fees and money-laundering offences in Germany and the UK', *Journal of Money Laundering Control*, 4(1): 76–88.

Giddens, A. (1991) *Modernity and Self-Identity*, Cambridge: Polity.

Giulianotti, R. and Robertson, R. (2007) 'Forms of glocalization: globalization and the migration strategies of Scottish football fans in North America', *Sociology* 41(1): 133–52.

Kirby, D. (2008) 'The European Union's gatekeeper initiative: the European Union enlists lawyers in the fight against money laundering and terrorist financing', *Hofstra Law Review*, 37(1): 261–311.

Lankhorst, F. and Nelen, H. (2004) 'Professional services and organised crime in the Netherlands', *Crime, Law and Social Change*, 42(2/3): 163–88.

Levi, M., Nelen, H. and Lankhorst, F. (2004) 'Lawyers as crime facilitators in Europe: an introduction and overview', *Crime, Law and Social Change*, 42(2/3): 117–21.

Middleton, D. and Levi, M. (2004) 'The role of solicitors in facilitating "organized crime": situational crime opportunities and their regulation', *Crime, Law and Social Change*, 42(2/3): 123–61.

Mitsilegas, V. (2006) 'Countering the chameleon threat of dirty money: "hard" and "soft" law in the emergence of a global regime against money laundering and terrorist financing', in A. Edwards and P. Gill (eds) *Transnational Organised Crime: Perspectives on Global Security*, Abingdon: Routledge, pp 195–211.

Nance, M.T. (2018a) 'Re-thinking FATF: an experimentalist interpretation of the Financial Action Task Force', *Crime, Law and Social Change* 69(2): 131–52.

Nance, M.T. (2018b) 'The regime that FATF built: an introduction to the Financial Action Task Force', *Crime, Law and Social Change* 69(2): 109–29.

Office for Professional Body Anti-Money Laundering Supervision (OPBAS) (2019) 'Anti-money laundering supervision by the legal and accountancy professional body supervisors: themes from the 2018 OBPAS anti-money laundering supervisory assessments', March, Available at: www.fca.org.uk/publication/opbas/themes-2018-opbas-anti-money-laundering-supervisory-assessments.pdf

Proceeds of Crime Act (POCA) (2002) Available at: www.legislation. gov.uk/ukpga/2002/29/contents

Robertson, R. (1995) 'Glocalization: time-space and homogeneity-heterogeneity', in M. Featherstone, S. Lash and R. Robertson (eds) *Global Modernities*, London: Sage, pp 25–54.

Roudometof, V. (2016) *Glocalization: A Critical Introduction*, New York: Routledge.

Roudometof, V. (2019) 'Cosmopolitanism, glocalization and youth cultures', *Youth and Globalization*, 1: 19–39.

Terry, L. (2010) 'An introduction to the Financial Action Task Force and its 2008 lawyer guidance', *Journal of the Professional Lawyer*, 2010: 3–68.

Van Hellemont, E. and Densley, J. (2019) 'Gang glocalization: how the global mediascape creates and shapes local gang realities', *Crime Media Culture*, 15(1): 169–89.

Xanthaki, H. (2001) 'Lawyers' duties under the draft EU money laundering directive: is confidentiality a thing of the past?', *Journal of Money Laundering Control*, 5(2): 103–14.

7

Responding to Money Laundering across Europe: What We Know and What We Risk

Karin van Wingerde and Anna Merz

Introduction

On 4 September 2018, the Netherlands Public Prosecution Service (NPPS) published a €775 million settlement with the Dutch bank ING Group NV, the largest financial services provider in the Netherlands, for serious and structural violations of the Money Laundering and Counter-Terrorist Financing (Prevention) Act (AML/CTF Act). The settlement, consisting of a fine of €675 million and a disgorgement of €100 million, is the largest ever agreed upon in the Netherlands.

The AML/CTF Act regulations require banks and other service providers to identify and prevent illicit financial flows by monitoring (potential) clients, and by signalling and reporting risks to the authorities. In other words, these service providers should act as gatekeepers to protect the integrity of the financial system; a role which ING had insufficiently fulfilled. As a result, criminals had been able to abuse ING accounts and launder large sums of money through Dutch accounts for several years.

Together with the settlement, the NPPS published an extensive statement of facts on the criminal investigation against ING (Netherlands Public Prosecution Service, 2018). The report presents a shocking picture of the bank's internal operations. Not only were client investigations not carried out properly, resulting in files being missing or incomplete, the internal risk monitoring system – which was specifically intended to pick up risks of money laundering – turned out to be capped at only three risks per day for some categories of risks (Netherlands Public Prosecution Service, 2018: 11). As a result, the bank had missed important signals of money laundering. According to the NPPS, these shortcomings were deeply rooted in the bank's corporate culture, in which cutbacks had come at the expense of compliance (Netherlands Public Prosecution Service, 2018: 17).

Around the time of the ING case, a similar case occurred in Belgium. In May 2018, the National Bank of Belgium imposed a fine of €300,000 on BNP Paribas Fortis, the largest bank in Belgium, for violations of anti-money laundering regulations (Bové and Broens, 2018). Here too, the bank failed to adequately monitor clients and transactions for many years. The former Libyan leader Muammar Gaddafi had an account with the bank which he used to transfer more than €80,000 for the purchase of more than 1,000 bulletproof vests (Bové and Broens, 2018).

Although similar in terms of the nature and extent of the violations involved, these cases triggered completely different responses. Whereas the ING case resulted in a criminal settlement and dominated the newspaper headlines, the case of BNP Paribas involved a regulatory fine that was published anonymously by the National Bank of Belgium in order 'not to cause the bank a disproportionate disadvantage' (Bové and Broens, 2018). The case did not receive any attention in the media until a journalist linked the fine to BNP Paribas. Yet, even then, public outcry failed to materialize.

These cases are just two recent examples of major European and global financial institutions being involved in, and being punished for, facilitating money laundering. The need to respond to these cases effectively has been a priority for national, supranational and international organizations for many years now (Gelemerova, 2011; Sharman, 2011; Bergstrom, 2018). Yet, previous studies have indicated that there are significant differences in the ways in which the AML/CTF Act regulations are implemented and enforced across EU member states (Levi and Reuter, 2006; Unger, 2006; Sharman, 2011; Verhage, 2015, 2017; Levi, 2018). This chapter maps similarities and differences in responses to anti-money laundering (hereafter AML) cases against banks in Europe, allowing us to better understand what is 'European' about responding to corporate and white-collar crime in Europe and to reflect on the implications for the effectiveness and legitimacy of AML efforts in the global financial system. Following our mapping exercise, we see a much more stringent and aggressive enforcement paradigm.

We then go on to argue for the need to be mindful of the adverse effects of such an aggressive approach for the legitimacy of the global AML regime as potentially undermining the willingness of banks and financial institutions to take on more responsibilities to fight money laundering.

Taking stock of money laundering cases against banks across Europe

Table 7.1 provides an overview of 47 AML cases against banks in Europe between January 2015 and January 2020. Using media reports and open source materials for verification, cases were selected when they resulted in sanctions imposed by European authorities. This focus on European responses was informed by the focus of this volume on corporate and white-collar crime and its enforcement across Europe. Yet, the transnational character of many AML cases implies that there are many cases involving European actors sanctioned by other authorities, like the United States for instance, that fall outside the scope of this chapter. Moreover, we have only included cases for which information about the case (bank, nature of violations and type and size of the sanction) was publicly available. Not all authorities disclose the type of sanction and the name of the offending organizations. Furthermore, as we have limited our search to breaches of AML requirements as the primary offence, we did not include cases regarding auxiliary offences, even though these may be related to money laundering, such as tax fraud, reporting failures, or sanctions violations. Finally, our sample is limited to those sources that have been published in the Dutch, English and German languages. This implies that our sample does not cover all AML cases against banks that have been pursued by European authorities. The results are therefore not generalizable to other cases in other countries. Even more so, based on the data presented here, we do not know what non-enforcement tells us. This may either be the result of our selection bias or actual non-enforcement. An understanding of the impact of AML enforcement will eventually require a more detailed overview of AML cases across and beyond Europe than the one presented here. However, we do believe that the data presented here is a first step in creating an evidence base for understanding AML enforcement.

Table 7.1 shows that eleven AML cases have led to criminal investigations. At the time of writing, five cases were still ongoing (UBS in France, Danske Bank in Denmark, Caixa Bank in Spain, ABN AMRO in the Netherlands, Swedbank in Sweden), but most cases resulted in criminal fines or deferred prosecution/ non-prosecution agreements, involving monetary sanctions.

Table 7.1: Overview of AML cases against banks across Europe

Criminal response				Regulatory response			
Bank	Jurisdiction	Year	Sanction	Bank	Jurisdiction	Year	Sanction
UBS*	France	2019	€4.5 billion (€3.7 billion fine + €800 million civil penalties)	Swedbank AB	Sweden	2019	€360 million; warning; publication of report and CEO dismissed
ING	Netherlands	2018	€775 million settlement (€665 million fine + €100 million disgorgement); publication of statement of facts and resignation of CFO	Deutsche Bank	UK	2017	€183.7 million (£163.1 million after 30% discount for early settlement; £154 million fine + £9.1 million disgorgement) + publication of report
HSBC	France	2017	€300 million settlement	Standard Chartered Bank	UK	2019	€115.1 million (£102.2 million after 30% discount for early settlement) + publication of report
HSBC	Belgium	2019	€294.4 million settlement	Barclays	UK	2015	€81.2 million (£72.1; £19.8 million fine + £52.3 million disgorgement) + publication of report
Credit Suisse	Italy	2016	€109.5 million settlement	BNP Paribas	France	2017	€10 million
Danske Bank*	Denmark & Estonia	2018	Reform order and reprimands (Denmark); order to close local branch & repay customer deposits (Estonia); CEO resigned & arrest of ten client managers	Nordea Bank	Sweden	2015	€5.4 million + warning + publication of report

Table 7.1: Overview of AML cases against banks across Europe (continued)

Criminal response				Regulatory response			
Bank	Jurisdiction	Year	Sanction	Bank	Jurisdiction	Year	Sanction
ING (Italian business)	Italy	2019	€30 million settlement (€1 million fine + €29 million disgorgement)	Société Générale	France	2017	€5 million + publication of report
UBS	Italy	2019	€10 million settlement (€2.125 million fine + €8.175 million disgorgement)	Banque Havilland	Luxemburg	2018	€4 million
ABN Amro*	Netherlands	2019	Ongoing investigation	Handelsbanken	Sweden	2015	€3.7 million + remark + publication of report
Caixabank*	Spain	2018	Ongoing investigation	Sonali Bank Limited	UK	2016	€3.7 million (£3.3 million after 30% discount for early settlement) Money laundering reporting officer (MLRO) fined £17,900 (after 30% discount for early settlement) and prohibition to perform MLRO position in regulated firms + publication of report + restriction on accepting deposits from new clients for 168 days
Swedbank AS*	Estonia	2019	Ongoing investigation	ABLV	Latvia	2018	€3.17 million
				Raiffeisen Bank International AG	Austria	2019	€2.748 million

(continued)

Table 7.1: Overview of AML cases against banks across Europe (continued)

Criminal response				Regulatory response			
Bank	Jurisdiction	Year	Sanction	Bank	Jurisdiction	Year	Sanction
				PrivatBank	Cyprus	2016	€1.5 million (eligible for 15% discount for early payment)
				Swedbank	Latvia	2016	€1.36 million
				FBME Bank	Cyprus	2015	€1.2 million + withdrawal of license
				Hellenic Bank	Cyprus	2016	€1.1 million (eligible for 15% discount for early payment)
				Rabobank	Netherlands	2018	€1 million
				Santander (Norwegian business)	Norway	2019	€1 million
				Canara Bank (Indian Bank)	UK	2018	€1.03 million; restriction, prevented from accepting deposits from new customers for 147 days
				RCB Bank	Cyprus	2017	€800,000 (eligible for 15% discount for early payment)
				Cyprus Development Bank	Cyprus	2018	€715,000 (eligible for 15% discount for early payment)
				Volksbank	Netherlands	2016	€500,000 and ordered improvements
				Hypo Vorarlberg Bank AG	Austria	2019	€414,000

Table 7.1: Overview of AML cases against banks across Europe (continued)

Criminal response				Regulatory response			
Bank	Jurisdiction	Year	Sanction	Bank	Jurisdiction	Year	Sanction
				ING (Belgian business)	Belgium	2019	€350,000
				BNP Paribas Fortis	Belgium	2018	€300,000
				Central Cooperative Bank	Cyprus	2016	€25,000
				DnB NOR	Norway	2019	€2,951 non-compliance fee
				ABLV	Latvia	2018	Temporary restriction on payments + withdrawal of license + voluntary liquidation
				Versobank	Estonia	2018	Withdrawal of license + liquidation
				Pilatus Bank	Malta	2018	Withdrawal of license
				Jyske bank	Denmark	2017	Administrative orders to revise risk assessment and AML policies
				Credit Suisse	Switzerland	2018	Appointment of monitor + ordered improvements until end 2019
				Triodos	Netherlands	2019	Ordered Improvements until end 2019
				Deutsche Bank	Germany	2018	Appointment of monitor
				Gazprombank	Switzerland	2018	Appointment of monitor + ordered improvement + prohibition of expansion private clients
				Swedbank	Lithuania	2018	Warning

Note: *ongoing investigations at time of writing

Together these fines amount to €6.018 billion. This was largely the result of a record fine of €4.5 billion issued against the Swiss bank UBS by a French court in February 2019, the largest single European fine ever levied against a bank. UBS was convicted for aiding its clients to hide billions of euros from French tax authorities between 2004 and 2012 and launder the proceeds. The conviction followed a seven-year investigation during which the bank had already rejected a previous settlement offer (Monroe, 2019).

Yet, most cases resulted in regulatory sanctions (*n*=36). This is in line with previous research showing that responses to corporate crime in general (van de Bunt and Huisman, 2007; Lord and Levi, 2015) and AML violations in particular (Bergström, 2018) are predominantly regulatory or administrative. Moreover, most of these cases resulted in monetary penalties (*n*=26). In these cases, fines range from €25,000 (Central Cooperative Bank, Cyprus) up to the €360 million fine for Swedbank AB (Sweden), issued in 2019. Together these fines amount to €789 million, with an average of €30.3 million. Apart from monetary sanctions, administrative responses to AML violations include the appointment of a monitor, stipulating measures for improvements, withdrawal of banking licenses and the liquidation of the bank.

In these 47 cases, the type of violation does not seem to account for the pursuit of either criminal or regulatory sanctions. Most cases involved inadequate AML systems (omission) that may have allowed money laundering to occur, rather than proof of the actual facilitation of money laundering (commission), and these cases have led to both criminal and regulatory sanctions. For example, the ING and BNP Paribas cases were similar in terms of the type of violations but have led to different responses.

Responding to money laundering in Europe: what we know

The above stocktaking of AML enforcement against banks in Europe is not just a simple mapping exercise but provides important insights into understanding what is 'European' about responding to money laundering in Europe. Two key findings emerge from this analysis: fragmentation and a more aggressive enforcement paradigm.

Fragmentation

Since its emergence on the international policy agenda in the late 1980s, the regulation and enforcement of money laundering, unlike most types of corporate and white-collar crime, has predominantly been organized and coordinated at the international level (Sharman, 2011; van den Broek, 2015; Verhage, 2015, Bergström, 2018). Moreover, the AML regime has been set up to become a 'truly global regime' (Levi and Reuter, 2006: 291). The rationale underlying this 'top-down' approach (Verhage, 2015) is that tackling money laundering effectively requires international coordination and cooperation since the offence itself almost always involves cross-border activities (van den Broek, 2015; Verhage, 2015, Bergström, 2018). Since the 1990s there have been numerous initiatives aimed at the harmonization of AML policies around the world. Six consecutive (Anti-)Money Laundering Directives (1991, 2001, 2005, 2015, 2018, 2020), have shaped the regulation and enforcement of money laundering across Europe. For example, the EU's Sixth AML Directive, which was to have been implemented in domestic legislation by the end of 2020, introduces a uniform definition of money laundering to improve cooperation across member states and establish a level playing field regarding criminal liability for money laundering. Yet, despite these attempts, countries across Europe still differ significantly in their interpretation, implementation and enforcement of the Directives (Unger, 2006; Sharman, 2011; Verhage, 2015, 2017). This is well illustrated by the differences in terms of the number, type and size of sanctions imposed in AML cases against banks in Europe and the way in which these cases are scattered across Europe.

As Table 7.2 shows, the 47 cases in our analysis were pursued in 18 different European countries. However, this may be the result of our selection bias. There may have been cases that were not publicly available, published in languages that we could not analyze or that we have missed or excluded for other reasons. Another reason might be that other countries did not encounter any AML violations in the past few years or imposed any formal legal sanctions. However, we find that highly unlikely given the transnational scope of many banks, increased public scrutiny of banking practices and heightened awareness of AML practices across the globe.

Second, in terms of the number of cases enforced, Cyprus imposed the highest number of sanctions, followed by the Netherlands and the UK. In terms of monetary value however, we can distinguish between two groups of countries: those that levied total fines over and under €100 million. Only six countries (France, the Netherlands, the UK, Sweden, Belgium and Italy) imposed fines above €100 million. Together, these six countries imposed 21 fines (out of 23 total sanctions) of which 8 were above €100 million. The other 12 countries imposed

Table 7.2: Sanctions levied on banks by European authorities, 2015–2020

Country	Number of cases (*n*=47)	Total fines levied (in million euros)
France	4	4,815
Netherlands	5	776.5
UK	5	384.73
Sweden	3	369.1
Belgium	3	295.05
Italy	3	149.5
Cyprus	6	5.34
Latvia	3	4.53
Luxemburg	1	4
Austria	2	3.162
Norway	2	1
Switzerland	2	No fines levied
Denmark	2	No fines levied
Estonia	2	No fines levied
Lithuania	1	No fines levied
Malta	1	No fines levied
Spain	1	No fines levied
Germany	1	No fines levied

24 sanctions, of which 13 were fines, which together amounted to €18.03 million, which is only 0.003 per cent of the total of €6.7 billion in fines imposed by the countries levying fines over €100 million. The highest fine in the group of countries levying fines under €100 million was a €4 million fine imposed by Luxembourgian regulators. Hence, there is a significant gap regarding the size of the fines between countries that levied fines over and under €100 million.

In sum, despite being organized and coordinated on the international level, our 'mapping exercise' illustrates that rather than a harmonized European approach, AML enforcement against banks remains highly fragmented in terms of the number, type and size of the sanctions imposed. This can partly be explained by differences in competence and mandate between the different European jurisdictions and regulators.

A more aggressive enforcement paradigm

Even though the regulation and enforcement of corporate and white-collar crime in Europe is generally presented as more lenient than in the United States (Lord and Levi, 2015), the current AML regime against banks across Europe illustrates a shift towards a more aggressive enforcement paradigm in which banks are increasingly being portrayed as (criminal) facilitators of money laundering rather than as gatekeepers (Bergström, 2018; see also Fenergo, 2019, 2020).

For example, in March 2019, the chairperson of Europe's Single Resolution Board (SRB), responsible for the resolution of failing banks, said that 'Europe has zero tolerance to money-laundering, therefore banks have to be very careful about their reputation' ('Europe has zero tolerance to money laundering', 2019). In April 2019, the European Parliament adopted a legislative resolution on a proposal to strengthen the role of the European Banking Authority (EBA) in the fight against money laundering by (among other mandates) developing regulatory and supervisory standards and giving the EBA a leading role in the coordination and cooperation between EU and national authorities.[1] Furthermore, several European countries (France, Germany, the Netherlands, Latvia and Spain) presented a joint statement to the European Commission, expressing their desire to harmonize the European regulatory framework and establish a European supervisory authority for the enforcement of AML measures (Ministers of Finance of France, Germany, Italy, Latvia, the Netherlands and Spain, 2019). Finally, AML violations by banks across Europe are increasingly subjected to more substantial penalties. The EU's Fourth AML Directive already introduced the possibility for regulatory authorities to impose turnover-related fines and required member states to adopt legislation aimed at disclosing information about the nature and circumstances of AML violations and to publish the names of financial institutions subject to enforcement. This trend towards more aggressive enforcement is supported by our mapping exercise of AML cases.

First, over the last couple of years, the number of AML fines against banks has been steadily increasing. Sixteen fines were imposed in 2018, another 14 in 2019, marking record years in terms of the number of AML-related fines imposed on banks in Europe (see also Fenergo, 2020). Furthermore, in terms of monetary value, fines are increasing up to the point that they exceed the profit margins of firms. For example, the €4.5 billion fine issued against UBS exceeded the bank's annual net profit (Fenergo, 2020: 4). Finally, a recent report by

Fenergo (2019) summarizing all European fines for AML, 'know your customer' and sanctions violations over the past decade, shows that the total amount of fines levied has increased gradually over the last ten years, and nearly tripled between 2017 and 2018.

Yet, it is not just monetary fines that seem to be on the rise. Sanctions at the top of the regulatory enforcement pyramid (Ayres and Braithwaite, 1992), such as the suspension or withdrawal of the license to operate, fit this war on money laundering. These sanctions were imposed three times in 2018 alone, in all cases for smaller, non-systemic banks (in Estonia, Latvia and Malta). Withdrawal of license and liquidation are direct interferences in the bank's authority and autonomy. It communicates the authorities' distrust in the bank being able to fulfil its 'prudential requirements' and its 'obligations towards its creditors' (European Central Bank, 2018: 25). To give one example, the Estonian banking supervisor discovered 'systemic and long-lasting' AML breaches at the Estonian bank Versobank AS (Estonian Financial Supervision and Resolution Authority, 2018). Therefore, the Estonian financial watchdog initiated the procedure for withdrawal of Versobank's licence and subsequent liquidation by the European Central Bank:[2]

> As financial intermediaries are one of the first and most important lines of defence combating money laundering and terrorist financing, we cannot tolerate any breaches of the law by them. The withdrawal of the authorisation of Versobank AS is a clear signal that Estonia will not tolerate breaches of anti-money laundering and combating of terrorism law. (Estonian Financial Supervision and Resolution Authority, 2018)

This discussion on enforcement raises the question as to whether European responses are increasingly assimilating US practices. One topic that emerges from our analysis is the role the US plays in driving AML enforcement across the globe. Many of the cases that we analyzed were initially led by or involved US authorities. For example, the cases of ING, Deutsche Bank, Danske Bank, ABLV, Pilatus Bank, Nordea and Swedbank were all initiated by US authorities. Although it is difficult to establish how and to what extent US law enforcement shapes European practices, it seems highly likely that European authorities tend to impose more significant penalties to ensure that the US refrains from taking enforcement actions, which often result in even more substantial fines and would significantly hinder commercial operations within the US for the banks involved (see also Levi and Reuter, 2006: 291). For example, Cypriot newspapers connected the increase in number of cases against banks with a campaign by the Cypriot authorities to improve the reputation of its financial system, especially regarding allegations of money laundering and allowing financial institutions to engage in cross-border activity (Orphanides, 2018).

Responding to money laundering in Europe: what we risk

The fragmented yet more aggressive enforcement paradigm in Europe raises significant concerns regarding the effectiveness and legitimacy of the global AML regime. Despite its emergence on the international policy agenda in the late 1980s, we still don't know much about the impact of the AML regime on reducing money laundering (Levi, 2002; Verhage, 2017; Pol, 2019, 2020a, 2020b). Not only is its impact difficult to assess due to a lack of comparable data (Verhage, 2017; Bank Policy Institute, 2018; Levi et al, 2018), but according to some commentators, while the regime might be effective in catching a few criminals it has almost no real impact on illicit flows of money and the crimes preceding illegal money (Pol, 2020b). Focusing enforcement efforts on the monitoring roles of gatekeepers is a way of dealing with this enforcement gap. The assumption is that threatening these gatekeepers with more severe penalties urges them to take their responsibilities more seriously, which would prevent future crimes. Unfortunately, however, existing research on corporate crime deterrence does not provide evidence that more severe penalties do in fact prevent future wrongdoing. A systematic review of all available evidence on corporate crime deterrence failed to find a deterrent effect (Simpson et al, 2014). Insofar as sanctions have a preventive impact on future wrongdoing, this effect is more indirect (Thornton et al, 2005). Sanctions may remind other regulatees to check whether they are still in compliance with rules and regulations and reassure 'good compliers' that violations are dealt with and that a level playing field is being established.

Yet, the analysis of our cases illustrates that, rather than a level playing field, the enforcement of AML cases across Europe is fragmented and uneven (see Verhage, 2017). This signals that other players may get away with AML violations or are punished less severely. Rather than preventing future violations, this may undermine compliance. Moreover, to remind other regulatees to check their own compliance, sanctions should communicate a moral message, explaining the causes of the violation, emphasizing that the penalized behaviour is condemned and creating consensus about the blameworthiness of the penalized offense (van Wingerde, 2016). The question is that of whether the current, more aggressive enforcement paradigm is sending just such a moral message. As the earlier summary of cases has illustrated, most AML cases against banks are regulatory cases. At the same time, however, criminal sanctions are often better suited to express the blameworthiness of the punished conduct and label it as a wrongful act, since, according to Simester and Von Hirsch (2011: 6), criminal law 'speaks with a moral voice'. Moreover, apart from a few exceptions, most sanctions imposed on banks that we have witnessed over the last few years have placed the size of the fine in the limelight. As such, these fines only fuel a rat race in which authorities increasingly propose harsher and more severe penalties. According to Rakké and Huisman (2020) the statement of facts in the ING case significantly contributed to change in the banking industry because it provided detailed explanations as to why and how the violations at the bank happened.

Furthermore, imposing these draconian fines on banks may be counterproductive, by undermining the legitimacy of the global AML regime. The global AML regime is built on the delegation of responsibilities for monitoring of clients and suspicious transactions to the private sector. Banks and financial institutions were the first assigned to this role, but since then AML requirements have expanded to the legal professions, real estate agents, car dealers, casinos and so on. This implies that these gatekeepers have been made jointly responsible for protecting public interests. However, the current enforcement paradigm subjects banks to (criminal) investigations and, rather than portraying banks as gatekeepers, this more aggressive enforcement discourse portrays banks and financial institutions as criminal facilitators. This may negatively impact their moral commitment for public–private cooperation.

There are already indications that this global war on money laundering undermines gatekeepers' willingness to take on more responsibilities in terms of the prevention of money laundering and cooperating with authorities. For example, in a study on financial companies, Gill and Taylor (2004) found that their respondents felt that the increased AML requirements alienated clients and consequently had a serious negative impact upon business. Similarly, in her research on legal professionals convicted for money laundering offences, Benson (2018) shows that the responsibilization of legal professionals raises significant concerns among lawyers about the consequences for confidentiality within the lawyer–client relationship and fears about the risks for lawyers. Moreover, in a study on US banks, Eren (2020) highlights the competing objectives AML compliance officers must deal with: compliance with AML requirements and limiting the risk of enforcement on the one hand and profit making on the other. Finally, forthcoming research on the experiences and perceptions of five groups of gatekeepers (notaries, lawyers, accountants, financial advisors and financial institutions) about their roles as gatekeepers illustrates that responsibilizing gatekeepers while strengthening enforcement generates internal and external tensions that drive crises of existence for AML compliance actors within regulated entities (van Wingerde, 2021, forthcoming). As a result, AML compliance actors tend to 'play it safe' by de-risking clients and services (see also Levi, 2018) or by overreporting suspicious transactions. But it also leads to what can be characterized as 'creative', 'cosmetic' or 'ritualistic' compliance (McBarnett, 2001; Krawiec, 2003; Edelman, 2007), which refers to compliance motivations that are geared towards anticipating and defusing possible state intervention so as to minimize risk to the business rather than a normative commitment to reduce flows of illicit finance. These findings suggest that the more aggressive enforcement paradigm of increased penalties may undermine the necessary conditions for the successful delegation of more supervisory responsibilities to business, increases distrust between regulatory authorities and gatekeepers, and may even be counterproductive.

Conclusion

Combating money laundering is one of the key issues on the international policy agenda (Bergström, 2018) and given its relatively uniform international legal framework it offers an ideal case study for comparative criminological inquiry. In this short chapter, we have summarized the responses in 47 AML cases across Europe. In line with previous research, this mapping exercise confirms that AML responses across Europe are highly fragmented in terms of the number, type and size of the sanctions imposed. At the same time however, AML violations by banks across Europe are increasingly subjected to more substantial and criminal penalties. Rather than contributing to the prevention of illicit flows of money, this may negatively impact upon gatekeepers' willingness to contribute to AML in the global financial system. As mentioned before, the data presented here has limitations and leaves many questions unanswered. For example, based on our data we cannot make conclusions on non-enforcement and the significance thereof for the impact of AML enforcement across the globe. Understanding the impact of AML regimes requires an understanding of the full extent of the AML problem, beyond the present knowledge. Moreover, fragmentation may also be the result of differences in compliance standards in comparable jurisdictions or differences in competence and responsibilities in different countries. Understanding these differences not only requires better insight into the AML problem but also into national policies and politics. Finally, what we do know from the deterrence literature is that a greater likelihood of detection is more of a deterrent than more punitive penalties. Based on the data presented here, however, we do not yet know whether detection probability is increasing or not. The evidence base presented here, however, is a first step in exploring these issues.

To understand the impact of the current enforcement paradigm, future research must consider the experiences of gatekeepers. Therefore, follow-up research is needed on how the current AML regime is perceived by gatekeepers and how they respond to it. Such research could take the form of in-depth ethnographic analysis of the experiences of AML compliance actors in various industries.

Notes

[1]   See: www.europarl.europa.eu/doceo/document/TA-8-2019-0374_EN. html?redirect

[2]   While other administrative responses are national in scope, a withdrawal of license is a European measure, involving the approval of the European Central Bank (2018: 25).

References

Ayres, I. and Braithwaite, J. (1992) *Responsive Regulation: Transcending the Deregulation Debate*, New York: Oxford University Press.

Bank Policy Institute (2018) 'Getting to effectiveness: report on U.S. financial institution resources devoted to BSA/AML & sanctions compliance', Available at: https://bpi.com/wp-content/uploads/2018/10/BPI-AML-Sanctions-Study-vF.pdf

Benson, K. (2018) 'Money laundering, anti-money laundering, and the legal profession', in C. Walker, C. King and J. Gurulé (eds) *The Palgrave Handbook of Criminal and Terrorism Financing Law*, London: Palgrave Macmillan, pp 109–33.

Bergström, M. (2018) 'The global AML regime and the EU AML directives: prevention and control', in C. Walker, C. King and J. Gurulé (eds) *The Palgrave Handbook of Criminal and Terrorism Financing Law*, London: Palgrave Macmillan, pp 33–56.

Bové, L. and Broens, B. (2018) 'BNP Paribas Fortis jarenlang te laks tegen witwassen', *De Tijd*, [online] 22 September, Available at: www. tijd.be/ondernemen/banken/bnp-paribas-fortis-jarenlang-te-laks-tegen-witwassen/10052091.html

Broek, M. van den (2015) *Preventing Money Laundering: A Legal Study on the Effectiveness of Supervision in the European Union*, The Hague: Eleven Publishers.

Edelman, L.B. (2007) 'Overlapping fields and constructed legalities: the endogeneity of law', in J. O'Brien (ed) *Private Equity, Corporate Governance, and the Dynamics of Capital Markets Regulation*, London: World Scientific Publishing, pp 55–90.

Eren, C.P. (2020) 'Cops, firefighters, and scapegoats: anti-money laundering (AML) professionals in an era of regulatory bulimia', *Journal of White Collar and Corporate Crime*. doi:10.1177/2631309X20922153

Estonian Financial Supervision and Resolution Authority (EFSA) (2018) 'The authorisation of Versobank AS has been withdrawn', [online] 26 March, Available at: www.fi.ee/en/news/authorisation-versobank-has-been-withdrawn

European Central Bank (2018) 'Guide to assessments of licence applications', Available at: www.bankingsupervision.europa.eu/ecb/pub/pdf/ssm.201803_guide_assessment_credit_inst_licensing_appl.en.pdf

Fenergo (2019) 'A fine mess we're in: AML/KYC/sanctions fines, a ten-year analysis (2008 – 2018): EMEA edition', Available at: https://go.fenergo.com/aml-kyc-sanctions-fines-emea.html

Fenergo (2020) 'Another fine mess: a global research report on financial institution fines and enforcement actions', Available at: www.fenergo.com/resources/reports/another-fine-mess-global-research-report-financial-institution-fines.html

Gelemerova, L.Y. (2011) *The Anti-Money Laundering System in the Context of Globalisation: A Panopticon Built on Quicksand?* Nijmegen: Wolf Legal Publishers.

Gill, M. and Taylor, G. (2004) 'Preventing money laundering or obstructing business?', *British Journal of Criminology*, 44(4): 582–94.

Krawiec, K. (2003) 'Cosmetic compliance and the failure of negotiated governance', *Washington University Law Quarterly*, 81: 487–544.

Levi, M. (2002) 'Money laundering and its regulation', *The ANNALS of the American Academy of Political and Social Science*, 582(1): 181–94. doi:10.1177/000271620258200113

Levi, M. (2018) 'Punishing banks, their clients and their clients' clients', in C. Walker, C. King and J. Gurulé (eds) *The Palgrave Handbook of Criminal and Terrorism Financing Law*, London: Palgrave Macmillan, pp 273–91.

Levi, M. and Reuter, P. (2006) 'Money laundering', *Crime and Justice*, 34(1): 289–375.

Levi, M., Reuter, P. and Halliday, T. (2018) 'Can the AML system be evaluated without better data?', *Crime, Law and Social Change*, 69: 307–28.

Lord, N. and Levi, M. (2015) 'Determining the adequate enforcement of white-collar and corporate crimes in Europe', in J. van Erp, W. Huisman and G. Vande Walle (eds) *The Routledge Handbook of White-Collar and Corporate Crime in Europe*, Abingdon: Routledge, pp 39–56.

McBarnet, D. (2001) 'When compliance is not the solution but the problem: from changes in law to changes in attitude', Centre for Tax System Integrity, The Australian National University, Available at: https://openresearch-repository.anu.edu.au/bitstream/1885/41635/2/WP18.pdf

Ministers of Finance of France, Germany, Italy, Latvia, the Netherlands and Spain (2019) 'Towards a European supervisory mechanism For ML/FT', Available at: www.moneylaundering.com/wp-content/uploads/2019/11/EU.Report.AMLSuperMechanism.110819.pdf

Monroe, B. (2019) 'Daily briefing: French court hits UBS with $5 billion fine, SC sets aside $900 million, and more', *ACFCS*, [online] 22 February, Available at: www.acfcs.org/news/439400/Daily-Briefing—French-court-hits-UBS-with-5-billion-fine-SC-sets-aside-900-million-and-more.htm

Netherlands Public Prosecution Service (NPPS) (2018) 'Investigation Houston: criminal investigation into ING Bank N.V.: statement of facts and conclusions of the Netherlands Public Prosecution Service', Available at: www.prosecutionservice.nl/binaries/prosecutionservice/documents/publications/fp/hoge-transacties/feitenrelaas/statement-of-facts-ing/statement_of_facts_houston.pdf

Orphanides, S. (2018) 'Cyprus Development Bank fined €0.7m for AML shortcomings'. *Cyprus Mail*, 22 May, Available at: https://cyprus-mail.com/2018/05/22/cyprus-development-bank-fined-e0-7m-for-aml-shortcomings/

Pol, R.F. (2019) 'The global war on money laundering is a failed experiment', *The Conversation*, [online] 21 October, Available at: https://theconversation.com/the-global-war-on-money-laundering-is-a-failed-experiment-125143

Pol, R.F. (2020a) 'Response to money laundering scandal: evidence-informed or perception driven?', *Journal of Money Laundering Control*, 23(1): 103–121. doi:10.1108/JMLC-01-2019-0007

Pol, R.F. (2020b) 'Anti-money laundering: the world's least effective policy experiment? Together, we can fix it', *Policy Design and Practice*, 3(1): 73–94. doi: 10.1080/25741292.2020.1725366

Rakké, J.T. and Huisman, W. (2020) 'Motieven voor naleving van de wettelijke anti-witwasmeldplicht', *Tijdschrift voor Bijzonder Strafrecht & Handhaving*, 1: 5–11.

Sharman, J.C. (2011) *The Money Laundry: Regulating Criminal Finance in the Global Economy*, Ithaca, London: Cornell University Press.

Simester, A.P. and von Hirsch, A. (2011) *Crimes, Harms, and Wrongs: On the Principles of Criminalization*, Oxford, Portland: Hart Publishing.

The Baltic Times (2019) 'Europe has zero tolerance to money laundering', 25 March, Available at: www.baltictimes.com/europe_has_zero_tolerance_to_money_laundering/

Thornton, D., Gunningham, N.A. and Kagan, R.A. (2005) 'General deterrence and corporate environmental behavior', *Law & Policy*, 27(2): 262–87.

Unger, B. (2006) 'The amounts and the effects of money laundering', Report for the Ministry of Finance, The Hague, Available at: www.rijksoverheid.nl/documenten-en-publicaties/rapporten/2006/02/16/onderzoeksrapport-the-amounts-and-the-effects-of-money-laundering.html

van de Bunt, H.G. and Huisman, W. (2007) 'Organizational crime in the Netherlands', in M. Tonry and C. Bijleveld (eds) *Crime and Justice in the Netherlands*, Chicago: University of Chicago Press, pp 217–60.

van Wingerde, C.G. (2016) 'Deterring corporate environmental crime: lessons from the waste industry in the Netherlands', in T. Spapens, W. Huisman and R. White (eds) *Environmental Crime in Transnational Context*, Abingdon: Routledge, pp 193–207.

Verhage, A. (2015) 'Global governance = global compliance? The uneven playing field in anti-money laundering', in J. van Erp, W. Huisman and G. Vande Walle (eds) *The Routledge Handbook of White-Collar and Corporate Crime in Europe*, Abingdon: Routledge, pp 471–85.

van Wingerde, K. (2021, forthcoming) *Tussen Wortel en Stok: En Empirische Studie Naar Poortwachters (Between Carrot and Stick: An Empirical Analysis of Anti-Money Laundering Gatekeepers)*, The Hague: Sdu.

Verhage, A. (2017) 'Great expectations but little evidence: policing money laundering', *International Journal of Sociology and Social Policy*, 37(7/8): 477–90. doi:10.1108/IJSSP-06- 2016-0076

PART III

White-Collar Crime: European Case Studies

8

Food Production Harms in the European Context: The EU as an Enabler or a Solution?

Ekaterina Gladkova

Introduction

Food is vitally important for human subsistence. Moreover, the nature of socio-environmental and politico-economic conditions is particularly intricate in the process of food production. This intricacy begs the question, 'who is producing what kind of food, for whose benefit, and to whose disadvantage?' (Moragues-Faus and Marsden, 2017: 281).

This chapter poses the question of whether food production-focused research can also become the lens that helps to open up new lines of inquiry about what is 'European' about European white-collar crime. Even though both isolated deviancy and systemic harm feature in the fabric of modern food systems, criminological engagement with intersections of food, crime and harm has not been prolific (see Walters, 2007; Cheng, 2011; Croall, 2012). Once the concept of food crime was introduced by Croall in 2007, avenues for research included food fraud, food poisoning (Tombs and Whyte, 2010), food mislabelling (Croall, 2012), trade practices and environmental law (Walters, 2006), food pricing, exploitation in food production (Tombs and Whyte, 2007) and cruelty to animals (Agnew, 1998; Yates, 2007).

The intersection of food and criminological research in the European context can be observed in *The Routledge Handbook of White-Collar and Corporate Crime in Europe* (2015), which invokes the topic of food crime in relation to food adulteration and hygiene regulation. Since then, European criminologists have developed a better understanding of the criminal acts embedded in the food chain through the analysis of food fraud (Lord et al, 2017; Flores Elizondo et al, 2018; Ruth et al, 2018) and harmful labour practices (Davies, 2018). Nevertheless, only 12 out of 42 contributors to the most recent edition of *A Handbook of Food Crime* (Gray and Hinch, 2018) come from European countries, with the majority of authors being North American and Australian researchers. It is evident that the European research on food crime needs to be problematized further. Moreover, the specificities of the European context might facilitate this task and provide additional opportunities for academic inquiry, thus advancing research into both food crime and European white-collar crime.

Echoing critical traditions in criminology, I suggest that focusing solely on food crime creates boundaries that do not allow us to venture beyond the rigid binary between criminal and lawful. Food production may involve serious harms that lie beyond traditional definitions of crime (Gray and Hinch, 2015), on the spectrum that Passas (2005) calls 'lawful but awful'. Therefore, in line with the socio-legal approach in green criminology, this chapter attempts to challenge the existing epistemology of food crime by discussing routine practices that govern meat production in the European context. The chapter highlights the manner in which meat production governance safeguards the interests of the powerful actors, despite the detrimental impacts of those interests on ecological systems and society.

Criminology scholars stress the importance of opening industrial farming for criminological exploration (Sollund, 2015). While industrial farming results in social and environmental grievances (Passas, 2005), the agri-food actors benefitting from it are highly resistant to regulation (Croall, 2012) and guarantee that the legal frameworks continue to protect their vested interests (Boekhout van Solinge, 2010). The topic of industrial farming thus intersects with the research on the crimes of the powerful, including white-collar crime. While the latter occasionally considers the role of high-profile actors and organizations in the pillaging of the environment, some authors nevertheless suggest that more 'greening' of crimes of the powerful research should take place (Bradshaw, 2014: 166).

To summarize the rationale outlined previously, in this chapter I identify the trajectories for the future white-collar crime research in relation to food production governance by revealing how European economic and regulatory contexts safeguard the interests of the powerful in the processes of meat production. I suggest that more criminological attention should be directed to analyzing existing regimes of power in European food production governance and discussing the Europe-specific circumstances that reinforce them. The chapter utilizes a case study of farming industrialization in Northern Ireland and discusses some of the findings as they relate specifically to the European context. Between 2011 and 2017, Northern Ireland witnessed a 68 per cent rise in the total number of intensive pig and poultry farms, from 154 to 259 (Davies and Wasley, 2017). The empirical evidence in this chapter originates from 29 semi-structured interviews conducted in November 2018–January 2019 with farming industry, political and non-governmental organization actors as well as members of communities affected by farming intensification. It is worth pointing out that Northern Ireland as a whole voted 'remain' during the referendum on the membership of the UK in the European Union (EU) that was held on 23 June 2016. The interviewees in this research, both in the farming industry and in local communities, saw Brexit as a significant challenge to the country's economic, environmental and social future. Nevertheless, this stance did not preclude them from identifying some flaws in the European meat production governance context, some of which will be outlined later in this chapter.

An elaboration is needed to clarify what is meant by 'Europe' in this chapter. Europe is a contested concept, laden with cultural and symbolic meanings. Yet, I limit the concept of Europe solely to the EU political project. While this approach has its limitations, it nevertheless allows exploration of how a supranational institutional framework that attempts to harmonize private business interests with public regulation and authority structures food production and potentially foments opportunities for harm in the routine processes of food production. This statement should not undermine some of the benefits associated with the European model of food production governance. The EU's Common Agricultural Policy (CAP) mechanism (which will be described in the next section in more detail) has been providing a common set of rules and regulations which have been instrumental in developing EU agriculture and farming; these rules guaranteed that EU farming is competitive globally, producers are supported financially through direct payments, fragile regions benefit from rural development policies and environmental and animal welfare concerns are addressed. Despite this, both the broader direction of the European model of food production governance as well as its national implementation (through the case of Northern Ireland) deserve further scrutiny and present a compelling case study for white-collar crime researchers. The EU specifically presents a case of a regulated market, thus providing a unique context for exploring white-collar crime and harm not driven by deregulation.

Another caveat in this chapter is that it is beyond the scope of this work to review the implications of Brexit on food production in the EU. The empirical basis of this chapter is Northern Ireland and, considering that it was written during the time of uncertainty around Brexit, I perceive the UK as a member of the EU to answer the research question posed here. The rationale behind it is that thus far the EU has, to a significant extent, governed the processes of food production in the UK, and the legislative change around that has not yet been finalized. Finally, the empirical research behind this chapter is focused on pig farming industrialization, and therefore, the discussion hereafter is mostly concerned with meat production in the European context.

The chapter is structured around three areas of concern that were mentioned by the Northern Irish agri-food industry actors, farmers and local residents, all of which relate to the EU. First, the implications of the EU common market's meat production goals and attendant opportunities for environmental and social harms are discussed. Second, meat production regulation in the EU and its potential consequences for the environment and society are examined. Third, this chapter elaborates on the technological solutions for addressing the impacts of industrial farming in the EU and invites further scrutiny of the contexts in which technology is embedded.

Meat production goals and opportunities in the EU common market

In the agricultural sector in the EU, the choices of the Committee for the Common Organisation of the Agricultural Markets (COM) determine the economies of production. The COM identifies competitiveness as the key sector of economy (Santonja et al, 2017). Competitiveness on the European market was also identified as one of the motivations for farming industrialization in Northern Ireland. According to one interviewee, 'there are very different costs of production within the EU and the countries that have high costs of production [like the UK] force their industries to go large to compete' (Ulster Farmers' Union, 2002). Uneven costs of production in the European Common Market foster an asymmetry. According to Passas (1999: 402), asymmetries, conceptualized as structural discrepancies, mismatches and unequal interactions in the realms of the economy, law, politics and culture, can be criminogenic. Economic asymmetry in this case paves the way for farming industrialization in Northern Ireland, leading to adverse environmental impacts and threatening the health and wellbeing of both non-human animals and humans. Moreover, farming industrialization may also be the result of overemphasizing competitiveness: state-corporate crime theorists maintain that the greater emphasis on goal attainment might result in socially injurious behaviour (Kauzlarich and Kramer, 1998).

Another important aspect of the economic performance on the COM's radar is efficiency, which is synonymous with the move towards economies of scale and agglomeration; in other words, larger farms in specialized regions (Santonja et al, 2017). These prescriptions are reflected in the latest data from the EU Farm Structure Survey. In the case of EU pig farms, the data show that half of the sows (female pigs) and three quarters of other pigs are reared by 1.7 per cent of the farms. Only ten countries (Belgium, Denmark, Germany, Spain, Italy, Luxembourg, the Netherlands, Finland, Sweden and the UK), whose production techniques are very specialized, are responsible for 75 per cent of all EU pork production. By contrast, only 3.8 per cent of other pigs are reared on small farms, which account for 73.3 per cent of all pig farms (Santonja et al, 2017). It has been shown that concentration of meat production is associated with harm to ecological systems and non-human animals (Schally, 2017).[1]

It is also vital to discuss the opportunity structure within the EU, designed to meet the goals set out on the European level (Michalowski and Kramer, 2006). Consumer demand for animal protein constitutes a part of this opportunity structure, as it provides a rationalization for meat production increases. Yet, this strategy is premised on the controversial premise of a pressing need to double global food production in light of population growth by 2050: the roots of this statistic do not have a normative agenda (they simply describe a potential scenario in the future and actually doubling food production would exacerbate the existing problems in the global food system) (Tomlinson, 2013). Meat consumers, by virtue of reproducing the social practice of meat consumption, continue to support the treadmill of meat production (Curran, 2017). Yet, meat producers' justification for increasing production, as a response to consumer demand for animal protein, also conceals the ideological rationale behind such increases, which is rooted in the growth-oriented political economy of neoliberal capitalism. Ultimately, production takes place before consumption and producers can influence consumer desires and needs (Gould et al, 2004), using the power they have to control the decisions around production.

Furthermore, a uniquely European mechanism, the CAP, can be called into question when discussing this opportunity structure. The CAP provides financial support to agriculture and the rural economy. Its focus is currently organized under two pillars: the Basic Payment Scheme and the Rural Development Programme. Yet, its direct payments based on the area of land in production have been criticized for their disproportionately favouring large-scale producers and marginalizing smallholder farmers (Kay, 2016). Subsidy benefits distribution is particularly uneven in countries such as Romania (where 1.1 per cent of subsidy beneficiaries receive 51.7 per cent of the CAP direct payments) and Bulgaria (where 1.1 per cent of subsidy beneficiaries receive 45.6 per cent of the CAP direct payments) (European Commission, 2015). The uneven distribution of subsidy benefits is also associated with the decline of small farms in Europe (see Kay, 2016).

Social harms associated with the decline of small farmers include rural unemployment and gradual erosion of rural community life that values local food cultures and traditions. As local markets disappear, food supply chains grow longer and transparency of food provenance is compromised and producers become more dependent on global food markets and have to confront its volatility (Kay, 2016). Finally, small-scale farming is associated with environmental protection and contributes to the safeguarding of biodiversity. Subsidies oriented to economic growth tend to sideline natural resource limitations and sustainability concerns.[2] Inadequate mechanisms of food production financial support may have adverse environmental and social effects, which echoes Spapens et al's (2018) statement that environmental harm is bound to involve a financial component. Despite this awareness, few criminologists (especially European criminologists) problematize harms associated with financial support for food production. Croall (2012) points out the problematic nature of corporate-governmental collusions in relation to subsidies, and Standing (2015) highlights the criminogenic role of private investment and public subsidies in fuelling illegal fishing. Yet, thus far none of these studies consider the role of subsidies in fuelling industrialization of farming.

European white-collar crime researchers might benefit from taking a closer look at the harms associated with food production goals and opportunities that exist in the EU common market. Williams (1996) claims that market-based explanations of environmental and social inequities do not reveal the structural processes behind them. Therefore, European white-collar crime researchers should examine who the main beneficiaries of the common market are, and how institutional assemblages of food production shape the uneven distribution of benefits and burdens. Moreover, as stated before, the European context provides a unique opportunity to explore a regulated market and its potential for white-collar crime and harm, as opposed to white-collar crime underpinned by forces of deregulation, privatization and globalization. The goals governing food production in the EU market are intertwined with the goals of global food production markets, where free-market opportunities are said to provide a façade for perpetrating systematic forms of injustice (White, 2014; Ezeonu, 2015; Khoury, 2018). However, some academics (Egan, 2001; Finger and Laperrouza, 2011; Tarko, 2017) claim that the EU provides a regulatory role, creating a context in which market liberalization and market regulation coexist peacefully, leading to a paradoxical state of 'freer markets, more rules'. It is, therefore, worth examining how certain components of the EU regulatory framework and its mechanisms of control are conducive to environmental harm and protection of the interests of the powerful in the processes of meat production governance.

Meat production regulation in the EU

The EU postulates that the impacts of large-scale farming must be regulated in accordance with the Integrated Pollution Prevention and Control (IPPC) Directive. The aim of the IPPC Directive is to apply 'Best Available Techniques' (BAT) to prevent or reduce emissions to air, land and water from these activities (Environment Agency, 2006). The BAT Reference Document (BREF) for Intensive Rearing of Poultry and Pigs is produced by the European IPPC Bureau. Yet, only the farms that house more animals than stated in the BREF are required to apply for a IPPC permit that covers all aspects of farm management,[3] from feed delivery to manure spreading. This benchmark regulation does not seem to account for cumulative environmental impact. Yet, according to one interviewee in Northern Ireland, 'sometimes they register a big [pig] breeding centre and give pigs to small farmers [under 2,000 animals] to avoid environmental impact assessments. I think it's an EU thing, which is fine in a country like Germany where you don't need to worry about 2,000 pigs. But it's not so fine in a smaller country like Northern Ireland, because 2,000 pigs is a big number. And if you have ten [such] farms next to each other, it's 20,000 pigs' (COM002). Cumbers et al (1995) claim that the difficulties in constructing a single market in food result from imposing a new set of regulations (including the IPPC regulations) on an existing national regulatory regime. The application of this regulation in the Northern

Ireland context and the disregard for regional differences within that context might result in the adverse environmental impacts that stem from an increased concentration of farms in one place. Interestingly, an increased concentration of farms may also result in more stringent environmental regulation. Schwägerl (2015) demonstrates that in both the Netherlands and Denmark – countries experiencing high levels of nitrogen pollution originating, among other things, from intensive farming – stricter nitrogen management plans have been established, with Germany also planning to follow suit. However, it has also been argued that the predicted decrease in emissions in the Netherlands did not occur and, conversely, some areas showed an increase in ammonia emissions from farming (Anker et al, 2019). Moreover, measures to decrease emissions from intensive meat production are often associated with technological achievement alone and do not require a reduction in the number of animals, meaning that the trail of harm continues. This particular regulation may also contribute to consolidation of power dynamics in the meat supply chain as it is the farms with less than 2,000 pigs that tend to be vertically integrated into meat supply chains in Northern Ireland, when large producers subcontract different stages of production to smaller farmers. Vertical integration and concentration of production have been subject to criticism – they pose a threat to the survival of small farmers (Grey, 2000) and reinforce the buyer dominance of the retailers (Morgan et al, 2006), thus contributing to the neoliberalization of agri-food governance (McMahon and Glatt, 2018), whereby corporate influence over the food system is secured. Moreover, small farmers – both those that are vertically integrated and not – are influenced by the ambitious production goals set from the top echelons of the supply chain. Yet, small farmers might not possess sufficient infrastructural and financial means to achieve those goals. Goals–means discrepancy is reported to fuel deviancy (Agnew, 2009), including deviancy in relation to the environment. Vertical integration restricts farmers' choices or dissuades them from a choice they would normally make, 'forcing them into the kinds of decisions that they otherwise would not have chosen for ethical or other reasons' instead (James, 2018). Farmers, thus, respond to the external pressures situated in global markets and the regulatory contexts associated with them (Donnermeyer and DeKeseredy, 2014).

Finally, it is worth exploring the manner in which economic forces of production are embedded in regulation and how the EU's food production regulations protect the interests of the powerful. Critical criminologists have long emphasized that economic interests have significant clout in the creation of law (Ruggiero, 2013). The EU provides a unique context for dissecting this issue: Egan (2001) suggests that due to a close relationship between public and private interests in the EU context, there exists a significant overlap between the regulators and the regulated – a statement that certainly holds true in the food production case. In some EU member states, such as France and Germany, food legislation has often been introduced to protect certain producer groups (Cumbers et al, 1995). Indeed, business has had a favoured position in agenda-setting at the institutional level in Europe (Coen, 2005) as Corporate Europe Observatory (2017) demonstrates that the corporate agri-food sector has influenced and continues to influence law making in the EU. The economic privilege of the industry guarantees its influence in environmental and planning decision making (Smith, 1990). Relationships around regulation are, therefore, organized in a manner that creates a favourable regulatory climate for capital accumulation. While these exact processes also take place on the level of individual nation-states, the EU is unique in its approach to regulation: Pelkmans and Renda (2014: 15) even suggest that 'the EU's "core business" is essentially the making, improving or removing of EU regulation'. Existing European standards ensuring that EU-wide benchmark objections are met have a significant symbolic power. In the case of meat production, this power is directed to consolidate a market-driven approach in regulation, rather than the one protecting the lives of humans and the health of the environment.

This insight into the intricacies of application of the EU regulations of meat production to each country's context has several implications for future research. It demonstrates that further attention needs to be directed towards scrutinizing and contextualizing the regulatory frameworks that underpin food production governance in Europe, the potential those frameworks have for changing national food regimes and how those frameworks come into being as a result of the state–industry collusion. European white-collar food crime scholarship may benefit from using the EU context to understand how food production regulations reproduce dominant class interests, preclude radical change (Pearce, 1976) and are 'geared to the protection of socioeconomic systems that are heavily orientated towards unfettered industrial growth, production and consumption' (Ruggiero, 2015: 85).

Technological innovation and meat production in the EU

Environmental damage resulting from industrial meat production is palpable. In addition to contributing to climate change, industrial meat production contributes to air (ammonia) and water (nitrogen) pollution. In 2015, 94 per cent of ammonia emissions in Europe originated from agriculture (European Environment Agency, 2019). The IPPC's Best Available Techniques discussed previously strongly encourage innovation in the production processes to address the rising environmental toll of industrial meat production. Therefore, it might be of interest for white-collar crime researchers in Europe to discuss the role of the EU context in technological innovation and the impacts of the national-level application of technological innovation. It needs to be highlighted here that the following discussion focuses specifically on the technologies that enable industrial meat production.

The implementation of technological solutions to feeding and air-cleaning systems and the adoption of technologies such as anaerobic digestion are perceived to be synonymous with the sustainable development doctrine. Agri-food industry interviewees in Northern Ireland often expressed admiration for the European technologies for agricultural emissions abatement and encouraged their subsequent replication in the Northern Irish context.

New technologies are being developed within and beyond the EU to meet the environmental challenges from livestock production. For instance, the ten European manufacturers that currently supply air-cleaning systems to livestock producers have to deal with various admission and assessment procedures in different nations. A joint initiative of parties from Denmark, the Netherlands and Germany has sought to 'develop common test protocols for testing and verification of these environmental technologies for agricultural production' in order to overcome this fragmentation, thereby 'saving time and costs in implementing eco-efficient technologies' (Verification of Environmental Technologies for Agricultural Production, 2010: 2–6) and promoting the wider use of these technologies. The initiative opens up opportunities for technology transfers, and close cooperation between the EU agri-food stakeholders is conducive to this process.

Yet, technology transfers are not merely technical but also political processes. The way technology is applied in the local context depends on the strength of domestic institutions and the enforcement of environmental policies (Hensengerth, 2018). Moreover, the introduction of a new technology incites social changes in the local environment (Hensengerth, 2018), and it is important to question who the beneficiaries of the transferred technology are. While technology producers may reap the financial benefits of the wider use of the technology, large meat producers will also benefit from technological transfers. It is worth emphasizing that technological innovation might lead to structural changes in farm sizes, as more efficient measures are only applicable to larger farms (Oenema et al, 2012). Such application of technology will only reinforce the dominance of environmentally disadvantageous industrial meat production, the impacts of which technology is aiming to address.

On a macro level, technological solutions do not stimulate environmental and social reform either: they simply 'green' capitalism, thus diverting any form of ecological critique (Gould et al, 2004). Powerful interests safeguard the doctrine of sustainable development, with the economically efficient use and management of resources at its core, but manage to dismiss the inherent contradiction between economic production in capitalism and nature, wherein capitalism must cause ecological disorganization by polluting nature (Lynch and Stretesky, 2014). Technological innovation thus becomes a condition for the continued expansion of capitalism (Harvey, 2010): it might mitigate the harmful impacts of intensive livestock farming but does not challenge or alter the unsustainable nature of the practice.

The uniqueness of the EU context in relation to technological innovation in industrial meat production is underlined by the fact that governments choose to engage private expertise (such as the production of abatement technology) for public purposes, thus incorporating market norms into the provision of public goods (Egan, 2001). The EU context also appears to facilitate transfers of technological innovation, as the leading actors in the industry work on making technology more available for others. White (2017) concludes that by examining the relations behind technology, criminologists can get a better understanding of whether technology and its applications serve the interests of social and ecological justice, or whether they reinforce existing regimes of power. Therefore, white-collar crime researchers in Europe may wish to more closely inspect the relationship between technology and food production, drawing on social and political contexts behind technological use and development, and examining how those contexts furnish opportunities for harm.

Conclusion

The chapter posed the question of whether food production-focused research can become a lens that opens up new lines of inquiry about what is 'European' about European white-collar crime, utilizing the case of farming industrialization in Northern Ireland to take a closer look at European meat production governance. Intensive livestock production is the dominant mode of meat production in the EU. Bernat and Whyte (2017: 77) argue that normal functioning of a broader system of production can produce criminogenic outcomes; this chapter shows how such outcomes are produced in Northern Ireland. First, the EU's regulated market model may create economic asymmetries that encourage industrialization of meat production. Its subsidy mechanism also serves the interests of larger, rather than smaller, farmers, thus providing perverse incentives. Moreover, EU regulatory frameworks are informed by the global political economic dynamics of meat production, where relationships between political and economic actors are organized to pursue the goal of capital accumulation in the context of a competitive global market rule ideology. For Northern Ireland, it may result in an increased farm concentration and power consolidation in the meat supply chain. Finally, the EU context reinforces existing power regimes in the technological realm by preserving the doctrine of ecological modernization that impedes any systemic change; it is achieved through promoting solutions rooted in technological innovation (Böhm et al, 2012). A supranational institutional regime appears to facilitate transfers of technological innovation and also allows for coordinated improvement and alignment of technological innovation in meat production. Additionally, the EU provides a unique context for coordinating research efforts into technological innovation, some of which may be aimed at sustaining industrial farming. Future research in white-collar crime in Europe may benefit from further problematization of food production harms in the European context and identification of the structural factors behind them, constituted by the European 'regimes of permission' (Whyte, 2014: 244) that are not only enabled by particular institutional relationships but originate from power architectures that lie beyond the observable empirical manifestations of power.

Notes

[1] Ruhl (2000: 266) gives an apt summary of the environmental implications of industrial farming: 'farms pollute ground water, surface water, air, and soils; they destroy open space and wildlife habitat; they erode soils and contribute to sedimentation of lakes and rivers; they deplete water resources; and they often simply smell bad'. Moreover, industrial farming is exceptional in its brutality towards farm animals: in the process, they are maimed, confined in appallingly crammed spaces, raised in artificial settings and fed unnatural diets (Fiber-Ostrow and Lovell, 2016).

[2] Rural development measures were allocated €14.3 billion of funding in 2018, while direct payments to farmers amounted to €40.1 billion (European Parliament, 2020).

[3] '(a) with more than 40,000 places for poultry; (b) with more than 2,000 places for production of pigs (over 30 kg), or (c) with more than 750 places for sows' (Santonja et al, 2017: xxxi).

References

Agnew, R. (1998) 'The causes of animal abuse: a social-psychological analysis', *Theoretical Criminology*, 2: 177–209.

Agnew, R. (2009) 'Revitalizing Merton: general strain theory', in F.T. Cullen, F. Adler, C.L. Johnson and A.J. Meyer (eds) *Advances in Criminological Theory: The Origins of American Criminology* (vol 16), New Brunswick, NJ: Transaction, pp 137–58.

Anker, H., Backes, C.W., Baaner, L., Keessen, A.M. and Möckel, S. (2019) 'Natura 2000 and the regulation of agricultural ammonia emissions', *Journal for European Environmental & Planning Law*, 16(4): 340–71.

Bernat, I. and Whyte, D. (2017) 'State-corporate crime and the process of capital accumulation: mapping a global regime of permission from Galicia to Morecambe Bay', *Critical Criminology*, 25: 71–86. doi:10.1007/s10612-016-9340-9

Boekhout van Solinge, T. (2010) 'Deforestation crimes and conflicts in the Amazon', *Critical Criminology*, 18(4): 263–77.

Böhm, S., Misoczky, M.C. and Moog, S. (2012) 'Greening capitalism? A Marxist critique of carbon markets', *Organization Studies*, 33(11): 1617–38. doi:10.1177/0170840612463326

Bradshaw, E. (2014) 'State-corporate environmental cover-up: the response to the 2010 Gulf of Mexico oil spill', *State Crime*, 3(2): 163–81.

Cheng, H. (2011) 'Cheap capitalism: a sociological study of food crime in China', *British Journal of Criminology*, 52(2): 254–73. doi:10.1093/bjc/azr078

Coen, D. (2005) 'Environmental and business lobbying alliances in Europe: learning from Washington', in D. Levy and P.J. Newell (eds) *The Business of Global Environmental Governance*, Cambridge: MIT Press, pp 197–220.

Croall, H. (2012) 'Food crime: a green criminology perspective', in N. South and A. Brisman (eds) *Routledge International Handbook of Green Criminology*, Abingdon: Routledge, pp 167–83. doi:10.4324/9780203093658.ch10

Cumbers, A., Leigh, R. and Smallbone, D. (1995) 'The Single European Market and the new regulatory regime in the food sector: the impact on small and medium-sized manufacturing firms', *British Food Journal*, 97(4): 13–18.

Curran, D. (2017) 'The treadmill of production and the positional economy of consumption', *Canadian Review of Sociology/Revue Canadienne de Sociologie*, 54(1): 28–47.

Davies, J. (2018) 'From severe to routine labour exploitation: the case of migrant workers in the UK food industry', *Criminology & Criminal Justice*, 19(3): 294–310.

Davies, M. and Wasley, A. (2017) 'Intensive farming in the UK, by numbers', The Bureau of Investigative Journalism, [online] 17 July, Available at: www.thebureauinvestigates.com/stories/2017-07-17/intensive-numbers-of-intensive-farming

Donnermeyer, J. and DeKeseredy, W. (2014) *Rural Criminology*, London, New York: Routledge.

Egan, M. (2001) *Constructing a European Market: Standards, Regulation, and Governance*, Oxford: Oxford University Press.

Environment Agency (2006) 'Integrated pollution prevention and control (IPPC): intensive farming how to comply guidance for intensive pig and poultry farmers', Available at: www.environment-agency.gov.uk

European Commission (2015) 'CAP expenditure in 2013 by MS', Available at: http://ec.europa.eu/agriculture/%0Astatistics/factsheets/pdf/eu_en.pdf

European Environment Agency (2019) 'Agriculture', Available at: www.eea.europa.eu/themes/agriculture/intro#tab-news-and-articles

European Parliament (2020) 'Financing of the CAP', Available at: www.europarl.europa.eu/ftu/pdf/en/FTU_3.2.2.pdf

Ezeonu, I. (2015) 'Capital and catharsis in the Nigerian petroleum extraction industry', in G. Barak (ed) *The Routledge International Handbook of the Crimes of the Powerful*, London, New York: Routledge, pp 89–104.

Fiber-Ostrow, P. and Lovell, J.S. (2016) 'Behind the veil of secrecy: animal abuse, factory farms and Ag-Gag legislation', *Contemporary Justice Review*, 19: 230–49.

Finger, M. and Laperrouza, M. (2011) 'Liberalization of network industries in the European Union: evolving policy issues', in M. Finger (ed) *International Handbook of Network Industries*, Northampton: Edward Elgar, pp 345–65.

Flores Elizondo, C., Lord, N. and Spencer, J. (2018) 'Food fraud and the Fraud Act 2006: complementarity and limitations', in C. Monaghan and N. Monaghan (eds) *Financial Crime and Corporate Misconduct: A Critical Evaluation of Fraud Legislation*, Abingdon: Routledge, pp 48–62.

Gould, K.A., Pellow, D.N. and Schnaiberg, A. (2004) 'Interrogating the treadmill of production: everything you wanted to know about the treadmill, but were afraid to ask', *Organization & Environment*, 17(3): 296–316.

Gray, A. and Hinch, R. (2015) 'Agribusiness, governments and food crime: a critical perspective', in R. Sollund (ed) *Green Harms and Crimes: Critical Criminology in a Changing World*, London: Palgrave Macmillan, pp 97–116. doi:10.1057/9781137456267_6

Gray, A. and Hinch, R. (eds) (2019) *A Handbook of Food Crime*, Bristol: Policy Press.

Greenpeace European Unit (2019) 'Feeding the problem: the dangerous intensification of animal farming in Europe', Available at: www.greenpeace.org/static/planet4-eu-unit-stateless/2019/02/83254ee1-190212-feeding-the-problem-dangerous-intensification-of-animal-farming-in-europe.pdf

Grey, M. (2000) '"Those bastards can go to hell!" Small-farmer resistance to vertical integration and concentration in the pork industry', *Human Organization*, 59(2): 169–76.

Harvey, D. (2010) *A Companion to Marx's* Capital, London: Verso.

Hensengerth, O. (2018) 'South–South technology transfer: who benefits? A case study of the Chinese-built Bui Dam in Ghana', *Energy Policy*, 114: 499–507. doi:10.1016/j.enpol.2017.12.039

James Jr., H. S. (2018) 'Ethical challenges facing farm managers', in A. Gray and R. Hinch (eds) *A Handbook of Food Crime*, Bristol: Policy Press, pp 61–76.

Kauzlarich, D. and Kramer, R. (1998) *Crimes of the American Nuclear State*, Boston: Northeastern University Press.

Kay, S. (2016) 'Land grabbing and land concentration in Europe – a research brief', Transnational Institute, Available at: www.tni.org/files/publication-downloads/landgrabbingeurope_a5-2.pdf

Khoury, S. (2018) 'Pesticideland: Brazil's poison market', in S. Bittle, L. Snider, S. Tombs and D. Whyte (eds) *Revisiting Crimes of the Powerful. Marxism, Crime and Deviance*, London, Routledge, pp 174–87.

Lord, N., Flores Elizondo, C. and Spencer, J. (2017) 'The dynamics of food fraud: the interactions between criminal opportunity and market (dys)functionality in legitimate business', *Criminology and Criminal Justice*, 17(5): 605–23.

Lynch, M. and Stretesky, P. (2014) *Exploring Green Criminology: Toward a Green Criminological Revolution*, London: Ashgate.

McMahon, M. and Glatt, K.L. (2018) 'Food crime without criminals: agri-food safety governance as a protection racket for dominant political and economic interest', in A. Gray and R. Hinch (eds) *A Handbook of Food Crime*, Bristol: Policy Press, pp 27–42.

Michalowski, R. and Kramer, R. (2006) *State-Corporate Crime*, New Jersey: Rutgers University Press.

Moragues-Faus, A. and Marsden, T. (2017) 'The political ecology of food: carving "spaces of possibility" in a new research agenda', *Journal of Rural Studies,* 55: 275–88. doi:10.1016/j.jrurstud.2017.08.016

Morgan, K., Marsden, T. and Murdoch, J. (2006) *Worlds of Food: Place, Power, and Provenance in the Food Chain*, Oxford, New York: Oxford University Press.

Oenema, O., Velthof, G. and Klimont, Z. (2012) 'Emissions from agriculture and their control potentials', International Institute for Applied Systems Analysis, Available at: http://ec.europa.eu/environment/air/pdf/TSAP-AGRI-20121129_v21.pdf

Passas, N. (1999) 'Globalization, criminogenic asymmetries and economic crime', *European Journal of Law Reform*, 1(4): 399–424.

Passas, N. (2005) 'Lawful but awful: "legal corporate crimes"', *The Journal of Socio-Economics*, 34: 771–86. doi:10.1016/j.socec.2005.07.024

Pearce, F. (1976) *Crimes of the Powerful*, London: Pluto Press.

Pelkmans, J. and Renda, A. (2014) *Does EU Regulation Hinder or Stimulate Innovation?* CEPS: Brussels.

Ruggiero, V. (2013) 'The environment and the crimes of the economy', in N. South and A. Brisman (eds) *Routledge International Handbook of Green Criminology*, London: Routledge.

Ruggiero, V. (2015) ' "Creative destruction" and the economy of waste', in R. Sollund (ed) *Green Harms and Crimes: Critical Criminological Perspectives*, London: Palgrave Macmillan, pp 79–96.

Ruhl, J. (2000) 'Farms, their environmental harms, and environmental law', *Ecology Law Quarterly*, 27: 263–349.

Ruth, S.M., Luning, P.A., Silvis, I.C.J., Yang, Y. and Huisman, W. (2018) 'Differences in fraud vulnerability in various food supply chains and their tiers', *Food Control*, 84: 375–81.

Santonja, G., Georgitzikis, K., Scalet, B., Montobbio, P., Roudier, S. and Sancho, L. (2017) 'Best available techniques (BAT): reference document for the intensive rearing of poultry or pigs', European Commission, Available at: https://ec.europa.eu/jrc/en/publication/eur-scientific-and-technical-research-reports/best-available-techniques-bat-reference-document-intensive-rearing-poultry-or-pigs

Schally, J.L. (2017) *Legitimizing Corporate Harm: The Discourse of Contemporary Agribusiness*, London: Palgrave Macmillan.

Schwägerl, C. (2015) 'With too much of a good thing, Europe tackles excess nitrogen', *Yale Environment 360*, [online] 14 April, Available at: https://e360.yale.edu/features/with_too_much_of_a_good_thing_europe_tackles_excess_nitrogen

Smith, M.J. (1990) *The Politics of Agricultural Policy Support: the Development of an Agricultural Policy Community*, London: Dartmouth.

Sollund, R. (2015) *Green Harms and Crimes: Critical Criminology in a Changing World*, London: Palgrave Macmillan.

Spapens, T., White, R., van Uhm, D. and Huisman, W. (eds) (2018) *Green Crimes and Dirty Money*, New York, London: Routledge.

Standing, A. (2015) 'Mirage of pirates: state-corporate crime in West Africa's fisheries', *State Crime,* 4(2): 175–97.

Tarko, V. (2017) 'Neoliberalism and regulatory capitalism: understanding the "freer markets more rules" puzzle', Available at: https://ssrn.com/abstract=3042734

Corporate Europe Observatory (2017) 'Lobby planet Brussels: the Corporate Europe Observatory guide to the murky world of EU lobbying', Available at: https://corporateeurope.org/en/lobbyplanet

Tombs, S. and Whyte, D. (2007) *Safety Crime*, Cullompton: Willan Publishing.

Tombs, S. and Whyte, D. (2010) 'Crime, harm and corporate power', in J. Muncie, D. Talbot and R. Walters (eds) *Crime: Local and Global*, Cullompton: Willan Publishing, pp 137–72.

Tomlinson, I. (2013) 'Doubling food production to feed the 9 billion: a critical perspective on a key discourse of food security in the UK', *Journal of Rural Studies*, 29: 81–90.

Verification of Environmental Technologies for Agricultural Production (VERA) (2010) 'Test protocol for air cleaning technologies', Available at: www.vera-verification.eu/app/uploads/sites/9/2019/05/VERA_Testprotocol_AirCleaner_V2_2018.pdf

Walters, R. (2006) 'Crime, bio-agriculture and the exploitation of hunger', *British Journal of Criminology*, 46(1): 26–45.

Walters, R. (2007) 'Food crime, regulation and the biotech harvest', *European Journal of Criminology*, 4(2): 217–35.

White, R. (2014) *Environmental Harm: An Eco-Justice Perspective*, Bristol: Policy Press. doi:10.1332/policypress/9781447300403.001.0001

White, R. (2016) 'The four ways of eco-global criminology', *International Journal for Crime, Justice and Social Democracy*, 6(1): 8–22. doi:10.5204/ijcjsd.v6i1.375

White, R. (2017) 'Technology, environmental harm and green criminology', in M.R. McGuire and T.J. Holt (eds) *The Routledge Handbook of Technology, Crime and Justice*, Abingdon: Routledge, pp 310–24.

Whyte, D. (2014) 'Regimes of permission and state-corporate crime', *State Crime,* 3(2): 237–46.

Williams, C. (1996) 'An environmental victimology', *Social Justice*, 23(4): 16–40.

Yates, R. (2007) 'Debating "animal rights" online: the movement-countermovement dialectic revisited', in P. Beirne and N. South (eds) *Issues in Green Criminology: Confronting Harms Against Environments, Humanity and Other Animals*, Cullompton: Willan Publishing, pp 140–57.

9

Understanding the Dynamics of White-Collar Criminality in Ukraine

Anna Markovska and Iryna Soldatenko

Introduction

This chapter examines the nature of white-collar criminality in Ukraine. Post-Soviet states have been described as 'states with flexible legality' (Wedel, 2005), where politicians, ministers and public officials have enjoyed unlimited powers. This chapter analyzes the concept of politically driven white-collar criminality and its harmful influence within otherwise legal entrepreneurship in the Ukrainian context as well as in overtly illegal activities.

The COVID-19 pandemic of 2020–21 has brought heightened consideration of the role of the state in planning a strategic response to economic upheaval. In the early 1990s, reaction to the collapse of the Soviet Union focused on reducing the role of the state and allowing the free market to drive economic recovery. Entrepreneurs and entrepreneurial culture were believed to be able to replace or invigorate state planning and production (Kovacs, 1994). However, the endemic conflicts of interest existing in the higher levels of the Soviet bureaucratic structure left those in charge of the vast industrial Soviet estate to identify opportunities for personal enrichment during privatization (Organized Crime Observatory, 2013; Kupatadze, 2015). An underdeveloped legal and regulatory framework effectively offered immunity for the political and business elite in their appropriation of state assets and transferring of ownership from state to private hands.

In this chapter we consider white-collar criminality involving the embezzlement of state funds by those with the ability to coerce political power. One of the best-documented examples of such political corruption is that of Pavlo Lazarenko, the former prime minister of Ukraine. Lazarenko abused his official role to issue contracts, permits and licenses in return for financial remuneration (Organized Crime Observatory, 2013). Applying Levi's (2008) fraud typology, it is possible to consider Lazarenko's crimes as pre-planned fraudulent activities using political and legal means. In 1995–96, Lazarenko was the Ukrainian deputy prime minister, with specific responsibility for the energy sector. He was thus able to 'leverage illegally procured gas into virtually any commodity through unregistered barter transactions; he could then trade the goods on the open world market' (Nichols, 2007: 10). Lazarenko's reforms of the energy sector allowed certain companies to acquire the monopoly of purchasing natural gas from Russia and engage in its resale in certain regions of Ukraine (Organized Crime Observatory, 2013). For example, he obtained a state guarantee to buy US$200 million worth of gas from the Russian majority state-owned energy corporation Gazprom (Organized Crime Observatory, 2013). However, following an obscure chain of events, a deliberately formed private company (United Energy International Limited) defaulted on payments to the state, and US$140 million was transferred to private accounts, leaving the state to cover the loss (Organized Crime Observatory, 2013). Generally, the most pressing issue for such private account holders is 'organising escape from criminal sanctions' (Levi, 2008: 395); Lazarenko, however, did not manage to avoid criminal sanctions and served 97 months in a US prison as a consequence of the scheme. There is currently an ongoing investigation concerning 'US$271 million and additional unspecified amounts held in accounts in financial institutions in Guernsey, Antigua and Bermuda, Switzerland, Liechtenstein and Lithuania' that remain unaccounted for (World Bank, 2017).

In Ukraine a spectrum of entrepreneurial activity exists, ranging from that of productive entrepreneurs, who invest in long-term economic and social development, to those who are unproductive or destructive, often in collusion with politicians for short-term personal gain (Baumol, 1990). Existing literature tends to focus on the unproductive and destructive aspects (Desai and Acs, 2007), or on politically motivated corrupt entrepreneurship often associated with transitional national economies. However, Audretsch and

Belitski (2017: 3) argue that entrepreneurship can be an important contributor to economic development, with the caveat that 'its decision-making does not happen in isolation from a local context where entrepreneurs operate'. Understanding the local context and economic environment are important factors in determining entrepreneurial success. Conversely, the case of Lazarenko illustrates political corruption as being a form of destructive political and legal entrepreneurship wherein public office and its associated legal power were employed to defraud the state budget. The redistribution of state funds linked to legal entrepreneurship were used to criminal effect, under conditions of negligible 'immediate enforcement or operational risks' (Levi, 2008: 392).

Ukraine is strategically important to both the European Union (EU) and the US. Restoring Ukraine's sovereignty is a foreign policy priority for both the EU and the US. Before the political crisis of 2014, Ukraine received US$200 million per year in US foreign aid (Masters, 2020). Strengthening the rule of law, fighting corruption and encouraging the privatization of state enterprises have been the core agenda linked to this aid (Masters, 2020). While a lot of attention has been given to corruption and the abuse of power in post-Soviet countries, the discussion of corruption as an indicator of organized white-collar criminality is often given little consideration.

In 2015, following the Maidan (or Euromaidan) protests (2013–14) and responding to significant pressure from the US and the EU, Ukraine established the National Anti-Corruption Bureau (NABU), an independent law enforcement organization with powers to prosecute high-level criminality. The NABU works in conjunction with Ukraine's specialist Anti-Corruption Prosecution Office (SAPO). While the actual transposition of legal and regulatory frameworks has proved to be relatively straightforward, their implementation and application has been challenging for the emerging economies of the countries of the former Soviet Union. Post-Soviet regions have experienced different levels of difficulty in reforming their economies. Thus far, it is very difficult to ascertain the level of success of both the previously named organizations in fighting corruption in Ukraine (Markovska and Duyne, 2020), where political collusion is still believed to be at a significant level (Home Office, 2019).

While there has been a major shift in public opinion regarding the importance of fighting corruption at the highest levels, Ukrainians still treat corruption with ambivalence, often accusing others in the hope that they will be punished (Markovska and Serdyuk, 2015). A 2014 study of corruption in the city of Kharkiv in eastern Ukraine suggested that people generally consider corruption to be necessary (Markovska and Serdyuk, 2015). Political collusion with businesses and organized crime is well documented in many sectors, from coal mining in the east to illegal amber and timber extraction in the west (Home Office, 2019). While illegal amber extraction sites and illegal logging are perceived as being corrupt and criminal activities, workers involved in these industries often have little alternative and thus view these corrupt activities as functional (Earthsight, 2018). It would be wrong to suggest this is only a Ukrainian phenomenon. An Earthsight (2018) report argues that illegally extracted Ukrainian amber and timber is generally available in European markets. This research suggests that EU companies are buying illegally exported timber from Ukraine by employing corporate intermediaries to do the importing on their behalf. We suggest, therefore, that understanding the realities of economic reform and associated criminal activity in any particular sector in Ukraine can potentially identify weaknesses in its anti-corruption measures and strengthen the diligence of European countries against indirect participation.

This chapter critically explores the nature of political collusion and the related potential for white-collar crime in Ukraine. We begin by contextualizing the consequences of weak political leadership and political involvement in the privatization of the Ukrainian mining and timber sectors before identifying further political collusion in illegal practices often related to labour regulations. We conclude by discussing the role of the Soviet legacy in creating and sustaining such destructive and politically motivated entrepreneurship and why this should matter for Europe in general.

Political collusion in context of Post-Soviet development and entrepreneurial corruption

We begin our discussion with the collapse of the Soviet Union and the legacy of the Soviet state. The 1990s was an exciting decade for Soviet scholars as they contemplated the past and future of the former Soviet economies often questioning the new entrepreneurial nature, and transformative politics, and privatisation agenda (Aslund, 1992; Kovacs, 1994), and attempting to identify an appropriate economic model for transition (Gaidar, 1993). Three major aspects of transition were identified, namely, stabilization and institutional and structural change (Ellman, 1993). Stabilization here meant monetary and real macroeconomic stabilization. Institutional changes involved economic institutions and the nature of economic planning; structural changes identified changes in the role of the military, primary production and manufacturing industries (Ellman, 1993). While all these factors are interrelated, they require the presence of strong political leadership to execute reforms for the common good and the involvement of entrepreneurs willing to invest in a productive future. Over the past 20 years, post-Soviet countries have often been requested or even instructed to harmonize their internal legislation with international norms, led by the EU and the US, with calls to fight money laundering, drug trafficking and corruption. Political corruption has created a challenging environment for post-Soviet enterprise, with both productive and destructive entrepreneurs finding ways of conducting business. For some post-Soviet countries, overcoming political corruption and its influence on public services was a legacy from previous centuries.

Mungiu-Pippidi (2015: 58) describes European legislation to suppress corruption as 'the only historically successful process of state building in which a long transition to ethical universalism has resulted in an equilibrium where opportunities for corruption are largely checked by societal control of rulers and reasonable reciprocal control by the government'. Such legislation is inspired by general principles of accountability and the rule of law. For example, in 19th-century Britain, debates concerning corruption were held at both the parliamentary and local civil levels (Mungiu-Pippidi, 2015). In contrast, reforms attempted in 19th-century Russia were overseen by monarchs who failed to develop any rapport with wider society. The ability of European states to control corruption has, however, varied in effectiveness over time and reflects progress in wider political and social reform (Fukuyama, 2012).

Mungiu-Pippidi (2015) proposes a theoretical model of corruption control that can be used in the categorization of white-collar criminality. In this model, the continuum of corruption is considered against the background of available opportunities and constraints. Opportunities for criminals include excessive red tape, lack of transparency, the concentration of power, large amounts of discretionary funding and the availability of foreign aid. Normative constraints are generally understood in terms of four distinct categories: social values, social capital, civil society and civic culture (Mungiu-Pippidi, 2015). For example, constraints may include the existence of an independent judiciary, independent media, an active civil society and demanding voters (Mungiu-Pippidi, 2015). Thus, the importance of transparent politics and the political will to fight corruption can be considered a crucial element in nation building. Kupatadze (2015) identifies the political nature of opportunities to engage in corrupt conduct and argues that the best way to discuss the various forms of organized criminality for financial gain is to consider their links with political corruption and collusion. He suggests that political competitiveness or the lack of it exemplifies two different types of state that emerged from the Soviet Union (Kupatadze, 2015). For example, Russia and Kazakhstan are centralized and practically non-competitive, whereas Ukraine and Georgia are similarly centralized, but politically more competitive. According to Kuptatzde (2015), levels of political competitiveness could be a significant predictor in our understanding of the presence and success of organized crime. Highly-centralized states with little political competitiveness do not allow as many opportunities for competition, and thus corruption where it exists is more centralized. In countries such as Ukraine, both political power and organized crime have the opportunity to compete for resources (Kupatadze, 2015), and when they do so, they are able to benefit from flexible legality (Wedel, 2005) and the ability to negotiate official prohibitions (Markovska and Zabyelina, 2019). Here, we critically consider examples of corruption as a form of destructive political and legal entrepreneurship in Ukraine and its wider European implications.

The early 1990s

Lotspeich (1995) identified the following criminogenic features of economic transition in post-Soviet countries: difficulties in law enforcement, changing economic regulations, a deterioration of the economy, incomplete economic reforms and certain features of social psychology. The post-Soviet period has witnessed several attempts to introduce effective economic reforms (Ellman, 1993). For example, the 1990s were subject to a 'totally different model of economic organization, characterised not only by large scale market relations but also by preponderant private ownership, liberal democracy and full membership of the international economic community' (Ellman, 1993: 1). Successful transition from the Soviet system required a stabilization of the economy and institutional and structural change (Ellman, 1993). Institutional change includes 'establishing a legitimate, elective government, privatising state enterprises' and introducing 'an enterprise-friendly system of criminal and commercial law which could fully protect private property against government appropriation, private theft, racketeering and appropriate labour relations' (Ellman, 1993: 8–9). These conditions characterize productive entrepreneurship. The structural approach to transition that dominated in the early 1990s was intended to introduce capitalism very quickly ('the 500 days strategy') without concentrating on implementation problems (Ellman, 1993: 8). Kosmarskii (1992) discusses the results of the All-Union Centre for Public Opinion and Market Research surveys conducted in Ukraine between December 1989 and March 1991. In December 1990, only 14 per cent of Ukrainians believed the government had a well thought out anti-crisis programme, with 55 per cent stating that they did not believe this to be the case. Kosmarskii (1992) noted that the results of the poll suggest that people view political struggles within parliament as being a struggle for power rather than policy. Regarding privatization, the early surveys quoted by Kosmarskii suggested that people were in favour of collective, rather than individual, ownership. In December 1990, 56 per cent of respondents stated that they regarded the sale of large state enterprises as negative (Kosmarskii, 1992).

Privatization of the Ukrainian mining sector provides an example of early attempts to transition to capitalism. Initially, the state emphasized the social aspects of reform: the welfare of employees and the economic development of those regions that relied on mining. However, the reality of transition proved very different. Zabyelina and Markovska (2019) discuss the predatory forms of capital accumulation in the 1990s that occurred in the Donbas region of Ukraine. Known for its rich deposits of extractable coal, the region had been the mining centre of the Soviet Union, and consequently became a target for opportunistic and destructive political entrepreneurs. Yakovlev (2013) describes a scheme that used a quasi-legal front company to siphon off state funds. To facilitate the purchase of equipment for the biggest state-owned mine in Ukraine, a company called Progress was registered under a fictitious address. This company was allocated a state tender for the purchase of equipment but was later found to be involved in the privatization of the mine. In effect, state funds were used to modernize the mine, but the funds would never benefit the state, as the subsequent privatization of the enterprise was politically facilitated in the interest of private investors (Yakovlev, 2013).

There are five steps that destructive political entrepreneurs typically use to illegally obtain state funds. These five steps were identifiable in the case of the privatization of Ukraine's state-owned mines (Yakovlev, 2013). The first step was to register a limited company that would mediate between the state and the mines. The second step was for the limited company to 'win' a state tender in order to receive a commission for supplying equipment and to be involved in any upgrading activities to be paid for by the state prior to privatization. The third step was to set up legal and illegal coal redistribution. The same front companies would then be used to sell coal produced by the state mine as well as coal produced illegally by unauthorized mining groups. Zabyelina and Markovska (2019) note that in the early 1990s some state-owned mines sold more coal than they produced, meaning that illegally produced coal formed not only part of the sales statistics, but was therefore also eligible for subsidies illicitly related to such illegal production. The issue here is one of public accountability, but in a corrupt system, standard mechanisms of accountability are shielded and subverted by political influence. The fourth step is when all production expenses appear in the state-owned mines' accounts and all the profits are registered to the front companies already created. Finally, the fifth step is the state announcing that the mine is no longer viable and should be privatized for a fraction of its official valuation. The transfer of ownership occurs under powerful political influence and protection. In reality, state officials act as destructive political entrepreneurs by creating the mechanisms for the selected mines to be upgraded at the state's expense, maximizing profit in the short term, and facilitating the eventual sale of selected mines at a reduced price. Similar corrupt procedures enable white-collar crime in many different sectors.

Two more recent examples of corrupt transfers are these of timber and amber extraction. Corruption in the export of illegally sawn timber in Ukraine is well documented. An Earthsight (2018) study suggests that the Ukrainian forestry sector evidences significant involvement of government officials who are prepared to breach the law. The EU is the largest purchaser of this timber, estimated at around 70 per cent of total Ukrainian production and to a value of €1 billion in 2017 (Earthsight, 2018). This is despite the fact that in 2015 the Ukrainian Parliament passed a law prohibiting the export of unprocessed logs (Verkhovna Rada, 2015). EU customs statistics record huge volumes of timber coming from Ukraine labelled as 'firewood'. Criminal groups involved in this timber trafficking include lawyers, bank officials and representatives of governmental agencies who can falsely obtain certificates of origin that will enable the export of timber abroad (Earthsight, 2018). Some major EU firms have recently been implicated in the investigation of such procedures (Earthsight, 2018). For example, Earthsight (2018) identifies the largest buyer of Ukrainian wood as Schweighofer, an Austrian-owned timber-processing firm. The company owns facilities located in Romania, close to the Ukrainian border. In 2017, 70 per cent of Ukrainian unprocessed logs were exported to this Austrian company. Earthsight (2018) reported that 'the Schweighofer Group subsidiary which handled most of the shipments until 2016' was directly implicated in Ukrainian corruption cases, including the 'fictitious marketing of services to offshore companies' controlled by a former Ukrainian forestry ministry chief (Earthsight, 2018: 6). In response to the Earthsight investigation, Schweighofer issued a number of statements suggesting its commitment to better diligence by utilizing external agencies to improve the resistance of the company to such Ukrainian criminal manipulation (Holzindustrie Schweighofer, 2019).

Ukraine has one of the world's largest reserves of amber and over the last 30 years amber exports from Ukraine have been steadily increasing (Wendle, 2017). While the major demand for this amber comes from China, Ukraine also exports to the EU. Much of this amber is supplied by criminal gangs employing illegal methods of extraction (Wendle, 2017; Earthsight, 2018). Ukraine's State Authority for Geology and Subsoil estimates that up to 300 tonnes of amber are illegally mined annually, and the black market for this is estimated to be worth US$500 million annually (Besser, 2020). According to Earthsight (2018), much of this illegally extracted amber is exported to Romania, Poland and Hungary. The 'Amber mafia' in Ukraine comprises criminal networks that include senior government officials, criminal gangs and local people (Kalczynski, 2020). Indeed, it is estimated that as many as 50,000 local people are involved in an illegal amber extraction operation that extends over more than 5,500 hectares (Ukrainian Liaison Office, 2018). In 2017, the Ukrainian parliament drafted a law intended to legalize amber mining as a legitimate occupation, but to date little progress has been made (President of Ukraine, 2019). The previous examples of timber and amber trading demonstrate collaboration between destructive political entrepreneurs in Ukraine and ostensibly productive entrepreneurs from the EU.

Political collusion with destructive entrepreneurship led to the rise of so-called 'business-administrative groups' (BAGs) in Ukraine. The development of these BAGs seriously undermined the power of the state while increasing that of political entrepreneurs. During the course of privatization, BAGs accumulated significant economic resources and started engaging with the state's administrative decision-making processes and in associated criminality (Balmaceda, 2008). The transition from 'building socialism' to 'embracing capitalism' brought opportunities for corruption in its vagueness. Where previously a factory belonged to the state, during the transition to capitalism ownership was transferred to the BAGs by employing various legal and semi-legal procedures, often leading to the impoverishment of local populations and a sharp increase in unemployment. Ellman (1993: 8) draws a comparison with the early communists who wanted to build socialism 'regardless of the short-term consequences'. Kovacs (1994) questions the assumption concerning the early transitional phase that still-active parts of the communist state structure were supposed to support the transition to capitalism. These included the accepted illegal and semi-legal transactions that formed part of a centrally planned economy. However, the further assumption that 'what was instrumental in undermining the old communist regimes might contribute to the integration of new democratic ones' proved erroneous (Kovacs, 1994: xv). By the late 1990s, illicit collusion between politicians, industry representatives and organized criminals became well established in many post-Soviet economies, including that of Ukraine (Kupatadze, 2015). Kupatadze (2015: 204) argued that political competition following Ukrainian independence had the capacity to 'foster corruption and collusive networks'. As politicians formed links with business, their managing elite and organized criminals 'sought to maintain the cracks and divisions in political control as a lack of any state monopoly benefited them in creating vulnerabilities, and enabled them to lower rents thus providing greater opportunities in the market for their patronage' (Kovacs, 1994: 204). At the international level it is important to consider the vulnerabilities of international operators when dealing with seemingly legitimate enterprises in Ukraine which are subject to such practices.

Schimmelfennig (2005: 108) discusses the role of the EU in promoting the values of liberal democracy to post-Soviet states, where the EU employs 'a strategy of political conditionality to promote liberal-democracy in Central and Eastern Europe' by encouraging governments to create structures which 'to comply with the norms of liberal democracy' (Schimmelfennig, 2005: 110). Schimmelfennig (2005: 124) points out that social justice factors present the biggest challenge in the implementation of such new principles; vulnerable as such economies are to the effects of destructive entrepreneurship as described previously. Nevertheless, it is also important to understand how legal entrepreneurship can affect the development of a transitional economy such as that of Ukraine. Consequently, we now consider the development of labour rights in Ukraine as an example of the political elite engaging in legal entrepreneurship.

The political exploitation of labour in Ukraine: the rise of legal entrepreneurship

Becker (1966) was interested in studying the cooperation between media, officials and the general public in a given state. He argues that the authorities can thereby use the legislative process to create a 'new moral construct of society, its code of right and wrong' (Becker, 1966: 145). We intend to apply this consideration to the concept of legal entrepreneurship and of workers' rights in Ukraine. Moral entrepreneurship in Becker's study was underpinned by political will and the private interests of privileged individuals while avoiding political collusion and destructive exploitation as previously discussed in the case of Ukraine.

Karl Marx famously argued that each worker should provide according to their ability and receive according to their need. This abstract principle described the ideals of a highly developed communist society and was adopted by the Bolsheviks under the leadership of V.I. Lenin as an ideological blueprint for the new socialist Soviet state. Berger (1994) notes that the Soviet state of workers and peasants very quickly dropped theoretical Marxist ideas in relation to labour remuneration in favour of the ruthless exploitation of its labour force. The resulting savings made on the remuneration of labour were part of a survival strategy for the newly established Soviet state with an impoverished population that was barely surviving following the devastation of the First World War. On the surface, such a practice could be labelled as organized state exploitation. However, the reality is more complex, and poor labour remuneration was often compensated for by social benefits such as free housing and subsidized transport (Berger, 1994). For ideological reasons the notion of 'exploitation' was never debated in the Soviet state, but rather state propaganda promoted an ideal of equality, justice and the communal building of a better future. Such Soviet ideology justifying minimal wages for labour has survived. In states such as Russia, China and Vietnam, the discussion of wages has been deeply problematic (Pringle and Clarke, 2011).

In the 21st century, the context of labour exploitation varied from that of undocumented migrants working in a limited range of sectors, to that of local populations working in their home country with little social resources or opportunities for secure or higher-paid employment. However, the underlying issue remains the same: political or controlling elites aim to save money at the cost of human labour. The nature of such exploitation is often opportunistic, facilitated by the legal and commercial context of a specific region or country. Many workers from post-Soviet states have become subject to labour exploitation abroad, given the numbers who are willing to migrate in search of better-paid employment. Davies (2018) argues that understanding the nature of labour exploitation requires moving beyond notions of traditional criminal justice and considering the normalization of exploitative labour practices in ostensibly legitimate contexts.

Labour exploitation in Ukraine: an old system but new players

Ukraine has, over the last decade, signed several international treaties aimed at protecting employment standards. The International Labour Organisation (ILO) reports that the Ukrainian Parliament has ratified a number of international conventions and adopted international labour standards to make progress in fulfilling 'its constitutional obligations related to reporting on such standards to ILO supervisory bodies, and submission to the national authorities of newly adopted standards' (International Labour Organisation, 2017: 7). Although Ukraine has addressed certain EU requirements to provide a framework for employment protection, such national legislation is widely viewed as protecting business interests rather than the rights of workers, and overall there is poor national compliance with EU directives (International Labour Organisation, 2017).

The Centre for Social and Labour Research (CSLR) (2017: 3) notes that labour relations in Ukraine have been organized under severe pressure from businesses, which have developed feudal'-type labour relationships and have no interest in their improvement. The CSLR (2017) observes that it is common for the directors of such enterprises to believe that they are 'above the law', often taking advantage of ineffective state legislation to suppress trade union membership and threaten workers in cases of industrial dispute. Ukrainian labour practices provide an example of systemic deviance, where the state is directly involved in exploitative labour practices due to poor or absent regulation. The consequences of this can be far reaching, often resulting in undeclared employment or involvement with criminal gangs.

Undeclared employment is defined by the European Commission (2020) as being 'any paid activities that are lawful as regards their nature but not declared to the public authorities, taking into account differences in the regulatory systems of Member States'. In 1998, the size of the undeclared economy was estimated at 'between 7% and 16% of the gross domestic product (GDP) of the European Union, or between 7% and 19% of total declared employment' (European Commission, 1998). The data on undeclared labour in Ukraine is similarly impressive. The ILO (2017) estimated that around 26 per cent of work is undeclared (representing that of 4.3 million citizens), however, the CSLR (2017) adjusts this number to six million undeclared workers. Around a third of the Ukrainian labour force is thus thought to be operating outside of the legal framework. In mitigation however, the 2019 Eurobarometer survey suggested that undeclared work remains a persistent problem in the EU, and half of Europeans believe that the risk of its detection is low (European Commission, 2020).

The ILO (2017) identifies four types of undeclared labour: 1) economic activities at unregistered enterprises; 2) 'cash in hand' informal employment in the formal sector; 3) hidden payments or 'envelope' employment, where the worker receives the state minimum salary officially and additional payment according to verbal contract 'in the 'envelope' (to avoid taxation and social security payments); 4) fictitious self-employment. Of these, informal employment within both the formal and informal sectors is most common in Ukraine, representing the employment of 48.2 per cent of the working population (International Labour Organisation, 2017). This can have serious consequences such as where breaches in health and safety regulations result in injury to a worker, who consequently has no legal right to compensation. With the COVID-19 epidemic response, the social protection of undeclared labour became a serious issue for most EU countries, where legal but unregistered workers were excluded from emergency financial assistance (Biletta, 2020).

Until 2016, Ukrainian labour legislation did not include official definitions of either informal labour or undeclared labour (International Labour Organisation, 2017). Even though these terms are mentioned in various cases of employment legislation. In Ukraine one of the most socially harmful practices is the payment of the minimum state salary and supplemented by a clandestine top up 'envelope'. Upon reaching pensionable age, workers so employed will receive only a minimum pension related to their officially recorded salary, thus leading to pensioner poverty. To date, the Ukrainian Parliament has failed to confront this practice by introducing a legal inspectorate of labour practices. Politicians who claim to want to protect the labour force are faced with a dilemma. On the one hand, Ukraine has to comply with the international regulatory framework, but on the other, politicians are too involved with business interests that are not concerned with long-term social development and as such are not interested in the welfare of the workforce.

The Ukrainian media has consistently highlighted the issue of labour exploitation and challenged the government on its lack of progress in regulating labour relations (Volkonskaya, 2018). There are examples of large companies with wage arrears calculated at around 15 million hryvnia (around €450,000 million), where the wealth of the owner of the company is estimated at around 12 billion hryvnia (ArgumentUA, 2011). Here, wage arrears exist not because there is a lack of available funds for their payment but because this practice has been semi-normalized by the state (ArgumentUA, 2011; Privalov, 2017) and attempts to address this practice through legislation have proved unsuccessful. Indirect evidence indicates collusion between political and business interests to block legislative progress in direct contradiction to what was supposed to be the new socially responsible ideology of the post-Soviet states, relying on entrepreneurship to rebuild the economy. As a result, Ukrainian wages are among the lowest in Europe, and Ukrainian migrant workers are stereotypically perceived to be the cheapest European workforce (Hyde, 2020).

Dudin (2015) argues that the Labour Code adopted in November 2015 is the most cynical document ever passed by the Ukrainian Parliament (see also Privalov, 2017). It allows for the possibility of a 12-hour working day, the introduction of video and listening devices to monitor workers and the practice of the 'sharing', where one employer is able to 'share' an employee with another for up to three months with no social protection for the employee and mandatory work on state and religious holidays. Pavlovski (in Privalov, 2017) notes that in any other European country such changes in the labour code would lead to public protests organized by trade unions. However, in Ukraine the new trade unions lack any real power, whereas the older ones are moribund and often inextricably linked to politicians (see Privalov, 2017). Labour regulations are one principal means of understanding the business environment. The study of them has the potential to guide us towards a better understanding of the nature of unproductive business relationships within and between economies. It can also help us to understand the choices people are forced to make when searching for employment in any country. Hence, in the Ukrainian context, extracting amber illegally under the protection of criminal gangs or working for illegal logging operations can be seen as a viable alternative to legal employment, in which employers fail to comply with even the most basic labour regulations.

Conclusion

This chapter has considered two important issues: the political corruption that facilitates white-collar criminality and underdeveloped and inadequate labour laws. Enabled by the competitive political sphere, the interaction of politicians with white-collar and organized criminals in Ukraine is complex and has the potential of influence beyond the country's borders. For example, Earthsight (2018) estimates that at least 40 per cent of the timber exported to the EU from Ukraine was either harvested or traded illegally. This suggests that governments in both Ukraine and the EU have failed to enforce existing legislation with appropriate diligence. Acknowledging just who is responsible for this situation and how opportunities for abuse arise will be an important step in developing preventative measures. This chapter argues that the focus on state corruption as an initiator of white-collar criminality is an efficient means of uncovering covert illegality in many sectors and is especially useful to all parties involved in developing sustainable commercial entities in Ukraine. For example, in response to the Earthsight (2018) investigation into logging, representatives of the industry considered the inefficiency of Ukrainian laws designed to protect biodiversity where 'the legislation is not clear and the interpretation is not clear ... . It is likely that some of the logging is illegal. It is likely that the uncertainties in the legislation are being used by some companies to do logging that they should not' (Harvey, 2020).

The selective and politically motivated drafting of ambiguous legislation has seriously affected not only specific industries, but also the Ukrainian labour market. As stated previously, limited opportunities to earn fair wages in Ukraine legally has encouraged people to seek employment outside of the legal economy, both in Ukraine and abroad. When abroad, Ukrainians are faced the popular stereotype that they are used to work for less and as such become more vulnerable to abuse. The Ukrainian Liaison Office (2018) reported that, among those who illegally extract amber are individuals from various sectors of society, even including retired school teachers and clergy. They justify their involvement as bringing tangible income for their families. In the east of the country, workers themselves organized the illegal extraction of coal in order to make an adequate living (Zabyelina and Markovska, 2019). Behind these examples exist criminal groups who offer protection to and cooperation with outwardly legitimate businesses and politicians.

For many years both the US and the EU have been concerned with encouraging the rule of law, fighting corruption and facilitating privatization in Ukraine. It is possible to argue that all these objectives have failed. Privatization has created opportunities for destructive political and legal entrepreneurship. Fighting corruption requires a political will to enforce legislation which is absent at high political levels and any attempt to organize public protest against corruption can trigger violent unrest. We note that further research is needed in order to inform any targeted international public campaign to challenge corrupt practices in particular industries. Earthsight (2018) has initiated work to understand corrupt European practices related to the Ukrainian timber industry, but further studies are required to follow their example in many other sectors.

References

ArgumentUA (2011) 'Ukraine: slave labour without the right to salary', Available at: https://golos.ua/i/626674

Aslund, A. (1992) 'A Critique of Soviet Reforms Plans', in A. Aslund (ed) *The Post-Soviet Economy: Soviet and Western Perspectives*, London: Pinter Publishers, pp 167–81.

Audretsch, D.B. and Belitski, M. (2017) 'Entrepreneurial ecosystems in cities: establishing the framework conditions', *Journal of Technology Transfer*, 42(5): 1030–51.

Balmaceda, M.M. (2008) *Energy Dependency, Politics and Corruption in the Former Soviet Union: Russia's Power, Oligarchs' Profit and Ukraine's Missing Energy Policy*, London: Routledge.

Baumol, W.J. (1990) 'Entrepreneurship: productive, unproductive and destructive', *Journal of Political Economy*, 98(5): 893–921.

Becker, H. (1966) *The Outsiders: Studies in the Sociology of Deviance*, London: The Free Press.

Berger, P.L. (1994) 'Observations on the transition in East-Central Europe', in J.M. Kovacs (ed) *Transition to Capitalism: The Communist Legacy in Eastern Europe*, New Brunswick: Transaction Publishers, pp 293–99.

Besser, L. (2020) 'Ukraine's illegal amber mining boom is scarring the earth and making criminal gangs rich', *ABC News*, [online] 21 January, Available at: www.abc.net.au/news/2020-01-21/illegal-amber-mining-creating-environmental-disaster-in-ukraine/11745470

Biletta I. (2020) 'All aboard: hauling undeclared workers onto the pandemic rescue boats', Eurofound, [online] 11 May, Available at: www.eurofound.europa.eu/publications/blog/all-aboard-hauling-undeclared-workers-onto-the-pandemic-rescue-boats

CitizensUK (2017) 'The Living Wage Campaign', Available at: www.citizensuk.org/campaigns/the-campaign-for-a-real-living-wage

Centre for Social and Labour Research (CSLR) (2017) 'Atypical labour in Ukraine', Available at: https://rev.org.ua/wp-content/uploads/2017/12/Atypical-Employment_Brochure.pdf

Davies, J. (2018) 'From severe to routine labour exploitation: the case of migrant workers in the UK food industry', *Criminology & Criminal Justice*, 19(3): 294–310.

Desai, S. and Acs, Z.J. (2007) 'A theory of destructive entrepreneurship', *Jena Economic Research Papers*, Available at: www2.wiwi.uni-jena.de/Papers/jerp2007/wp_2007_085.pdf

Dudin, V. (2015) 'Ukraine's labour reform', Available at: www.opendemocracy.net/en/odr/ukraines-labour-reforms- threaten-its-already-precarious-workers/

Earthsight (2018) 'Complicit in corruption: how billion dollar firms and EU governments are failing Ukraine's Forests', Available at: www.earthsight.org.uk/investigations/complicit-in-corruption

Ellman, M. (1993) 'General aspects of transition', in P.H. Admiraal (ed) *Economic Transition in Eastern Europe*, Oxford: Blackwell, pp 1–42.

European Commission (1998) *Communication of the Commission on Undeclared Work*, Available at: http://aei.pitt.edu/5111/

Fukuyama, F. (2012) *The Origins of Political Order*, London: Profile Books.

Gaidar, E.T. (1993) 'Inflationary pressures and economic reform in the Soviet Union', in P.H. Admiraal (ed) *Economic Transition in Eastern Europe*, Oxford: Blackwell, pp 63–91.

Harvey, F. (2020) 'Timber from unsustainable logging allegedly being sold in EU as ethical', *The Guardian*, [online] 23 June, Available at: www.theguardian.com/environment/2020/jun/23/timber-unsustainable-logging-allegedly-sold-eu-ethical

Holzindustrie Schweighofer (2019) 'Holzindustrie Schweighofer: update regarding timber imports from Ukraine', Available at: https://hs.at/fileadmin/files/all_en/Press/190228_Update_regarding_timber_imports_from_Ukraine.pdf

Home Office (2019) 'Country policy and information note: Ukraine: organised crime and corruption (version 3)', Available at: www.gov.uk

Hyde, L. (2020) 'Ukraine's trapped migrant workers look for roads back to Europe', *Politico*, [online] 31 May, Available at: www.politico.eu/article/coronavirus-ukraine-migrant-workers-trapped/

International Labour Organisation (ILO) (2017) 'Ukraine: decent work country programme, 2016–2019', Available at: www.ilo.org/wcmsp5/groups/public/---europe/---ro-geneva/---sro-budapest/documents/genericdocument/wcms_467704.pdf

Kalczynski, N. (2020) 'The underground economy of amber: a destabilizing threat to Ukraine', *International Policy Digest*, [online] 6 January, Available at: https://intpolicydigest.org/2020/01/06/the-underground-economy-of-amber-a-destabilizing-threat-to-ukraine/

Kovacs, J.M. (ed) (1994) *Transition to Capitalism: The Communist Legacy in Eastern Europe*, New Brunswick: Transaction Publishers.

Kosmarskii, V. (1992) 'Public attitudes to the transition', in A. Aslund (ed) *The Post-Soviet Economy: Soviet and Western Perspectives*, London: Pinter Publishers, pp 25–39.

Kupatadze, A. (2015) 'Political corruption in Eurasia: understanding collusion between states, organised crime and business', *Theoretical Criminology*, 19(2): 198–215.

Lotspeich, R. (1995) 'Crime in the transition economies', *Europe-Asia Studies*, 47(4): 555–89.

Levi, M. (2008) 'Organized fraud and organizing fraud: unpacking research on networks and organization', *Criminology and Criminal Justice*, 8(4): 389–419.

Markovska, A. and Serdyuk A. (2015) 'Black, grey or white? Finding the new shade of corruption in Ukraine', in P.C. van Duyne, A. Maljevic, G. Antonopoulos, J. Harvey and K. Von Lampe (eds) *The Relativity of Wrongdoing: Corruption, Organized Crime, Fraud and Money Laundering in Perspective*, Oisterwijk: Wolf Legal Publishers, pp 21–43.

Markovska, A and Van Duyne, P. (2020) 'Power and trust networks in the organisations of crime in Ukraine', in Hufnagel, S. and Moiseienko, A. (ed) *Criminal Networks and Law Enforcement: Global Perspectives on Illegal Enterprise*, London: Routledge, pp 162–178.

Masters, J. (2020) 'Ukraine: conflict at the crossroads of Europe and Russia', Council on Foreign Relations, [online] 5 February, Available at: www.cfr.org/backgrounder/ukraine- conflict-crossroads-europe-and-russia

Mungiu-Pippidi, A. (2015) *The Quest for Good Governance: How Societies Develop Control of Corruption*, Cambridge: Cambridge University Press.

Nichols, P.M. (2007) 'United States v. Lazarenko: filling in gaps in support and regulation of transnational relationships', *Legal Studies and Business Ethics Papers*, Available at: repository.upenn.edu/lgst_papers/44

Organized Crime Observatory (2013) 'Ukraine and the EU: overcoming criminal exploitation toward a modern democracy?', Available at: www.o-c-o.net/wp-content/uploads/2013/11/Ukraine-and-the-EU-Overcoming-criminal-exploitation-toward-a-modern-democracy.pdf

President of Ukraine (2019) 'President on the struggle against the illegal amber mining: no "schemes" will help escape responsibility', [online] 12 August, Available at: www.president.gov.ua/en/news/zhodni-shemi-ne-dopomozhut-uniknuti-vidpovidalnosti-preziden-56817

Privalov, A. (2017) 'Draft labour code in Ukraine: expert analysis', *Rabcom*, [online] 31 March, Available at: https://rabcom.info/2017/03/31/trudovoy-kodeks-rasschitannyiy-na-stranyi-tretego-mira/

Schimmelfennig F. (2005) 'The EU: promoting liberal-democracy through membership conditionality', in T. Flockhart (ed) *Socializing Democratic Norms*, London: Palgrave Macmillan, pp 106–26.

Tombs, S. and Whyte, D. (eds) (2003) *Unmasking the Crimes of the Powerful: Scrutinising States and Corporations*, New York: Peter Lang.

Ukrainian Liaison Office (2018) 'The leprosy of the land', 23 May, Available at: https://ukraineoffice.blogactiv.eu/2018/05/23/leprosy-of-the-land-illegal-amber-mining-turns-ukraine-landscape-to-lunar-like

Verkhovna Rada (2015) 'On peculiarities of state regulation of business entities associated with the sale and export of timber' [in Ukrainian], *Ministry of Justice of Ukraine*, Available at: https://zakon.rada.gov.ua/laws/show/325-19#Text

Volkonskaya, I. (2018) 'How to save yourself from slavery in Ukraine', Available at: https://golos.ua/news/

Wedel, J.R. (2005) 'Flex organising and clan-state: perspectives on crime and corruption in new Russia', in W.A. Pridemore (ed) *Ruling Russia: Law, Crime and Justice in a Changing Society*, Oxford: Rowman and Littlefield, pp 101–17.

Wendle, J. (2017) 'The dramatic impact of illegal amber mining in Ukraine's wild west', *National Geographic*, [online] 31 January, Available at: www.nationalgeographic.com/news/2017/01/illegal-amber-mining-ukraine/

World Bank (2017) 'Asset recovery watch', Available at: https://star.worldbank.org/corruption-cases/node/18566

Yakovlev, V. (2013) 'Destruction is not a reform' [in Russian], *Ostrov*, [online] 29 March, Available at: www.ostro.org/general/economics/articles/417163

Zabyelina, J. and Markovska, A. (2019) 'Ukraine: organised crime, politics and "frozen" conflicts', in F. Allum and S. Gilmour (eds) *Handbook of Organised Crime and Politics*, London: Edward Elgar, pp 105–18.

10

Labour Exploitation and Posted Workers in the European Construction Industry

Jon Davies

Introduction

In late 2019, the European Trade Union Confederation (ETUC) announced that a construction worker who had been waiting three years for over €8,000 in unpaid wages was among the cases of worker exploitation referred to the new European Labour Authority (ELA) for investigation (European Trade Union Confederation, 2019). Cases such as this represent how construction workers experience labour exploitation across European countries and industries. Given that the European construction industry is expected to continue growing in the foreseeable future (Building Information Modeling, 2018),[1] it represents an increasingly important area of investigation for issues associated with labour exploitation and corporate criminology. Labour exploitation can be broadly understood as a spectrum, ranging from criminalized practices such as forced labour, to 'routine' breaches of labour or employment legislation (Murphy et al, 2019). The purpose of this chapter is to consider what is 'European' about white-collar and corporate crime throughout the European construction industry, with an emphasis on exploitative labour practices and the 'posting' of workers. 'Posting' refers to the temporary migration of workers sent by their employers to work on projects abroad, which is facilitated under EU free movement of services rules (Lillie, 2012).[2] It is hoped that this chapter will help to frame labour exploitation in the European construction industry through a corporate criminology lens, especially concerning why businesses are able to exploit posted workers in the context of 'free movement', as well as how governance gaps serve to maintain weak standards of accountability in this area.

White-collar and corporate crimes in European construction

Discussion of criminal activity in European construction industries is not new. For example, Savona (2010) analyzes the infiltration of the Italian construction industry by organized crime groups; in Dutch construction, van Duyne and Houtzager (2005) frame concerns over the 'black labour market', whereas van de Bunt (2010) focuses on cartels and construction fraud scandals; and Kankaanranta and Muttilainen (2010) examine economic crimes and the 'grey economy' in Finnish construction. More recently, concerns revolving around human trafficking and other forms of 'modern slavery' have generated significant European interest regarding the protection of (migrant) workers, as well as the role of states and corporations in facilitating exploitation (Caro et al, 2015; Chartered Institute of Building, 2018; Focus on Labour Exploitation, 2018a; Fundamental Rights Agency, 2019; Murphy et al, 2019).

While this body of literature is not usually framed from explicit white-collar or corporate crime perspectives, corporate criminology can play a significant role in helping to explain how and why exploitative practices occur in European construction, as well as interventions to address them. Firstly, a corporate criminology perspective facilitates an understanding of business decision-making processes when temporarily moving workers from one country to another (worker posting), who may then be vulnerable to exploitation. The issue of posted workers is one example of how many construction companies use otherwise legal processes and routine business practices in order to remain competitive, and thereby can wittingly or unwittingly facilitate labour exploitation. Secondly, corporate criminology provides opportunities to examine regulatory spheres within which businesses operate; in the case of posted workers, this may include discussion of pan-European frameworks such as the Posted Workers Directive 96/71/EC. In short, the intersections of legitimate business practices, limited regulatory oversight and market dynamics that expose workers to labour exploitation arguably provide a dynamic area of investigation for corporate criminology in this industry.

In a broader context, (migrant) labour exploitation can be considered as a subcategory of corporate crime due to its emphasis on criminal, illegal, and other 'dubious' business practices and the individuals associated with them (Alvesalo et al, 2014; Davies and Ollus, 2019). There are numerous social harms not legally branded as 'criminal' that occur in the construction industry, such as non-payment or underpayment of wages (Focus on Labour Exploitation, 2018a; Fundamental Rights Agency, 2019), which provide opportunities for corporate criminological analysis. In recent years, there has been a significant increase in academic and policy attention given to the central role of businesses in facilitating labour exploitation across their product and labour supply networks (Meardi et al, 2014; Crane et al, 2019). Given that businesses are arguably in a dual position to exploit labour but also help prevent such practices, there are key questions concerning how to achieve such prevention. Part of the answer involves considering supranational trends and policies, including at the European level, especially since the process of labour exploitation can and does occur across borders, both within and beyond Europe.

As part of recent developments, 9 out of 21 surveyed EU countries identified construction as the sector that is most vulnerable to labour exploitation (Fundamental Rights Agency, 2015). An estimated 6 per cent of the European workforce is based in the European construction industry (Building Radar, 2016), and organizations such as the Fundamental Rights Agency (FRA) (2019) point to growing concerns of labour exploitation across this industry amid a somewhat slow recovery from the 2008–09 global financial crisis. Materials used in the construction industry, including bricks, cement and timber, may be sourced, produced, processed and assembled under exploitative conditions (KnowTheChain, 2019: 4). Construction industry work is characterized by short-term projects, extensive subcontracting as part of fragmented supply chains, informal work, hazardous conditions and poor treatment of workers, including payment problems – all of which are key vulnerabilities to labour exploitation (Elliott, 2014; Focus on Labour Exploitation, 2018a). Most construction work has to be completed on-site, which limits the ability of companies to outsource production to less expensive locations within or beyond Europe – therefore, labour and materials are routinely key costing factors. Perhaps one of the most recent well-known examples of labour exploitation in European construction involves the 'Space Egg' EU headquarters being built with the aid of undocumented migrants, who at times went without pay, partly due to complex subcontracting arrangements (Boffey, 2019).

Although there are common trends and issues across the European construction industry, there is also significant diversity within Europe concerning issues related to construction, as well as broader factors such as migration patterns. First, according to European Construction Monitor (2018), although there are varying levels of growth between north western, southern, and eastern European countries, profit margins are under pressure most in the north west due to relatively high labour costs, whereas the south and east are less affected by such pressures. These challenges are significant because narrow profit margins encourage many businesses to reduce labour costs by outsourcing or informalizing employment relationships (Davies and Ollus, 2019).

In contrast, construction costs in southern and eastern countries have risen less than the European average, or have even declined in some cases due to a slower recovery from the 2008–09 global financial crisis (European Construction Monitor, 2018: 7). This slow recovery, in conjunction with fewer projects and less competitive work, has encouraged many businesses and workers from southern/ eastern countries to bid for projects and migrate to the north or west in order to improve their prospects (Caro et al, 2015). For example, long-term high unemployment rates and structurally low wages in countries such as Greece and Portugal have seen increases in emigration, especially among young people (Gorjão Henriques, 2011). As is well documented elsewhere, such labour migration has associated risks to exploitation, since many workers are unfamiliar with host countries or rely on intermediaries when searching for work and accommodation (Berntsen and Lillie, 2016).

Second, and related to the first point, European migration patterns traditionally follow east-to-north-west and south-to-north-west trajectories, which means that migrant workers are particularly vulnerable to exploitative practices linked to companies trying to reduce their costs and business pressures. This pattern has been especially prominent following the 2004 accession of Eastern European countries to the EU. These factors have important implications for corporate criminology, since they would benefit from a pan-European discussion on how and why vulnerabilities develop, and how they can be addressed at organizational, regulatory and political-legal levels. The intention of this chapter is not to resolve these issues; a more wide-ranging and in-depth discussion would be required in order to begin doing so. However, an issue often linked to the pan-European labour market, and therefore Europe-wide regulation, is that of posted workers.

Posted workers in European construction

The notion of 'posted workers', which, as noted previously, refers to the temporary migration of workers sent by their employers to work on projects abroad, has become increasingly common throughout the European construction industry (Caro et al, 2015). The posting of workers is a distinctly European, or at least EU practice, since this process does not occur in the same form beyond EU borders. As a side note, the UK's withdrawal from the EU means that, at the time of writing, it is unlikely to continue using posted workers, and instead may increase the use of Temporary Labour Migration Programmes (TLMPs)[3] in order to meet fluctuating demand in sectors such as construction (Focus on Labour Exploitation, 2018b). Posted migration is substantively different from those migrating to work in other EU countries as individuals, since employers arrange this posting with host countries strictly on a temporary basis (no more than 24 months) as part of their business needs.

Posted workers are a relatively small proportion of the overall European labour force: 2 million postings, or approximately 1 per cent of the total number of employed people in the EU (Darvas, 2017). In practice these figures may be higher, since some labourers may not be officially registered as posted workers due to short-term work tasks, frequent travel between home and work over shorter distances, and employers failing to register them by notifying relevant state authorities (European Commission, 2019). Nevertheless, at face value, worker posting may appear to deliver benefits to businesses and workers in the form of labour flexibility, as well as intra-EU labour mobility. The posting of workers, unlike individual migration, is not covered by usual freedom of movement rules, but by freedom of services, since it is businesses that instigate posting for their own needs (Lillie, 2012: 153). In addition, there are different forms of posting that reflect categories of employment, including agency work and self-employment, as well as regular posting, which further complicates the availability of accurate figures on numbers of workers involved in this scheme.

However, there have been concerns across Europe which suggest that the posting of workers allows companies to avoid labour regulation, and exposes workers to exploitation due to increased segregation from local populations, payments below local labour standards and unfair deductions from salaries (Lillie, 2012). Studies from countries including Finland, Germany, Spain, Sweden, the Netherlands and the UK suggest that there are connections between the posting of workers and labour exploitation, including in construction (Lillie, 2012; Meardi et al,

2014; Thörnqvist and Bernhardsson, 2015; Wagner, 2015; Berntsen, 2016). Posting as a form of intra-EU mobility is not new, since this goes back at least as far as the 1957 Treaty of Rome. However, the Posted Workers Directive of 1996 sets out base level requirements, including minimum rates of pay, minimum paid annual leave, health and safety protocols and maximum work periods and minimum rest periods (Lillie and Greer, 2007).

Perhaps the most significant change over time has been that the facilitation of posted workers has become less state managed and more driven by the independent actions of businesses and workers. In other words, worker posting has become less like controlled migration between national labour markets, and more like a pan-EU labour market (Caro et al, 2015). In particular, there are postings concentrate in two sectors: low-wage jobs, including general labouring, where migrant labour streams flow from Eastern and Southern Europe to countries in the north-west; and high-wage jobs, such as IT experts, which are focused in the north-west, and where streams work more equally both ways. As part of these flows, classic patterns of seasonal migration persist, but are becoming increasingly fragmented, less network driven and more employer arranged (Caro et al, 2015: 1602). Hence, posted workers do not necessarily have the same rights as individual migrants who choose to move, live and work in another EU country, which has consequences regarding vulnerability to exploitation. This increased role of businesses risks them developing a dominant 'voice' on issues such as working conditions, since they frequently discourage workers from mixing with other local workers by providing separate accommodation.

Segregation and exploitation are not inevitable consequences of posted working, since to an extent this also depends on individual decisions of workers and personal circumstances of migration. However, as Caro et al (2015) note, posted working organized by employers is temporary by design, which means that there is less incentive for workers to integrate within the host society. In addition, while in many countries posting is marketed as a safer form of labour migration due to employers providing accommodation, this arguably reduces workers' independence from them (Thörnqvist and Bernhardsson, 2015). Employers may take advantage of this temporary nature of posted work by driving down work conditions, deducting expenses from salaries for accommodation, transport and 'administration' costs, as well as encouraging workers to socialize only with coworkers in order to discourage integration with the host society. For example, when discussing the case of posted Polish construction workers in

Sweden, Thörnqvist and Bernhardsson (2015: 25) found that the Polish workers were being paid less than their Swedish colleagues, and were routinely exceeding the maximum number of working hours that was written into their contracts. Companies also did not pay overtime for work during night shifts and during public holidays. Such mistreatment is hardly new, but workers' posted status adds an additional layer of vulnerability, in that employers primarily control the process, thereby making workers more dependent on their employers than they otherwise would be in their home countries or as individual migrant workers.

More recently, the EU announced revisions to posted worker arrangements which are intended to address some of the concerns noted earlier in this section; member states should have implemented these changes during 2020. Specifically, posted workers will be entitled to the same remuneration as local workers if they are conducting the same work in the same place (Laboris, 2018) – although this is problematic because there is no 'equal pay principle' among local (national) workers in any country, along with associated factors such as gender (Darvas, 2017). After 12 months of working in the same position, posted workers will also be entitled to all mandatory working conditions of the host member state, and the principle of equal treatment between agency workers and permanent employees will apply to posted temporary agency employees. Not all parties have welcomed these changes. Some speculate that changing the Posted Workers Directive will have little impact in practice, and instead argue for a stronger emphasis on tackling bogus self-employment and undeclared work as ways to enhance protection for workers (Darvas, 2017). Regardless of how these changes affect European construction industries in the short and longer term, it is clear that the posting of workers will remain a significant European dynamic that is worthy of attention from white-collar and corporate criminology.

These gaps in the regulatory oversight of posted workers, as well as the vulnerabilities to labour exploitation that these gaps may result in, mean that employers and businesses are in a prominent position to mistreat workers. Mistreatment of employees and workers is a key criterion for corporate criminology to address, and runs parallel with similar developments in criminology that emphasize the growing problem of labour exploitation across European countries (International Labour Organization, 2017). The challenge for white-collar and corporate criminologists here is in deciding to what extent they should emphasize the European-level regulatory framework of posted workers, or national-level labour market policies and, by extension, individual companies. Pursuing the former is likely to be helpful in the sense that posting is an EU-wide phenomenon, so data on numbers of workers, types of businesses, migration patterns and enforcement mechanisms, however flawed, all provide sources of information from which to develop macro analyses of ongoing challenges such as labour exploitation.

However, if pursuing the latter, it will be possible to develop in-depth case studies of local and/or national labour markets, as well as how individual businesses manage associated pressures through their use of posted workers – thereby providing regular meso and micro analyses in line with previous research (Thörnqvist and Bernhardsson, 2015; Wagner, 2015; Berntsen, 2016). Ultimately, Europe-wide and national/localized case studies are worthy of attention, but the distinct European dynamic of posted workers is continually evolving, thereby making this subject an important one during the next decade. Such evolving policy is especially important as the EU seems to move towards further integration of its regulatory agenda, as evidenced by the newly formed ELA, which will play a role in upholding labour rights and resolving disputes across EU labour markets (European Trade Union Confederation, 2019).

Conclusion

This chapter has outlined some challenges that relate to white-collar and corporate crime; specifically in the area of labour exploitation across the European construction industry. The role of construction businesses in facilitating exploitation has been introduced with regards to the topic of posted workers. Given that the European construction industry is now growing after a slow recovery from the 2008–09 global financial crisis (European Construction Monitor, 2018), the issue of labour exploitation is also becoming more prominent across European countries and sectors (Fundamental Rights Agency, 2019). Although posted workers remain a relatively small sub-group of migrant workers in European construction, the vulnerabilities they face can be significant, and the posting of workers adds a distinctly European (or at least, EU) element to the question of what is 'European' about white-collar and corporate crime.

As others in this edited collection will have made clear, examining supranational challenges – in this case, at the European level – provides opportunities to analyze corporate structures, their processes, and the consequences of their actions in a way that is not as feasible when considering localized case studies or national factors. Due to space constraints, this chapter cannot discuss all such Europe-level factors on labour exploitation with the rigour they deserve. However, in some respects, the Europe-level policy agenda can prove to be helpful to workers, and less helpful or at least more complex, in others. Regarding posted workers, amending the Posted Workers Directive in order to improve working conditions may theoretically seem helpful, yet others cite concerns over differences between policy and practice (Darvas, 2017), which risks little changing 'on the ground'. The challenge for white-collar and corporate criminology regarding labour exploitation is to consider how far a 'one size fits all' policy approach at the European level is going to be a key trend in the foreseeable future, and if so, how it can position itself among the advantages and drawbacks of these approaches.

Notes

[1] At the time of writing, it is not yet fully clear what impact the ongoing COVID-19 crisis will have across European construction industries, but many self-employed workers and small-and-medium-sized businesses have voiced significant concerns over their future in construction, as well as growth rates (The Construction Index, 2020).

[2] This employer-led worker posting contrasts with individual labour migration, which is governed by EU principles of freedom of movement for workers.

[3] TLMPs involve the provision of time-limited work visas, often for seasonal or other production where there is fluctuating demand for labour. The posting of workers is comparable to TLMPs in terms of purpose, but each scheme is governed by different regulatory and enforcement frameworks: that is, posted workers by EU Directive 96/71/EC and TLMPs by national immigration regimes.

Acknowledgements

This project has received funding from the European Research Council (ERC) under the European Union's Horizon 2020 research and innovation programme (grant agreement no. 756672). I would like to thank Nicholas Lord, Rita Faria and Hanna Malik for commenting on earlier versions of this chapter, as well as the members of the European Working Group on Organisational Crime for facilitating a broader discussion on the issues at its 2019 workshop in Manchester.

References

Alvesalo, A., Jokinen, A. and Ollus, N. (2014) 'The exploitation of migrant labour and the problems of control in Finland', in P. Van Aerschot and P. Daenzer (eds) *The Integration and Protection of Immigrants: Canadian and Scandinavian Critiques*, Surrey: Ashgate Publishing Limited, pp 121–38.

Berntsen, L. (2016) 'Hyper-mobile migrant workers and Dutch trade union representation strategies at the Eemshaven construction sites', *Economic and Industrial Democracy*, 37(1): 171–87.

Boffey, D. (2019) 'EU headquarters built by undocumented migrants, workers claim', *The Guardian*, [online] 20 December, Available at: www.theguardian.com/world/2019/dec/20/eu-headquarters-built-by-undocumented-migrants-workers-claim?CMP=share_btn_link

Building Information Modeling (2018) 'The future of construction: a European overview', *BIM*, [online] 5 February, Available at: www.bimcommunity.com/news/load/631/the-future-of-construction-an-european-overview

Building Radar (2016) 'Construction industry in Europe', *Building Radar*, [online] 25 February, Available at: https://buildingradar.com/construction-blog/construction-industry-europe/

Caro, E., Berntsen, L., Lillie, N. and Wagner, I. (2015) 'Posted migration and segregation in the European construction sector', *Journal of Ethnic and Migration Studies*, 41(10): 1600–20.

Chartered Institute of Building (CIOB) (2018) *Construction and the Modern Slavery Act: Tackling Exploitation in the UK*, Bracknell: CIOB.

The Construction Index (2020) 'EU urged to class Covid-19 as a "force majeure"', *The Construction Index*, [online] 24 March, Available at: www.theconstructionindex.co.uk/news/view/europe-urged-to-class-covid-19-as-force-majeure

Crane, A., LeBaron, G., Allain, J. and Behbahani, L. (2019) 'Governance gaps in eradicating forced labour: from global to domestic supply chains', *Regulation & Governance*, 13(1): 86–106.

Darvas, Z. (2017) 'Revision of the Posted Workers Directive misses the point', *Bruegel*, [online] 18 October, Available at: https://bruegel.org/2017/10/revision-of-the-posted-workers-directive-misses-the-point/

Davies, J. and Ollus, N. (2019) 'Labour exploitation and human trafficking as corporate crime: supply chain activities in food production and cleaning services', *Crime, Law and Social Change*, 72(1): 87–106.

Elliott, J. (2014) *The Umbrella Company Con-Trick*, London: UCATT.

European Commission (2019) *Practical Guide on Posting*, Luxembourg: European Commission.

European Commission (2020) 'European construction sector observatory', Available at: https://ec.europa.eu/growth/sectors/construction/observatory_en

European Construction Monitor (2018) *2017–2018: A Looming New Construction Crisis?* Amsterdam: Deloitte.

European Trade Union Confederation (ETUC) (2019) 'Unions refer first exploitation cases to new European labour authority', *ETUC*, [online] 15 October, Available at: www.etuc.org/en/pressrelease/unions-refer-first-exploitation-cases-new-european-labour-authority-investigation

Focus on Labour Exploitation (2018a) *Shaky Foundations: Labour Exploitation in London's Construction Sector*, London: FLEX.

Focus on Labour Exploitation (2018b) *Preventing Exploitation in the Shadow of Brexit: The Risks of Temporary Migration Programmes*, London: FLEX.

Fundamental Rights Agency (2015) *Severe Labour Exploitation: Workers Moving Within or into the European Union*, Vienna: Fundamental Rights Agency.

Fundamental Rights Agency (2019) *Protecting Migrant Workers from Exploitation in the EU: Workers' Perspectives*, Vienna: Fundamental Rights Agency.

Gorjão Henriques, J. (2011) 'Young people are fleeing Portugal in droves. But is this a bad thing?', *The Guardian*, [online] 8 January, Available at: www.theguardian.com/commentisfree/2011/jan/08/portugal-emigration-young-generation

International Labour Organization (2017) *Global Estimates of Modern Slavery*, Geneva: ILO.

Kankaanranta, T. and Muttilainen, V. (2010) 'Economic crimes in the construction industry: case of Finland', *Journal of Financial Crime*, 17(4): 417–29.

KnowTheChain (2019) *Forced Labour in the Construction Sector*, San Francisco: KnowTheChain.

Laboris, I. (2018) 'EU states have until 2020 to implement revised Posted Workers Directive', *SHRM*, [online] 12 October, Available at: www.shrm.org/ResourcesAndTools/legal-and-compliance/employment-law/Pages/global-EU-posted-workers-directive.aspx

Lillie, N. (2012) 'Subcontracting, posted migrants and labour market segmentation in Finland', *British Journal of Industrial Relations*, 50(1): 148–67.

Lillie, N. and Greer, I. (2007) 'Industrial relations, migration, and neoliberal politics: the case of the European construction sector', *Politics & Society*, 35(4): 551–81.

Meardi, G., Martín, A. and Lozano Riera, M. (2014) 'Constructing uncertainty: unions and migrant labour in construction in Spain and the UK', *Journal of Industrial Relations*, 54(1): 5–21.

Murphy, C., Doyle, D.M. and Murphy, M. (2019) '"Still waiting" for justice: migrant workers' perspectives on labour exploitation in Ireland', *Industrial Law Journal*, 49(3): 318–51.

Savona, E.U. (2010) 'Infiltration of the public construction industry by Italian organised crime', in K. Bullock, R.V. Clarke and N. Tilley (eds) *Situational Prevention of Organised Crimes*, Cullompton: Willan Publishing, pp 130–50.

Thörnqvist, C. and Bernhardsson, S. (2015) 'Their own stories: how Polish construction workers posted to Sweden experience their job situation, or resistance versus life projects', *Transfer*, 21(1): 23–36.

van de Bunt, H. (2010) 'Walls of secrecy and silence: the Madoff case and cartels in the construction industry', *Criminology & Public Policy*, 9(3): 435–53.

van Duyne, P.C. and Houtzager, M.J. (2005) 'Criminal sub-contracting in the Netherlands: the Dutch 'koppelbaas' as crime-entrepreneur', in P.C. van Duyne, K. von Lampe, M. van Dijck and J.L. Newell (eds) *The Organised Crime Economy: Managing Crime Markets in Europe*, Nijmegen: Wolf Legal Publishers, pp 163–88.

Wagner, I. (2015) 'Rule enactment in a pan-European labour market: transnational posted work in the German construction sector', *British Journal of Industrial Relations*, 53(4): 692–710.

11

Struggles in Cooperation: Public–Private Relations in the Investigation of Internal Financial Crime in the Netherlands

Clarissa Meerts

Introduction

News about fraud and other white-collar crimes is apparent in many of the global headlines. Major companies, such as banks, are under public scrutiny when it comes to their own alleged criminal behaviour, but also with regard to their efforts to prevent crime by others. For example, in the recent ING scandal, the Dutch bank settled with the Dutch Public Prosecution Service for an amount of €775 million, to avoid prosecution after being suspected of large-scale negligence with regard to anti-money laundering efforts (National Office for Serious Fraud, Environmental Crime and Asset Confiscation, 2018). The ING case is intriguing and brings to the fore one of the paradoxes that surround efforts to combat white-collar crime. On the one hand, the state is dependent on cooperation by and with private parties, while on the other these private parties may be the culprits.

It has long been acknowledged that the state is not able to fulfil all of the security demands of society (see, for example, Jones and Newburn, 2006). Private sector involvement in crime control is widespread (White, 2014; Gurinskaya and Nalla, 2018). When it comes to white-collar and corporate crime, an area in which the involvement of the criminal justice system has historically been limited, the situation seems to be even more pronounced.

The growth of private policing is a global phenomenon (see, for example, De Waard, 1999). However, scholarship on private policing and public–private relationships is predominantly Anglo–American and has a distinctly neoliberal focus. The rhetoric (focused on privatization and responsibilization) used in the public–private security debate fits better with laissez-faire, market-driven economies than with the welfare state model, which is more prevalent in Europe. What is more, the rhetoric seems to be an uncomfortable fit for corporate investigations as well. One reason for this is that dominant conceptualizations of private policing tend to make no distinction between different forms of private policing and, as a consequence, fail to appreciate the nuances between them. This calls for an alternative approach that counterbalances the hegemony of Anglo–American scholarship on private policing. Using the Netherlands as a case study representing a European welfare state, it is advocated here that such an approach should be developed from a European perspective.

This chapter discusses public–private relations in the context of internal financial crime within organizations. The reason for this delineation is twofold. First, the category of 'white-collar crime' is too broad and contains too many different situations for a thorough inspection of public–private relationships. Internal financial crime is still a broad category, however, it narrows the scope to criminal actions that are committed inside an organization. Organizational crime, committed *by* the organization, therefore falls outside the scope of this chapter. Second, internal crime has some characteristics which make it especially interesting from a perspective focusing on public–private relations. Internal crime is committed within a labour relationship.[1] One implication of this is that the organization in which the crime occurs has multiple options to investigate the alleged crime without recourse to the police. As an employer, the organization has a right to certain information regarding its employees (Meerts, 2019a). While the necessity to cooperate may be less pressing from the perspective of private actors in this context, the criminal justice system relies for an important part on the information provided by organizations. As such, one might argue that cooperation is more vital to the criminal justice system than to private parties.

While law enforcement authorities may investigate ex officio, as a result of information received from for example other criminal investigations, in many instances information flows to the criminal justice system only after corporate investigations have been concluded (for more on the reasons for this see Meerts, 2019a). Many incidents of internal financial crime never reach the criminal justice system (see also PricewaterhouseCoopers, 2019). Research suggests that organizations faced with internal crime tend to order a private investigation before deciding whether or not to report to criminal justice authorities (Gottschalk, 2016; Meerts, 2018). Corporate investigators investigate these matters within the private sphere. Four main groups of investigators can be identified: investigators working for private investigation firms, in-house security departments, forensic accountancy firms and forensic (departments of) law firms. The choice of a particular investigator may be guided by different considerations, such as the applicable legal framework. For example, an internal investigation may be protected by the legal privilege of a legal investigator. This 'forum shopping' by clients based on legal frameworks is potentially problematic in terms of transparency and fairness of the procedure, but it could also hamper public–private cooperation efforts (for more on this see Meerts, 2019a).

While a case may be internal to an organization and often is dealt with accordingly, it may have national, regional or even global consequences (for example, for the financial system at large). It is notoriously difficult for national policing organizations to cooperate, even in an EU context.[2] Corporate investigators, however, are able to move relatively quickly across national jurisdictions and have, in this way, the potential to more effectively deal with the harms caused by transnational internal financial crimes (Meerts, 2019a). This chapter uses the Dutch situation as a case study to look at the question of public–private relations. Insights derived from multiple qualitative research projects are used to shed light on public–private relationships with respect to Dutch internal financial crime. The chapter, then, should be read as a reflection based on previous research by the author and others. The next section of this chapter starts with a discussion of some more common forms of public–private relationships, after which some relevant recent changes in the context in which cooperation should take place are discussed. Finally, it is argued that corporate investigators' operational autonomy limits contact or cooperation with law enforcement agencies and, as such, public–private 'separation' is often a better conceptualization than 'cooperation' (Meerts, 2019b). Given this de facto separation, it is argued that concepts such as privatization, responsibilization and the blurring of private and public fail to capture this autonomy.

Public–private relationships

Formally structured cooperation efforts

Even though both the public and the private sides have ample possibilities to investigate independently from each other, a call for cooperation has been heard for decades. The theme first occurred in Dutch safety and security policy midway through the 1980s (Van Dijk and De Waard, 2001). These calls for cooperation are often shaped as formal agreements or Public–Private Partnerships (PPPs). The PPP is a popular method to formalize cooperation, however, there is some controversy about its definition. Generally, though, PPPs consist of at least one public sector and one private sector actor who form a cooperation with a substantial duration. This cooperation involves a common goal, in which all parties involved have a stake. In addition, tasks are divided between the partners and there is no hierarchy between parties (Rooseboom et al, 2006). PPPs may be utilized as governance tools by governments to 'transfer the responsibility for the design and realisation of public service delivery to the private sector through long term contracting' (Reynaers and De Graaf, 2014: 120). This form of cooperation fits with ideas of privatization, responsibilization and multilateralization, often mentioned in private security research (Meerts, 2019b).

PPPs are not uncommon in the security field more generally, but they are less prevalent with regard to corporate investigations. The few examples that do exist focus on crimes that are committed from outside (and against) the organization, such as hacking, skimming, attacks on ATM machines (Dutch Banking Association, 2016) or insurance fraud.[3] Another example of a formalized, structural PPP is the Electronic Crimes Task Force (ECTF), which is a joint task force of the Dutch Public Prosecution Office, the Dutch Police organization and the major Dutch banks that is focused on digital crimes.

With regard to internal financial crimes specifically, interesting attempts towards formalized cooperation have been made with two pilot projects.[4] These pilot projects were focused specifically on private investigation firms and their possible contribution to a criminal justice procedure. Even though the pilot projects are generally considered to have been unsuccessful, they represent an interesting attempt to formalize the process in which private investigation firms participate in criminal justice investigations. Private investigation firms were to deliver a full investigative report to the police, who would then, with minimal effort, investigate further and send the case to the Public Prosecution Office to take to court (Friperson et al, 2013; Kuin and Wilms, 2015).

This is essentially the situation that already exists in practice on a more ad hoc basis. Even though the cooperation between public and private was considered fruitful in both pilot projects, an important side note is that while the word 'cooperation' is used, it is questionable whether this is justified. According to the evaluation report of the first pilot project, cooperation was limited to the alignment of the type of information necessary for a substantial report (Friperson et al, 2013).[5]

Ad hoc cooperation efforts

In the relative absence of formalized types of cooperation, many public–private relations revolving around internal financial crime remain ad hoc and rely on individual efforts of public and private investigators (Meerts, 2019a). These more fleeting public–private contacts may, however, take the form of a thorough cooperation, in which information is shared and actions are coordinated. Public–private contact most commonly is not very extensive, however. It often revolves around the transfer of information from corporate investigators to the criminal justice system, usually in the context of an official report to the police. This information transfer may be voluntary (information is provided as a result of a client's wish to report the crime) or may be obligatory (when information is subpoenaed by criminal justice actors through the use of powers of investigations). The contact between public and private is very limited in these cases and usually ends with the official report. In other instances, some information may flow from the criminal justice system to corporate investigators and clients. In this process of minor mutual information sharing, corporate investigators still provide the majority of information to law enforcement authorities, however, they also receive information in return. At the far-end of the spectrum of public–private cooperation we can find the actual cooperation. Here, actions are coordinated, information is shared on a near equal basis and the internal financial crime may be investigated as a joint effort (Meerts, 2019a).

The ad hoc public–private relations described here largely revolve around information sharing. In the above, information may be shared with regard to a specific case of financial crime, a specific suspect or a specific victim. In these cases, information sharing is often difficult as a result of different factors, an important one being legal regulations. However, public and private parties involved in the investigation of internal financial crime share more general information, such as new phenomena and modus operandi, in the different professional networks in which they are involved. In addition to these formal networks, informal networks between public and private investigators may be used to either receive information that one should not have, or to find a point of reference within an external organization. Both corporate investigators and police officers may use their personal and professional network in this way. This use of 'old boys networks' is often mentioned as a risk of the transfer of knowledge and personnel from the police to the private sector.[6] There have been cases of investigators abusing their informal network to illegally obtain information,[7] however, there is little evidence suggesting that this happens on a large scale (Klerks et al, 2001). Another use of informal contacts seems more prevalent: procedural questions may be posed within the informal network, helping a corporate investigator to find the best location to file a report (or conversely, a police officer to find a contact within an organization). The central points of reference within the Dutch Police organization may serve as a formalized alternative to this informal route. In addition to the central point of contact for expertise on financial crime ('Knooppunt FINEC'), recently, regional front offices for financial crime have been instated. Each regional police force has such a front office, which is meant to serve as an information point for both professionals within and outside of the Dutch Police organization (Politie, 2018). Whether or not they will actually serve this purpose of formalizing ad hoc contacts in practice is a question to be answered in future research.

Despite the aforementioned possibilities of public–private cooperation and information sharing, public and private largely remain in their separate sphere (Meerts, 2019b). In many cases, corporate investigators provide their clients with a report in which the results of the investigations are stated and on the basis of which further steps can be taken. The crime may be reported to law enforcement authorities, however, this is just one option – others being the use of the civil justice system, contract law, labour law or internal regulations. In this way, corporate investigators are often able to act independently from the criminal justice system, providing the organization faced with internal crime with the option of a solution that remains entirely in the private legal sphere and outside the view of the criminal justice system (Meerts, 2019a). In what follows, some reasons for this situation of separation are explicated.

Some complicating factors for cooperation

The nature of the corporate investigations market

There are some factors which, despite good intentions, complicate cooperation in practice. The first category of complicating factors involves the nature of the corporate investigations market. The second flows from changes in the (legal) context within which cooperation takes place. With regard to the nature of the corporate investigations market, we may return to the two pilot projects briefly described earlier. As mentioned, the pilot projects are generally considered to have been unsuccessful. This is mostly due to a very limited influx of cases. While there are procedural reasons for this low number of reported cases, it is also partly due to the logic of corporate investigations: many clients do not wish to report the crime to law enforcement authorities (Friperson et al, 2013).[8] This fact identifies a key reason why formalized, long-term cooperation between corporate investigators and the criminal justice system remains difficult. Corporate investigators work for clients, who are focused on their own interests. Even though common-good arguments may be involved in the decision whether or not to report, private interests often prevail. The willingness of corporate investigators to cooperate with law enforcement authorities thus largely depends on the client. This complication cannot be overcome by a formalized PPP structure, agreed upon between corporate investigators and law enforcement authorities, without involving the client whose interests are at stake.

Another factor that is connected to the nature of the corporate investigations market is its fragmented character. There are many corporate investigators, who work for many different clients. The agreement necessary for a successful PPP is very challenging to produce when there are so many players involved. Corporate investigators are not united in one representative organization – rather, different corporate investigators have different representative organizations. In addition, not all corporate investigators are part of a representative organization (Meerts, 2019a). Even if such an overarching representative organization would exist it would be difficult to unify the sector within a PPP. Apart from in-house investigators, corporate investigators work on contract basis for many different clients. This makes the nature of their work ad hoc and fragmented.

Changes within the (legal) context

A major change in the legal context within which the cooperation between public and private investigators takes place is the recent change in privacy regulation. As of May 2018, the EU-wide General Data Protection Regulation (GDPR) has come into force. The new privacy regulation has a major impact on the way organizations handle personal data, especially with regard to the administrative actions and safeguards that need to be taken. However strict the new regulation may appear, the GDPR still leaves room for the collection and processing of personal data. One of the reasons for processing personal data, defined as legitimate by the law, is the protection of a legitimate interest, such as the prevention of fraud. Principles of law such as proportionality and subsidiarity have an important function in the decision whether there is legitimate reason in a certain case (Schermer et al, 2018). Even though the GDPR leaves room to both collect and process personal data, and to come to public–private cooperation, it remains to be seen what the effects of the new legislation are. Preliminary fieldwork by the author suggests, however, that both law enforcement professionals and corporate investigators are wary of breaking the law. As a result, they tend to turn away from cooperation and information sharing, rather than towards it. This is not surprising and it fits with a wider tendency (especially among police officers), identified in earlier research, to be reluctant to share information. Knowledge of rules is often merely general, and the absence of detailed knowledge on what could be shared often leads to a situation in which nothing is shared (Van Ruth and Gunther Moor, 1997; Meerts, 2019a). It is too soon to tell what the effects of the GDPR are on public–private cooperation and related subjects such as whistleblowing, but initial information points towards it complicating cooperation (although the evidence is merely anecdotal at this point).

Another complicating factor is the major reorganization which has taken place in the Dutch Police. As mentioned previously, cooperation is largely dependent on individuals. Individual law enforcement actors (both police and prosecutors) who are willing to cooperate with corporate investigators and who have expertise on financial crime are essential to successful cooperation. With the reorganization, the structure of the Dutch Police organization has altered and people have been relocated. Respondents suggests that this makes it more difficult to find the right person. Interestingly, the introduction of the front offices for financial crime should provide a (formalized) entrance into the Dutch Police organization. Preliminary fieldwork by the author suggests, however, that the front offices are, as of yet, not widely known among corporate investigators.

The consequence of the separation that may be discerned in practice is that we lack a useful conceptual framework to further our understanding of public–private relations in the context of internal financial crime. The reason for this is that most existing literature assumes a blurring or convergence, in one shape or another, between public and private. In the conclusion to this chapter, I will turn my attention to this issue.

Conclusion

The earlier discussion provides a broad overview of public–private relations between the actors involved in the investigation and settlement of internal financial crime in the Netherlands. In this final section of the chapter, we return to the question posed in this volume: what is European about that? On the face of it maybe not that much. The processes discussed here occur throughout the world and are not unique to Europe. On a regulatory level – for example, with regard to the regulation of private investigator permits – there is even much diversity within Europe. What is distinctly European, however, is the (theoretical) approach towards public–private relations. While most European nation-states are a version of the welfare state model, in the public–private security debate a rhetoric is used that fits better with laissez-faire, market-driven economies. Privatization and responsibilization are tools for small and less interventional (neoliberal) governments to provide their population with security services (resulting in a shift from government to governance, see Garland, 1996). As Shearing (1992) has previously explained, the redefinition of private security as a 'junior partner' to the police (essentially responsibilizing the private sector) removed the threat it posed to the monopoly of violence held by the state. It is not surprising that this narrative is persistent in countries, such as the welfare states of Europe, that put emphasis on the importance of the state in the provision of public services (such as security). It is important to note, however, that this narrative has been developed in the context of security and safety (Sanders and Langan, 2019) but is too often uncritically applied to private investigations (the development of which has been quite different from private security more generally). Whether or not the narrative is successful with regard to private security in Europe is not a question that can be answered in this chapter, however, with regard to corporate investigations into internal financial crime we should be cautious with its application.

Anglo–American scholarship on public–private relations tends to emphasize the perceived blurring of boundaries between public and private security providers, into a hybrid form of security provision – be that through processes of privatization, responsibilization or multilateralization. In this context, an emphasis is placed on cooperation, joint efforts and security networks. Although on a more abstract level one might discern this kind of blurring, on an operational level the separation seems to hold strong (see Meerts, 2019b). Since much of the work of corporate investigators remains entirely out of sight of the criminal justice system, one may claim that public and private investigations into, and reactions to, internal financial crime are largely separate, albeit while overlapping in some instances. Using concepts such as responsibilization and multilateralization would, then, prove insufficient to grasp public–private relationships in the context of internal financial crime.

Looking at the context of internal financial crime within (European) companies, I believe our approach should shift focus from the state to private actors. Letting go of concepts that put emphasis on how private actors are used by state actors to further their own objectives allows us to investigate the potential of corporate investigators to (partly) address issues such as the transnational consequences of internal financial crime, as well as the potential for public–private cooperation. This is a pressing matter, since in the context of internal financial crime criminal justice actors are largely dependent on information provided by organizations who might have been the victim or the culprit of the crime.

For this, we need to be aware of the relative operational autonomy of the sector. However, such an approach flies in the face of much scholarship to date and requires both more empirical corroboration and academic debate. The approach advocated in this chapter is still in an early phase, however, it is important for European criminological scholarship to develop it further and open up the debate with Anglo–American scholars. One question to be posed in future is whether the mechanisms delineated in this chapter are distinctly (Western) European or whether the critique on the applicability of dominant concepts of privatization, responsibilization and multilateralization can also be applied to corporate investigations in other contexts.

Notes

[1] However, 'internal' is somewhat of a flexible category, often also including, for example, subcontractors.

[2] Mutual Legal Assistance Treaties and Memoranda of Understanding enable countries to share information and cooperate (Black et al, 2019). Cooperation also takes place through EU agencies such as Europol, Eurojust and the European Anti-Fraud Office, however, cooperation efforts between different national agencies often remains challenging. It will be interesting to see how the field develops after the European Public Prosecution Office becomes operational; see: https://ec.europa.eu/info/law/cross-border-cases/judicial-cooperation/networks-and-bodies-supporting-judicial-cooperation/european-public-prosecutors-office_en

[3] See: www.verzekeraars.nl/media/3328/kaderconvenant-samenwerking-aanpak-verzekeringsfraude-en-gerelateerde-criminaliteit-def.pdf

[4] Not all crimes included in this pilot project were internal to the organization.

[5] The aforementioned pilot project involving insurance fraud has a similar aim with regards to external crime.

[6] 'Moonlighting' by police officers as private investigators is not allowed under Dutch law, contrary to many US jurisdictions (see, for example, Stoughton, 2017).

[7] See, for example, ruling ECLI:NL:RBSGR:2004:AO9348 (2004) in the Court of The Hague, in which the judge ruled that a former police officer, now working as a private investigator, abused his network within the Dutch Police organization to illegally obtain information.

[8] For more on this, see Meerts (2019a). The decision not to report may work against the organization in the situation where the crime does come to light later on. This may be a consideration that compels the organization to report after all.

References

Black, C., Bowden, T., Coppens, K., Hodge, R. and Binding, C. (2019) 'The increasingly cooperative world of cross-border investigations', *Global Investigations Review – The Law and Practice of International Investigations*, [online] 10 June, Available at: https://globalinvestigationsreview.com/benchmarking/europe-the-middle-east-and-africa-investigations-review-2019/1193857/the-increasingly-cooperative-world-of-cross-border-investigations

De Waard, J.J. (1999) 'The private security industry in international perspective', *European Journal on Criminal Policy and Research*, 7: 143–74.

Dutch Banking Association (2016) *Factsheet Veiligheid en Fraude*, Amsterdam: Nederlandse Vereniging van Banken.

Friperson, R., Bouman, S. and Wilms, P. (2013) *Samen Opgespoord? Eindrapport "Pilot Samenwerking Particuliere Onderzoeksbureaus met Politie en OM"*, The Hague: WODC.

Garland, D. (1996) 'The limits of the sovereign state: strategies of crime control in contemporary society', *British Journal of Criminology*, 36(4): 445–71.

Gottschalk, P. (2016) 'Limits of private internal investigations of white-collar crime suspicions: the case of Scandinavian bank Nordea in tax havens', *Cogent Social Sciences*, 2(1): 1–14.

Gurinskay, A. and Nalla, M.K. (2018) 'The expanding boundaries of crime control: governing security through regulation', *The ANNALS of the American Academy of Political and Social Science*, 679(1): 36–54.

Jones, T. and Newburn, T. (2006) 'Understanding plural policing', in T. Jones and T. Newburn (eds) *Plural Policing. A Comparative Perspective*, Abingdon: Routledge, pp 1–11.

Klerks, P., Van Meurs, C. and Scholtes, M. (2001) *Particuliere Recherche: Werkwijzen en Informatiestromen*, The Hague: ES&E.

Kuin, M.C. and Wilms, P.J.M. (2015) *Publiek-Private Opsporing: Vele Handen Maken Licht Werk? Eindrapport Evaluatie Vervolgpilot Samenwerking Particuliere Onderzoeksbureaus met Politie en Openbaar Ministerie*, The Hague: WODC.

Meerts, C.A. (2018) 'The organisation as the cure for its own ailments: corporate investigators in the Netherlands', *Administrative Sciences*, 8(3): 106–20.

Meerts, C.A. (2019a) *Corporate Investigations, Corporate Justice and Public-Private Relations: Towards a New Conceptualisation*, London: Palgrave Macmillan.

Meerts, C.A. (2019b) 'Corporate investigations: beyond notions of public-private relations', *Journal of Contemporary Criminal Justice,* 36(1): 86–100.

National Office for Serious Fraud, Environmental Crime and Asset Confiscation [Functioneel Parket] (2018) 'ING betaalt 775 miljoen vanwege ernstige nalatigheden bij voorkomen witwassen', Available at: www.om.nl/@103953/ing-betaalt-775/

Politie (2018) 'Jaarverantwoording politie 2017', Available at: www.politie.nl/binaries/content/assets/politie/jaarverslag/2017/jaarverantwoording-2017.pdf

PricewaterhouseCoopers (2019) *Economic Crime Survey Nederland 2019*, Amsterdam: PricewaterhouseCoopers.

Reynaers, A. and De Graaf, G. (2014) 'Public values in public-private partnerships', *International Journal of Public Administration,* 37: 120–28.

Rooseboom, S.J., Driessen, F.M.H.M. and Völker, B.G.M. (2006) *Regionale Platforms Criminaliteitsbeheersing, een Evaluatie*, The Hague: WODC.

Sanders, C.B. and Langan, D. (2019) 'New public management and the extension of police control: community safety and security networks in Canada', *Policing and Society*, 29(5): 566–78.

Schermer, B.W., Hagenauw, D. and Falot, N. (2018) *Handleiding Algemene Verordening Gegevensbescherming*, The Hague: Ministerie van Justitie en Veiligheid.

Shearing, C.D. (1992) 'The relation between public and private policing', *Crime and Justice: A Review of Research*, 15: 399–434.

Stoughton, S.W. (2017) 'Moonlighting: the private employment of off-duty officers', *University of Illinois Law Review,* 2017: 1848–1900.

Van Dijk, F. and De Waard, J.J. (2001) *Publieke en Private Veiligheidszorg, Nationale en Internationale Trends*, The Hague: Ministerie van Justitie.

Van Ruth, A. and Gunther Moor, L. (1997) *Lekken of Verstrekken? De Informele Informatie-Uitwisseling Tussen Opsporingsdiensten en Derden*, Ubbergen: Uitgeverij Tandem Felix.

White, A. (2014) 'Politics, economics and security', in M. Gill (ed) *The Handbook of Security*, London: Palgrave Macmillan, pp 89–106.

12

Cartel Cases: From State Negligence to Direct Political Interest in Hungary

Éva Inzelt and Tamás Bezsenyi

Introduction

The aim of this chapter is to elucidate the characteristics of cartels as a type of corporate crime in Hungary and consider the implications of such corporate crimes for the European region. In 1990, 40 years of socialist rule in Hungary ended. The former regime was a one-party system and planned economy with a hegemonic Marxist-Leninist ideological framework. This change moved the country towards a capitalist society based upon parliamentary democracy, a market economy, social, cultural and political pluralism, the protection of human rights and membership in the political, economic and military organizations of the 'Western' countries.

Corporate crime has been on the rise since the change of regime. Different forms of white-collar crimes had always existed under all of the previous political and economic systems in Hungary, but the transition period produced special opportunities for white-collar criminal activities, mostly for those who were close to the political parties and/or had good connections with the establishment (Inzelt, 2015). Several cases of corporate crime in Hungary that occurred between 1989 and 2000 have been analyzed in detail, such as the bank scandals involving Ybl Bank, Lupis brokerage, Agrobank and Postabank, the conversion of the Hungarian Venture Development Foundation, privatization irregularities, criminal bankruptcy and phantomization of firms,[1] fraudulent reclaiming of VAT, the so-called 'Energol case',[2] healthcare insurance fraud, cartels and the corruption of politicians (see Inzelt, 2011).

It is of the utmost importance to understand the circumstances which promote cartels and corporate crime, as cartel-associated behaviours, such as restrictive agreements and unfair competition practices, generate significant harms to the morals of society and to victim organizations (those businesses which lose out due to cartel activities), as well as damaging public confidence (Jávor and Jancsics, 2013). More specifically, this chapter explores and elucidates the complex interrelationships between corporate crime and the functioning of the Hungarian market economy (Tóth, 1995).

In Hungary, European competition law has been implemented into the legal system. The Hungarian Competition Authority (HCA) and the Hungarian courts have to apply EU competition law to all restrictive agreements and dominant abuses applied (or applied in parallel) by Hungarian competition law and which may affect trade between EU member states. The effect of trade among EU member states is a complex topic, which means that conduct can have an actual, potential, indirect or direct impact on competition in an international dimension. Therefore, the European Commission (EC) can also investigate cartel cases. The EC has the right to take action against EU member states in order to enforce European Community competition law and to initiate infringement proceedings against the concerned member state before the European Court of Justice. The EC can investigate and punish such matters independently of the Hungarian procedures.

With this in mind, this chapter analyzes cartel cases from the HCA to answer the following core question: what is the role of the state in responding to cartel cases and in ensuring freedom of competition in the market? Our analysis reveals that the state has different approaches to dealing with corporate crime like cartels. In some cases, the state itself initiates the cartel (see the watermelon case, later on), in other incidents, the state facilitates the process (see the cash register case, later on). In light of such state involvement, this chapter draws on the theoretical framework of 'state-corporate crime' (Aulette and Michalowski, 1993) to inform our contribution. Based on the authors' own research, it can be seen that the circumvention of EU legislation on unfair and restrictive market practices is a kind of Hungarian specialty. However, ideas for circumventing competition rules that operate under similar state regulations may arise in other EU countries. Thus, based on an examination of cases from different periods in Hungary after the change of regime in 1989–90, and including different types of markets and companies (small, medium, multinational), it is our contention that connections between state regulations and the regulatory agencies' practices assists – directly or indirectly – cartel cases in Hungary.

Defining cartels

The EC defines cartels as a group of similar, independent companies which join together to fix prices, limit production or share markets or customers between them. Article 101 of the Treaty on the Functioning of the European Union (TFEU) prohibits agreements between companies which prevent, restrict or distort competition in the EU, and which may affect trade between member states (anti-competitive agreements). These include, for example, price fixing or market sharing cartels. Anti-competitive agreements are prohibited regardless of whether they are concluded between companies that operate at the same level of the supply chain (horizontal agreements) or at different levels (vertical agreements).

The Organisation for Economic Co-operation and Development (OECD) defines cartelism as 'an anticompetitive agreement, anticompetitive concerted practice, or anticompetitive arrangement by competitors to fix prices, make rigged bids (collusive tenders), establish output restrictions or quotas, or share or divide markets by allocating customers, suppliers, territories or lines of commerce' (Organisation for Economic Co-operation and Development, 1998). Similarly, the International Competition Network states that the main forms of cartelism are as follows: an agreement between competitors to restrict competition through price fixing, output restrictions, market allocation or bid rigging (International Competition Network, 2005).

According to the HCA, restrictive agreements can be both horizontal agreements (between competitors) and vertical agreements (between undertakings operating on different levels of the production and distribution chain, for example, between manufacturers and distributors). Restricting competition is prohibited and corresponding agreements void according to the Hungarian Competition Act (Act LVII of the Prohibition of Unfair and Restrictive Market Practices 1996). Agreements between competitors deemed of minor importance (that is, when the joint market share of the participating undertakings does not exceed ten per cent) are not prohibited, and where the undertakings engaged in are not independent of each other, their agreement does not qualify as restrictive under the Competition

Act (Hungarian Competition Authority, 2020). This regulation is basically in harmony with the EU Market Abuse Regulation. The interesting part of that picture is that the HCA stipulates that European Community competition law is directly applicable to Hungarian undertakings as well. The effect on trade between member states is a complex question. The practice of the HCA to use the European competition regulations can vary case by case.

The legal background of the operation and the applicable law of the HCA

The HCA is – in theory – an autonomous public administrative authority safeguarding freedom and fairness of competition in the market. It reports directly to the Hungarian Parliament. The HCA began operation on 1 January 1990 when Act LXXXVI of the Prohibition of Unfair Market Practices 1990 entered into force. The most recent and currently effective version of the Competition Act (it has been amended several times), Act LVII of the Prohibition of Unfair and Restrictive Market Practices 1996, entered into force on 1 January 1997. The Competition Act defines the rules of Hungarian competition law, the legal status of the HCA, its organizational and operational framework and its proceedings. Hungary's accession to the EU represented a turning point in the history of the authority. It resulted in the HCA becoming a member of the European Competition Network. It also meant that the HCA had to start to apply EU competition law (Hungarian Competition Authority, 2014). The Competition Act contains general prohibitions on unfair competition, though certain practices are listed, such as the disparagement of competitors, the unfair acquisition or making use of business secrets, boycott appeals, imitation and the infringing of the fairness of any bidding process.

The most harmful restrictive agreements are those of the so-called 'hard core cartels'. These agreements stipulate direct or indirect fixing of purchase or sale prices or other business terms and conditions that redefine the allocation of the market. It is worth mentioning that the most harmful type of cartel is regulated not just by the Competition Act, but also by the Criminal Act (Act C of the Hungarian Criminal Code 2012), which has been in force since 1 September 2005. According to the Criminal Act, bid rigging agreements in restraint of competition in public procurement and concession procedures are penalized. It prohibits: a) any agreement that restricts competition in a public procurement or concession tender procedure by fixing the prices (fees) and other contractual terms and conditions or by market sharing for the purpose of manipulating the outcome of the tender, and b) concerted activities, or participation in decision making, by an association of undertakings in order to restrict competition. The Criminal Act qualifies the above acts as crimes, punishable with imprisonment of one to five years. In our view, this means that hard core cartels that are dangerous to society should also be prosecuted under the criminal law. Unfortunately, in cases of agreement in restraint of competition in public procurement and concession procedures there have been no criminal investigations for years.

The initiation of competition supervision proceedings that examine competitive conduct is not the only means that the HCA has at its disposal to promote competition. It can also collect general information about the competitive process in a given sector or on a given market. The Competition Act authorizes the president of the HCA to order a sectoral inquiry if market processes in a given sector suggest that the competitive process in the sector is restricted or distorted. In the course of the inquiry, a report is made as a result of the detailed analysis of the information collected from the market participants. The implementation of sectoral inquiries is not unknown in European practice, as the EC also has the right to use sectoral inquiries to bring to light competitive problems in certain markets.

One recent European sectoral inquiry was in connection with a dominant gas supplier in Central and Eastern Europe. On 24 May 2018, the EC adopted a decision (European Commission, 2018a) removing obstacles created by the Russian majority state-owned energy corporation Gazprom which affected free flow of gas in Central and Eastern Europe and imposing on Gazprom a set of obligations for its future conduct. Gazprom is the dominant gas supplier in a number of Central and Eastern European countries. In April 2015, the EC set out its concerns that Gazprom breached EU antitrust rules by pursuing an overall strategy to partition gas markets along national borders in eight member states: Bulgaria, the Czech Republic, Estonia, Hungary, Latvia, Lithuania, Poland and Slovakia. This strategy enabled Gazprom to charge higher gas prices in five of these member states (Bulgaria, Estonia, Latvia, Lithuania and Poland). To address the EC's competition concerns, Gazprom was asked to comply with a set of obligations aimed at ensuring the free flow of gas at competitive prices across Central and Eastern Europe. These obligations on Gazprom will be in place for eight years. They reflect feedback from stakeholders in a market test, which the EC launched in March 2017.

There are four parts to Gazprom's obligations. First, Gazprom's customers are no longer restricted from reselling purchased gas across national borders. Second, they have more flexibility on where they want Gazprom to deliver their gas (some parts of Central and Eastern Europe, namely the Baltic states and Bulgaria, are still isolated from other member states due to the lack of interconnectors). Third, customers receive an effective tool to make sure their gas price reflects the price level in competitive Western European gas markets, especially at liquid gas hubs. Fourth, Gazprom cannot act on any advantages concerning gas infrastructure. Combined, these obligations address the EC's competition concerns and contribute to its objectives of enabling the free flow of gas in Central and Eastern Europe at competitive prices. The EC decided to make these obligations (so-called 'commitments') legally binding on Gazprom, which means that if the company breaks any of these obligations, the EC can impose a fine of up to 10 per cent of Gazprom's worldwide turnover.

European Community competition law

European Community competition law is directly applicable to Hungarian undertakings since the country's accession to the EU. The competition rules laid down in Articles 81 and 82 of the Treaty Establishing the European Community (hereafter the Treaty) prohibit, in respect to the common market, the conclusion of agreements that restrict competition, as well as the abuse of a dominant position. In case there is a suspicion of infringement, the HCA is authorized and also obliged to apply European Community law (namely to start proceedings against the supposed infringement of European Community competition law, which may affect trade between member states), where it would apply Hungarian competition law for the supposed infringement of its provisions. In the proceedings, the HCA applies as substantive law Articles 81 and 82 of the Treaty, secondary European Community legislation (regulations and EC notices), furthermore, the legal principles arising from the decision making practice of the EC and the case law of the European Court of Justice. European Community law is applied in procedures that are governed by the procedural law laid down in the Competition Act, while the substantive provisions of the Competition Act may be applied in parallel with the substantive European Community rules. In applying the competition provisions of the Treaty, the members of the European Competition Network cooperate closely in order to ensure the efficiency and uniformity of law enforcement.

Previous criminological studies on cartels

In order to understand the nature and structure of cartels we need to learn what causes the existence of cartels in general. Previous criminological studies emphasize the fact that different motives and opportunities facilitate individuals and/or organizations to get involved in cartel agreements. According to Geis (1987: 130) the following factors promote cartels: 'the avoidance of uncertainty, the formalization and predictability of outcome, the minimization of risk'. We agree with Benson and Simpson (2009) that high barriers for market entry, a low number of players in the market (high market concentration) and homogeneity of products can be seen as opportunities for cartel agreements. Jaspers (2020: 116) points out that 'business people can find competition law abstract and complex or might not support the moral wrongfulness of cartel conduct'. He also emphasizes that cartels are integrated in traditions within certain markets and cartelists have internalized justifications of their practices in the market (Jaspers, 2020: 121).

The core theoretical frame of our analysis is the concept of state-corporate crime, which refers to illegal or socially injurious social actions that are the collective product of interaction between a business corporation and a state agency engaged in a joint endeavour (Kramer and Michalowski, 1990). The state has different approaches to dealing with corporate crime, like cartels, which will clearly be visible in the three cases evaluated in the following. We analyze how different state regulations have changed and how these changes related to cartel cases. We see who, or what factors, can influence the outcome of an investigation of a cartel according to the Hungarian practice. The following cases illustrate the attitude and the interest of the state to respond or not to a cartel. These cases are typical examples of the different approaches of the state towards investigating cartels.

Case Study 1: The sale and servicing of cash registers in Hungary

Introducing the market for the sale and servicing of cash registers, we uncover the failures of state involvement and the limits of its possible control. The HCA conducted major investigations against cash register companies. We present how state negligence after the regime change resulted in cartelism.

The first chosen case was initiated against György Sipos, who worked as a service technician in the field of cash registers (Hungarian

Competition Authority, 2000). At the beginning of the 1990s, Mikrosystem, a small corporation, later transformed to a limited liability company, dealt with the distribution of cash registers. It was accompanied by the development of a service network that operated in accordance with the relevant Hungarian Tax and Financial Control Office (APEH) regulations. With the approval of the APEH, the 18-member service network was responsible for the distribution, commissioning and servicing of approximately 4,000 imported cash registers, either CASIO 108 SR and 109 SR models or models manufactured by BEKO.

In Budapest and Pest county, four companies, one of which belonged to György Sipos, were eligible to operate within this service network. In the meantime, the import of these types of machines ceased. The number of machines was also decreasing as a result of scrapping and the usability of the cash registers. At the end of 2000, there were approximately 250,000 cash registers for consumer use, with 320 service repair agents. On 1 January 1996, regulatory changes on cash register use and provision came into force. The Ministry of Finance decreed that only APEH-authorized cash register distributors could operate in the market. Mikrosystem was liquidated in June 1997, but it had to take care of servicing the sold cash registers. Therefore, on 18 June 1997, the liquidator appointed Sipos as an exclusive after-sales service provider responsible for servicing those registers and, in accordance with current legislation and the rules of the APEH, notified to the National Cash Register and Taxameter Technical Committee. The APEH Committee informed the liquidator on 7 August 1997, approving the exclusive right of Sipos and the non-exclusive right of the E51 Deposit Company, but added it to the national service list. Thus, only these two actors of the cash registers in question were eligible for servicing because the other 16 service centres were no longer considered eligible to conduct repairs by the APEH. The service network was not officially informed of the decision of the APEH, and in mid-1999 it became apparent that the right to lawfully service cash registers could only be obtained with the assistance of György Sipos – who was granted the right and obligation of the 1997 approved service selection right (Hungarian Competition Authority, 2000).

Many (at least 50) companies were contacted to sign a contract with György Sipos. Sipos established his 34-member network (including himself and the E51 Limited Partnership)on the basis of his own judgement and connections. He signed a contract with 13 out of the 16 formerly authorized service providers. Sipos remained as a service technician, mainly in Budapest and Pest county. In order to offset his own economic role, he also commissioned two other companies to work in these two areas. György Sipos, in his capacity as a contractor, contractually ensured that the selected companies could perform their repair tasks (course maintenance, documentation, provision of parts and other relevant aspects) (Hungarian Competition Authority, 2000). Due to the aforementioned events, the state effectively gave Sipos a monopoly on servicing cash registers.

The network created by György Sipos has become an element of state revenue control with the APEH approving Sipo's selections. The HCA, on the basis of the Unfair Market Competition Act, initiated proceedings against Sipos for the abuse of a dominant position. The outcome of the proceeding considered the infringement to be of a minor nature, which it considered to be eligible for the award of contracts to the victims of the competition violations.

This case clearly falls under the term state-facilitated corporate crime (or state-facilitated cartel), which occurs when a certain government regulatory institution, in this case the Hungarian Tax and Financial Control Office, fails to restrain deviant business activities, either because of direct collusion between business and government or because they adhere to shared goals whose attainment would be hampered by aggressive regulation (Michalowski and Kramer, 2007). State-corporate crime, as defined previously, involves the active participation of two or more organizations, at least one of which is private and one of which is public, which contribute towards the harmful result of an interorganizational relationship between business and government (Kramer and Michalowski, 1990). This corporate involvement intertwines with governmental policy and political intention. State-corporate crime is a relatively recent and contemporary concept, which is becoming increasingly relevant in a more globalized and business-centric political era, but crimes stemming from the relationship between policies of the state and policies and practices of commercial corporations can be identified long before it was academically titled as such, as we have seen in the case of György Sipos.

To further establish the aforementioned definitions, Friedrichs (2010) created a five-point typology of state-corporate crimes. He separated the wide-ranging phenomenon into state-initiated corporate crimes, state-facilitated corporate crimes, corporate-initiated states crimes, corporate-facilitated state crimes and those that are the consequence of collusion and corruption (Friedrichs, 2010: 1–33). Within this detailed typology, initiation suggests that crimes were committed at the direction, or with the tacit approval, of the initiator. The claim being that economic inequality clearly intrudes into the realm of political governance and therefore there is neither economics nor politics, political economy (Kramer and Michalowski, 2007). In order to attempt an explanation of state-corporate crime, it is crucially important to first examine the state-created social conditions that promote state-corporate crime. An anti-regulatory, pro-business climate enables corporations to avoid prosecution while their pursuit of wealth is encouraged by the state, regardless of potential wider implications.

Case Study 2: Cartels without direct state intervention – cartel circles in the insurance market

The following case illustrates how the HCA deals with cartels if the participants are multinational companies, with a particular focus on multinational enterprises that have misused their dominant position in the insurance market. The investigation of the HCA into this case was very delicate because the involved companies provide special services, which are determined by EU legislation. In its decision of 21 December 2006, the Competition Council of the HCA concluded that Allianz Hungária Biztosító, Generali-Providencia Biztosító, the Hungarian Association of Automotive Dealers (GÉMOSZ), Hungarian Peugeot Dealers Insurance Brokers, Hungarian Opel Sales Brokers and Porsche Biztosítási Alkusz had been restricting competition over the preceding few years. The relationship among the aforementioned actors was based on formal relationships between insurance and automotive repair companies. Hungarian insurance companies, including Allianz and Generali-Providencia, agreed once a year on the terms and conditions applicable to the repair services to be paid by the insurer in the event of damage to insured vehicles by their repairers and their national association. These car repair workshops carried out repairs directly, on the basis of terms and fees approved by the insurer (Hungarian Competition Authority, 2005). The HCA, after finding that the agreements in question were restrictive of competition in the car insurance and car repair services markets, prohibited the continuation of anti-competitive conduct and imposed fines on the companies concerned.

The affected companies contested the result of the procedure in the Hungarian courts. The Hungarian Supreme Court, as part of the formal review procedure, waited until 2013 for the decision of the European Court of Justice to determine whether the agreements in question were intended to exclude, restrict or distort competition in the market. In its judgment, the European Court of Justice recalled that agreements for that purpose are prohibited without the need to examine their effects on competition. The final judgment of the European Court of Justice established the liability of the parties. In addition, they stipulated the clear connections and the common interests between insurance and car repair firms in this case.

The European Court of Justice then found that the agreements in question combined two, in principle, independent activities, namely remuneration for the repair of damaged motor vehicles and remuneration of car insurance. In that regard, the court emphasized that, although the link between the two activities was established, that did not automatically imply that the agreements in question were restrictive of competition, but may still have constituted an important element in assessing whether, by their nature, those agreements were detrimental to the proper functioning of normal competition. In that regard, the court noted that, although these were vertical agreements, that is to say, between non-competing undertakings, they may have had the object of restricting competition (European Court of Justice, 2013).

The court further stated that the purpose of the agreements was to be assessed in light of the two concerned markets. Due to this aspect, the court pointed out that the Hungarian Supreme court had to examine – in view of the economic and legal context in which the vertical agreements are compatible – whether particular agreements were sufficiently detrimental to competition in the car insurance market in order to qualify as a targeted restriction of competition. This was particularly the case where vehicle dealers acted as intermediaries or insurance brokers. According to the European Court of Justice, Hungarian law requires that such brokers maintain independence from insurance companies (European Court of Justice, 2013). In addition, the anti-competitive intention of these agreements had been proven even if competition was likely to be eliminated or significantly weakened in the vehicle insurance market as a result of the conclusion of the agreements in question.

The European Court of Justice concluded that the Hungarian courts had to take into account the fact that these agreements were concluded on the basis of decisions by GÉMOSZ. The so-called 'recommended' (that is, fixed) prices were provided by the car repair companies as part of the agreements in question in the context of the market for vehicle repair services ('Tiltott megállapodásokat kötöttek az autójavítók és a biztosítók', 2013). The Hungarian Supreme Court decided that the agreements in question were unlawful. In their judgment they concluded that insurance companies directly cooperated with GÉMOSZ. The significance of the investigation in the insurance market was not merely a huge fine but the acceptance of the fact that European competition law takes responsibility to create accurate findings for courts of the member states (European Court of Justice, 2013).

Case Study 3: A cartel case resulting from political gain (state-initiated cartelism)

This final case study involves a cartel case in which, due to the social status of the actors involved, the procedure of the HCA was questioned. The members of the governing party handled the investigation of the HCA unethically, in what could be considered to be a violation of national values. The case investigated Gyula Budai, the state secretary at the Ministry of Rural Development, for giving state aid to Hungarian watermelon producers. The result being that while primary producers did not voluntarily set up a price cartel, with the involvement of a state actor they enjoyed the equivalent benefits. The Ministry of Rural Development in the summer of 2012 agreed with major retail store networks that in their shops the per kilo prices of watermelon would not go below 99 Hungarian forints (approximately 33 euro cents). With this gesture of the government, the cheap resale of imported watermelons, arriving to Hungary, was impossible. Due to the issue of import shipments, compliance with the requirements of EU regulation, in addition to domestic competition law, has also become questionable ('Itt az állami kérésre született dinnyekartell', 2012).

In this particular case, the newspapers quickly raised the question of whether the Competition Authority had just launched a procedure to avoid EU-wide investigation. To make EU competition law more effective, the EC facilitated cooperation within the European Competition Network (ECN). In this particular case, the HCA launched a competitive oversight procedure for ALDI Hungary Food Co., Auchan Magyarország Kft., CBA Commercial Ltd., Lidl Magyarország Kereskedelmi Bt., SPAR Magyarország Kereskedelmi Ltd., and TESCO-GLOBAL Department Stores. Ltd., as well as the Hungarian Melon Association and the Hungarian Vegetable-Fruit Intergovernmental Organization and Product Board. The accusation being that these parties had agreed on the prices of watermelons grown in Hungary from mid-July 2012. Furthermore, that they had concurred that watermelons produced outside of Hungary would not be marketed, or only at a discriminatory price (Hungarian Competition Authority, 2012). In the autumn of 2012, the Hungarian Parliament amended the so-called Inter-Professional Law.[3] According to this new legislation, in cartel proceedings concerning agricultural products, the HCA is required to seek the opinion of the Minister for Rural Development on the applicability of domestic competition law and may only proceed on the basis of that position. This regulation is a clear violation of EU competition law.

Correlations in cartel cases following the change of regime

On the basis of the watermelon cartel case, the possibilities and spirit of European and national competition law can be clearly demonstrated. The Ministry of Rural Development, together with the government, has put in place regulations that will continue to provide opportunities for price cartels in the field of agricultural products. This was a case of a state-initiated corporate crime/state-initiated cartel, which occurs when corporations, employed by the government, engage in organizational deviance at the direction of or with the tacit approval of the government (Kramer and Michalowski, 2007). The concept in its modern form seeks to bridge concepts of economic crimes and political crimes by creating a new lens through which the ways crimes and social injuries often emerge from intersections of economic and political power can be examined (Kramer and Michalowski, 2007). With economic crimes, economics and politics are often inseparable in relation to their aims and ambitions and regularly collaborate to achieve success. Economists need political actors to enable them act in ways which provide them with the best opportunity to prosper from the societal conditions; a structured legal framework may allow or forbid certain activity, but providing corporate criminality is met with the states seal of approval, there are few regulatory institutions capable of intervening. Politicians require economists to provide them with wealth, bargaining leverage and power, meaning investment can be focused and calculated.

In the 1990s, the Hungarian cartel cases were able to develop due to the negligence of state actors and regulators. In the years following Hungary's accession to the EU, the HCA has been successful in dealing with giant companies dealing with services, and serious fines have been imposed on companies with foreign backgrounds. After transformation of the national economy, following the change of the government in 2010, state-initiated cartel cases appeared. We can clearly state that these corporate crimes arose based on political purposes, rather than the criminogenic effect of the capitalist economy, which we have experienced from 1990, after the change of regime, until 2010. In

Hungary, in the past twenty years, we have reached from cartel cases arising from state negligence to cartel cases implemented by the state in order to protect certain market participants. In the 1990s, the state was negligent with regards to its regulation of the cash register market. Thanks to the goals set for the post-2010 national economy, the state itself has consciously developed possible cartel cases in the field of agricultural products. Based on our own research, it can be seen that the circumvention of EU legislation on unfair and restrictive market practices is a kind of Hungarian specialty. However, ideas for circumventing competition rules that operate under similar state regulations may arise in other EU countries.

Conclusion

The main focus of this chapter was on the role of the state in responding to cartel cases and in ensuring freedom of competition in the market. Analyzing three types of cases demonstrated that the state has different approaches to dealing with cartels. In some cases, the state itself initiated the cartel (the watermelon case study), in other incidents, the state facilitated the process (the cash registers case study), while in the case of foreign multinational companies (the insurance firms case study) the reaction from the state was strict.

Political elites rarely act without the prompting or support of at least some economic elites (Kramer and Michalowski, 2007), and in which both parties have something to gain. We can clearly examine this in the watermelon case. When considered through a lens of self-interest and dominance, government elites are able to enhance resources, suppress resistance and strengthen repression through state-corporate crime while corporate elites are able to take advantage of favourable market conditions, limited competition and cheap business (see the cash register case study). The mutual benefits and maintenance of power that state-corporate crime entails are major reasons for its regularity and continuance. More research into state-corporate crimes would potentially help us to prevent their occurrence: through trend identification, pinpointing responsible involvement and raising awareness of their proportional harm.

There are two overriding problems with legislation, which from a criminal perspective appear to complement each other and open the environment for the emergence of state-corporate crime. Using regulatory rather than criminal law systems to address harms caused by corporate and governmental elites reflects the interests of those actors, political and corporate, that the system was intended to control (see

Pearce, 1976). Regulatory laws result in far less serious sanctions and penalties, therefore offering white-collar criminals the chance to avoid life-altering punishment. It is possible that the elites encouraged this move to avoid more invasive laws or even to ensure that the regulatory law would have little or no effect on their covert operations, due to its application only being available within such narrow parameters.

Notes

[1] The expression 'phantomization' of firms means after the bankruptcy of a firm with a substantial debt the firm was sold legally with the participation of a lawyer's office, however, the purchaser used a false identification (sometimes they used stolen passports).

[2] The state – for reasons connected to social policy – had for a long time subsidized oil used as fuel in burners for heating by selling it at a lower price. They colorized it by adding a dye, however, it was very easy to remove by a treatment with sulfuric acid; as such, there was a great opportunity for abuse. The oil importer Energol was found to be involved in illegal tampering and resale of subsidized oil.

[3] Act CXXVIII on interbranch organizations and certain issues of agricultural market regulation 2012 (so-called: Inter-Professional Law).

Acknowledgements

The project is supported by the National Research, Development and Innovation Office (no. FK 124968).

References

Aulette, J.R. and Michalowski, R. (1993) 'Fire in Hamlet: a case study of state-corporate crime', in K.D. Tunnell (ed) *Political Crime in Contemporary America: A Critical Approach*, New York: Garland, pp 171–206.

Benson, M.L. and Simpson, S.S. (2009) *White-Collar Crime: An Opportunity Perspective,* New York: Routledge.

European Commission (2013) 'Procedures in anticompetitive agreements', Available at: https://ec.europa.eu/competition/antitrust/procedures_101_en.html

European Commission (2018a) 'Commission decision: case 39816: upstream gas supplies in Central and Eastern Europe', Available at: http://ec.europa.eu/competition/elojade/isef/case_details.cfm?proc_code=1_39816

European Commission (2018b), 'Report on competition policy', Available at: https://ec.europa.eu/competition/publications/annual_report/2018/part1_en.pdf

European Court of Justice (2013) 'Case C–32/11: judgement of the court', Available at: http://curia.europa.eu/juris/document/document.jsf?docid=135021&text=&dir=&doclang=EN&part=1&occ=first&mode=lst&pageIndex=0&cid=5037779

Friedrichs, D.O. (2010) *Trusted Criminals: White Collar Crime in Contemporary Society*, Belmont: Wadsworth Cengage Learning.

Geis, G. (1987) 'White collar crime: the heavy electrical equipment antitrust cases of 1961', in M.D. Ermann and R.J. Lundmann (eds) *Corporate and Governmental Deviance: Problems of Organizational Behavior in Contemporary Society*, New York: Oxford University Press, pp 139–56.

Hungarian Competition Authority (2000) 'Case no. Vj-6/2000/9: proceedings of the Hungarian Competition Authority', Available at: www.gvh.hu/dontesek/versenyhivatali_dontesek/dontesek_2000/2537_hu_vj-620009.html

Hungarian Competition Authority (2005) 'Case no. Vj-51/2005/184: proceedings of the Hungarian Competition Authority', Available at: www.gvh.hu//data/cms1022542/Vj051_2005_m.pdf

Hungarian Competition Authority (2012) 'Case no. Vj-62/2012: proceedings of the Hungarian Competition Authority', Available at: www.gvh.hu//data/cms994461/Vj062_2012_VV_jo.pdf

Hungarian Competition Authority (2014) 'Amit a Gazdasági Versenyhivatalról tudni kell', Available at: www.gvh.hu/data/cms1026781/GVH_vkk_kiadvanyok_amit_a_gvh_rol_tudni_kell_2014_03.pdf

Hungarian Competition Authority (2019) 'Restrictive agreements', Available at: www.gvh.hu/en/legal_background/rules_for_the_hungarian_market/competition_act/restrictive_agreements

International Competition Network Group on Cartels (2005) *Defining Hard Core Cartels Conduct, Effective Institutions, Effective Penalties*, Bonn: European Communities ICN.

Inzelt, É. (2011) 'White-collar crime during the political and economic transition in Hungary', *US-China Law Review*, 8: 359–79.

Inzelt, É. (2015) 'White collar crime in countries of transition: the lesson of Hungary', in J. van Erp, W. Huisman and G. Vande Walle (eds) *The Routledge Handbook of White-Collar and Corporate Crime in Europe*, Abingdon: Routledge, pp 182–97.

'Itt az állami kérésre született dinnyekartell' (2012) *Index.hu*, [online] 19 July, Available at: https://index.hu/gazdasag/magyar/2012/07/19/legalis_kartell_allami_keresre/

Jaspers, J.D. (2020) 'Leniency in exchange for cartel confessions', *European Journal of Criminology*, 17(1): 106–24.

Jávor, I. and Jancsics, D. (2013) 'The role of power in organizational corruption: an empirical study', *Administration & Society*, 48(5): 527–58.

Kramer, R.C. and Michalowski, R. (1990) 'Toward an integrated theory of state-corporate crime', paper presented at the American Society of Criminology, 9 November, Baltimore, MD.

Michalowski, R.J. and Kramer, R.C. (2007) 'State-corporate crime and criminological inquiry', in H. Pontell and G. Geis (eds) *International Handbook of White-Collar and Corporate Crime,* Boston: Springer, pp 200–15.

Organisation for Economic Co-operation and Development (OECD) (1998) 'Recommendation of the OECD Council concerning effective action against hard core cartels', Available at: www.oecd. org/daf/competition/2350130.pdf

OECD (2019) 'Recommendation of the Council concerning effective action against hard core cartels', Available at: https://legalinstruments. oecd.org/en/instruments/OECD-LEGAL-0452/

Pearce, F. (1976) *Crimes of the Powerful: Marxism, Crime, and Deviance,* London: Pluto Press.

'Tiltott megállapodásokat kötöttek az autójavítók és a biztosítók' (2013) *Napi.hu*, [online] 14 March, Available at: www.napi.hu/magyar_ vallalatok/tiltott_megallapodasokat_kotottek_az_autojavitok_es_a_ biztositok.547954.html

Tóth, M. (1995) 'Piacgazdaság és büntetőjog', in M. Lévay (ed) *A Piacgazdaság Kiépülése és a Gazdasági Bűnözés*, Budapest: Magyar Kriminológiai Társaság, pp 4–35.

PART IV

Responding to White-Collar Crimes in Europe

Silencing Those Who Speak Up against Corporate Power: Strategic Lawsuits against Public Participation (SLAPPs) in Europe

Judith van Erp and Tess van der Linden

Introduction

On 31 May 2016, Resolute Forest Products, a Canadian pulp and paper manufacturer, filed suit against Greenpeace and Stand.earth, environmental organizations that had been engaged in a campaign against Resolute regarding its allegedly unsustainable forestry activities. Resolute accused Greenpeace of racketeering under the United States' Racketeer Influenced and Corrupt Organizations (RICO) Act, arguing that Greenpeace is a criminal enterprise. Resolute claimed that Greenpeace is a 'global fraud' and that it has 'fraudulently induced people throughout the United States and the world to donate millions of dollars based on materially false and misleading claims about its purported environmental purpose and its "campaigns" against targeted companies'. According to Resolute, 'maximizing donations, not saving the environment, is Greenpeace's true objective'.[1] After a long legal battle in which the case was transferred to the Northern District of California, the US District Court for the Northern District of California dismissed the RICO charges on 22 January 2019, and ordered Resolute to pay part of the defendants' legal fees. Resolute had previously filed a similar defamation case against Greenpeace Canada and two of its staff members for allegedly distorting the truth in order to raise money. Resolute also lost this case as the Ontario Supreme Court stated that there was not a single example of Greenpeace engaging in the alleged behaviour. The court described the allegations as 'scandalous and vexatious'. Greenpeace was also sued in relation to its campaign against the Dakota Access Pipeline, by Energy Transfer, in a $900 million case led by Resolute's lawyers. The District Court of North Dakota dismissed these claims as well.

These cases are not unique. Non-governmental organizations (NGOs), and other public watchdogs, such as journalists and academics, are frequently sued for criticizing corporate behaviour. These lawsuits exemplify how corporate actors may strategically and aggressively litigate against public watchdogs to discourage them from speaking out against corporations. Although it is difficult to establish malicious motives behind a lawsuit, these suits are viewed as strategic as their real objective is not to win the case or remedy real harm, but to deter criticism against powerful actors. They are therefore named strategic lawsuits against public participation (SLAPPs). Even though corporations often lose these court cases, they can form a huge threat to civil society actors and their abilities to criticize corporations in the public arena. SLAPPs are said to have a so-called 'chilling effect', which entails that public interest advocates may be reluctant to express concerns regarding an issue of a public nature, because of the legal costs of a court procedure and the threat of subsequent liability (Gleason, 2003; Barylak, 2010; Shapiro, 2010; Biché, 2013).

SLAPPs originate in the US, but have been filed all over the world against civil society organizations and actors in the past few decades. Since the 1990s and the 2000s, SLAPPs have spread, for instance, to Canada (Lott, 2004; Sheldrick, 2014), Australia (Ogle, 2010) and South Africa (Murombo and Valentine, 2011). European public watchdogs have not been spared either. Libel suits have been filed against NGOs and journalists in the UK, with the 'McLibel' case, pitting McDonalds Restaurants against London Greenpeace activists Helen Steel and David Morris, in 1997 and the Trafigura lawsuit against *The Guardian* and the BBC in 2009 being landmark cases. The most important and recent source of concern in Europe is the case of Maltese journalist Daphne Caruana Galizia. Caruana Galizia frequently reported on money laundering, corruption and bribery of Maltese politicians by their business associates. These reports led to 42 libel suits against her, filed by a plethora of business actors and politicians. Caruana Galizia was murdered by a car bomb in October 2017. The criminal investigation into her assassination found relations between her murderer and the Maltese corporate-political elite and resulted in the resignation of Malta's prime minister in December 2019.

These developments have raised the question of to what extent SLAPPs are a cause for concern in Europe and whether additional legislation to increase legal protection is necessary. This question has been raised, for example, in the Council of Europe and by members of the European Parliament following the murder of Daphne Caruana Galizia (Prévost, 2019). This chapter explores the topic of strategic libel and defamation suits by corporate actors against NGOs and journalists in Europe in relation to corporate environmental crime and corruption – issues that are often related. This chapter adopts a criminological perspective by placing strategic litigation in the broader context of corporate strategies to conceal corporate crimes and harms. Corporations employ a variety of tactics to shield themselves from critiques about their harmful behaviour, ranging from reputation management, manipulation of information and litigation to straightforward threats and attacks against critics (Bradshaw, 2015; Wahlin, 2019). Criminologists also emphasize the role of the social control of crime in addition to state control. This chapter therefore first discusses the role of civil society in the social control of corporate harm, and the importance of open debate about corporate actions. The chapter continues by reviewing a variety of SLAPP cases that have emerged in Europe to identify some of the forms and consequences of SLAPPs in the European context, although by no means providing an extensive overview. Last, we discuss recent legislative reforms in North America to protect free speech and public interest litigation, as well as calls for such reforms in the EU.

Public watchdogs and defamation lawsuits

An open society, as the European ideal envisions, is based on the principles of liberal democracy and the rule of law. This ideal is based on a balance of powers between the state, entrepreneurs and civil society, to protect individual liberties and civic rights. Freedom of expression, contestation and, if necessary, contradiction of the powerful are the premises of an open society, crucial to exposing truths and untruths (Salama and White, 2017). In this respect, the role of independent media, civil society and civic activism are crucial in open societies. Such civil society actors include NGOs, grassroots and informal organizations, individual citizens, lawyers, academics and other experts, politicians, investigative journalists and media outlets. A multitude of national, EU and international policy initiatives now recognize that civil society actors help strengthen the democratic state under the rule of law (see European Commission, 2017; OECD, 2014, 2018; UN, 2011). Not only do they serve to control the state, they are also acknowledged as crucial in the control of negative impact of businesses on the environment or human rights.[2] In addition to transparency and accountability, free speech is also a fundamental condition for civil society actors to investigate, expose and confront more powerful state and corporate actors and thus act as watchdogs.

Salama and White (2017) identify three core strategies of social movements: dissent and protest, investigation and litigation. Dissent can include advocacy by NGOs through raising awareness and lobbying for new norms, but also naming and shaming of individual corporations to challenge their image of sustainability and corporate social responsibility (Salama and White, 2017). Investigations, by journalists, academics, whistleblowers or, again, NGOs, can uncover harmful activities or the manipulation or strategic framing of information by powerful actors. Investigation also involves disclosing and reporting findings. Finally, NGOs increasingly move from advocacy and investigation to active enforcement of (international) law in the absence of state action. This is manifested in civil litigation against corporations and political elites for causing or facilitating environmental damage, human rights violations or corruption (Eilstrup-Sangiovanni and Sharman, 2019). NGOs are empowered to do so by the increased opportunities in national and international legislation to seek justice in courts and to bring cases to court directly rather than reporting them to criminal justice authorities.

It should be noted that NGOs can also use public interest lawsuits as a platform to raise awareness and put environmental and corruption issues on the agenda. Salama and White (2017) discuss the example of the extensive legal battles around the Australian company Carmichael Coal Mines. Various environmental groups overwhelmed Carmichael with legal disputes to hinder the execution of its mining projects. Although the judgements of the lawsuits have mostly been in favour of Carmichael, each decision provided grounds for appeal and thus another opportunity to postpone the company's activities, legal costs permitting. Academics have warned against the risk of 'vigilante justice' through inaccurate accusations by NGOs, although they also argue that NGO enforcement often operates to fill rule-of-law vacuums in which state criminal justice fails to act (Eilstrup-Sangiovanni and Sharman, 2019).

Civil litigation against corporations, as well as other forms of activism, involves the public disclosure of potentially damaging information about powerful corporate or political actors. Hence, civil society actors engaging in this disclosure can become the subject of defamation lawsuits involving damage claims, or injunctions and 'gag orders' preventing publication. Defamation laws protect the interests and reputations of persons and corporations against unjust allegations. In such defamation cases, the right to protect corporate or political reputation should be balanced by the right to free speech as laid down by Article 10 of the European Convention of Human Rights (ECHR), thereby taking into account all the circumstances of the case. On the basis of the case law of the European Court of Human Rights (ECHR), NGOs, journalists, academics and other public watchdogs are worthy of a high – although not absolute – level of protection, as long as their statements are based on facts, contribute to the public debate and their underlying research is conducted thoroughly (Peeters, 2018; Van der Linden, 2020).

This high level of protection is, however, not an obstacle for SLAPP litigators to file suit. The academic literature around SLAPPs has clearly found that strategic litigation has the purpose to hinder the exercise of political rights and free speech, rather than enforce a right (Pring, 1989). In other words, litigation can be considered strategic and instrumental when a positive outcome of the individual lawsuit is not the primary purpose. Strategic litigation by corporate powers becomes problematic when the claim is frivolous, for instance when there is no valid interest to be protected under defamation laws, and the only aim of the lawsuit is to harm the opponent. Such strategic litigation fits in a pattern in which not action, but information becomes more and more strategic and contested, as in debates about 'junk science', fake news and misinformation. Against this background, it may become increasingly difficult to distinguish malicious strategic litigation from 'genuine' pursuit of legitimate goals. Whether a lawsuit is filed with malicious intent is, obviously, difficult to establish. It is, therefore, challenging to ban these lawsuits altogether, especially since judges have to respect the fundamental right of access to the courts (Article 6 of the ECHR).

In the European context, complicating factors are the diverging legal cultures, and differences between defamation and procedural laws between EU member states. These factors provide additional strategic opportunities for corporations to file claims in forums that offer advantageous conditions. This leads to forum shopping in respect to defamation and procedural laws, or 'libel tourism' (Prévost, 2019), making it more difficult for civil society actors to defend their case.[3] Vexatious litigation not only affects the position of the defendants, but also the position of the judiciary, as it may affect judges' workload and may constitute an abuse of procedural rights and public means (Van der Linden, 2020). The concept of SLAPPs however draws attention to the impact of strategic lawsuits beyond individual cases: chilling, and so-called 'Streisand', effects.

Potential impacts of defamation lawsuits: 'chilling' and 'Streisand' effects

SLAPPs can involve injunctions (preventing publication) or damage claims. In both cases, the immediate consequence is that the defendant stops expressing the statements causing the SLAPP. This may hinder the publication of information and debate about facts, including media reporting, publication of (counter-)evidence, expert opinions and political debate. When a corporation wins a SLAPP from an NGO, the devaluation and undermining of the credibility and reliability of the NGO, and the legitimation of the corporation and its strategies, are side-effects. This may undermine trust in the rule of law (Curry Jansen and Martin, 2015).

The impact of SLAPPs, however, reaches well beyond the individual case to future opposition: they are said to have a 'chilling' or deterrent effect on public participation (Schauer, 1978), meaning that other civil society actors are reluctant to engage in any kind of (future) public participation. The chilling effect may be caused by both the legal costs of lawsuits in themselves and by the prospect of the imposition of liability. In Gordon v Marrone, 590 [1991] New York S2d 649, 659, the New York Supreme Court stated that, 'The ripple effect of such suits in our society is enormous. Persons who have been outspoken on issues of public importance targeted in such suits or who have witnessed such suits will often choose in the future to stay silent. Short of a gun to the head, a greater threat to First Amendment expression can scarcely be imagined'.

However, attempts to suppress reputational damage may backfire by drawing more negative attention to a certain case than would have occurred without the attempt to stop publicity. Censorship may thus become counterproductive – an effect known as the 'Streisand effect', named after attempts of Barbra Streisand to forbid publication of photos of her Malibu residence in a California coastline repository, for violation of her privacy. Before the lawsuit, the photo of Streisand's residence had been downloaded six times, but the publicity following her legal action triggered hundreds of thousands of downloads within a month (Curry Jansen and Martin, 2015). Such 'censorship backfire' occurs when efforts to prevent the publication or spreading of potentially damaging or embarrassing information are exposed, and lead to the ridiculing or shaming of the censor (Curry Jansen and Martin, 2015).

Examples of SLAPPs in Europe

Although SLAPPs are best known in the Northern American context, they have also raised concern in Europe. Three types of SLAPPs can be distinguished: SLAPPs against journalists, against NGOs and against academics. A well-known British case is the successful injunction obtained by the commodities trader Trafigura against British media outlets, following a report by BBC Newsnight about the *Probo Koala* scandal in the Ivory Coast. The *Probo Koala*, a ship registered in Panama, carried what are believed to be toxic slops and dumped these in the city of Abidjan without proper waste treatment. A confidential report about the harmful nature of the waste was obtained by *The Guardian* in 2009. Trafigura issued an injunction against *The Guardian* that prevented the paper from publishing the report. Moreover, *The Guardian* was issued a so-called 'superinjunction' banning all mention of the original injunction. Trafigura eventually lifted the injunctions following an internet uproar after Carter-Ruck, libel specialists employed by Trafigura, threatened to extend the injunction to any coverage of parliamentary debates around the *Probo Koala* scandal – a clear example of the Streisand effect. Later, however, the BBC was forced to apologize to Trafigura and to withdraw a statement suggesting a connection between the slops and health consequences (including deaths) of the inhabitants of Abidjan (van Erp et al, 2015).

A recent UK case that is considered a SLAPP is that of businessman Arron Banks against journalist Carole Cadwalladr. Cadwalladr uncovered the Cambridge Analytica scandal and investigated the finances of Banks as funder of the pro-Brexit Leave.EU campaign. Banks filed a defamation lawsuit against Cadwalladr over her suggestions that Banks received funding from the Russian government, statements which he denies. The defamation suit is widely considered to serve the purpose of stifling public debate about election campaign financing.

One of the most notorious recent examples of SLAPP suits centre around Maltese investigative journalist Daphne Caruana Galizia, whose articles covered corruption of state officials and organized crime. She had 42 libel suits against her by Maltese politicians, and their business associates, including four brought by the Maltese minister for the economy (Allaby, 2019). She was killed by a car bomb in October 2017, supposedly in relation to her reporting. After her death, the court cases against her have passed on to her family – Caruana Galizia's husband has had to appear in court twice a week since her death. Similarly, journalists in Croatia, Italy (Allaby, 2019) and Belgium (Cochez, 2017) reporting on allegations of corruption of politicians and state officials (Allaby, 2019) have claimed to be very frequent subjects of libel cases. Journalists having experienced a SLAPP say that it is harassing and intimidating even when the claim is unsuccessful. While it is not unusual for a claim to 'fizzle out', it remains very time consuming and also costly in financial terms, as the journalists often have to pay for legal costs and the burden of proof is often on the defendant. Journalists state that European judges are unfamiliar with SLAPPs and, therefore, are less aware of the strategic uses of libel suits by powerful actors (Donson, 2010).

Daphne Caruana Galicia's case points to a more serious threat than libel suits, however: physical harassment and even murder of journalists who attempt to uncover money laundering and corruption. The murder of journalist Jan Kuciak in Slovakia, and the assault on Bulgarian journalist Hristo Geshov are two other recent cases that point in the direction of the most serious undermining of media freedom, hence the Council of Europe's recently founded Platform to Promote the Protection of Journalism and Safety of Journalists (Council of Europe, 2015).

The earlier cases are examples of SLAPPs against European journalists reporting on allegations of corruption and money laundering of what is referred to as the 'oligarchs': the elite at the state-corporate nexus. SLAPPs against NGOs – the main category of SLAPP defendants in the US – seem less common but can also be observed. Without doubt the most well-known libel case in Europe that could be labelled as a SLAPP by a corporation against an NGO: the case of McDonalds against Helen Steel and Dave Morris, two activists of the local NGO London Greenpeace (not a part of Greenpeace International). The case was originally issued against five London Greenpeace activists for issuing a critical pamphlet against McDonalds. After significant threats by McDonalds, three activists apologized, but Helen Steel and Dave Morris stood by their statements. This led to a ten-year libel suit against them. The case was ruled mostly in favour of McDonalds in 1997. Steel and Morris subsequently brought their case before the ECHR. In 2005, the ECHR ruled that the UK had violated the activists' right to a fair trial, referring to the right of NGOs to contribute to public debate by disseminating information and ideas on matters of public interest, such as health and the environment.[4] Other examples include criminal and civil lawsuits by Chevron in Poland against anti-fracking environmental activists protesting at a shale gas site, and the Portuguese eucalyptus pulp producer Celtejo filing suit against an environmental activist who accused the company of polluting the Tejo (Tagus) River.

A last category affected by SLAPPs is academics. Despite the principle of academic freedom, and similar protections under Article 10 of the European Convention on Human Rights, several cases are known of scholars investigating white-collar or other crimes of the powerful who were prevented from publishing their findings. Most prominently, the founding father of white-collar crime research, Edwin Sutherland, did not publish the names of the corporations he found convicted of white-collar crimes in the first edition of his book *White Collar Crime* (1949), as his publisher faced a libel suit. The 'uncut' version was published in 1983. A similar fate was met by the authors of one of the chapters of *The Routledge Handbook of White-Collar and Organisational Crime in Europe* (van Erp et al, 2015). Academic publishers may be channels through which a chilling effect manifests, but academics also face direct threats from corporations. Dutch criminologist Willem de Haan (2019) investigated complicity of chemical corporation Akzo Nobel with crimes against humanity in Argentina, and was threatened with a publication restriction by Akzo. However, the journal *Business History* published the story and Akzo did not follow through on its threat. One of the rare cases of an organization attempting to obtain an injunction against an academic institution is the recent court case of the Jehova's Witnesses in the Netherlands against Utrecht University researchers who had investigated the treatment of victims of sexual abuse in the Jehova's Witness community (Van den Bos et al, 2020). The report, commissioned by the Dutch ministry of Justice and Safety, concluded that victims were unsatisfied with the way the community treated victims of sexual abuse, and the board of the Jehova's Witnesses considered the report incorrect and defamatory. The judge, however, ruled in favour of the academics, as the findings were well substantiated and the report clearly served the public interest (de Rechtspraak, 2020). This verdict once again demonstrates that the legal threshold to prevent publication of academic research is very high.

Conclusion

This chapter has discussed the risk of SLAPPs hindering publications about white-collar and corporate crimes in Europe. It has argued that given the unequal distribution of power between corporations and civil society, corporations have the benefit of withholding negative information about their activities from the public. A critical watchdog role of civil society, investigating corporate activities and disclosing information, serves the public interest in democracies, under the condition that this information is accurate and carefully prepared. Given widespread secrecy of many corporate actors, however, the publication of incorrect and incomplete information by journalists cannot be completely ruled out.

Our discussion of developments around SLAPPs in Europe and of recent cases, including not only libel suits but also physical threats to journalists and injunctions and threats to academics, show that SLAPPS are an actual risk in Europe. This raises the question of to what extent European laws adequately protect rights to free expression. This question is particularly relevant as anti-SLAPP legislation is being introduced in the US both at state and federal level.

In the US, SLAPP defendants may argue that their statements fall within the scope of the First Amendment of the US Constitution, and that they are, therefore, not liable for any harm to the corporation's business opportunities or business relations. In addition to this general constitutional protection, a majority of US states have recognized the risk of SLAPPs to public participation and has adopted anti-SLAPP legislation. Some states even provide SLAPP defendants with the possibility to 'SLAPP back' by filing a counterclaim. If the SLAPP is judged to be vexatious, SLAPP defendants (the plaintiffs in the counterclaim) may collect damages. On a federal level, the bipartisan SPEAK FREE Act 2015 (which stands for 'Securing Participation, Engagement, and Knowledge Freedom by Reducing Egregious Efforts Act') has been proposed, but its adoption has become uncertain after the change in the US Congress in 2017.

Neither EU member states nor the EU itself have installed specific anti-SLAPP legislation (Donson, 2010). In Europe, a broad consortium consisting of politicians and media advocacy groups, including the European Centre for Press and Media Freedom (ECPMF), the Committee to Protect Journalists, PEN International, Article 19 and Reporters Without Borders, are lobbying for the introduction of an anti-SLAPP directive in EU legislation. The main aim is to protect journalists against vexatious lawsuits and chilling effects of such litigation, as well as to prevent forum shopping with respect to defamation laws, or 'libel tourism' (Costa, 2019). A group of 27 European NGOs led by the Greenpeace European Unit have also called upon the European Commission to include NGOs in this EU anti-SLAPP legislation (Business & Human Rights Resource Centre, 2020). Several members of the European Parliament have supported these claims, and European commissioner Vera Jourova (Values and

Transparency) has committed to protecting journalists from vexatious lawsuits. This commitment and the support of members of the European Parliament render it quite likely that some form of legislation will be adopted over the coming years. In the meantime, it seems imperative to make judges in Europe more aware of the strategic use of defamation lawsuits and to strengthen legal support for those who speak up against power in the public interest.

Notes

[1] Resolute Forest Products vs. Greenpeace, Case 1:16-cv-00071-JRH-BKE, filed 31 May 2016. See also: www.washingtonpost.com/news/volokh-conspiracy/wp-content/uploads/sites/14/2016/05/complaint.pdf?tid=a_inl

[2] See Directive PE-CONS 47/14 of the European Parliament and the Council amending Directive 2013/34/EU as regards disclosure of non-financial and diversity information by certain large undertakings and groups, July 2014. Available at: http://register.consilium.europa.eu/doc/srv?l=EN&f=PE%2047%202014%20INIT

[3] See Declaration by the Committee of Ministers on the Desirability of International Standards dealing with Forum Shopping in respect of Defamation, 4 July 2012, Parts 5–10.

[4] Steel and Morris v United Kingdom, 68416/01 [2005], European Court of Human Rights.

References

Allaby, E. (2019) 'After journalist's murder, efforts to combat SLAPP in Europe', *Columbia Journalism Review*, [online] 24 April, Available at: www.cjr.org/analysis/slapp-daphne-caruana-galizia-malta.php

Barylak, C. (2010) 'Reducing uncertainty in anti-SLAPP protection', *Ohio State Law Journal*, 71(8): 845–81.

Biché, T. (2013) 'Thawing public participation: modelling the chilling effect of strategic lawsuits against public participation and minimizing its impact', *Southern California Interdisciplinary Law Journal*, 22: 421–62.

Bradshaw, E. (2015) 'Blacking out the gulf: state-corporate environmental crime and the response to the 2010 BP oil spill', in G. Barak (ed) *The Routledge International Handbook of the Crimes of the Powerful*, New York: Routledge, pp 363–72.

Business and Human Rights Resource Centre (2020) '27 NGOs call on European Commissioner to include all parties impacted by SLAPPs in new EU legislation', Available at: www.business-humanrights.org/en/latest-news/27-ngos-call-on-european-commissioner-to-include-all-parties-impacted-by-slapps-in-new-eu-legislation/#c203022

Cochez, T. (2017) '"Chilling": als journalisten moeten zwijgen', *Apache*, [online] 15 December, Available at: www.apache.be/2017/12/15/chilling-als-journalisten-moeten-zwijgen/

Costa, M. (2019) ' "I will keep my promises to Caruana Galizia family" – Vera Jourova', *Malta Today*, 7 October, Available at: www.maltatoday.com.mt/news/national/97904/i_will_keep_my_promises_to_caruana_galizia_family__vera_jourova#.YEH-6S2l1QI

Council of Europe (CoE) (2015) *Platform to promote the protection of journalism and safety of journalists*, Available at: www.coe.int/en/web/media-freedom

Craig, S. (2016) 'Court dismisses "vexatious" allegations by Resolute Forest Products against Greenpeace', *Financial Post*, [online] 2 September, Available at: https://financialpost.com/commodities/agriculture/court-dismisses-vexatious-allegations-by-resolute-forest-products-against-greenpeace

Curry Jansen S. and Martin, B. (2015) 'The Streisand effect and censorship backfire', *International Journal of Communication*, 9(1): 656–71.

de Rechtspraak (2020) *Uitspraken - ECLI:NL:RBMNE:2020:227*, Available at: https://uitspraken.rechtspraak.nl/inziendocument?id=ECLI:NL:RBMNE:2020:227

De Haan, W. (2019) 'To know or not to know: silent complicity in crimes against humanity in Argentina (1976–1983)', *Business History*, [online] 12 February. doi:10.1080/00076791.2018.1523393

Donson, F. (2010) 'Libel cases and public debate: some reflections on whether Europe should be concerned about SLAPPs', *RECIEL*, 19(1): 83–95.

Eilstrup-Sangiovanni, M. and Sharman, J. (2019) 'Enforcers beyond borders: transnational NGOs and the enforcement of international law', *Perspectives on Politics*, [online] 18 October, Available at: www.cambridge.org/core/journals/perspectives-on-politics/article/enforcers-beyond-borders-transnational-ngos-and-the-enforcement-of-international-law/BB3570687DDE8F22C23785E749BD30A4

European Commission (2017) 'Better regulation guidelines (European Commission)', Available at: www.emcdda.europa.eu/system/files/attachments/7906/better-regulation-guidelines.pdf

Fiset, M-C. (2019) 'U.S. Federal Court dismisses $900 million pipeline company lawsuit against Greenpeace', *Greenpeace*, [online] 14 February, Available: www.greenpeace.org/canada/en/press-release/7538/u-s-federal-court-dismisses-900-million-pipeline-company-lawsuit-against-greenpeace/

Gleason, J. (2003) 'Strategic lawsuits against public participation', in S. Stec (ed) *Handbook on Access to Justice under the Aarhus Convention*, Hungary: The Regional Environmental Center for Central and Eastern Europe, pp 59–60.

Lott, S. (2004) 'Corporate retaliation against consumers: the status of strategic lawsuits against public participation (SLAPPs) in Canada', Available at: www.piac.ca/wp-content/uploads/2014/11/slapps.pdf

Murombo, T. and Valentine, H. (2011) 'SLAPP suits: an emerging obstacle to public interest environmental litigation in South Africa', *SAJHR*, 27(1): 82–106.

Organisation for Economic Co-operation and Development (OECD) (2014) 'Regulatory enforcement and inspections', Available at: www.oecd.org/gov/regulatory-enforcement-and-inspections-9789264208117-en.htm

OECD (2018) 'OECD regulatory policy outlook 2018', Available at: www.oecd.org/governance/oecd-regulatory-policy-outlook-2018-9789264303072-en.htm

Ogle, G. (2010) 'Anti-SLAPP reform in Australia', *RECIEL*, 19(1): 35–44.

Peeters, M. (2018) 'About silent objects and barking watchdogs: the role and accountability of environmental NGOs', *European Public Law*, 24(3): 449–72.

Pegg, D. (2019) 'Judge makes preliminary ruling in Carole Cadwalladr libel case', *The Guardian*, [online] 12 December, Available at: www.theguardian.com/law/2019/dec/12/judge-makes-preliminary-ruling-in-carole-cadwalladr-libel-case]

Prévost, E. (2019) 'Study on forms of liability and jurisdictional issues in the application of civil and administrative defamation laws in Council of Europe member states', Council of Europe, Available at: https://rm.coe.int/study-on-forms-of-liability-and-jurisdictional-issues-in-the-applicati/168096bda9

Pring, G.W. (1989) 'SLAPPs: strategic lawsuit against public participation', *Pace Environmental Law Review*, 7(1): 3–19.

Salama, O. and White, R. (2017) 'Dissent, litigation, and investigation: hitting the powerful where it hurts', *Critical Criminology*, 25(4): 523–37.

Schauer, F. (1978) 'Fear, risk and the First Amendment: unraveling the chilling effect', *Boston University Law Review*, 58: 685–732.

Shapiro, P. (2010) 'SLAPPs: intent or content? Anti-SLAPP legislation goes international', *Review of European, Comparative & International Environmental Law*, 19(1): 14–27.

Sheldrick, B. (2014) *Blocking Public Participation: The Use of Strategic Litigation to Silence Political Expression*, Waterloo: Wilfrid Laurier University Press.

SPEAK FREE Act (2015) H.R.2304, Available at: www.congress.gov/bill/114th-congress/house-bill/2304

Sutherland, E. (1949) *White Collar Crime*, New York: Holt, Rinehart and Winston.

United Nations (UN) (2011) 'Guiding principles on business and human rights', Available at: www.ohchr.org/documents/publications/guidingprinciplesbusinesshr_en.pdf

van den Bos, K., Schiffelers, M., Bal, M., Grootelaar, H., Bertram, I. and Jansma, A. (2020) *Seksueel Misbruik en Aangiftebereidheid Binnen de Gemeenschap van Jehova's Getuigen*, The Hague: Boom juridisch.

Van der Linden, T.E. (2020) 'Strategisch procederen tegen activisten: over strategic lawsuits against public participation (SLAPP's) in Nederland', *Nederlands Tijdschrift voor Burgerlijk Recht*, 37(3): 65–78.

van Erp, J., Huisman, W. and Vande Walle, G. (eds) (2015) *The Routledge Handbook of White-Collar and Corporate Crime in Europe*, Abingdon: Routledge.

van Erp, J., Spapens, T. and van Wingerde, C. (2015) 'Legal and extralegal enforcement of pollution by seagoing vessels', in T. Wyatt (ed) *Hazardous Waste and Pollution: Detecting and Preventing Green Crimes*, New York: Springer, pp 163–77.

Wahlin, M. (2019) 'Defenders at risk: attacks on human rights and environmental defenders and the responsibility of business', Swedwatch, Available at: https://swedwatch.org/wp-content/uploads/2019/12/MR-fo%CC%88rsvarare_191209_uppslag.pdf

14

Same Difference? Reflections on the Comparative Method in White-Collar Crime Research in Ireland and the United States

Joe McGrath and Deirdre Healy

Introduction

Comparative socio-legal and criminological research is notoriously complex and fraught with difficulties (Harrendorf, 2011; Huisman et al, 2015). This is particularly true of research that relies on official statistics to study comparative trends in crime and punishment. Official statistics are shaped not only by international developments but also by a variety of local factors, including policing, prosecutorial and recording practices, which can vary by jurisdiction. The task is even more challenging in the case of cross-national research involving countries with non-shared (and non-English) languages. Comparative European white-collar crime research is especially difficult due to the variety of languages, cultures and legal systems that exist within the continent. Consequently, comparative researchers cannot always be sure that they are comparing like with like, though attempts have been made to produce standardized cross-national data, including the *European Sourcebook of Crime and Criminal Justice Statistics* (Aebi et al, 2014/2017). Notwithstanding these difficulties, the fields of comparative socio-legal and criminological research are valuable and thriving disciplines which have the potential to make important contributions to theory and practice. Comparative methodologies allow scholars to escape ethnocentric biases and preconceptions and test the seeming universalism of legal claims and theories in new social, political and economic contexts. Such methods can also highlight global challenges and identify opportunities for collective action to address them. Additionally, comparative research can provide the basis for law reform by illuminating examples of international best practice.

Comparative white-collar crime research is in its early stages, though a number of valuable international collections have emerged to provide an overview of knowledge across different jurisdictions (for example, Pontell and Geis, 2007; van Erp et al, 2015; Van Slyke et al, 2016). This chapter seeks to add to this field of study by comparing responses to white-collar crime in the United States and Ireland. These jurisdictions were chosen as comparators for several reasons. On the one hand, their similarities allow for meaningful comparison. The two countries have a shared history as former British colonies, are English-speaking and operate according to common law systems. They are also both stable Western democracies with neoliberal political economies (see Cavadino and Dignan, 2006). On the other hand, the countries are sufficiently unalike to facilitate interesting explorations of their differences. For instance, the Irish prosecution system is not politicized and the legal system has a single-tier structure (unlike the multi-tier federal and state system in the US). Most importantly for our purposes, responses to white-collar crime are more highly developed in the US than Ireland. While this chapter focuses specifically on the US and Ireland, the analysis is also relevant to debates on European white-collar crime scholarship more generally. The issues raised here are likely to bedevil any European scholar who seeks to compare their jurisdiction against an international exemplar. Indeed, scholarly attention to jurisdictions outside Europe is becoming essential as the effects of globalization make borders increasingly porous. Ireland is an interesting case in point due to its dual orientation towards the US and Europe, with one former tánaiste (deputy prime minister) describing Ireland as spiritually 'closer to Boston than Berlin' (cited in Fischer, 2014: 81).

The analysis draws on quantitative data compiled by the national statistical agencies in each jurisdiction as well as a qualitative, contextual analysis of both criminal justice landscapes. Two statistical sources were used for this analysis, namely the Bureau of Justice Statistics (BJS) Integrated Data Series which contains detailed records on criminal defendants in the US and the Central Statistics Office (CSO) recorded crime series which contains data on crime and justice in Ireland (currently published under reservation due to concerns about data quality[1]). This analysis is used as a springboard for a critical reflection on the methodological challenges and opportunities that arise during comparative research on white-collar crime. The discussion focuses on two issues in particular: the data limitations that hamper high-quality quantitative and qualitative research and the utility of mixed-methods approaches.

Methodological issues

Official crime statistics are at best a proxy for actual crime rates, and their scope, accuracy and quality are shaped for better or worse by wider political, sociocultural and institutional forces. Comparative socio-legal or criminological analysis based on official statistics is therefore most effective when it takes account of the broader generative conditions which produce that data (Nelken, 2009). Indeed, it has been suggested that comparative researchers should treat the criminal justice system as a variable in its own right because of its uneven application within and between nations (Nelken, 2009). From a measurement point of view, national statistics may conceal as much as they reveal. Aggregate summary data may hide significant within-country diversity. For example, the national imprisonment rate in the US obscures large variations across individual states (O'Donnell, 2004). Furthermore, some cases may be 'lost' to the criminal justice system (and therefore to official statistical records) at particular decision points, such as the decision to report a crime to the police or the decision to prosecute a case. This is particularly the situation with white-collar crimes, because people do not always know they have been victimized, offences are rarely reported to the authorities and cases are often filtered out of the criminal justice system. From a comparative perspective, it can be difficult to determine whether cases are lost at the same points in the criminal justice process across different jurisdictions, or at the same rate (Pakes, 2019). Moreover, official criminal justice statistics do not capture every population that is subject to regulatory mechanisms. The partial nature of official criminal justice data is exacerbated with regard to white-collar criminality because these cases are often dealt with outside the usual criminal justice channels, through responsive, compliance-oriented strategies, with criminal law treated as the sanction of last resort (Ayres and Braithwaite, 1992; Hawkins, 2002). Notwithstanding these challenges, official statistics constitute a valuable source of information but must always be subjected to careful and critical interpretation, contextualized with an in-depth understanding of the data production process and triangulated with other sources (Pakes, 2019).

Compounding matters, there is significant disagreement as to how to define and measure white-collar crime (Benson et al, 2016). In particular, there is continuing debate as to whether it ought to be defined by reference to the elite status of the offender (Sutherland, 1949) or by reference to specific offences (Edelhertz, 1970). Even within the offence-based approach, there is significant disagreement as to what offences best capture the essence of white-collar criminality. The researchers in the Yale Studies on White Collar Crime series identified eight 'quintessential' white-collar offence categories including bank embezzlement, bribery and anti-trust (Wheeler et al, 1988). Though widely employed thereafter, they have become dated over the last three decades given the increased access to credit cards, information technology, electronic banking and so on. In light of this, Healy and McGrath (2019) added four new offences (computer fraud, bank fraud, healthcare fraud and selected tax offences), to create a list of twelve quintessential white-collar crimes (see Table 14.1). Because not all of these offences are committed by persons of high social respectability and high social status, some researchers would not identify these offences as white-collar crimes, reflecting the lack of consensus in the field. There are also disagreements as to whether other harmful and unethical – but legal – behaviours should be included in the definition (for example, tax avoidance). Further difficulties arise when engaging in comparative analysis with the US, not just because crime is prosecuted in both state and federal courts, but also because US statistics often include lots of separate crime categories, so some aggregation is often required for further analysis. Accurate measurement is further constrained by the scope of available data. Official datasets rarely contain information on the status of the offender, as is the case with the data provided by the BJS and the CSO. Consequently, researchers often have no choice but to employ the offence-based approach, as was the case in the current analysis.

The following analysis draws on crime and criminal justice statistics published by the CSO in Ireland and the BJS in the US to illustrate some of the challenges faced by comparative white-collar crime researchers. The first issue concerns the incompatibility of different data sources. The national statistical agencies in Ireland and the US use different crime classification systems. To illustrate, the CSO figures aggregate white-collar crimes into a category called 'fraud, deception and related offences'. This includes falsification of accounts, offences contrary to company law, money laundering, embezzlement, counterfeiting notes and coins, and corruption (see Table 14.1). There is little overlap between this list of offences and the

Table 14.1: Definitions of white-collar crime

Central Statistics Office

Fraud, forgery and false instrument offences

Fraud, deception, false pretence offences

Forging an instrument to defraud

Possession of an article for use in fraud, deception or extortion

Falsification of accounts

Offences under the Companies Act

Offences under the Investment Intermediaries Act

Offences under the Stock Exchange Act

Other fraud

Money laundering

Embezzlement

Fraud against the European Union

Importation/sale/supply of tobacco offences

Counterfeiting currency and related offences

Counterfeiting notes and coins

Corruption

Corruption (involving public office holder)

Bureau of Justice Statistics

Bank embezzlement

Tax fraud[2]

Fraud – lending and credit institutions

Bank fraud

Mail/wire fraud

Securities fraud

False claims and statements

Credit card fraud

Computer fraud

Healthcare fraud

Bribery

Antitrust

European Sourcebook of Crime and Criminal Justice Statistics

Receiving or handling stolen property

(continued)

Table 14.1: Definitions of white-collar crime (continued)

Forgery of documents, passports and so on

Tax and customs offences

Subsidy fraud

Fraud involving welfare payments

Money laundering

Forgery of money/payment instruments

Computer fraud

Consuming goods or services

Breaches of trust or embezzlement

---

offence classifications that appear in the BJS dataset. The offence of embezzlement provides a particularly good illustration of the difficulties involved in selecting offences for comparison as there is no equivalent in the BJS dataset. The closest comparable offence is bank embezzlement, which represents just one form of embezzlement. Further complicating matters, there is no statutory offence of embezzlement in Irish law, so it is unclear what activities are being represented in the CSO data, though it is presumably being prosecuted as a subset of theft, as defined in Section 4 of the Criminal Justice (Theft and Fraud Offences) Act 2001. Comparing case progression over time also proves complicated. Both the CSO and the BJS publish information on the progression of cases through the criminal justice system but utilize different time periods. The BJS records fiscal year data from 1996 to 2014 while the CSO records annual data for 2003 to 2014, with some data published under reservation due to concerns about its quality. The most recent statistics in both countries relate to 2014, reflecting the time it takes to record and compile this kind of longitudinal data.

International datasets which employ standardized definitions allow researchers to overcome some of these difficulties. The *European Sourcebook of Crime and Criminal Justice Statistics* (Aebi et al, 2014/2017) uses standardized offence definitions and also provides information on criminal procedures and data recording practices to enhance the comparability of national data. With regards to white-collar crime, it records information on fraud offences against computer data systems and money-laundering, though again these offences do not neatly map onto their Irish and American counterparts (see Table 14.1). The offence of fraud, for example, as defined by the *Sourcebook*, consists of 12 sub-categories, including forgery of documents, tax and customs offences, money laundering, computer fraud, breaches of trust and embezzlement (Harrendorf, 2012). While the *Sourcebook* and the BJS dataset specify computer-related fraud as a standalone category, this type of white-collar crime does not feature in the CSO dataset, making comparison difficult. While the *Sourcebook* is undeniably useful for comparative research within Europe, the absence of comparable US data inhibits the scope for international comparative research.

In the absence of comparable official statistics, researchers often turn to victimization surveys. Victimization surveys, like the Global Economic Crime and Fraud Survey (PricewaterhouseCoopers, 2018a, 2018b), can provide researchers with some understanding of corporate victimization in Ireland and the US. They demonstrate similar levels of victimization in both jurisdictions, with 49 per cent of Irish respondent organizations and 53 per cent of US respondent organizations reporting victimization in 2018. However, victimization trends over time differ in both jurisdictions. Reported victimization in Ireland increased from 26 per cent in 2009 to 53 per cent in 2018 but has risen from a higher base in the US, from 35 per cent in 2009 to 53 per cent in 2018. The International Criminal Victimisation Survey (ICVS) also documents standardized victimization rates for countries such as Ireland and the US and includes data on ten white-collar crimes, including consumer fraud (with detailed analysis of internet fraud and credit card fraud) and corruption. In 2003–04, the most recent data available, 12.5 per cent of American respondents reported that they were victims of consumer fraud in the previous year. This is slightly higher than the overall victimization rate of 11 per cent and significantly higher than the Irish rate of 8 per cent. Drilling down further into the consumer fraud figures, the data indicated higher rates in America than Ireland of victimization relating to fraud while shopping on the internet and credit card fraud. Victimization rates for corruption, defined as being asked for bribes by public officials, was also higher in the US (0.5 per cent) than in Ireland (0.3 per cent), but was quite low overall in both jurisdictions. It should also be noted that PricewaterhouseCoopers and the ICVS define white-collar crime in ways that do not map on to the legal and operational definitions used in Ireland, the US and the *Sourcebook*, creating further complexity for researchers to unpack. Despite their many benefits, self-report surveys also have several limitations (for a comprehensive overview see Mosher et al, 2002). Victimization surveys tend to be limited in scope (for example, victimless crimes are usually excluded) and accuracy can be impeded by poorly phrased questions and imprecise operational definitions of crime. Samples may be too small or unrepresentative of the population at large, particularly since some groups are less willing, or able, to participate (including very affluent, marginalized and institutionalized groups). Respondents may also introduce error through forgetfulness, vague responses, misinterpreting questions, fear, dishonesty or the desire to present a favourable self-image. Survey responses are also rarely subjected to independent corroboration.

Gathering these threads together, it is clear that comparative quantitative research is often frustrated by the absence of an agreed definition of white-collar crime, the lack of standardized definitions for various offence categories and concerns about the quality and comparability of national and international data. In the absence of high-quality comparative data, the challenge of generating standardized offence definitions is significant. This may be particularly pronounced for certain offence types. Harrendorf (2012) found that countries' ability to provide data that conformed to the *Sourcebook* definitions varied by offence type. Money laundering data showed relatively high levels of conformity, possibly because this offence has been targeted by several European and international crime-fighting campaigns. In contrast, fraud data were quite inconsistent across the countries studied, probably because of a lack of precision in the definition of fraud, which is usually framed quite broadly, as discussed further in the next section. At the same time, many researchers believe that attempts to produce standardized definitions or complete descriptions are misguided and risk over-simplification through a flattening out of differences. Scholars, such as Pakes (2019), regard definitional ambiguities as not only unavoidable but also potentially fruitful if viewed through a qualitative, conceptual lens which enables researchers to understand the reasons behind observed convergences and divergences.

Legal issues

The complexities that surround the measurement of white-collar crime are mirrored by the ambiguities that exist within legal definitions of white-collar crimes. For instance, different countries may define similar-sounding crimes in different ways. This means that the same crime label can attach to very different forms of wrongdoing in different jurisdictions. This is a source of significant complexity for researchers who want to ensure that data is truly comparable. As Harrendorf (2012: 24) states, 'simply comparing statistical categories bearing the same, yet translated, headline is like comparing apples with oranges disguised as apples'. Take fraud, for example. There is no stand-alone offence of fraud in US federal law, though there are a variety of offences which criminalize types of fraud, including mail and wire fraud, bank fraud and so on. Podgor (1999: 740) has noted, 'the scope of fraud is problematic in that there is no specific group of statutes designated in the federal code as fraud statutes and no consistent definition to create the boundaries of what is encompassed within the term'. Similarly, there is no single offence of fraud in Irish law, though the Law Reform Commission recently determined that 'fraud' refers to five distinct offences in the Criminal Justice (Theft and Fraud) Act 2001: making gain or causing loss by deception, obtaining services by deception, unlawful use of a computer, false accounting and suppression of documents.

The offence of deception, however, is interesting in that it shows how legal systems may converge and diverge around a single offence. Deception is a broad offence in Irish law and is committed when a person dishonestly intends to cause the making of a gain for him/herself or a loss to someone else, whether by doing or refraining from doing an act. There is no requirement to prove an actual gain or loss (Campbell et al, 2010: 759). A person deceives when he/she creates a false impression, prevents the acquiring of information which would correct a false impression or fails to correct a false impression which he/she created or reinforced. The Irish definition of deception stems from Section 223.3 in the US Model Penal Code, which sets out draft provisions for individual states to implement so that they may have criminal law provisions that are harmonious with each other. This construction was adopted into Irish law following a recommendation from the Irish Law Reform Commission Report on Dishonesty of 1992 (Law Reform Commission, 1992). Unfortunately, there no equivalent federal offence in the US, which frustrates direct comparisons between the US and Ireland.

There is, however, the common law offence of conspiracy to defraud in Ireland, and a statutory offence of conspiracy to defraud in US federal criminal law. The federal conspiracy to defraud offence in US law criminalizes any conspiracy to commit an offence against the United States or to defraud the United States or its agencies (18 U.S.C. § 371). The conspirator must agree to a conspiracy with an illegal object, intend to participate in it, and there must be an overt act which furthers the agreement. It is so broad as to have 'no fixed meaning', which makes it useful from a prosecutor's perspective (Goldstein, 1959: 408). Understandably, for this reason, Judge Learned Hand stated it was the 'darling of the modern prosecutor's nursery' (Harrison v United States, 7 F.2d 259, 263 [2d Cir. 1925]). The conspiracy to defraud offence in Irish law is also a very broad common law offence. Justice Geoghegan of the Irish High Court in Myles v

Sreenan [1999] 4 IR 294 at 298, following English case law, stated that the 'best definition' of the offence is 'an agreement by two or more by dishonesty to deprive a person of something which is his or to which he is or would be or might be entitled, or ... an agreement by two or more by dishonesty to injure some proprietary right (of the victim's)'. Unlike the US equivalent, there is no requirement, for example, to commit an overt act. Conspiracy was subsequently placed on a statutory footing by Section 71 of the Criminal Justice Act 2006, as amended in respect of 'serious' offences punishable by four years imprisonment or more, but remains a common law offence for other forms of conspiracy.

The Irish Supreme Court did determine, however, that the Irish offence of conspiracy to defraud is comparable to an entirely different US federal offence. The Irish Supreme Court in Attorney General v Oldridge [2000] 1 IR 593 considered whether the offence was comparable to the US federal wire fraud offence in order to determine whether to extradite the respondent to face trial for this offence in America. Wire fraud is committed by 'whoever, having devised or intending to devise any scheme or artifice to defraud, or for obtaining money or property by means of false or fraudulent pretences, representations, or promises, transmits or causes to be transmitted by means of wire, radio, or television communication in interstate or foreign commerce, any writings, signs, signals, pictures, or sounds for the purpose of executing such scheme or artifice' (18 USC § 1343). The alleged criminality in Oldridge involved defrauding three banks of US$28 million in loans secured on assets which did not exist. The Supreme Court did not engage in direct comparisons of the elements of each offence but did accept that the wrongdoing in question could be prosecuted for conspiracy to defraud in Irish law. The Law Reform Commission (2018: 655) subsequently determined that Oldridge 'made it clear that conspiracy to defraud effectively occupied the same niche in Irish law as the wire and mail fraud offences do in the federal US system', so there would be no point in recommending that a similar offence be introduced into Irish law.

Taken together, this discussion shows that difficulties arise when comparing particular white-collar crimes in Ireland and the US because terms like fraud have no fixed meaning and because when given meaning they are disaggregated into different kinds of broad and narrow offences in each jurisdiction. There is also significant disagreement among scholars about what offences constitute white-collar crimes, creating an additional layer of complexity. Moreover, these offences have different elements, exhibit some familiarity with state law and not federal law and differ in their origins in statute or common law. In addition, some of these offences are so broad that even when they specify different elements, like conspiracy to defraud and wire fraud, they may still be used to prosecute the same wrongdoing, making it difficult to precisely identify the core conduct each offence addresses. Criminal justice decision makers may also use their discretion to classify crime incidents in ways that increase the likelihood of a successful case outcome, creating further conceptual confusion. For instance, Lord (2014) reports that German prosecutors often prosecute transnational bribery cases as 'fraud' or 'breach of trust'. In the absence of standardized quantitative data and legal definitions what exists is a patchwork of information, not always comparable, that sheds light on aspects of white-collar crime but never the whole.

Conclusion

Comparative research is a difficult and complex task but can prove invaluable in terms of developing sharing understandings, identifying current (and sometimes evolving) problems and highlighting examples of international best practice. It is important because it can help to boost our understanding of foreign law and offers the potential to improve our own national laws and perhaps even to standardize legal rules in some cases. Using official statistics as the basis for this research can, however, pose problems when researchers are not sure that they are comparing like with like. Terms like white-collar crime and fraud have no fixed legal meaning in any one country, let alone across multiple jurisdictions. Even when certain offences are called the same thing in different jurisdictions, they may address different forms of misconduct. Equally, the same misconduct can be addressed by offences with different names, requiring different proofs in different jurisdictions. In addition, official statistics say little about the background influences which shape and generate these statistics. International and European datasets use standardized definitions to overcome these difficulties, shoehorning offences into broad categories, but these data do not map easily onto each other or onto national crime classification systems, impeding international comparative work.

The solution to this impasse may be a qualitative, or mixed methods, case study approach, which many scholars (for example, Nelken, 2009) regard as superior to quantitative methodologies. A number of monographs on white-collar and corporate crime also showcase the importance of looking behind official criminal justice statistics in Ireland and the US to reveal the economic, political and cultural contexts that produce these data. McGrath's (2015) examination of white-collar crime in Ireland, for example, discusses how the state's models of corporate enforcement contain internal contradictions. Traditionally, the Irish state invoked its most powerful weapon of state censure, the criminal law, but was remarkably lenient in practice because the law was not enforced. The contemporary model is much more reliant on cooperative measures and civil orders, but also contains remarkably punitive and instrumental measures to surmount the difficulties of proving guilt in criminal cases. McGrath (2015) locates this change in architecture to the broader transition from a highly agrarian, closed state to a much more open, global centre for commerce and finance. A deeper understanding of these cultural, historical, social, political and economic nuances clearly adds colour to any attempts at cross-national comparison.

Similarly, work by Garrett (2014) in the US has moved beyond examining official criminal justice data to show what really happens when companies are prosecuted for crimes. Garrett notes that while official criminal justice data demonstrate that criminal fines imposed on companies have risen considerably since the 20th century, he delves behind that data to show that a small number of companies have paid a significant portion of those fines. In fact, Garrett (2014) demonstrates that most companies pay lower fines than expected (with some spectacular exceptions), that approximately two thirds of settlement agreements are not accompanied by the prosecution of the individuals that run those companies and that there is no corporate monitor appointed to oversee corporate governance changes in three quarters of all agreements. In doing so, he describes the 'hidden world' of corporate prosecutions that is not captured by official data on the number of prosecutions or in official press releases announcing large fines, prompting us to ask whether these tactics and strategies are working effectively. The significance of both McGrath's and Garrett's work is that they demonstrate how contemporary practices depend on historical conditions and look beyond legal outcomes to consider the generative forces which have shaped and produced these outcomes. They show that differing regulatory responses to white-collar criminality reflect the level of knowledge within, and political objectives of, government, as informed by the economic, social, and cultural contexts at various points in time. From a methodological point of view, they illustrate how a purely quantitative approach to the study of white-collar crime can obscure as well as reveal the reality of the criminal justice landscape and highlight the added value of case study approaches.

At the same time, it is important to note that no methodological approach is capable of offering perfect insights into the subject of inquiry. The selection of any methodological approach inevitably involves trade-offs between specificity and generalizability: approaches that operate at a macro level of analysis can provide clear and useful theoretical frameworks to guide other researchers in the field but may also lead to oversimplification and conceal differences between jurisdictions (O'Donnell, 2004). Comparative qualitative research is of course extremely resource intensive but could be facilitated through cross-national collaborations and research partnerships. The best approaches triangulate different data sources, operate at multiple levels of analysis and situate findings within the historical, cultural, social, political and legal contexts of the comparator countries. Accordingly, qualitative and mixed-method approaches involving multiple, embedded case studies may prove especially valuable in this field (for practical methodological suggestions on how to conduct such research, see Maesschalck, this volume). In particular, in-depth, context-sensitive studies of corporate and white-collar crime enforcement in each jurisdiction may provide the basis for more nuanced comparative research and add depth, breadth and richness to statistical mapping exercises.

Notes

[1] Quality reviews highlighted issues such as the non-recording of reported crimes, misclassification of reported crimes, incorrect use of crime counting rules, delays in recording incidents, failure to provide explanations for marking crimes as invalid (that is, the label given to incidents when a crime is deemed not to have occurred); failure to record prosecution information on detected incident records (see, for example, Central Statistics Office, 2018).

[2] Includes tax fraud offences such as 'Income tax, evade or defeat'; 'Income tax, other felony'; 'Income tax, failure to file'; 'Income tax, other misdemeanour'; 'Fraud, excise tax, other'; 'Fraud, wagering tax, other'; 'Fraud, other tax'.

References

Aebi, M., Akdeniz, G., Barclay, G., Campistol, C., Caneppele, S., Gruszczyńska, B., Harrendorf, S., Heiskanen, M., Hysi, V., Jehle, J.-M., Jokinen, A., Kensey, A., Killias, M., Lewis, C.G., Savona, E., Smit, P. and Þórisdóttir, R. (2014/2017) *European Sourcebook of Crime and Criminal Justice Statistics*, Helsinki: Hakapaino Oy.

Ayres, I. and Braithwaite, J. (1992) *Responsive Regulation: Transcending the Deregulation Debate*, Oxford: Oxford University Press.

Benson, M., Van Slyke, S. and Cullen, F. (2016) 'Core themes in the study of white-collar crime', in S. Van Slyke, M. Benson and F. Cullen (eds) *The Oxford Handbook of White-Collar Crime*, Oxford: Oxford University Press, pp 1–21.

Campbell, L., Kilcommins, S. and O'Sullivan, C. (2010) *Criminal Law in Ireland: Cases and Commentary*, Dublin: Clarus Press.

Cavadino, M. and Dignan, J. (2006) 'Penal policy and political economy', *Criminology and Criminal Justice*, 6(4): 435–56.

Central Statistics Office (2018) 'Review of the quality of recorded crime statistics based on 2017 data provided by An Garda Síochána', Available at: www.cso.ie/en/media/csoie/releasespublications/documents/crimejustice/2017/Review_of_Quality_Crime_2017.pdf

Edelhertz, H. (1970) *The Nature, Impact, and Prosecution of White-Collar Crime* (vol 2), Washington, DC: National Institute of Law Enforcement and Criminal Justice.

Fischer, J. (2014) 'Boston or Berlin? Reflections on a topical controversy, the Celtic Tiger and the world of Irish Studies', *The Irish Review*, 48(1): 81–95.

Garrett, B. (2014) *Too Big to Jail: How Prosecutors Compromise with Corporations*, Harvard: Harvard University Press.

Goldstein, A. (1959) 'Conspiracy to defraud the United States', *The Yale Law Journal*, 68(3): 405–63.

Harrendorf, S. (2011) 'How to measure punitiveness in global perspective: what can be learned from international survey data', in H. Kury and E. Shea (eds) *Punitivity: International Developments. Vol. 1: Punitiveness: A Global Phenomenon?* Bochum: Universitatsverlag Dr N. Brockmeyer, pp 125–48.

Harrendorf, S. (2012) 'Offence definitions in the European Sourcebook of Crime and Criminal Justice Statistics and their influence on data quality and comparability', *European Journal on Criminal Policy and Research*, 18(1): 23–53

Hawkins, K. (2002) *Law as Last Resort: Prosecution Decision-Making in a Regulatory Agency*, Oxford: Oxford University Press.

Healy, D. and McGrath, J. (2019) 'Simple rhetoric and complex punitiveness: federal criminal justice responses to white-collar criminality', *Justice Quarterly*, 36(7): 1258–83.

Huisman, W., van Erp, J., Vande Walle, G. and Beckers, J. (2015) 'Criminology and white-collar crime in Europe', in J. van Erp, W. Huisman and G. Vande Walle (eds) *The Routledge Handbook of White-Collar and Corporate Crime in Europe*, Abingdon: Routledge, pp 1–21.

Law Reform Commission (1992) *LRC 43-1992, Report on the Law Relating to Dishonesty*, Dublin: Law Reform Commission.

Law Reform Commission (2018) *LRC 119-2018, Report Regulatory Powers and Corporate Offences*, Dublin: Law Reform Commission.

Lord, N. (2014) 'Responding to transnational corporate bribery using international frameworks for enforcement: anti-bribery and corruption in the UK and Germany', *Criminology and Criminal Justice*, 14(1): 100–20.

McGrath, J. (2015) *Corporate and White-Collar Crime in Ireland: A New Architecture of Regulatory Enforcement*, Manchester: Manchester University Press.

Mosher, C.J., Miethe, T.D. and Hart, T.C. (2011) 'Self-report studies', in C.J. Mosher, T.D. Miethe and T.C. Hart (eds) *The Mismeasure of Crime* (2nd edn), London: Sage, pp 117–50.

Nelken, D. (2009) 'Comparative criminal justice: beyond ethnocentrism and relativism', *European Journal of Criminology*, 6(4): 291–311.

O'Donnell, I. (2004) 'Interpreting penal change: a research note', *Criminal Justice*, 4(2): 199–206.

Pakes, F. (2019) *Comparative Criminal Justice*, Abingdon: Routledge.

Podgor, E. (1999) 'Criminal fraud', *American University Law Review*, 48(4): 729–68.

Pontell, H. and Geis, G. (eds) (2007) *International Handbook of White-Collar and Corporate Crime*, New York: Springer.

PricewaterhouseCoopers (2018a) 'Shining a light on fraud: Irish economic crime survey 2018', Available at: www.pwc.ie/publications/2018/economic-crime-survey-2018.pdf

PricewaterhouseCoopers (2018b) '2018 global economic crime and fraud survey – US perspectives: pulling fraud out of the shadows', Available at: www.pwc.com/us/en/forensic-services/assets/2018-global-economic-fraud-survey.pdf

Sutherland, E.H. (1949) *White Collar Crime*, New York: The Dryden Press.

van Erp, J., Huisman, W. and Vande Walle, G. (eds) (2015) *The Routledge Handbook of White-Collar and Corporate Crime in Europe*, Abingdon: Routledge.

Van Slyke, S., Benson, M. and Cullen, F. (eds) (2016) *The Oxford Handbook of White-Collar Crime*, Oxford: Oxford University Press.

Wheeler, S., Mann, K. and Sarat, A. (1988) *Sitting in Judgment: The Sentencing of White-Collar Criminals*, New Haven: Yale University Press.

15

Settling with Corporations in Europe: A Sign of Legal Convergence?

Liz Campbell

Introduction

A growing number of jurisdictions now permit Deferred Prosecution Agreements (DPAs), or some equivalent, to be negotiated with corporations, entailing suspension or avoidance of criminal prosecution as long as the entity meets certain conditions (King and Lord, 2018; Campbell, 2019; Hawley et al, 2020). Though certainly not uncontroversial, DPAs are seen as a pragmatic response to difficulties in pursuing corporate misconduct through the standard criminal trial process, given the evidential burdens that must be surmounted and the risks and resources involved in prosecution.

Much has been made of the differences between DPAs as initially developed and applied in the United States and their equivalents and subsequent iterations in Europe and elsewhere, as well as the concerns about oversight, review, prosecutorial overreach, fairness, consistency and transparency. Less attention has been paid to the fact that these mechanisms were formed in a common law/adversarial system, but now have gained traction in both common law and civil law contexts, albeit in more moderate and formalized configurations.

This chapter analyzes how DPAs have been defined, developed and deployed in different European jurisdictions, in an effort to identify the extent to which this is shaped by the dominant model of criminal procedure (Damaska, 1973) in a given country. Although the classification of criminal processes is complex and contested, it is still a novel and valuable lens through which to analyze the introduction and operation of DPAs. Indeed, the common law/civil law distinction has particular salience given the imminent departure of the United Kingdom from the European Union (EU), insofar as it left Ireland as the only common law jurisdiction in the EU. This chapter asks to what extent the models of criminal procedure shed light on the form that DPAs take, and whether their growing adoption is indication of an organic convergence or transnationalization in the response to white-collar and corporate crime (Freiberg, 2011).

First, this chapter describes DPAs and cognate mechanisms across Europe. Then, it outlines characteristics of common law and civil law jurisdictions, emphasizing how some forms of settlement have emerged in both traditions. I examine the extent to which DPAs are necessitated by common law and civil law norms and practices, and consider how they are resulting in legal convergence. These pragmatic responses to corporate crime often relate to transnational corporations and to multi-jurisdictional crime, explaining why some degree of harmonization is preferred. That said, there are unresolved issues regarding 1) double jeopardy where action/settlements are possible in more than one jurisdiction, 2) recidivist corporate offenders and 3) the ultimate effectiveness of such settlements. These shared problems underline the significance of a pan-European dialogue, as well as implying the centrality of settlements in wider European conversations on responses to corporate misconduct.

Describing DPAs (and other non-conviction-based criminal law settlements)

The Organisation for Economic Co-operation and Development (OECD) (2019: 11) describes 'non-trial resolutions' as any agreement between a legal or natural person and an enforcement authority to resolve a case without a full trial on the merits, with sanctions and/or confiscation, irrespective of whether it is a conviction (for example, plea deals) or a non-conviction mechanism (for example, non-prosecution or DPAs). My focus is narrower, on agreements with legal persons that do not involve prosecution or conviction, but which are situated in the criminal realm. I could call these non-conviction-based criminal law settlements, but for clarity and brevity's sake, I'm going to refer to and focus on DPAs, given that these are my starting point, and given that my vantage point is that of a common law criminal lawyer.

DPAs enable prosecutors to enter into agreements with corporations to defer or suspend criminal proceedings despite or indeed because of the admission of wrongdoing. They empower the state to intervene and impose conditions on corporations for criminal behaviour, while permitting legal persons to make reparations without the consequences of a conviction. It has been proposed that DPAs avoid 'the uncertainty, expense, complexity or length of a criminal trial' (Ministry of Justice, 2012: 3), and are endorsed as a pragmatic response to corporate crime, insofar as they add to the suite of regulatory devices available to the state.

DPAs are tailored settlements between the state and corporations which seek to encourage self-reporting as a way of revealing and enabling responses to corporate misconduct. The purported advantages operate in both ways. The state's difficulty in detecting and addressing corporate crime is said to be mitigated by the purported incentivizing of self-reporting (though this is no longer a prerequisite in the UK, according to the settlement with Airbus SE; see Serious Fraud Office, 2020), while the corporation benefits from the predictability, relative speed and confidentiality of the process, in addition to its control over it, when compared to criminal investigation and trials.

First developed in the US as a means of diverting young offenders from the conventional criminal justice process, somewhat ironically DPAs have been used with increasingly regularity in relation to corporate crime by both the US Department of Justice and the Securities and Exchange Commission since 1992 (Epstein, 2011; Garrett, 2014; Rakoff, 2015; King and Lord, 2018). In the US, DPAs are available to both individual and corporate defendants, and are extrajudicial settlements, insofar as there is limited judicial oversight of the process. Courts are not involved in the weighing of the terms of DPAs, and rather serve as repositories for agreements at the end of negotiations. This is a consequence of the interpretation of the separation of powers in the US, which precludes direct judicial involvement in prosecutorial decisions, as well as being a specific legacy of the US preoccupation with plea bargaining in prosecutions.

Since their development in the US, DPAs have gained traction in various other common law jurisdictions. There is no indication that any country has contemplated and rejected DPAs. They have been in place on a statutory basis in England and Wales since 2013, in Canada[1] and Singapore[2] since 2018, are likely to be introduced in Australia (see Campbell, 2019), and have been recommended by the

Irish Law Reform Commission (2018). In the European context, comparable mechanisms have developed and are used in numerous jurisdictions such as France,[3] the Netherlands,[4] Italy[5] and Switzerland[6] (see Corruption Watch, 2016; Organisation for Economic Co-operation and Development, 2019). These measures take different forms, with varying degrees of judicial and prosecutorial involvement, consequences and conditions. Such differences are due to the fact that each mechanism/system is grounded in the particular legal traditions. Despite these differences, there is a uniformly growing preference for them: the 2014 OECD Foreign Bribery Report found that 69 per cent of the cases successfully concluded by countries party to the OECD Anti-Bribery Convention were resolved through non-trial resolutions (NTRs), while by 2018 78 percent of the 890 successfully concluded foreign bribery cases since 1999 were through NTRs (Organisation for Economic Co-operation and Development, 2019: 13).

I have argued elsewhere (Campbell, 2019) that DPAs are necessitated by, but also misconstrued as, a way of offsetting problems with corporate criminal liability. Moreover, and paradoxically, while DPAs are introduced in an effort to remedy such issues, they are deployed also to mitigate the inevitable consequences of conviction, like debarment from certain contracts, diminution of share price and possible liquidation. DPAs therefore both serve to supplement as well as to dilute corporate criminal liability. DPAs were introduced, in part, as a way of addressing the identification doctrine (Serious Fraud Office, 2018), a means of ascribing corporate criminal liability in common law contexts, whereby persons who control or manage the affairs of a company are deemed to embody the company itself (Tesco Supermarkets Ltd v Nattrass [1972] AC 153). As long as issues with the identification doctrine are not resolved, DPAs will be both necessary as well as ineffective. Moreover, though much has been written about DPAs in common law jurisdictions (Epstein, 2011; Garrett, 2014; Bronitt, 2017; Comino, 2018; King and Lord, 2018; Lewis, 2018), there has been no examination of the extent to which they are a necessary consequence of the common law/adversarial process, or whether their adoption is a manifestation or a diminution of adversarialism. Another description of the 'negotiated justice' focused on by King and Lord (2018) in their analysis of DPAs could be 'non-adversarial' justice, though that is not a term used explicitly in their book. Overall, none of the existing literature addresses directly DPAs' relationship to the underlying nature of the criminal justice process.

Models of criminal procedure

It is instructive to consider whether the prevailing model of criminal procedure has impacted upon the introduction and operation of DPAs, and conversely, the extent to which the ubiquity of DPAs in different guises is resulting in a convergence of legal systems.

The conventional view of the English and other common law criminal processes is as accusatorial, in which the prosecution constructs a case for convicting the defendant and the defendant attempts to undermine or discredit that case in an adversarial process. In opposition to this is the idea of an impartial inquiry into the case by a neutral official, with an active role for the fact finder, characterized by truth seeking rather than proof making.

So, the criminal justice model in England and Wales and the Anglosphere in general is regarded as an adversarial one in which two parties in a position of theoretical equality (the state and the accused) present their arguments before an impartial court which determines the outcome (Damaska, 1973: 563; McEwan, 1998: 1–32). The partisan lawyers for each party interrogate witnesses and present the evidence to the court. The aim of the procedure is to settle a conflict stemming from an allegation of criminal conduct, and to determine whether the prosecution has discharged the burden of proof (Devlin, 1981: 60).

Common law adversarialism generally is contrasted with what is often described (by English speakers!) as inquisitorialism. This term has a great deal of pejorative and problematic historical baggage (Damaska, 1973: 561; Weinreb, 1977: 11), and so I will use the term 'civilian' systems. Roughly speaking, in civilian systems the judge determines the law and finds as to the facts by active investigation at trial (Damaska, 1973: 525). Such proceedings are not structured as a dispute per se, but as an official inquiry which seeks to determine whether a crime has been committed, and the judge may interrogate the accused and the witnesses. The process is simpler, with fewer technicalities, and in principle all reliable sources of information may be used (Damaska, 1973: 564).

Of course, these dichotomous ideal types overlook the complexity and nuances of the common law/civil law distinction, both in theory and in practice. Indeed, many systems now seem to be 'mixed procedural' types, situated between the 'extremes' of the accusatorial and inquisitorial systems. And efforts have been made to characterize the criminal justice models to convey more accurately the empirical reality. For instance, the use of plea bargaining, which is a practical prerequisite in terms of maintaining the viability of a criminal justice system, seems to betray the precepts of adversarialism. Despite this, it has been argued that in the US in particular plea bargaining is so prevalent that it should not be considered an exception to the standard trial-based adversarial model but must be considered a part (and indeed a practical requirement) of the process itself (Lynch, 1998). Plea bargaining is a way of mitigating difficulties with the rigid application of common law standards which would otherwise compromise the very workings of the criminal justice system. Gerard Lynch (1998) describes this as part of an 'administrative' system of criminal justice. An alternative conception has been offered by Jenny McEwan (2011), who identified a series of ad hoc reforms to the English criminal justice system that depart to a significant degree from its adversarial heritage, but far from moving closer to the European model, mean that criminal procedure is dominated increasingly by 'managerialist' concerns.

Beyond these critiques, the 'theory of convergence' suggests that the trend in Europe has been away from a clear dichotomy of approaches and towards a more unified framework, influenced by the European Convention on Human Rights. However, the dynamics here are not straightforward (Campbell et al, 2019: 439). While it might be overstatement to talk of convergence per se, not least because legal traditions and jurisdictional cultures play a powerful role in the way that these developments emerge and crystallize, there is at least some growing commonalities. And while it is questionable to measure actual legal systems against an ideal type of the accusatorial or inquisitorial system (Campbell et al, 2019: 439); it is still helpful to make sense of legal changes by reference to a spectrum of norms and traditions.

DPAs as evidence of convergence?

Is the adoption of DPAs and comparable settlements indication of an organic convergence (Freiberg, 2011) across different legal traditions in the response to transnational white-collar and corporate crime? The OECD (2019: 19) notes that while non-trial resolutions may have once been perceived as incompatible with the inquisitorial approach traditionally found in civil law jurisdictions, most of the parties to the European Convention on Human Rights have some form of non-trial resolution for natural and legal persons, including a number of civil law countries like Germany, Italy, Argentina and France, which now have mechanisms equivalent to common law plea bargaining (Tulkens, 2002: 662; Langer, 2004: 37). Less has been written on how DPAs incorporate and import civil law elements into common law settings, and on what this means for the harmonization of procedures against corporate wrongdoing. I examine if and how such settlements indicate legal convergence.

One charge placed against the adversarial system is that its complicated matrix of evidentiary rules results in the acquittal of factually guilty individuals. This is compounded in respect of legal persons, not least due to the mechanisms for ascribing the fault element of offences that require proof of mens rea. In contrast, in civilian systems the defendant may be used as an evidentiary source before any other evidence has been examined at the trial (Damaska, 1973: 529–30). This may suggest that the burden on the prosecution is less onerous than in adversarial trials. However, Damaska notes that as the majority of defendants plead guilty in the adversary system and so do not have a full trial, the prosecutorial burden is in fact greater in inquisitorial proceedings (Damaska, 1973: 551–2).

It is this prosecutorial burden that is sought to be mitigated by the use of DPAs, which incentivize self-reporting. Self-reporting is a particularity of corporate regulation that is uncommon in other criminological contexts but represents a central element of routine corporate reporting and compliance (Lord, 2013: 136–7). Of course, self-reporting and disclosure of criminality in the corporate sphere may result in criminal investigations and/or charges, but is often also met with leniency in proceedings and outcome. While DPAs seek to incentivize self-reporting, this is not a prerequisite for a corporation to be regarded as cooperative (Serious Fraud Office, 2012), as was made clear in the agreements with *Rolls-Royce* and *Airbus*.[7] Regardless, I suggest that one civilian characteristic which has been transplanted by the DPA is the view of the accused as a source of information for the state. This co-option of the corporate accused, who, needless to say, may benefit later from this, is indicative of a more consultative model of criminal procedure against corporate wrongdoers. Of course, with corporations, any information provided as part of this co-option goes through a stringent process of internal legal oversight before being communicated, so the narrative is constructed and framed strategically. It is doubtful that this is comparable to the provision of evidence by an individual accused in court to the investigating judge under interrogation, or cross examination in the common law setting.

As noted previously in Campbell et al (2019: 439), if the essence of the accusatorial system is that of the parties' control over proceedings then there is no pure accusatorial system, because ethical duties to the court and exclusionary rules have always limited the ability of the parties to conduct proceedings in the manner that they want. I suggest that increased party control outside of any court proceedings mean

DPAs are both strengthening and weakening adversarialism. In DPAs in common law jurisdictions the power remains with the parties, albeit with some judicial oversight (very little in the US, a lot in England and Wales, somewhere in the middle in the proposed Australian model). This is akin to the adversarial norm. And even in England and Wales, which entails the most interventionist judicial oversight model, all seven DPAs have been approved, exemplifying that party determinations remain key.

The contested judicial trial is seen as the core of the adversarial approach. However, as Baer (2016: 1122) reminds us, trials are the exception for corporate suspects. This is not necessarily because of DPAs, and research from the US suggests that DPAs are not replacing other criminal justice settlements against corporations. Alexander and Cohen (2015: 540) identified and analyzed all non-prosecution agreements (NPAs), DPAs and plea agreements entered into by public corporations in the US between 1997 and 2011, reviewing over 486 agreements. They found that DPAs and NPAs did not replace traditional plea agreements during that time; rather, the number of traditional plea agreements with corporate defendants remained steady while DPAs and NPAs grew in popularity. Accordingly, they conclude that the availability and use of DPAs and NPAs has effectively 'expand[ed] the reach of criminal enforcement' (Alexander and Cohen, 2015: 572). I am less sanguine, and argue that these figures should be read as indicative of the scale of offending and as representing several missed opportunities for contested criminal prosecution. There are only a tiny number of contested corporate prosecutions in the US: between 1992 and 2021, 310 NPAs were approved, 269 DPAs, and 2022 plea agreements. There were 545 dismissals, 28 declinations, and 52 trial convictions.[8] Analyzing the DPAs in England and Wales was rather more straightforward, given that there have been just nine (see Hawley et al, 2020)! For this reason, it is difficult to ascertain whether there is any statistically significant difference in how corporate crime is being addressed in the UK since their introduction, and so whether there is a diminution in adversarialism in the corporate criminal law context. Where there is less adversarial pursuit is in respect of individuals. In the US, DPAs and NPAs are typically not accompanied by prosecutions of individuals (Garrett, 2014), and of the nine DPAs agreed in England and Wales, the situation regarding individuals is mixed. There were no associated proceedings against any individuals in relation to Standard Bank's (SB) failure to prevent bribery by Stanbic Bank Tanzania (a bank in SB's division) to influence members of the Tanzanian Government. Three directors and managers in Sarclad were charged with conspiring to bribe to secure contracts in foreign jurisdictions but were acquitted; the prosecution of three Tesco directors for false accounting and fraud collapsed; the investigation into the conduct of individuals in Rolls-Royce has been dropped; and while three individuals were charged with conspiracy to make corrupt payments in relation to Güralp's scheme of corrupt payments to South Korean public official, they were acquitted. Two directors from Serco Geografix Ltd have been charged with false accounting and fraud in relation to the scheme to dishonestly mislead the UK Ministry of Justice as to the true extent of the profits made from its contract for the provision of electronic monitoring services of prisoners; the trial will be heard in 2021. Likewise, the Airbus SE investigations are ongoing, and no proceedings have been taken in relation to the G4S Care & Justice Services and Airlines Services Ltd DPAs (for further details see Campbell, 2019 and 2021; Hawley et al, 2020; Serious Fraud Office, nd).

What is significant also is the adversarial alternative to DPAs and other settlements. The value of DPAs as a tool of preventive justice, such as it is, is predicated on there being an incentive to enter into a DPA, and even more importantly, on a robust and meaningful alternative in the form of criminal prosecution of both individual and corporate persons. The US DPA scheme is underpinned by the expansive doctrine of *respondeat superior*, whereby the corporate entity is liable for acts of its employees and agents, as well by as sanctions that are regarded as severe, comparatively speaking, as in the US Supreme Court case of New York Central & Hudson River Railroad Co. v United States 212 U.S. 481 (1909) (King and Lord, 2018: 246). In contrast, the UK and Ireland (as well as Singapore, Canada and Australia) rely on the 'identification doctrine' in ascribing corporate criminal liability, whereby persons who control the affairs of a company embody the company itself. The application of this doctrine means that conviction is more difficult in these common law jurisdictions than in the US, a matter which undermines the efficacy of DPAs by virtue of the alternative being less likely and less robust. If corporations agree to DPAs but this is followed by individuals subsequently being acquitted this sounds alarm bells for corporations in future in respect of agreeing DPAs, and in terms of the desirability of contesting charges in court (Campbell, 2019). This raises some interesting questions about timelines and interplay between legal actions against corporations, and whether individuals should be prosecuted before DPAs are finalized, though this would render the processes even more protracted. Failure to address the flaws in the dominant mechanism of attributing corporate criminal liability critically undermines any positive impact of DPAs, and indeed the likelihood of corporations agreeing to them.

Such settlement responses to corporate crime often relate to transnational corporations and relate to multi-jurisdictional behaviour. The OECD (2019: 14) notes the steady increase in the use of coordinated multi-jurisdictional NTRs over the past decade and suggests that one of their advantages over trials is that multi-jurisdictional cases can be resolved between several authorities at the same time, giving both prosecution and companies some certainty in the outcome and in particular combined financial penalty. The OECD uses Rolls-Royce as an example. Rolls-Royce Civil Aerospace and Defence Aerospace as well as its former energy business used a network of agents to bribe officials in at least seven countries to win contracts over three decades, with an overall estimated profit of £258 million. As Judge Brian Leveson stated in his judgment on the DPA,

> My reaction when first considering these papers was that if Rolls-Royce were not to be prosecuted in the context of such egregious criminality over decades, involving countries around the world, making truly vast corrupt payments and, consequentially, even greater profits, then it was difficult to see when any company would be prosecuted. (*Serious Fraud Office v Rolls-Royce Plc* [2017] 1 WLUK 189 [61])

His ultimate approval of the DPA with Rolls-Royce exemplifies the growing unlikelihood of contested proceedings for corporate wrongdoing.

There are further unresolved issues regarding coordinated multi-jurisdictional NTRs, that are shared across Europe and beyond:

- 'Double jeopardy', where NTRs could be reached in more than one jurisdiction, such as occurred with regards to Airbus in 2020 in the UK, the US and France for failing to prevent persons associated with Airbus SE from bribing others concerned with the purchase of aircraft by customers across multiple jurisdictions (including Malaysia, Sri Lanka, Taiwan, Indonesia, Ghana); or where an NTR and prosecution in different jurisdictions may be pursued.
- Recidivism, in that repeat offenders are not precluded from comparable agreements.
- Effectiveness, given that there is no evidence that DPAs, whether domestic or multi-jurisdictional, prevent future misconduct or crime improve corporate behaviour.

To elaborate on these briefly, currently there is no consistent international approach to the question of whether a DPA in one jurisdiction will operate as a bar to a prosecution in another (Laird and Hardcastle, 2018; Organisation for Economic Co-operation and Development, 2019: 165–70). It seems to be the case that the Serious Fraud Office in England and Wales views a DPA as engaging the principle against double jeopardy at an international level: for example, a DPA in the US concerning certain conduct would preclude a prosecution in respect of the same facts in the UK. In contrast, the US and France emphasize that the jurisdiction of their courts should not be constrained by proceedings elsewhere. While the essential principle of double jeopardy seeks to guard against trial and punishment for the same set of facts and acts, I suggest that the multi-jurisdictional nature of the offending, and the victimized constituents, indicate that the latter approach is preferable, in leaving open the possibility of action in different states.

Furthermore, domestically and inter-jurisdictionally, repeat offenders are not precluded from comparable settlement agreements. This is of particular concern in respect of multi-jurisdictional corporations with complex structures. HSBC, one of the largest banks in the world, which is based in the UK, is a prime example of this, having multiple US DPAs, as well as settlements in Switzerland (Garrett, 2014: 102; Garside, 2015). Furthermore, there is no evidence that DPAs, whether domestic or multi-jurisdictional, prevent future misconduct or crime (Campbell, 2019: 13).

Conclusion

A European dialogue on DPAs and other negotiated settlements with corporations brings to the fore their shared rationales across jurisdictions, as well as indicating how the different legal models influence their form and use. DPAs are described by Simon Bronitt (2017: 211, 225) as a new form of justice, a hybrid model of legal responsibility in line with the use of civil penalties and settlements rather than criminal procedure as the dominant regulatory norm. Similarly, this chapter has presented DPAs, in their 'negotiated justice' paradigm, as sitting between adversarial and inquisitorial models, and incorporating elements of each. This sheds new light on DPAs themselves as well as on the models of criminal procedure. Analyzing the nature and traction of DPAs using the dichotomous models of criminal procedure in Europe is useful analytically, as well as being of practical value. It illustrates how these settlements cohere with and exemplify inherent characteristics of different legal systems in Europe, and how pragmatism influences the agreement of settlements with corporate actors regardless of the legal system. It also illustrates how much traction such settlements have across the continent and globally, notwithstanding their dubious effectiveness.

Notes

[1]   A remediation agreement, in accordance with Section 715.32 of the Criminal Code.

[2]   Criminal Procedure Code, Part VIIA.

[3]   Sapin II - Law no 2016-1691 of 9 December 2016. One such settlement was the Judicial Public Interest Agreement reached in 2020 between the French National Prosecutor's Office at the Paris District Court and Airbus SE; see: www.agence-francaise-anticorruption.gouv.fr/files/files/CJIP%20AIRBUS_English%20 version.pdf

[4]   Article 74 of the Dutch Criminal Code and the Directive on Large and Special Transactions. For example, in 2018 the ING bank entered into a settlement agreement with the Dutch Public Prosecution Service relating to investigations regarding requirements for client on-boarding and the prevention of money laundering and corrupt practices (ING, 2018).

[5]   The '*patteggiamento*' under Articles 444–8 of the Code of Criminal Procedure is a form of plea bargain. In 2014, AgustaWestland SpA and AgustaWestland Ltd (a helicopter design and manufacturing company) requested and entered into a *patteggiamento* in relation to alleged bribery (Organisation for Economic Co-operation and Development, 2019: 177).

[6]   A 'reparation' under Article 53 of the Swiss Criminal Code. For instance, the Geneva public prosecutor accepted the abandonment of the proceedings against HSBC pursuant to Article 53, in exchange for the payment of 40 million Swiss Francs in favour of the State of Geneva (Garside, 2015).

[7]   *Serious Fraud Office v Rolls-Royce Plc* [2017] 1 WLUK 189; *Director of the Serious Fraud Office v Airbus SE* [2020] 1 WLUK 435

[8]   The Corporate Prosecution Registry, run by the University of Virginia School of Law and Duke University School of Law, provides comprehensive information on federal organizational prosecutions in the United States. See: http://lib.law. virginia.edu/Garrett/corporate-prosecution-registry/browse/browse.html

References

Alexander, C. and Cohen, M. (2015) 'The evolution of corporate criminal settlements: an empirical perspective on non-prosecution, deferred prosecution, and plea agreements', *American Criminal Law Review,* 52: 537–93.

Baer, M. (2016) 'Too vast to succeed', *Michigan Law Review*, 114: 1109–35.

Bronitt, S. (2017) 'Regulatory bargaining in the shows of preventive justice: deferred prosecution agreements', in T. Tulich, R. Ananian-Welsh, S. Bronitt and S. Murray (eds) *Regulating Preventive Justice: Principle, Policy and Paradox*, Abingdon: Routledge, pp 211–27.

Campbell, L. (2019) 'Trying corporations: why not prosecute?', *Current Issues in Criminal Justice*, 31: 269–91.

Campbell, L., Ashworth, A. and Redmayne, M. (2019) *The Criminal Process* (5th edn), Oxford: Oxford University Press.

Comino, V. (2018) 'The GFC and beyond – how do we deal with corporate misconduct?', *Journal of Business Law*, 2018: 15–39.

Corruption Watch (2016) 'Out of court, out of mind – do deferred prosecution agreements and corporate settlements deter overseas corruption?', *Corruption Watch*, March.

Damaska, M. (1973) 'Evidentiary barriers to conviction and two models of criminal procedure: a comparative study', *University of Pennsylvania Law Review*, 121: 506–89.

Devlin, P. (1981) *The Judge*, Oxford: Oxford University Press.

Epstein, R. (2011) 'Deferred prosecution agreements on trial: lessons from the law of unconstitutional conditions', in A. Barkow and R. Barkow (eds) *Prosecutors in the Boardroom: Using Criminal Law to Regulate Corporate Conduct*, New York: New York University Press, pp 38–61.

Freiberg, A. (2011) 'Post-adversarial and post-inquisitorial justice: transcending traditional penological paradigms', *European Journal of Criminology*, 8: 82–101.

Garrett, B. (2014) *Too Big to Jail: How Prosecutors Compromise with Corporations*, Harvard: Harvard University Press.

Hawley, S., King, C. and Lord, N. (2020) 'Justice for whom? The need for a principled approach to deferred prosecution in England and Wales', in T. Søreide and A. Makinwa (eds) *Negotiated Settlements in Bribery Cases: A Principled Approach*, Cheltenham: Edward Elgar, Available at: www.research.manchester.ac.uk/portal/files/135142584/Hawley_et_al_2020_DPAs.pdf

ING (2018) 'ING reaches settlement agreement with Dutch authorities on regulatory issues in the ING Netherlands business', [online] 4 September, Available at: www.ing.com/Newsroom/News/Press-releases/ING-reaches-settlement-agreement with-Dutch-authorities-on-regulatory-issues-in-the-ING-Netherlands-business.htm

King, C. and Lord, N. (2018) *Negotiated Justice and Corporate Crime: The Legitimacy of Civil Recovery Orders and Deferred Prosecution Agreements*, London: Palgrave Macmillan.

Laird, K. and Hardcastle, K. (2018) 'International double jeopardy and deferred prosecution agreements', *Criminal Law Review*, 12: 946–60.

Langer, M. (2004) 'From legal transplants to legal translations: the globalization of plea bargaining and the Americanization thesis in criminal procedure', *Harvard International Law Journal*, 45(1): 1–64.

Lord, N. (2013) 'Regulating transnational corporate bribery: anti-bribery and corruption in the UK and Germany', *Crime, Law and Social Change*, 60(2): 127–45.

Lynch, G. (1998) 'Our administrative system of criminal justice', *Fordham Law Review*, 66: 2117–51.

McEwan J. (1998) *Evidence and the Adversarial Process*, Oxford: Hart.

McEwan, J. (2011) 'From adversarialism to managerialism: criminal justice in transition', *Legal Studies*, 31: 519-546.

Ministry of Justice (2012) 'Deferred prosecution agreements: government response to the consultation on a new enforcement tool to deal with economic crime committed by commercial organisations: response to consultation CP(R)18/2012', Available at: https://assets.publishing.service.gov.uk/government/uploads/system/uploads/attachment_data/file/236000/8463.pdf

Organisation for Economic Co-operation and Development (2019) 'Resolving foreign bribery cases with non-trial resolutions settlements and non-trial agreements by parties to the Anti-Bribery Convention', Available at: www.oecd.org/daf/anti-bribery/Resolving-foreign-bribery-cases-with-non-trial-resolutions.pdf

Rakoff, J. (2015) 'Justice deferred is justice denied', *The New York Review of Books*, [online] 19 February, Available at: www.nybooks.com/articles/2015/02/19/justice-deferred-justice-denied/

Serious Fraud Office (2012) 'Corporate self-reporting', Available at: www.sfo.gov.uk/publications/guidance-policy-and-protocols/corporate-self-reporting/

Serious Fraud Office (2020) 'SFO enters into €991m deferred prosecution agreement with Airbus as part of a €3.6bn global resolution', 31 January, Available at: www.sfo.gov.uk/2020/01/31/sfo-enters-into-e991m-deferred-prosecution-agreement-with-airbus-as-part-of-a-e3-6bn-global-resolution/

Serious Fraud Office (nd) 'Deferred prosecution agreements', Available at: www.sfo.gov.uk/publications/guidance-policy-and-protocols/deferred-prosecution-agreements/

Garside, J. (2015) 'HSBC pays out £28m over money-laundering claims', *The Guardian*, [online] 5 June, Available at: www.theguardian.com/business/2015/jun/04/hsbc-fined-278m-over-money-laundering-claims

Tulkens, F. (2002) 'Negotiated justice', in M. Delmas-Marty and J.R. Spencer (eds) *European Criminal Procedures*, Cambridge: Cambridge University Press, pp 641–87.

Weinreb, L. (1977) *Denial of Justice: Criminal Process in the United States*, New York: Free Press.

PART V

Observations from Outside of Europe

16

Observations on European White-Collar Crime Scholarship from the United States

Melissa Rorie

Introduction

The fundamental question that this book seeks to answer is 'what is "European" about white-collar and corporate crime in Europe?' The chapters do an excellent job of explaining how looking at Europe as a whole contributes to an understanding of how crime (and responses to crime) compares between countries within the continent, as well as making comparisons between Europe and other regions of the world. In this chapter, I would like to consider a slightly different version of the original question. I will discuss what I think is European about white-collar and corporate crime scholarship in Europe.

I have been incredibly fortunate to have worked with and around European white-collar crime scholars since graduate school. Judith van Erp and Wim Huisman were some of my earlier European influences, who introduced me to other student scholars at the time (like Aleksandra Jordanoska and Karin van Wingerde) as well as many others (as a few examples, Michael Levi, Nicholas Lord and Benjamin van Rooij). All of these individuals have had an incredible impact on my own research and my understanding of white-collar crime. Early on, I recognized some of my 'American privilege' as a white-collar crime scholar: notably, Wim Huisman introduced himself to me at an American Society of Criminology conference and remarked that my dissertation topic was similar to something he had written a few years earlier. I believe he said something along the lines of "I made a great mistake in only publishing it in Dutch!" That conversation really opened my eyes to the notion that I might be missing out on important research – mainly because I wasn't looking hard enough for it. I hope with this chapter that I can impart to the reader how a failure to recognize European scholarship in the white-collar crime domain (and in criminology more broadly) limits our ability to build knowledge.

To that end, I have gathered information on four different questions comparing European and North American white-collar and corporate crime research. These include the following:

- where is white-collar and corporate crime research generated?
- what topics or crime types do European authors cover more often or more thoroughly than North American authors?
- what methods or strategies are used by European researchers compared to North American researchers?
- what theories are used by European scholars compared to those used by American scholars?

In addition to examining the chapters in the present volume to answer these questions, I wanted to take a systematic approach to understanding the differences between European and North American scholarship in this domain more broadly. To that end, I culled articles published between January 2019 and April 2020 in journals known to publish white-collar crime research most often.[1] Specifically, the 21 journals were (in alphabetical order):

- *American Sociological Review*
- *American Journal of Sociology*
- *British Journal of Criminology*
- *Canadian Journal of Criminology and Criminal Justice*
- *Crime & Delinquency*
- *Crime, Law and Social Change*
- *Criminal Justice and Behavior*
- *Criminology*
- *Criminology & Public Policy*
- *Critical Criminology*
- *European Journal of Criminology*
- *Journal of Criminal Law and Criminology*

- *Journal of Research in Crime and Delinquency*
- *Journal of Quantitative Criminology*
- *Journal of White-Collar and Corporate Crime*
- *Justice Quarterly*
- *Law & Society Review*
- *Social Forces*
- *Social Justice*
- *Social Problems*
- *Theoretical Criminology*

Within each journal, I used six search terms to identify articles related to white-collar and corporate crime. These were:

- corporate crime
- white-collar crime
- government crime
- occupational crime
- organizational crime
- environmental crime

From this search, I identified 79 articles whose focus was on some form of white-collar crime (including organized crime, occupational crime, corporate crime, state and state-corporate crime, cybercrime and so on). My focus here is on empirical knowledge, so I removed all 'review' articles (for example, book reviews or articles describing the current status of a topic). This brought me to 66 empirical studies (53 of which are from European or North American authors, see the references section of this chapter) that will serve as the foundation of my comments in this chapter, although I use the extant literature as well. I coded each of the 66 studies for the following information:

- author names;
- first author's academic discipline (based on the discipline of their PhD, or – if that information was not available – the discipline in which they are currently employed);
- country of first author's employment;
- article title;
- journal name;
- country in which the study took place;
- theoretical approach or conceptual umbrella;

- crime type being studied;
- method used – quantitative, qualitative, or multiple methods?

Based on this review, and on the chapters of this volume and previous literature, I believe that I can accurately state that European white-collar crime scholars more generally offer a rich, qualitative approach to studying these crimes, whereas North American authors are more likely to take a quantitative, probabilistic approach. The European authors in my review also use a wider variety of theories to inform their research. In examining these questions, I emphasize the unique contributions that my European colleagues make to the white-collar crime literature.

Where is white-collar and corporate crime research generated?

Reading two recent meta-analyses of white-collar and corporate crime (Simpson et al, 2014; Pusch and Holtfreter, 2020; see also Schell-Busey et al, 2016; Rorie et al, 2018), one might believe that European scholarship is woefully underrepresented in the white-collar crime literature. Simpson et al (2014) found that 78 per cent of their effect sizes came from studies conducted on the United States, while Pusch and Holtfreter (2019) found that 7.9 per cent of their dataset came from Europe and 87.3 per cent of their dataset came from North America. It is crucial to note, however, that almost by definition, meta-analyses combine quantitative data sources to determine the overall magnitude of a relationship between two variables (Lipsey and Wilson, 2001). Systematic reviews (for example, 'vote-counting') are often done on qualitative studies, but none to my knowledge have examined white-collar or corporate crime using qualitative research.

As described later on, however, European scholars seem to use qualitative methods much more often than their North American counterparts. This is reflected in the articles reviewed for this chapter, which tell a very different story than the aforementioned meta-analyses about where white-collar and corporate crime research originates. Of the 66 articles, only 19 (28.8 per cent) were written by lead authors in North America. In contrast, 35 (53 per cent) were authored by scholars in Europe. With regards to which areas are being studied, 26 (39.4 per cent) examined white-collar and corporate crime in Europe while only 17 (25.8 per cent) used data or cases in North America.

What topics or crime types do European authors cover more often or more thoroughly than North American authors?

To examine how topics differed across studies by European and North American authors, I coded the study topics into 13 different crime types. It should be noted, however, that within each of these crime types scholars examined things like regulatory responses, offender motivations, prevention efforts, deterrence and so on; as such, this is an admittedly broad-brush approach to examining differences between the two continents, but the data are available from the author for further analyses. For now, Table 16.1 compares the frequency of articles by the crime type they are most focused on.

Clearly, the information here does not allow us to make sweeping generalizations about European and North American white-collar crime scholarship, but it is interesting to note that environmental

Table 16.1: Focus of articles from European and North American white-collar crime scholars

Crime type	Number (%) of European manuscripts	Number (%) of North American manuscripts
Environmental crime	5 (14%)	3 (17%)
Bribery/corruption	5 (14%)	3 (17%)
General/multiple types of white-collar crime	3 (9%)	5 (28%)
Securities crimes	3 (9%)	1 (6%)
Organized crime	3 (9%)	0 (0%)
Fraud (general)	3 (9%)	1 (6%)
Corporate crime (multiple types)	3 (9%)	1 (6%)
Tax crimes	2 (6%)	0 (0%)
Crimes of the powerful/state crime (general)	2 (6%)	3 (17%)
Corporate financial crimes	2 (6%)	0 (0%)
Cartel behaviour	2 (6%)	0 (0%)
Cybercrime	1 (3%)	1 (6%)
Corporate violence (not environmental)	1 (3%)	0 (0%)
Total	35 (100%)	18 (100%)

crime, bribery/corruption and general white-collar crime are topics of interest shared by scholars in both regions. It seems like organized crime and corporate financial crime might be a higher priority for European scholars than North American scholars (see also Meerts, this volume; Benson, this volume; Wilson, this volume) – perhaps because of the easy permeability of borders within the EU (see, for example, van Duyne, 1993; Sallavaci, 2018) and the current financial uncertainty surrounding Brexit (see Pasculli and Futter, 2019; van Erp and Lord, 2020: 4). State crime or crimes of the powerful seem to have more representation in the United States – this, in turn, could have reflected the political environment under President Donald Trump (see DeKeseredy, 2019; Friedrichs and Rothe, 2020).[2]

One might think that demands on law enforcement would motivate the study of such crimes more so than political concerns – if certain crime types are particularly prevalent in certain areas of the world then scholars in those areas would be more attuned to those. However, examining the United Nations Office on Drugs and Crime (UNODC) crime data for environmental crime, fraud crime and money laundering, as well as Transparency International's corruption data, contradicts this. Although environmental crime is a popular subject for scholars in both regions, the UNODC records of environmental pollution convictions, police-recorded offenses and convictions for illegal trade of species all demonstrate that these crimes are more prevalent in Europe than in all of the Americas (including North America, Central America, South America, and the Caribbean).[3] Similarly, despite the fairly equal treatment of fraud across regional scholarship, the number of police-recorded fraud cases in Europe is more than twice that of all American countries.[4] I have often noticed that money-laundering seems to be studied more often by European scholars than North American scholars (see, for example, Meerts, this volume; Benson, this volume; van Wingerde and Merz, this volume, as well as Table 16.1). According to the UNODC, there were indeed far more police-recorded money laundering offenses in Europe (80,538) than in the Americas (4,528) between 2013 and 2016.[5] Finally, although corruption received fairly equal treatment across the regions over the past year, Transparency International gives American countries a far worse corruption score (43.72) than European countries (66.03).[6]

Recognizing that data on white-collar crimes remain notoriously difficult to come by 80 years after it became a subject of systematic study (Simpson, 2019) and that law enforcement priorities are likely impacting differences in crime statistics, it is problematic to state that true crime prevalence is likely to be driving crime scholarship. What else might be influencing the choice of topics? Without accurate statistics on crime, it seems reasonable that crime scholars focus on the offenses that are of most concern to the public or that they feel should be of more concern to the public. Media coverage and political concerns are likely filling the vacuum left behind by the lack of white-collar and corporate crime data (see Hughes, 2000; Jewkes and Linnemann, 2017).

What methods or strategies are used by European researchers compared to North American researchers?

As mentioned previously, the most obvious difference between European and North American scholars, to me, is the emphasis on quantitative or qualitative research methods. In the review of journal articles, 22 (62.9 per cent) out of the 35 manuscripts authored by European authors relied on qualitative methods (for example, case studies, interviews or ethnographies). This is notably the most common strategy of the empirical articles within the present book (see, for example, Davies, this volume; Gladkova, this volume; Inzelt and Bezsenyi, this volume; Meerts, this volume) and is in stark contrast to the North American articles, of which 5 (27.8 per cent) of the 18 used qualitative methods. The raw number of articles using quantitative methods (for example, secondary or archival data, content analyses or surveys) were about the same across both regions, although North American authors were disproportionately more likely to use such methods. Specifically, 13 (72.2 per cent) of the North American articles took a quantitative approach compared to 12 (34.3 per cent) of the European articles.

What theories are used by European scholars compared to those used by North American scholars?

Something that struck me as I read through the chapters of the current volume was a lack of theoretical specificity. The chapter by Maesschalck explicitly uses grid-group theory, responsive regulation and social systems theory as its framework, while Gladkova explicitly takes a critical criminological approach. However, most of the other chapters talk broadly about the literature related to their topic without couching their research approach within a specific theoretical framework. This could simply be due to the nature of book chapters (which are often more review-oriented than empirical research endeavours), or it might be due to the methodological preferences of European scholars as described in the previous section. Qualitative research is often more inductive in nature; these scholars begin with a broad (often understudied) topic, gather a tremendous amount of data, then establish patterns from the data and create theoretical propositions from those patterns. Quantitative research, on the other hand, is much more often deductive, beginning with theoretical propositions and collecting data to examine the extent to which those theories can help us understand and prevent crime (Worrall, 2000).

Notably, however, when looking at the review of published manuscripts in peer-reviewed journals, one sees that European authors are very theoretically oriented, albeit in some unique ways compared to North American authors – in other words, European scholars use very different types of theories compared to their North American counterparts. Of course, this is a limited sample over a short period of time, but interestingly European authors used a wider variety of traditional criminological theories (for example, routine activities, self-control, techniques of neutralization, differential association, deterrence) compared to North Americans, and uniquely used 'southern theory' and green criminological approaches in the current review. Europeans also seemed more inclined to use a psychological or biosocial approach compared to North American authors. North American authors were more likely to use integrated theories (for example, control-balance theory, the integrated theory of state-corporate crime) or multiple (separate) theories in their manuscripts.

Conclusion

Overall, I think it is fair to state that European white-collar crime scholarship has been thriving in recent years. Not only were European studies overrepresented in major criminological journals in the 14 months prior to the writing of this chapter, scholars from this region are using a wider variety of methods and theories to guide their research. However, according to other current reviews of white-collar crime scholarship (Simpson et al, 2014; Pusch and Holtfreter, 2019), this is not obvious; a finding that necessitates further consideration. Although European white-collar crime scholarship is clearly making strong contributions to the literature, we all too often think of quantitative research as 'generalizable' or better at reflecting the 'reality' of a broad research topic, whereas qualitative research is considered to be an in-depth look at a specific (often 'sensational') situation. The emphasis in systematic reviews is often on including 'methodologically rigorous' studies (see, for example, Sherman et al,

1997) in order to strengthen inferences about causal relationships; this emphasis means that qualitative research is rarely included in reviews. To that end, systematic reviews and meta-analyses are often lauded as providing a sense of what research within a domain as a whole can say about the causal relationships of interest to the field (but see Rorie et al, 2018). A failure to review the multitude of qualitative research in the white-collar crime domain means that we are missing a large part of the research agenda – we have heretofore prioritized the North American perspective and neglected much of the European perspective. It is also likely that we are missing important studies that spoke directly and at length to offenders, victims and other stakeholders (and thus is more authentic); furthermore, qualitative research seeks to identify larger patterns and situate itself within the broader criminological domain (Copes et al, 2016). I encourage scholars to consider doing a narrative systematic review that could better assess the contributions of qualitative research and include more diverse perspectives.

All consumers of white-collar crime scholarship would benefit from efforts to delve into the European perspective, but North American white-collar crime scholars in particular would benefit greatly by looking to organizations like the European Working Group on Organisational Crime (EUROC) for opportunities to network with these scholars. For a long time it has been obvious to me that the 'European' approach to research is much deeper, thorough and effortful than the survey research I do regularly. Although many North American scholars do incredible research, I believe we all could learn from European scholars to engage in more case-specific, in-depth research to understand often highly individualized mechanisms of compliance and offending – mechanisms that simply cannot be examined using surveys and experiments (Tewksbury, 2009). Furthermore, North American scholarship would be greatly enhanced by considering more non-traditional criminological theories that might be better suited for studying the crimes of the powerful. I hope that this review encourages far more collaboration across continents in the future, but at the very least I encourage my colleagues to seek out publications from European journals more deliberately, using such publications as a guide for improving their own research.

Notes

[1]   I used citation studies by McGurrin et al (2013) and Lynch et al (2004) as well as discussions with the 2019 Awards Committee Chair from ASC's Division of White-Collar and Corporate Crime to determine the most appropriate journals

for this review. These journals were chosen for their prestige in the criminological domain, their international scope and/or their critical criminological perspective.

² It would be interesting to update this review after 2020 – the political upheaval surrounding COVID-19 responses in both continents, the US presidential election and the transition of Britain out of the EU are likely to change the priorities of many scholars in the coming years.

³ See data at: www.unodc.org/unodc/en/data-and-analysis/crime-and-criminal-justice.html. Here, you can see that from 2006 to 2011, pollution convictions totaled 552 in the Americas compared to 8,292 in all of Europe. For police-recorded pollution from 2006 to 2011, there were 394 offenses in the Americas compared to 65,250 offenses in Europe. Regarding illegal trade, from 2006 to 2011 there were 6 convictions in the Americas and 492 offenses in Europe.

⁴ See data at: https://dataunodc.un.org/data/crime/fraud, in which European cases total 7,347,261 compared to American cases of 2,938,527 between 2013 and 2016.

⁵ See data at: https://dataunodc.un.org/data/crime/money-laundering

⁶ See report at: www.transparency.org/en/cpi/2019/results/table

References

Articles marked with an asterisk were part of the comparative analysis of North American and European white-collar crime scholarship between January 2019–April 2020.

★ Andresen, M.S. and Button, M. (2019) 'The profile and detection of bribery in Norway and England and Wales: a comparative study', *European Journal of Criminology*, 16(1), 18–40.

★ Angeletti, T. (2019) 'The differential management of financial illegalisms: assigning responsibilities in the Libor scandal', *Law & Society Review*, 53(4): 1233–65.

★ Aziani, A., Favarin, S. and Campedelli, G.M. (2020) 'A security paradox: the influence of governance-type organized crime over the surrounding criminal environment', *British Journal of Criminology*, 60(4): 970–93.

★ Bautista-Beauchesne, N. (2020) 'Corruption and anti-corruption: a folklore problem?', *Crime, Law and Social Change*, 73(2): 159–80.

★ Box, M., Gratzer, K. and Lin, X. (2019) 'The asymmetric effect of bankruptcy fraud in Sweden: a long-term perspective', *Journal of Quantitative Criminology*, 35(2): 287–312.

★ Campedelli, G.M., Calderoni, F., Comunale, T. and Meneghini, C. (2019) 'Life-course criminal trajectories of mafia members', *Crime & Delinquency*, 67(1): 111–41.

★ Ceresola, R.G. (2019) 'The US government's framing of corruption: a content analysis of public integrity section reports, 1978–2013', *Crime, Law and Social Change*, 71(1): 47–65.

Copes, H., Tewksbury, R. and Sandburg, S. (2016) 'Publishing qualitative research in criminology and criminal justice journals', *Journal of Criminal Justice Education*, 27(1): 121–39.

DeKeseredy, W.S. (2019) 'Defenders of freedom or perpetrators and facilitators of crimes? Beyond progressive retreatism in the Trump era', *Victims & Offenders*, 14(8): 925–39.

★ Evertsson, N. (2019) 'Corporate tax avoidance and neutralization techniques: a case study on the Panama Papers', *Critical Criminology*, 28: 721–38.

★ Friedrichs, D.O. and Rothe, D.L. (2020) 'Regulatory rollback and white-collar crime in the era of Trump: the challenges of perspective', *Journal of White Collar and Corporate Crime*, 1(2): 95–102.

★ Galvin, M.A. (2020) 'Substance or semantics? The consequences of definitional ambiguity for white-collar research', *Journal of Research in Crime and Delinquency*, 57(3): 369–99.

★ Ghazi-Tehrani, A.K. and Pontell, H.N. (2020) 'Corruption in the United States and China: codes of conduct vs crackdowns', *Crime, Law and Social Change*, 73(1): 73–92.

★ Gladkova, E. (2020) 'Farming intensification and environmental justice in Northern Ireland', *Critical Criminology*, 28: 445–61.

★ Gooch, K. and Treadwell, J. (2020) 'Prisoner society in an era of psychoactive substances, organized crime, new drug markets and austerity', *British Journal of Criminology*, 60(5): 1260–81.

★ Gottschalk, P. and Benson, M.L. (2020) 'The evolution of corporate accounts of scandals from exposure to investigation', *British Journal of Criminology*, 60(4): 949–69.

★ Graves, J.T., Acquisti, A. and Anderson, R. (2019) 'Perception versus punishment in cybercrime', *Journal Criminal Law & Criminology*, 109(2): 313–64.

★ Greener, J. (2019) 'Performative compliance and the state–corporate structuring of neglect in a residential care home for older people', *Critical Criminology*, 28: 651–88.

★ Greife, M.J. and Maume, M.O. (2019) 'Do companies pay the price for environmental crimes? Consequences of criminal penalties on corporate offenders', *Crime, Law and Social Change*, 73: 337–56.

★ Györy, C. (2020) 'The institutional context of financial fraud in a post-transition economy: the Quaestor scandal', *European Journal of Criminology*, 17(1): 31–49.

★ Harbinson, E., Benson, M.L. and Latessa, E.J. (2019) 'Assessing risk among white-collar offenders under federal supervision in the community', *Criminal Justice and Behavior*, 46(2): 261–79.

★ Healy, D. and McGrath, J. (2019) 'Simple rhetoric and complex punitiveness: federal criminal justice responses to white-collar criminality', *Justice Quarterly*, 36(7): 1258–83.

★ Hiah, J. (2019) 'The client side of everyday corruption in Central and Eastern Europe: the case of Chinese migrant entrepreneurs in Romania', *European Journal of Criminology*, 17(6): 877–95.

Hughes, G. (2000) 'Understanding the politics of criminological research', in V. Jupp, P. Davies and P. Francis (eds) *Doing Criminological Research*, London: Sage, pp 235–48.

★ Hunt, D.E. and Topalli, V. (2019) 'To control or be controlled: predicting types of offending in a corporate environment using control-balance theory', *Journal of Quantitative Criminology*, 35(3): 435–64.

★ Jaspers, J.D. (2020a) 'Leniency in exchange for cartel confessions', *European Journal of Criminology*, 17(1): 106–24.

★ Jaspers, J.D. (2020b) 'Strong by concealment? How secrecy, trust, and social embeddedness facilitate corporate crime', *Crime, Law and Social Change*, 73(1): 55–72.

Jewkes, Y. and Linnemann, T. (2017) *Media and Crime in the US*, London: Sage.

★ Jönsson, E. (2019) 'Risky business: corporate risk regulation when managing allegations of crime', *Crime, Law and Social Change*, 71(5): 483–501.

★ Jordanoska, A. and Lord, N. (2020) 'Scripting the mechanics of the benchmark manipulation corporate scandals: the "guardian" paradox', *European Journal of Criminology*, 17(1): 9–30.

★ Lampkin, J.A. and Wyatt, T. (2019) 'Utilising principles of earth jurisprudence to prevent environmental harm: applying a case study of unconventional hydraulic fracturing for shale gas in the United Kingdom', *Critical Criminology*, 28: 501–26.

★ Lemaitre, S. (2019) 'Illicit financial flows within the extractive industries sector: a glance at how legal requirements can be manipulated and diverted', *Crime, Law and Social Change*, 71(1): 107–28.

★ Leon, K.S. and Ken, I. (2019) 'Legitimized fraud and the state-corporate criminology of food: a spectrum-based theory', *Crime, Law and Social Change*, 71(1): 25–46.

★ Ling, S., Raine, A., Yang, Y., Schug, R.A., Portnoy, J. and Ho, M-H.R. (2019) 'Increased frontal lobe volume as a neural correlate of gray-collar offending', *Journal of Research in Crime and Delinquency*, 56(2): 303–36.

Lipsey, M.W. and Wilson, D.B. (2001) *Practical Meta-Analysis*, London: Sage.

* Logan, M.W., Morgan, M.A., Benson, M.L. and Cullen, F.T. (2019) 'Coping with imprisonment: testing the special sensitivity hypothesis for white-collar offenders', *Justice Quarterly*, 36(2): 225–54.

* Lord, N.J., Campbell, L.J. and van Wingerde, K. (2019) 'Other people's dirty money: professional intermediaries, market dynamics and the finances of white-collar, corporate and organized crimes', *British Journal of Criminology*, 59(5): 1217–36.

Lynch, M.J., McGurrin, D. and Fenwick, M. (2004) 'Disappearing act: the representation of corporate crime research in criminological literature', *Journal of Criminal Justice*, 32(5): 389–98.

* McGrath, J. (2020) ' "Walk softly and carry no stick": culture, opportunity and irresponsible risk-taking in the Irish banking sector', *European Journal of Criminology*, 17(1): 86–105.

* McGrath, J. (2019) 'Regulating white-collar crime in Ireland: an analysis using the lens of governmentality', *Crime, Law and Social Change*, 72(4): 445–65.

* McGregor, R. (2019) 'James Ellroy's critical criminology: crimes of the powerful in the Underworld USA Trilogy', *Critical Criminology*. doi:10.1007/s10612-019-09459-3

McGurrin, D., Jarrell, M., Jahn, A. and Cochrane, B. (2013) 'White collar crime representation in the criminological literature revisited, 2001–2010', *Western Criminology Review*, 14(2): 3–19.

* Milburn, T. and Guertin-Martín, F.A. (2019) 'Tapping into environmental harm in brewing: an exploration of pollution and waste in beer production', *Critical Criminology*, 28: 407–23.

* Moosavi, L. (2019) 'Decolonising criminology: Syed Hussein Alatas on crimes of the powerful', *Critical Criminology*, 27(2): 229–42.

* Natali, L. and de Nardin Budó, M. (2019) 'A sensory and visual approach for comprehending environmental victimization by the asbestos industry in Casale Monferrato', *European Journal of Criminology*, 16(6): 708–27.

Pasculli, L. and Futter, A. (2019) 'Seeds of systemic corruption in the post-Brexit UK', *Journal of Financial Crime*, 26(3): 705–18.

* Patten, D. (2019a) 'Motivations, opportunities, and controls of environmental crime: an empirical test of Kramer and Michalowski's integrated theoretical model of state-corporate crime', *Crime, Law and Social Change*, 72(2): 195–210.

* Patten, D. (2019b) 'Criminogenic policy as a crime of the powerful: a case study on NAFTA's negotiation process', *Critical Criminology*, 27(2): 243–60.

★ Peeters, M., Denkers, A. and Huisman, W. (2020) 'Rule violations by SMEs: the influence of conduct within the industry, company culture and personal motives', *European Journal of Criminology*, 17(1): 50–69.

★ Pusch, N. and Holtfreter, K. (2020) 'Individual and organizational predictors of white-collar crime: a meta-analysis', *Journal of White Collar and Corporate Crime*, 2(1): 5–23.

★ Ranson, J.W.A., Arnio, A.N. and Baumer, E.P. (2019) 'Extending research on neighborhoods and crime: an examination of mortgage fraud across Chicago census tracts', *Journal of Quantitative Criminology*, 35(3): 465–91.

★ Ribeiro, R., Silva, B., Pimenta, C. and Poeschl, G. (2019) 'Why do consumers perpetrate fraudulent behaviors in insurance?', *Crime, Law and Social Change*, 73: 249–73.

★ Ribeiro, R., Sousa Guedes, I. and Cruz, J.N. (2019) 'White-collar offenders vs. common offenders: a comparative study on personality traits and self-control', *Crime, Law and Social Change*, 72(5): 607–22

Rorie, M., Alper, M., Schell-Busey, N. and Simpson, S.S. (2018) 'Using meta-analysis under conditions of definitional ambiguity: the case of corporate crime', *Criminal Justice Studies*, 31(1): 38–61.

★ Russell, B. and Cheng, H. (2019) 'A critical analysis of securities crime in Canada', *Canadian Journal of Criminology and Criminal Justice*, 61(1): 86-104.

Sallavaci, O. (2018) 'Strengthening cross-border law enforcement cooperation in the EU: the Prüm network of data exchange', *European Journal on Criminal Policy and Research*, 24(3): 219–35.

Schell-Busey, N., Simpson, S.S., Rorie, M. and Alper, M. (2016) 'What works? A systematic review of corporate crime deterrence', *Criminology & Public Policy*, 15(2): 387–416.

★ Schoultz, I. and Flyghed, J. (2019) 'From "we didn't do it" to "we've learned our lesson": development of a typology of neutralizations of corporate crime', *Critical Criminology*, 28: 739–57.

Sherman, L.W., Gottfredson, D., MacKenzie, D., Eck, J., Reuter, P. and Bushway, S. (1997) 'Preventing crime: what works, what doesn't, what's promising', US Department of Justice, Available at: www.ncjrs.gov/pdffiles1/Digitization/165366NCJRS.pdf

Simpson, S.S. (2019) 'Reimagining Sutherland 80 years after white-collar crime', *Criminology*, 57(2): 189–207.

Simpson, S.S., Rorie, M., Alper, M., Schell-Busey, N., Laufer, W.S. and Smith, N.C. (2014) 'Corporate crime deterrence: a systematic review', *Campbell Systematic Reviews*, 10(1): 1–105.

* Singh, D. (2019) 'Challenging corruption and clientelism in post-conflict and developing states', *Crime, Law and Social Change*, 71(2): 197–216.

* Sollund, R.A., and Runhovde, S.R. (2020) 'Responses to wildlife crime in post-colonial times. Who fares best?', *British Journal of Criminology*, 60(4): 1014–33.

* Tankebe, J. (2019) 'Cooperation with the police against corruption: exploring the roles of legitimacy, deterrence and collective action theories', *British Journal of Criminology* 59(6): 1390–410.

Tewksbury, R. (2009) 'Qualitative versus quantitative methods: understanding why qualitative methods are superior for criminology and criminal justice', *Journal of Theoretical & Philosophical Criminology*, 1(1): 38–58.

* Tudor, K. (2019) 'Symbolic survival and harm: serious fraud and consumer capitalism's perversion of the causa sui project', *British Journal of Criminology*, 59(5): 1237–53.

* van de Weijer, S.G.A., Leukfeldt, R. and Bernasco, W. (2019) 'Determinants of reporting cybercrime: a comparison between identity theft, consumer fraud, and hacking', *European Journal of Criminology*, 16(4): 486–508.

Van Duyne, P. (1993) 'Implications of cross-border crime risks in an open Europe', *Crime, Law and Social Change*, 20(2): 99–111.

van Erp, J. and Lord, N. (2020) 'Is there a "European" corporate criminology? Introduction to the Special Issue on European corporate crime', *European Journal of Criminology*, 17(1): 3–8.

* van Uhm, D.P. and Nijman, R.C.C. (2020) 'The convergence of environmental crime with other serious crimes: subtypes within the environmental crime continuum', *European Journal of Criminology*. doi:10.1177/1477370820904585

Worrall, J.L. (2000) 'In defense of the "quantoids": more on the reasons for the quantitative emphasis in criminal justice education and research', *Journal of Criminal Justice Education*, 11(2): 353–61.

17

What Is 'European' about White-Collar Crime in Europe? Perspectives from the Global South

Diego Zysman-Quirós

Introduction

It is truly a pleasure for me to be able to provide my point of view to such a relevant work that brings together such prestigious authors and interesting lines of inquiry. My contribution is based on certain impressions of European works on white-collar and corporate crime that I have read previously and, in a more analytical way, of the contributions to this volume. To offer a complementary view from South and Central America, such a vast territory, it is necessary to briefly introduce myself. I am a former magistrate and current trial lawyer in economic crime courts in Buenos Aires, Argentina, where I graduated and where I am currently a professor. I previously lived and studied in Barcelona, where I got my PhD specializing in the criminology and sociology of punishment. Academic activity has continued to connect me with Europe and the United States, and more recently with Australia. This has led me to become very interested in the similarities and differences in the explorations of the criminal justice system and of criminological theory and to participate in the reflection on a criminology of the Global South, or 'southern criminology'.

Most of the countries of South and Central America constitute Latin America (along with Mexico in North America). The Spanish and Portuguese colonization not only defined an important historical heritage, with national and cultural varieties and two Romance languages, but also a criminal legal tradition of civil law and an inquisitive system typical of continental Europe, which only in the last 30 years has been shaken by important reforms towards the adversarial system of English-speaking countries, although particularly toward that of the US (Langer, 2007). Compared to the US and Canada, South and Central America has a lot of historical and cultural diversity, beyond a common past provided by colonization. Adding to this, there are series of subaltern indigenous theories, practices and institutions that have wide differences according to the territory, and which are beginning to inspire the literature of 'green criminology'. On the other hand, for those countries that participate in what is usually called the Global South, both North America and Europe are part of the Global North axis and we necessarily treat Anglo–American countries as part of the same legal and criminological community.

Regional economic institutions or agreements in Latin America – like Mercosur – are neither comparable in development nor regulatory power to the regulations and guidelines of the European Union because they are younger but also highly subject to regional crises and political changes. However, some issues are somewhat similar. The influence of the so-called Americanization of economic crimes is discussed, as well as the influence of international organizations such as the Financial Action Task Force (FATF), the Organisation for Economic Co-operation and Development (OECD), the World Trade Organization (WTO), the World Bank and the United Nations (UN) and the agreements that universalize the legal practices and legal reforms of a large number of countries in the area of money laundering and terrorist financing (in Brazil with harsh policies on lawyers, see Benson, this volume, on Europe), public and private corruption, compliance and responsibility of legal entities, and tax agreements, among other areas. Much more established is the legal discussion and the political impact regarding institutions similar to plea bargaining in common law crimes with regards to white-collar and corporate crimes in Latin American justice systems (see Zysman-Quirós, 2019). Very novel and still very limited in academia are theory and jurisprudence on leniency programs, Deferred Prosecution Agreements, insider traders, whistleblowers, compliance and even details of corporate criminal liability. Likewise, there is no great academic tradition in white-collar crime research beyond journalistic coverage and political discussions. Nonetheless, I believe that some studies on corporate responsibility for human rights violations, both during authoritarian rule and now in terms of expansion mining of forests like the Amazon and water control, are beginning to be more visible on the agenda of critical criminology (see Rodriguez Goyes, 2019; Böhm, 2020).

The private sector and domestic transnational corporations are very few in number and much less powerful than those of the Global North, and as such there is less in need of harmonizing law than in Europe (Nieto Martin, 2007). The American style in legal reforms was usually influenced by those legal transformations in the jurisprudence and theory of countries such as Germany, Italy or Spain, important references in our criminal legal tradition. But it is probable that, in recent times, globalization and the shaping of an international agenda have had an impact on the speed and course of these reforms, which today are less likely to depend so much on this European mediation.

Provocation

I also want to add a provocative statement. What was the first thing that I noticed about the works and reflections on white-collar and corporate crime in Europe in this volume? It was not the kind of cases that are analyzed, nor the theoretical categories used to describe or explain them. Nor was it the difficulties in comparing statistics (pointed out by McGrath and Healy, this volume), the methodologies of the investigations (addressed by Lord et al, this volume) or the differences in criminal proceedings and punishments (see Campbell, this volume). What continues to be imposed explicitly or implicitly in a large majority of the European works that I have been able to access is that the white-collar crime scholarship in Europe is constantly defining itself from a single referent, towards which it gravitates. European states share a very extensive common history and the problems of capitalist, democratic and industrialized societies, but they continue to be examined based on their similarities, differences or proximity to the US. However, I believe that this 'identity by opposition', which reflects the difficulty of a definition in the – certainly – great European heterogeneity, leaves unexplored some of the most distinctive qualities of the European tradition and the diversity among its countries that would be much more productive for a European definition of white-collar crime scholarship.

Sutherland's success, as a notable exponent of American criminology, in imposing terminology in academia, journalism and other areas of common language, beyond constant discussion and typology, is clear. So too is his achievement in installing white-collar crime studies and corporate crime on the criminological agenda in a way that persists in the present. On these bases, since the 1970s there have been numerous and important theoretical North American academic publications and empirical investigations on white-collar and corporate crime that have developed concepts, categories, types and relevant discussions about this matter. Also, the current role of the US and the weight of its cultural industry has given wide publicity in other parts of the world to US scandals like Watergate and more recent financial scandals (for example subprime mortgage lending frauds) that motivated new conceptual discussions and important legal reforms in US which soon went on to influence a large number of countries in the new millennium. On the other hand, we cannot ignore the current overwhelming importance of the American economy in the world, especially on business regulation; even less the Anglophone dominance in criminology in general (see van Erp et al, 2015; Faraldo-Cabana, 2018). These reasons, among others, can easily explain North American leadership in this matter and the difficulty of moving away from the North American agenda and the type of cases that North American academic thought and that of its penal system regard as white-collar crime around the world.

However, the world is large, and today it is more connected than ever. Europe throughout the centuries has been the cradle of modern Western criminal law and scientific criminology, as well as adversarial and inquisitive criminal prosecution systems. But in addition to this, throughout the 20th century, Europe has shown such wide variations in national economic and political systems that we can still find cases in the experience of socialist, social democratic and liberal countries in economic matters that we would easily call 'white collar'. All this offers a comparative basis that we would not find elsewhere. To all this, Europe adds different national histories, cultures and languages but also a common concern as a bloc against other territorial spaces. In this way, bodies created under the axis of the EU and its institutions, aimed at harmonizing economic and other crimes as well as business regulation, were established (Nieto Martin, 2007). But despite this, this European tradition – perhaps due to the historical rivalries that have made it difficult to think beyond sovereign stories – does not necessarily appear in a prominent position in European academic publications. For a Latin American academic this can be a bit disconcerting.

Southern ideas for European debates

Of course, perhaps I am not exposing anything that has not been floating in the air for a long time. For these reasons, it seems to me that my view from the Global South can contribute better by recalling some of the theoretical and especially criminological reflections that were critically developed in Latin America – although not exclusively – regarding the role of knowledge and its dissemination between the Global North and the Global South. While insightful, these contributions are not mainstream social science in Latin America. In addition, naturally, these publications were written to question the subordinate knowledge of the countries in the Global South, but somehow I think they can also help us rethink what can be traced and is not usually highlighted in the idea of the Europeanness of white-collar crime.

In brief, postcolonial studies, de-colonial studies and 'southern' sociology share the idea that the production of academic knowledge in the world is unequal (among others, see Dussel and Mignolo, 2007). It has been pointed out that the US and the UK are responsible for more than half of all the output of the social sciences (Graham et al, 2011: 19), and the most widespread publications, in general, are in the English language, with a great predominance of Eurocentric or Anglocentric perspectives. These ideas also come close to what was expressed by the Portuguese sociologist Boaventura de Souza Santos, widely recognized for questioning the lack of 'cognitive justice' (de Sousa Santos, 2008) in academic knowledge. In light of the 2008–09 global financial crisis in Europe, de Sousa Santos warned that social injustice is an epistemological product of cognitive injustice and that this is due to the denial of world knowledge other than what Western science has considered as valid. Instead of reductionism or dualism, he promotes intercultural thinking and ways of knowing that escape the colonizing effects of the global episteme. Similarly, southern sociology also had an initial and important development in the former colony of Australia (Connell, 2007) and highlights that the hegemony of social scientific thought is based in experiences of a small number of societies in the Global North who are stakeholders in capitalist modernity and what is understood by 'civilization'. These divisions between North and South are not so much geographical as conceptual and the product of social construction; they also are encompassed by other distinctions such as industrialized or deindustrialized societies, developing or developed countries, the 'first world' and others. Anyway, it is affirmed that this led to a model of science accepted as universal and timeless deriving from thought in the 'metropole'. This produces a large number of global generalizations about phenomena that are not necessarily universal.

In turn, the Global North draws conclusions by studying the cases of countries in the Global South as if they were raw data in the process of being 'data mined', that is, inputs to validate their theories

(Connell, 2007). But very little attention is paid to new subaltern ideas or theories that come from these countries and which could question this universality. Given this, a 'situated knowledge' is proposed, a concept originally introduced in feminist studies to think about points of view and the particularities of certain scientific postulates according to the perspective from which they are produced. It is a concept that also reinforces the need to look beyond the universal and attend to variations in different stories and contexts.

Based on some of these lines of research, southern criminology (Carrington et al, 2016; Carrington et al, 2019) points out that criminology has been a fundamentally a product of the Global North, which is reluctant to enrich itself with the experiences and ideas of the Global South. This, until very recently, has not been a focus of imagination for criminology. On the contrary, it has maintained a position practically subordinate to the theories and concepts developed by the North. Most of the time, they have assumed them uncritically to try to apply them in very different realities. People only need to think about Lombroso's interest in Australia, New Zealand or South America to find examples of 'atavistic' criminals, the centrality of urban versus rural spaces for the first Chicago criminologists and the difficulty of considering functionalist theories in peacetime for large areas of the world living in warfare (Carrington et al, 2019).

Furthermore, it is highlighted that currently criminology is dominated by a number of English-speaking countries and their publications, conferences, universities and publishers (Faraldo-Cabana, 2018). Understood as a new lingua franca, such 'academic products' in English undoubtedly contribute to exchange, but without other initiatives they also contributes to the marginalizing of such products in other languages (and Europe has many).

While postcolonial approaches are often critical of and directly reject this dominance of the North, southern criminology is more seduced by a horizontal (and not vertical) collaboration and an intellectual motivation or revitalization motivated by processes and forces that transcend national limits (Carrington et al, 2016; Carrington et al, 2019). This also bets on a fuller consideration of the implications of a globalized era, with a myriad of problems and where the relations of cause and effect as well as the behaviours and social damages that they produce, transcend countries. Scholarship has been aware of the consequences of globalization on business expansion and also of the new opportunities and modalities for corporate crimes and social, economic and environmental damage that link decision making in Global North countries with effects on other parts of the world and discuss the traditional importance of sovereignty and nation-states against certain international regulatory bodies and large transnational corporations (Friedrichs 2010; Rothe and Friedrichs 2015; van Wingerde and Lord, 2020).

However, this recognition has not necessarily modified the epistemological bases of the Global North to think about corporate crimes and harms, nor has it opened curiosity about certain cases or thoughts forged in countries in subordinate positions in the field of knowledge, as mentioned previously. Europe can represent the Global North geographically. But within it, historically, it has had different relations of subordination.

Also the need to recover cultural traditions and insights that run through some works (see Lord et al, this volume; Maesschalck, this volume) should lead us to important clarifications about the sense in which we use the concept of culture: which can be very different when we speak of Mediterranean culture, the culture of late modernity or business culture. Simultaneously, it could be very insightful to pay attention to legal and even linguistic variations between the different European countries that allow for describing cases or explaining them in another way, understanding the various public attitudes to crimes, breaking pre-established postulates and showing counterintuitive realities that should not be ruled out for contradicting general sentences. I think that this search also comes close to some studies on the comparative criminal justice system carried out by European authors who have also shown a research interest in white-collar crime (see Nelken, 2011; Karstedt, 2012).

European essence or European diversity?

According to what has been said previously, I tend to believe that looking for a European essence that is univocal and differentiated from the North American tradition – and also, of course, from anywhere else – in the characteristics of cases or the traditions of academic studies or legal practices in relation to white-collar and corporate crime can be a complex or unnecessarily forced endeavour that, more than solidity, shows its fragility.

I think it would most likely end up integrating a few comparable European countries and in some way denying others. I have no concrete information on Europe regarding citation analysis on white-collar crime but I would be encouraged to consider that a methodologically acceptable cross between studies similar to those based on citations (that is, Cohn et al, 2014) and criminological publications in various

European languages (see Faraldo-Cabana, 2018) would also show a significant concentration of authors – probably male – and universities in Anglophone countries or close to this tradition than some other European countries, such as the Mediterranean, for example.

However, I do see it as possible and inspiring to unleash European multiplicity, its cultural, legal and language diversity that is probably impossible to replicate anywhere else. This gives added value to points of view that can coexist. Not only as a 'European lab' for testing theories or 'what works' in prevention (Maesschalck, this volume) but as a concert where you can enjoy the solos of multiple instruments.

I am not trying here to romanticize the European theoretical virtues, the plurality of languages and cultures, because they are necessarily intertwined with centuries of complex economic, political and social history of conquests, wars, colonization, religious disputes and internal conflicts.

However, I cannot forget that Europe has a much older record and discussion of economic crimes than America. Various authors have pointed out offenses from ancient Greece that we could study today as white-collar crime (Geis, 2007; Walburg, 2020). Furthermore, in Italy 900 years ago the first discussions took place on the possibility of corporate criminal liability against transgressions of European principalities and universities. Hence, the famous expression of the *ius commune*, '*societas delinquere non potest*', which has so far marked one of the most recurrent philosophical-legal oppositions to the prosecution of corporations.

The existence of a criminal law and even less an economic criminal law can hardly be affirmed prior to the birth of modern criminal law during 18th century. Although it might be more proper to say not before the 19th century, when state regulation and intervention in the economy in unified Germany and other countries developed an extensive criminalization unthinkable for the laissez-faire model (Vervaele and Hernández, 2011).

That moment is also the birth of the positivist criminology that would build the first attempts to scientifically explain criminal behaviour and Lombroso will already express, from his anthropological perspective, some considerations about 'latent' delinquent men, of great power and masked in their social position (Geis, 2007). It is in the face of the challenges of these changes that Adolphe Prins, Gérard Van Hamel and Frank Von Liszt created the Internationale Kriminalistische Vereinigung (IKV). At the beginning of the 20th century, the criminologist William Bonger, strongly inspired by the descriptions and theorizations of Karl Marx and Friedrich Engels and their criticisms of the criminal behaviour of capitalist society, became interested in the 'capitalist production of crime' (Heberecht, 2015).

To be consistent with what has been said previously, we must also be aware of the number of other contributions and discussions by authors from European countries that have been subordinated and that need to be recovered. I am thinking of theoretical contributions and authors from the past that are worth recovering, but perhaps also of contemporaries who write about economic, financial or environmental crimes or what we would identify today as a white-collar crime who have had less international diffusion. Naturally, this is true both for works in English and in other regional languages, and for works from academic criminology and from other related social disciplines. Hebberecht (2015) has made us rethink the foundational value of Bonger's writings. Surely we could find other very interesting exponents. In Latin America it has been done better and more systematically in literature or poetry, but certain journeys in the history of criminology in countries such as Argentina, Brazil or Colombia, to name a few, frequently bring us forgotten theories or approaches (Carrington et al, 2019).

Europe has also given rise, since the 12th century, to the accusatory and inquisitive traditions of criminal prosecution, that have been widely reformed to this day in their countries, as well as to the civil law and common law systems. These differences may be much less sharp in recent decades than they were half a century ago, but they still produce significant variations in understanding criminal proceedings and sentencing in Europe.

The links of the Nazi regime with large corporations has given rise to a few investigations on white-collar and corporate crime (see Matthews, 2006; Friedrichs, 2010; Van Baar and Huisman, 2012). These general references (although not always based on these academic works) together with the concept of state-corporate crime have been present in Latin American thinking about the corporate civil and administrative corporation's responsibility and criminal responsibility of managers of large international and local companies for the violation of human rights during Latin American dictatorships. This body of scholarship has been developed much more in Argentina in recent years than in other Latin American countries, due to the number of investigations and criminal sentences regarding 'transitional justice' cases (Centro de Estudios Legales y Sociales, 2015; Asciutto et al, 2017).

Furthermore, after the Second World War, the division into two opposed economic systems in Europe offers a privileged setting for research and discussion in studies on white-collar crime (see

Braithwaite, 1988). The fall of the Berlin Wall, the fragmentation of the Soviet Union and the transition to capitalism of Western Europe in the 1990s generated a large number of hypotheses and national histories that, I understand, go far beyond studies on public and private corruption during the transitions from communism to capitalism.

This also renews the challenge of explanations based on Anglo–American theories and categories and studies within the framework of strong and stable welfare state cultures (Meerts, this volume). In all the Americas we could not find comparable examples. Furthermore, white-collar crime research has become interested in cultural differences (cultural embedding) and diverse political economies. These differences in turn must play with a common market where business regulation has begun to follow in the footsteps of EU legislation and standards and the idea of harmonization. This harmonization is indeed a challenge of its own to the responses of the European criminal law (Nieto Martin, 2007).

It has already been pointed out (Friedrichs, 2015), but it appears as a distinctive note, and from my point of view, a promising one, that compared to the US, European criminology balances more mainstream criminology with critical criminology. This, perhaps, has been particularly present in the UK, Belgium, Germany, Italy and Spain, and translates into much more comprehensive inquiry lines and provocative and ingenious hypotheses; some that are so controversial that we would hardly find them elsewhere (see Tombs and Whyte, 2015).

Conclusion

Europeanness in white-collar and corporate crimes scholarship can hardly be found to have a European essence. This European essence would also be counterproductive, most likely denying the qualities of many of the countries that do not share credentials that are normatively defined as prestigious in terms of their criminal legal systems or their criminological academic development. But this Europeanness can be built from a territorial history and a diversity and multiplicity of academic voices that recognizes the relevance of cultural differences, political economy, legal systems and plurality of languages.

The thinking of southern criminology and the aforementioned postcolonial and de-colonial Latin American studies does not constitute mainstream social science and will not give lessons (nor does it claim to do so). But perhaps they can offer inspiration for rethinking the European criminology of white-collar and corporate crime through the value of diversity. Concepts such as 'situated knowledge' have proposed that all knowledge is produced in particular historical and social situations and, therefore, a questioning of scientific knowledge as universal and neutral just as devoid of political, cultural and social considerations that make it applicable and create a different form of objectivity. These ideas have also pointed out the importance of recovering dissonant voices or forgotten authors who did not integrate mainstream scholarship according to Western scientific canons. These conceptions promote greater horizontality in the production and recognition of knowledge between regions or countries and this idea would be especially enriching in Europe for its great historical, economic, political, cultural and legal diversity.

I have been attentive to the role played by allegations of political and royal corruption in Spain and legal reforms targeting political financing in Italy. I do not have an in-depth knowledge of the criminal policy of Portugal regarding corporations during the rapid recovery from the 2008–09 global financial crisis. I have read that there has been a great questioning of the environmental policies of the Nordic countries. Anyway, I am sure that in these places we would find theoretical approaches that enrich those of white-collar crime that other European countries produce from categories or cases that happened in the US and elsewhere.

I finish writing these lines in a still uncertain year, marked by the COVID-19 pandemic, in which commerce, academic life and other interactions are becoming highly digitized. On the other hand, large and small corporations are redefining their ways of working and future production, and a growth in the pharmaceutical industry is expected internationally and probably also from the ethical and legal implications of many of its decisions at the global level. It will be interesting to read this collection again in a few years and look back.

References

Asciutto, E., Hidalgo, C. and Izaguierre, I. (eds) (2017) *Negocios y Dictadura: La Conexión Argentino-Italiana*, Buenos Aires: Imago Mundi.

Böhm, M.L. (2020) *Empresas Transnacionales, Recursos Naturales y Conflicto en América Latina: Para una Visibilización de la Violencia Invisible*, Buenos Aires: UBA.

Braithwaite, J. (1988) 'White-collar crime, competition, and capitalism: comment on Coleman', *American Journal of Sociology*, 94: 627–32.

Carrington, K., Hogg, R. and Sozzo, M. (2016) 'Southern criminology', *British Journal of Criminology*, 56(1): 1–20.

Carrington, K., Hogg, R., Scott, J., Sozzo, M. and Waters, R. (2019) *Southern Criminology*, London: Routledge.

Carrington, K., Dixon, B., Fonseca, D., Rodríguez Goyes, D., Liu, J. and Zysman, D. (2019) 'Criminologies of the Global South: critical reflections', *Critical Criminology*, 27: 163–89.

Centro de Estudios Legales y Sociales (2015) 'Responsabilidad empresarial en delitos de lesa humanidad: represión a trabajadores durante el terrorismo de estado', Ministerio de Justicia, Buenos Aires, Available at: www.cels.org.ar/web/publicaciones/responsabilidad-empresarial-en-delitos-de-lesa-humanidad-represion-a-trabajadores-durante-el-terrorismo-de-estado-tomo-i/

Connell, R. (2007) *Southern Theory: The Global Dynamics of Knowledge Social Science*, Crows Nest: Allen and Unwin.

Cohn, E.G., Farrington, D.P. and Iratzoqui, A. (2014) 'Citation analysis in criminology and criminal justice', in E.G. Cohn, D.P. Farrington and A. Iratzoqui (eds) *Most-Cited Scholars in Criminology and Criminal Justice, 1986–2010,* New York: Springer, pp 1–13.

de Sousa Santos, B. (ed) (2008) *Another Knowledge Is Possible: Beyond Northern Epistemologies*, London: Verso Books.

Dussel, E. (2016) *Filosofías del Sur. Descolonización y Transmodernidad*, México: Akal.

Faraldo-Cabana, P. (2018) 'Research excellence and Anglophone Dominance: the case of law, criminology and social science', in K. Carrington, R. Hogg, J. Scott and M. Sozzo (eds) *The Palgrave Handbook of Criminology and the Global South*, New York: Springer, pp 163–81.

Friedrichs, D.O. (2010) *Trusted Criminals: White Collar Crime in Contemporary Society* (4th edn), Belmont: Cengage Learning/ Wadsworth.

Friedrichs, D.O. (2015) 'White-collar crime in Europe: American reflections', in J. van Erp, W. Huisman and G. Vande Walle (eds) *The Routledge Handbook of White-Collar and Corporate Crime in Europe,* Abingdon: Routledge, pp 570–82.

Geis, G. (2007) *White-Collar and Corporate Crime*, Upper Saddle River: Pearson.

Graham, M., Hal, S.A. and Stephens, M. (eds) (2011) *Geographies of the World's Knowledge* (ed. Flick, C.M.), London: Convoco Edition.

van Erp, J., Huisman, W., Vande Walle, G. and Beckers, J. (2015) 'Criminology and white-collar crime in Europe', in J. van Erp, W. Huisman and G. Vande Walle (eds) *The Routledge Handbook of White-Collar and Corporate Crime in Europe*, Abingdon: Routledge, pp 1–21.

Hebberecht, P. (2015) 'Willem Bonger: the unrecognized European pioneer of the study of white-collar crime', in J. van Erp, W. Huisman and G. Vande Walle (eds) *The Routledge Handbook of White-Collar and Corporate Crime in Europe*, Abingdon: Routledge, pp 147–54.

Karstedt, S. (2012) 'Comparing justice and crime across cultures', in D. Gadd, D.S. Karstedt and S.F. Messner (eds) *The SAGE Handbook of Criminological Research Methods*, London: Sage, pp 373–90.

Langer, M. (2007) 'Revolution in Latin American criminal procedure: diffusion of legal ideas from the periphery', *The American Journal of Comparative Law*, 55(4): 617–76.

Matthews, R.A. (2006) 'Ordinary business in Nazi Germany', in R.J. Michalowski and R.C. Kramer (eds) *State-Corporate Crime*, New Brunswick: Rutgers University Press.

Mignolo, W.D. (2007) 'Introduction: Coloniality of power and de-colonial thinking', *Cultural Studies*, 21(2/3): 155–67.

Nelken, D. (ed) (2011) *Comparative Criminal Justice and Globalization*, London: Routledge.

Nieto Martin, A. (2007) 'Americanización o europeización del Derecho Penal económico?', *Revista Penal*, 19: 120–36.

Rothe, D.L. and Friedrichs, D.O. (2015) *Crimes of Globalization: New Directions in Critical Criminology*, New York: Routledge.

Rodriguez Goyes, D. (2019) *Southern Green Criminology: A Science to End Ecological Discrimination*, Bingley: Emerald.

Sutherland, E.H. (1949) *White Collar Crime*, New York: The Dryden Press.

Tombs, S. and Whyte, D. (2015) *The Corporate Criminal: Why Corporations Must Be Abolished*, Abingdon: Routledge.

Van Baar, A. and Huisman, W. (2012) 'The oven builders of the Holocaust: a case study of corporate complicity in international crimes', *British Journal of Criminology*, 52: 1033–50.

van Wingerde, K. and Lord, N. (2020) 'The elusiveness of white-collar and corporate crime in a globalized economy', in M. Rorie (ed) *The Handbook of White-Collar Crime*, Hoboken: Wiley-Blackwell, pp 469–83.

Vervaele, J.A. and Hernandéz, H. (2011) 'Un enfoque histórico al derecho penal económico y financiero', in *Estudios de Derecho Penal Económico y Financiero. Reflexiones Jurídicas y Políticas*, *3*, Available at: http://dspace.library.uu.nl/handle/1874/235900

Walburg, C. (2020) 'White-collar and corporate crime: European perspectives', in M. Rorie (ed) *The Handbook of White-Collar Crime*, Hoboken: Wiley-Blackwell, pp 335–46.

18

Learning (Multiple) Lessons from Europe: Criminological Scholarship on White-Collar Crime

Fiona Haines

For those of us despairing at the state of our own countries' attitude towards corporate crime and corporate harm, fed in part by a toxic relationship between business and government, we often look to Europe as the – albeit relative – beacon of hope. European commitment to social welfare (Taylor-Gooby et al, 2017), human rights (Blauberger and Schmidt, 2017), unionization and union representation in management and control of business (Hall and Soskice, 2001) and the promotion of the precautionary principle in terms of risk reduction (Davis and Abraham, 2011), as well as the relatively more progressive attitude to environmental damage (Neslen, 2017), are aspects that most readily come to mind. Each of these has significance in terms of reducing corporate crime: inequality, generated in part by an abdication to the demands of capital, breeds division and crime (Pickett and Wilkinson, 2010); a strong union presence in workplaces reduces income disparity and generates higher standards of workplace health and safety (Walters and Nichols, 2009); and the push for more meaningful action on climate change, in which Europe has been at the forefront, both in terms of the activities of European governments but also NGOs and citizens, keeps governments accountable (Urgenda Foundation, 2019).

The chapters in this book act as an important counter to this one-sided view. They document and demonstrate the pervasive nature of corporate and white-collar crime across Europe. But the chapters do much more than this. Taken together, they shed considerable light on the contribution of a European perspective on a literature often dominated by US perspectives and Anglophone perspectives more broadly.

This reflection is framed around several critical questions that may assist in pushing this initiative further, concerning units of analysis, addressing challenges in comparative work, orientations toward the study of white-collar crime and finally thinking through different ways to collaborate. Certainly, there are significant insights provided in the chapters to these questions, yet in what follows I outline how continued attention to them may reap further benefits.

Firstly, there is continued benefit in asking questions concerning how choices around units of analysis, in addition to the foci of analysis, shape what is seen as critical to developing European perspectives or a European character to the study of white-collar crime. Not surprisingly, in a volume that is aimed at fleshing out European contributions, the unit of analysis geographically is often focused on how the national context interacts with the European project. Alongside this, a related focus is on specific offences, forms of corporate harm or control strategies. Geographical location, together with their respective legal and regulatory institutions are used to shed light on the nature of corporate or regulatory behaviour, while that behaviour in turn is used to shed light on questions of geography and institutional design. Between these two dimensions, rich insights are gained into both place and behaviour.

Keeping hold of both dimensions while questioning, more specifically, what the unit of analysis is, is a challenging task. But it is important. So, in terms of place – does the unit of analysis focus on local, national or regional levels? Moving to behaviour, is this defined by offence, harm or legal category? Critically, how does the unit of analysis bring both place and behaviour together? When these concerns are rigorously addressed, research can explore both commonality and difference in a meaningful way, as several chapters in this volume show. In the final section of this chapter, I offer a field perspective as a potential complementary method of thinking about how to take proper account of place and behaviour and the relationship between the two. Such an approach can also acknowledge more general influences outside of a specific field as well as resonance between different locations and different forms of corporate misbehaviour and attempts at control.

The second set of questions encompass critical criminological concerns related to the vantage point of the scholar and the substance of their concern. The study of corporate and white-collar crime spans distinct orientations of scholarship: from a comparative analysis that seeks to 'fix' the object of study (whether in attempting a unitary definition of what is and what is not white-collar crime, or what is and is not corruption and so on), to the more interpretive traditions that take the ambiguity of definitions in law and scholarship as a starting point for deeper interrogation into place and its political and economic contours, within which ambiguity arises. Finally, white-collar crime is well served by radical or critical criminology. Within this latter orientation there are important differences in instances where businesses are held to account through criminal or other forms of penalty. For example, those arguing within a frame of Gramscian counter-hegemony might take heart from these instances of accountability in terms of the partial leverage they may provide to chart a path to more thoroughgoing change. Those adhering to a more thoroughgoing structural (including, but not limited to Marxist) orientation would be more likely to view the same instances as problematic, as a distraction and an illustration of wasted effort that allows business and government to sidestep the structural change that is necessary.

Finally, given the very different perspectives and entry points into the questions generated by the chapters of this volume, this contribution invokes the question of collaboration. It reflects on what kind of collaboration between the scholars here and the broader network might generate the greatest potential for extending criminological knowledge and intervention in to the political and policy landscape governing the actions of business.

Deciding on the unit of analysis

There are a wide variety of answers to the question of what constitutes a European perspective, as provided by the chapters in this volume. Not surprisingly, geography and (in particular EU) institutions feature prominently. For some chapters, Europe is primarily represented by one country within the region (see, for example, Meerts, and McGrath, this volume; Healy, this volume), comparison between a selection of individual European countries (van Erp and van der Linden, this volume) or the statistics produced by European bodies. In other chapters it is the difference between one or more countries within Europe and those outside, for example whether white-collar crime (such as market abuse) is understood as 'victimless' or not (Wilson, this volume) or the impact of a European multinational MNC on less well-resourced countries outside of Europe.

The exclusive focus on European nations and EU institutions as providing the primary foci of analysis with respect to place provides a timely reminder that a focus on Europe independent from comparison outside the region has significant benefits. Firstly, it is a critically important region in its own right and secondly, for those of us from outside of the region, it provides an important comparator to research coming from outside of Europe with explicit or implicit claims regarding what is 'normal' when it comes to white-collar crime or the response to it. It is a timely reminder of how place shapes regulatory norms, such as the role of lawyers in reporting money laundering (Benson, this volume) or the emphasis on administrative law in combatting market abuse (Wilson, this volume).

Furthermore, reading many of the chapters it is the (arguably ever increasing) diversity and variation within Europe, and indeed within European countries themselves, that is striking. This variation provides rich terrain for comparison within Europe (Lord et al, this volume), with the suggestion made by Maesschalck that European countries provide the ingredients for comparative analysis in the form of a natural experiment where key similarities provide the ideal context for searching out variation and the reasons behind that variation between European countries. This diversity and the particularity of place is critical to understanding the challenges of tackling labour exploitation in post-Soviet Ukraine (Markovska and Soldatenko, this volume), for example, and whether the hope of EU directives simply legitimate ongoing impunity or are able to effect meaningful change.

A particularly interesting study within the collection is undertaken by Davies in his analysis of how labour exploitation between EU nations is contoured. This study highlights the value of both the common EU context (in assessing the value of European directives) as well as exploring how diversity drives exploitation. As Davies explains, labour exploitation is driven by the wealth of the northwest and its ability to exploit cheap labour from within the south and east of the EU. A key question arises as to the role common EU standards are playing here with the central question of whether these standards ameliorate such abuse or, given the lack of enforcement, act as a veneer to allow ongoing exploitation. The answer, as Davies points out, is a complex one, in which legal and regulatory dynamics are met by economic practices of lengthening supply chains and political decisions regarding the temporary nature of worker postings. The value of this study is how the unit of analysis, exploitation of labour market within the EU, can reveal the economic and political character to relationships within the EU that are shaped at several intersecting levels.

The Davies study, along with several others, also hold significant potential for reflecting back on the nature of the EU 'dream' (akin to it 'American' counterpart) and the way different institutional components of that dream shape the nature of corporate harm and potential points of entry in reducing it. It seems to me that it matters a lot whether exploitation is largely derived from elements and pressures found within borders of the EU, since this forms a critical component to evaluating whether regulatory and broader control strategies are able to articulate in a meaningful way with the dynamics of place.

The complexities of geography and deciding where the boundaries of geography are best set are, for any study, met by analysis of particular behaviours or regulatory strategies of interest. A particularly striking analysis of how national (yet, at the same time, European) institutions shape commonly mandated regulatory strategies is Campbell's analysis of Deferred Prosecution Agreements (DPAs). DPAs are used as a heuristic device to reflect on blending of civil and adversarial legal systems. The focus on the regulatory strategy then is tied to the challenges found within the different countries that make up the EU.

A key benefit of thinking carefully about the unit of analysis that connects place and offence, harm or regulatory strategy is to be able to understand what is possible in terms of comparison with other studies with a similar link. Comparison (either in part or whole) requires being able to critically analyze what aspect of the research, with its stated boundaries of study, resonates with other studies associated with developing the European perspective, with white-collar crime research more broadly, and to identify what is unique.

Thinking carefully about uniqueness and resonance may be of particular use to case study research, which is common in scholarship on white-collar crime. As Stake (1998), Flyvberg (2001) and others have argued, a qualitative case can do much more than simply provide insight into a given location and its specific dynamics. To do this, though, requires careful examination of how the specific case is related to a broader context. For some, significance derives from their uniqueness (what Stake terms an essential case) and the analysis may end there in terms of broader significance. However, I suspect many, if not most, of us seek a broader significance to our work – that is, our cases are in some sense what Stake terms an 'instrumental' case. If this is right, then how broader lessons can be learnt is critical. The key to broader significance here is *not* necessarily one of representativeness (cf. Shover and Hochstetler, 2002); rather, it is the relationship between the specific case and the dynamics of the underlying economic, social and political system within which it is embedded. In terms of understanding an instrumental case, attention to the case as 'deviant', and, therefore, unrepresentative, may miss the point. Rather, their value may lie in interrogation of *how* this case came to light, *why* is was vulnerable to public scrutiny and *what* that public scrutiny did or did not lead to in terms of fundamental changes to those underlying dynamics. In the words of Whyte (2014), it is the relationship between the 'moment of rupture' where the case emerges and the light it does or does not shed on the 'regime of permission' that underpins it. For this collection, then, a key question is which of the themes within the chapters can be understood to hold broader relevance, how these lessons resonate with each other and what insights can be gained from this. Taking the earlier argument, this may be as much a question of relationships as it is of discrete phenomena and their representativeness of the broader class or population of such phenomena. Nonetheless, what remains important is not to use those similarities to gloss over important differences and distinctions.

To this end, the key questions posed by Maesschalck are exactly on point. Speaking in the context of control, his questions of 'what works, for whom and under what circumstances' seem well designed to tease apart the significance of context. The earlier discussion would perhaps add to this in terms of how the control/accountability/enforcement effort is understood, and what boundaries are placed around where it begins and ends. That is to ask, which elements of context are co-constituted with the control measure (for example, that tie together the focus of study – offence, control measure or harm – and what are amenable to travel) and, if a control measure is the primary focus, what is possible in terms of experimentation in other jurisdictions? Questions such as these invite a deeper interrogation of similarities that can be followed by thoughtful analysis of what some of the striking differences are and to question what might be some of the reasons for those differences. A conscious approach such as this allows for a building of comparative analyses that follows a more inductive loop to build a rich and robust sense of the challenges of white-collar crime that we face in the present.

Meerts's chapter provides one example that grapples with these complexities of uniqueness and resonance. What is interesting in this chapter on public–private partnerships in fraud investigations is the way she looks to the greater emphasis on the welfare state as opposed to the neoliberal state in the Netherlands (and northern Europe more broadly) as a way to retheorize the nature of these kinds of partnerships in Europe. The particular elements she highlights are important – the contractual nature of many private investigations, the distinct interests of the company as client when compared to investigation by state police or regulatory agencies and how this shapes what collaboration is possible. Some of her work clearly resonates more broadly (see, for example, Williams, 2005). However, with Brexit there is an opportunity to tease out how the tension between privacy (and specifically the EU's General Data Protection Regulation 2016/679) and the desires underpinning investigation (whether by public or private investigators) develops. There is rich theoretical terrain here, too, in terms of understanding the different valences attached to what is private (and the different meanings of that word) and that which should be public and in being so is in the interests of the public to be known (for a discussion in the EU context see Andrew and Baker, 2019). How these contours are drawn have the potential to provide critical insight into how public discourse between the public and private are determined, and the impact of this on business behaviour and the possibilities of more effective control of business crime.

In sum, there is considerable richness to the chapters in terms of how comparison might be undertaken. Thinking further about units of analysis (that tie together what is taken as 'European' and what is taken as 'white-collar crime') and exploring different grounded methods of comparison promises rich rewards.

What is white-collar crime? Orientation to scholarship

The rich criminological work on white-collar crime in the Anglosphere has distinct perspectives on how best to approach the phenomenon of white-collar crime itself. Here, I offer some reflection on how the chapters in this volume resonate with, depart from and extend such scholarship. My purpose here is not to pin down definitions, but rather to tease out the implications of any definition for understanding the relationship between crime, control and place. Firstly, what was notable in several chapters was the emphasis on legal as opposed to largely empirical analysis. That is, the criminological was brought together more explicitly with the legal and socio-legal in a manner often absent in broader white-collar crime scholarship. This seems a very welcome development, particularly when questions of that law are asked: how it is constructed and enforced, what it allows, what is sees as the harm and to whom. The specific legal apparatus, then, is not necessarily only important for its own sake but rather because of the features of the broader context that allow it to be seen as legitimate or fragile, strong or weak, comprehensive or limited. These reflections (and critically the *capacity* to reflect) are made all the richer when there is deep knowledge about that law.

Yet, there were also more familiar criminological strands. The chapter from McGrath and Healy reflected a dominant (and elusive) historical quest for clear definitions and a consensus of what is and what is not criminal before comparison can begin (for a discussion see Nelken, 1997). Their work highlighted well the significant challenges in such an endeavour, while recognizing it as perhaps essential for much comparative quantitative analysis. In doing so, however, what is discarded as distracting from the cleanliness needed for statistical comparison may hold considerable value and point to how quantitative and qualitative approaches might be combined. Qualitative work might be directed to analyzing what has been discarded, to explore potentially different pathways that lead to the emergence of specific forms of white-collar harm as offences. Further, this might allow for examination of tension and disparity between business behaviour and legal definition, to reveal different place-specific trajectories and dynamics in the production of both. The benefit of doing this is to broaden the horizon of how white-collar crime might be compared (that is, the similarities and differences in how pathways to present definitions arise in different places).

There was a wealth of insight in those chapters that emanated from a more interpretivist position, exploring how ambiguity around criminalization or sanction can shed light on the way political and economic context shapes what is normal, illegal and criminal. In doings so, these chapters resonate with early arguments that the study white-collar harm is more suited as an exploration and critique of the society within which it is found (Aubert, 1952; Carson, 1974). Here, there is the interesting analysis by Wilson into market abuse that highlights the different moral valences attached to abuse between Europe and the US, and between different harms and illegalities. Of particular interest is her comment that understanding how white-collar crime and related behaviours are seen in Europe requires analysis of how the behaviour is framed with regards to a broader European project of maintaining peace and security. What is seen as criminal or harmful depends on how it is related to broader goals, while at the same time business behaviours can in turn shape what is considered as consistent or antithetical to those goals. So, the rich analysis of different terms associated with non-payment of taxes is instructive with a shifting focus from tax evasion/avoidance to tax abuse. The shifting from evasion to avoidance is familiar terrain, but the term tax abuse highlights something else by resonating with a deeper social harm than that of the 'game playing' that is associated with avoidance (Wilson). Despite this terminology, the sanctions remain administrative. This is intriguing.

The chapter by van Erp and van der Linden provides a second example of work that reflects an interpretivist approach in their analysis of strategic lawsuits against public participation (SLAPPs), what constitutes a SLAPP and how this differs between the US and Europe. Their chapter places SLAPPs within the context of a European ideal 'based on a balance of powers between the state, entrepreneurs and civil society, to protect individual liberties and civic rights'. This alerts the reader as much to how SLAPPs shape and undermine the European ideal as it does to the particularities of specific examples of the litigation itself. To this end, they compare the potential 'chilling' effect of such lawsuits with the way they may backfire and bring more attention to problematic corporate behaviour. Their reflections on the differences between the EU and US examples are, however, important and chilling in their own right. While much of the literature on SLAPPs pertains to their use by corporations against NGOs, the authors point to their use in Europe against journalists by governments as well as against academics.

This analysis demonstrates the potential of taking an interpretivist stance. Here, the activity (SLAPPs) is used to trace the challenges to the European ideal. The argument is nuanced. It demands that the reader take account of the contradictory tensions within Europe of a growing authoritarianism within some member states as well as the potential for an EU-wide response in terms of the potential for EU anti-SLAPP legislation.

Their work, too, asks for closer interrogation of the question of the relationship between business and government in different geographical contexts. Both can use litigation to silence criticism, and in both this can backfire against the plaintiff. Both can resort to violence. For me, there are additional lines of enquiry to this important project of teasing out the particular relationship between business and government within European states and using SLAPPs, together with related means of quelling dissent, to understand what a robust relationship between the two looks like.

In one way, the strengths of the European ideal premised on strong tripartite relationships, at least in some member states, may also lead to particular vulnerabilities. Understanding how particular institutional relationships can be both beneficial and problematic may provide a more robust understanding of how responses to white-collar and corporate harm can be anchored in and resonate positively with place – what I have labelled as understanding the importance of regulatory character (Haines, 2009, 2005). The analysis of cartel behaviour in Hungary in Inzelt and Bezenyi's chapter, and what it reveals about the (close) relationship between the state and business in that country and in response to EU directives, provides further rich material for understanding how the relationship between business and the state can both generate socially desirable outcomes and undermine them.

Less common were chapters explicitly identifying with the radical tradition. To be sure, this may be as much a reflection of the volume itself than of European criminological scholarship as a whole. Nonetheless, the chapter by Gladkova was clearly placed within this radical tradition, eschewing tight definitions of white-collar crime to uncover underlying power relations that serve the interests of capital. Her chapter traces a rich tapestry of connections between subsidies and the development of technology on continued capital accumulation. What is notable in her analysis is the way she focuses on the nexus between EU policies, goals (of competitiveness between the EU and outside, efficiency, pollution control) and greater market concentration to the detriment of local cultures, animal welfare and ecological resilience. In doing so, she follows diverse economic scholarship (including both Marxist and neo-classical variants) on the way that markets tend towards capital accumulation and regulations (whether aimed at market control or, in her case, pollution control) enhance that process.

There is much to like about this chapter, but perhaps the assertion of a common end point (enriching capital) distracts from critical elements of the puzzle. From an outside perspective, there are clear tensions in the European project as it aims at economic viability, respect for human rights and ecological sustainability. To be sure, managing these tensions may (and perhaps often) involve strong negative economic impacts on the most vulnerable in the pursuit of fiscal discipline or narrow economic goals. But the answer that this tension always supports the needs of capital risks glossing over the way structure is constantly being reinvented and reproduced – and in that reproduction there are potential vulnerabilities that might provide a different way forward (Jessop, 1990). Continued attention to what the unit of analysis is here seems particularly important. Perhaps revisiting, too, the questions of Maesschalck posed earlier, but posed in a slightly different manner; namely, what has disrupted the reproduction and extension of capital accumulation in meat production (even if only temporarily), what benefits were experienced from this and to whom, under what conditions were those disruptions possible and how might they be reproduced and extended? This research might usefully look to growing technologies around meat substitution and its impact on meat-related harms as a way of thinking through which harms are, or are not, associated with capital accumulation (Parker et al, 2018; Seehafer and Bartels, 2019), as well as to scholarship on empowered labour rights (de Sousa Santos and Rodriguez-Garavito, 2005) and work that extends beyond laws, regulation and state-based initiatives and their impact to explore different sites of resistance, for example the food sovereignty movement (Patel, 2009).

Conclusion

In this final section, I map out some of my own recent work and that of my colleagues that has attempted to come to grips with this challenge of drawing on interpretivist insights, the importance of taking account of substantive differences, yet trying to move this in a more radical direction. This work may offer a complementary set of tools for advancing the scholarship in this volume. My starting point is our collective knowledge that both illegal and 'lawful but awful' (Passas, 2005) corporate behaviour – what we might term 'business as usual' – is rapidly depleting the planet environmentally and exacerbating social injustices from modern forms of slavery to dispossession from land and livelihood. At the same time, it creates livelihoods and promises of a brighter future by ameliorating poverty in some areas (while creating it in others). The current system is not just harmful, it also brings considerable benefits – albeit unequally and unjustly shared.

There are significant pressures and incentives to continue down the path of destruction. Part of the challenge is that legal and regulatory strategies ostensibly for control of specific harms can end up collectively supporting the dynamic towards industrial monocultures, as Gladkova's chapter on the food industry shows (see also Haines and Parker, 2018; Parker and Haines, 2018). There is a critical need to examine the 'natural experiment' that Maesschalck sees as represented by Europe, to understand where different futures are being explored and are proving beneficial, and to understand how this might work more broadly.

For this to be productive it needs to meet (at least) three conditions. First, it must respect place: the location where something occurs is important if we are to learn from what is happening. The unit of analysis must be able to recognize how place matters while also taking account of broader influences. Second, there is a need to go beyond a singular focus on a single kind of problem (food, money laundering, occupational crime and so on) that is seen as amenable to discrete control measures. Third, there needs to be collaboration both within and beyond criminology.

In response to the first challenge, I have been exploring the value of a field of struggle orientation as a partial answer to meeting these three conditions (Haines and Macdonald, 2019). From this perspective, the focus of analysis is to understand the rules of the game governing business behaviour – what is and is not allowed and what strategies might be effective in changing those rules and ameliorating harm. My colleague Kate Macdonald and I have used this approach to understand the value of 'soft law' non-judicial mechanisms (NJMs) to provide redress for those subjected to human rights abuse by multi-national corporations. These are often heavily criticized as useless (with justification), but our work suggests a more complex picture. To see what is, and what is not, possible NJMs need to be analyzed in combination with the multiple sources of leverage and obstacles to redress as they appear in a given place. Critically important then, as Rodriguez-Garavito (2017) points out, is not to have an 'all or nothing' view of ways forward; whether the solution is seen as stronger law, enforcement or, in the case of multi-national business conduct, appeals to a treaty on business and human rights. The question becomes how a particular initiative (criminalization, for example) be used as a progressive tool, in combination and in place.

We have adapted the literature on fields of struggle as our primary unit of analysis to be able to make sense of how changing the rules around business behaviour might be achieved. To this end, we have framed the boundaries of struggle around the prize of influencing those rules in a given field. Consistent with a fields of struggle approach, close attention is directed towards specific actors (business, government, workers, local communities, activists and so on) who are drawn into and take part in that struggle to either push for change or maintain the status quo. Importantly, geography or legal jurisdiction does not necessarily determine the field, although it is brought into the struggle in important ways. The field is defined by the actors that are involved in a particular struggle, actors which may be located within different jurisdictions but who nonetheless are involved in either retaining or changing the status quo around a particular harm and its production or amelioration. When the identification of actors and the nature of the struggle is complete, the role law and law enforcement is playing (potentially within multiple jurisdictions depending on the location of the actors) in either supporting or challenging the status quo becomes clearer. The role laws are playing may change with the unfolding struggle. Further, the relationship between those laws and the rules of the game governing a particular struggle are complex. Law, including soft law, together with law enforcement, appear alternatively to be both constituting those rules and strategies to change or maintaining the rules. A field of struggle approach also directs attention to the boundaries that determine who is, and who is not, seen as a legitimate in a given field. Extending or contracting boundaries becomes a key site of contestation between actors, and where extending or narrowing boundaries is successful it can hold considerable potential in changing what is and what is not acceptable business behaviour by bringing in particular actors. Hence, a weak mechanism of control, such as being beholden to a non–judicial mechanism, can effect change if the boundaries of the field are successfully extended to include that mechanism (together with associated actors) and where it comprises just one of a number of strategies to minimize business harm.

This may be particularly relevant to scholarship on Europe. For example, there may be a particular case of corporate harm located outside of Europe, but where the home country of the perpetrator resides within Europe or within the EU. In this case, the supply chain, and which actors along the supply chain are seen as 'legitimate' in the field and, therefore, as able to challenge that behaviour, becomes a key site of contestation. Those who wish for said harm to be seen as a domestic matter for the host country may challenge the legitimacy of those who actors who seek to enter the struggle from outside the host country. Here, the presence or absence of specific actors, including those who can challenge those boundaries and successfully enter the field, have the potential to change the rules of the game. In the European context, for example, a particular country or a particular EU institution which becomes established as a legitimate actor may hold significance for the outcome. One example might assist in clarifying my point here. In corporate accountability research, of which I am a part,[1] one of our case studies is of the mining company Vedanta. Vedanta sought to remove local tribal people (the Dongriah Kondh and Kutia Kondh) from their land in Odisha India to establish a bauxite mine. They were prevented from doing so through a series of hard and soft law decisions in multiple locations, largely orchestrated from within India and specifically by the Dongria and Kuta Kondh themselves. The multiple locations involved were linked through the actors who joined the struggle to prevent (or in some cases aimed to assist) the development of the mine. Vedanta premised its right to access to the land by virtue of a problematic engagement with the local legal system, by which it gained permission to do so. The boundaries of the field were expanded beyond India in part when the Government Pension Fund of Norway decided to divest its holdings of Vedanta because of the protest by the Dongriah Kondh and their allies. Vedanta was forced to take account of their investors' actions, which had a chilling effect on their actions. Further, Vedanta was listed in the UK, and so was negatively affected by the finding of a UK body (the UK National Contact Point) that Vedanta has breached the Organisation for Economic Co-operation and Development (OECD) Guidelines for Multinational Enterprises. However, the success of the Dongria and Kuta Kondh was ultimately secured in a decision by the Indian Supreme Court that required final approval to be gained for the mine locally through the *gram sabha* or village councils. Approval was rejected. To understand this case and its complexities, successes and failures requires close attention to the diverse actors in the struggle and how their presence or absence was or was not legitimated and then to how this combination of actors changes or maintains the status quo. The implication for the research in this book and the European focus is that, depending on the specific dynamics of the field and the actors within that field, there are not only national but also EU institutions that may come into play and significantly affect the capacity to control (or indeed facilitate) corporate harm. Whether specific actors are successful in their pursuit of access to EU institutions depends on membership of the EU of the specific country in question and, in terms of the companies along the supply chain, at least one of those companies being located in an EU member country.

The second condition, going beyond a singular focus, can also be seen as related to the third: exploiting the potential for collaboration. The desire for collaboration is certainly reflected in this collection, whether between quantitative and qualitative approaches or through efforts at building on past research through a deliberative dialogue (Lord et al, this volume). In pursuing collaboration, it is worth critically reflecting on the different forms it can take. Often, collaboration is understood as a joint effort towards a common goal, and integrative synthesis (the dominant view in this collection). However, as Barry and Born (2013) have pointed out, collaboration can take diverse forms beyond this egalitarian synthesis. Collaboration can be characterized more by implicit or explicit hierarchical assumptions where one perspective or conceptual approach is structured to serve the interests of another. This form of collaboration can stifle critique. Their third ideal type seeks to reap the benefits of collaboration without the need for shared goals, an approach they name agonistic collaboration. The idea is to assist and work through a systematic process where lessons can be learnt from other disciplines to assist each in achieving their (separate) goals. The purpose might be as much about mutual learning but also potentially creativity and innovation (also evident in antagonistic forms that militate against the idea of instrumental goals predominating research). The benefit of these agonistic forms is the way they encourage learning from different approaches without the need for erasing those differences. Arguably, it may form the basis for those with divergent views to ask each other difficult questions, rather than speak primarily to those of a like mind, albeit in a manner that does not seek to erase those differences. The effect of this can be that of enhancing the rigour of each project individually, rather than necessarily forcing them into a coherent whole.

In sum, there is considerable richness in the chapters that make up this volume. Taken together, their insights both reflect the literature more broadly, but they also highlight the importance of bringing together complex constituent elements that point to the significance of that resonance while not sacrificing important differences. To assist this valuable project, I have suggested there is continued value in interrogation of the different units of analysis within the chapters that link together what is understood as European as well as what constitutes white-collar crime and its control. This interrogation of boundaries and linkages within those boundaries can then shed greater light on how broader context shapes, and is shaped by, the dynamics at the centre of the study. I have suggested that case study methods that force attention towards the boundaries of the case provide one way of doing this, taking a fields of struggle approach is another. Finally, what constitutes collaboration is also worthy of more attention. Shared goals may be important; but equally so are questions around whose goals and to what end. For me, ideas of agonistic collaboration hold considerable appeal in their capacity to enhance this important initiative.

Note

[1] See: https://corporateaccountabilityresearch.net/research-team

References

Andrew, J. and Baker, M. (2019) 'The general data protection regulation in the age of surveillance capitalism', *Journal of Business Ethics*. doi:10.1007/s10551-019-04239-z

Aubert, W. (1952) 'White collar crime and social structure', *American Journal of Sociology*, 58: 263–71.

Barry, A. and Born, G. (2013) 'Interdisciplinarity: reconfigurations of the social and natural sciences', in A. Barry and G. Born (eds) *Interdisciplinarity: Reconfigurations of the Social and Natural Sciences, Culture, Economy and the Social*, London: Routledge, pp 1–56.

Blauberger, M. and Schmidt, S.K. (2017) 'The European Court of Justice and its political impact', *West European Politics*, 40: 907–18. doi:10.1080/01402382.2017.1281652

Carson, W.G. (1974) 'Symbolic and instrumental dimensions of early factory legislation: a case study in the social origins of criminal law', in R. Hood (ed) *Crime, Criminology and Public Policy: Essays in Honour of Sir Leon Radnowicz*, London: Heinemann, pp 107–38.

Davis, C. and Abraham, J. (2011) 'A comparative analysis of risk management strategies in European Union and United States pharmaceutical regulation', *Health, Risk & Society*, 13: 413–31. doi:10.1080/13698575.2011.596191

de Sousa Santos, B., and Rodriguez-Garavito, C.A. (2005) *Law and Globalization from Below: Towards a Cosmopolitan Legality*, Cambridge: Cambridge University Press.

Flyvberg, B. (2001) *Making Social Science Matter: Why Social Inquiry Fails and How It Can Succeed Again*, Cambridge: Cambridge University Press.

Haines, F. (2005) *Globalization and Regulatory Character: Regulatory Reform after the Kader Toy Factory Fire*, Dartmouth: Ashgate.

Haines, F. (2009) 'Regulatory failures and regulatory solutions: a characteristic analysis of the aftermath of disasters', *Law & Social Inquiry*, 34: 31–60.

Haines, F. and Parker, C. (2018) 'Moving towards ecological regulation: the role of criminalisation', in C. Holley and C. Shearing (eds) *Criminology and the Anthropocene: Criminology at the Edge*, Abingdon: Routledge, pp 81–108.

Haines, F. and Macdonald, K. (2019) 'Grappling with injustice: corporate crime, multinational business and interrogation of law in context', *Theoretical Criminology*. doi:10.1177/1362480619872267

Hall, P.A. and Soskice, D. (2001) *Varieties of Capitalism: The Institutional Foundations of Comparative Advantage*, Oxford: Oxford University Press.

Jessop, B. (1990) 'Regulation theories in retrospect and prospect', *Economy and Society*, 19: 153–216. doi:10.1080/03085149000000006

Marshall, S. and Balaton-Chrimes, S. (2016) 'Tribal claims against the Vedanta bauxite mine in Niyamgiri, India: what role did the UK OECD National Contact Point play in instigating free, prior and informed consent?', Corporate Accountability Research, Available at: https://corporateaccountabilityresearch.net/njm-report-ix-vedanta

Nelken, D. (1997) 'White-collar crime', in M. Maguire, R. Morgan and R. Reiner (eds) *The Oxford Handbook of Criminology* (2nd edn), Oxford: Oxford University Press, pp 891–924.

Neslen, A. (2017) 'Controversial glyphosate weedkiller wins new five-year lease in Europe', *The Guardian*, [online] 27 November, Available at: www.theguardian.com/environment/2017/nov/27/controversial-glyphosate-weedkiller-wins-new-five-year-lease-in-europe

Parker, C. and Haines, F. (2018) 'An ecological approach to regulatory studies?', *Journal of Law and Society*, 45: 136–55. doi:10.1111/jols.12083

Parker, C., Haines, F. and Boehm, L. (2018) 'The promise of ecological regulation: the case of intensive meat', *Jurimetrics*, 59: 1–26.

Passas, N. (2005) 'Lawful but awful: "legal corporate crimes"', *Journal of Socio-Economics*, 34: 771–86.

Patel, R. (2009) 'Food sovereignty', *The Journal of Peasant Studies*, 36: 663–706. doi:10.1080/03066150903143079

Pickett, K. and Wilkinson, R. (2010) *The Spirit Level: Why Equality is Better for Everyone*, London: Penguin.

Rodriguez-Garavito, C. (ed) (2017) *Business and Human Rights: Beyond the End of the Beginning, Globalization and Human Rights*, Cambridge: Cambridge University Press.

Seehafer, A. and Bartels, M. (2019) 'Meat 2.0 – the regulatory environment of plant-based and cultured meat', *European Food & Feed Law Review*, 14: 323–31.

Shover, N. and Hochstetler, A. (2002) 'Cultural explanation and organizational crime', *Crime, Law and Social Change*, 37(1): 1–18.

Stake, R.E. (1998) 'Case Studies', in N.K. Denzin and Y.S. Lincoln (eds) *Strategies of Qualitative Inquiry*, Thousand Oaks: Sage, pp 86–109.

Taylor-Gooby, P., Leruth, B. and Chung, H. (2017) *The Context: How European Welfare States Have Responded to Post-Industrialism, Ageing Populations, and Populist Nationalism, After Austerity*, Oxford: Oxford University Press.

Urgenda Foundation (2019) 'Landmark decision by Dutch Supreme Court', Available at: www.urgenda.nl/en/themas/climate-case/

Walters, D. and Nichols, T. (2009) *Workplace Health and Safety: International Perspectives on Worker Representation*, Basingstoke: Palgrave Macmillan.

Whyte, D. (2014) 'Regimes of permission and state-corporate crime', *State Crime Journal*, 3(2): 237–46.

Williams, J.W. (2005) 'Reflections on the private versus public policing of economic crime', *British Journal of Criminology*, 45: 316–39.

Index

Page numbers in **bold** refer to tables. References to endnotes show both the page number and the note number (231n3).

A

ABLV (bank) **107**, **109**, 114
advice and persuasion approach 19, 21, 23
Aebi, M. 221, 226
African Union 49
aggressive enforcement paradigm 9, 104, 110, 113–15, 116–17
aggressive tax planning 85n6
agri-food industry 128, 133, 134
AgustaWestland SpA 248n5
Airbus SE 239, 243, 245–6
Akzo Nobel 215
ALDI Hungary Food Co. 198
Alexander, C. 244
Allianz Hungária Biztosító 196
All-Union Centre for Public Opinion and Market Research 149
Almond, P. 19, 23
Americanization of economic crimes 272
American privilege 255
American Society of Criminology 255
Amsterdam 58
Angola 57
anti-bribery compliance 59
anti-competitive
  agreements 189
  conduct 196
  intention 197
Anti-Corruption Prosecution Office (SAPO) 145
anti-EU sentiments 4–5
Antigua 144
anti-money laundering (AML) 9–10, 103–5, 113–18, 175
  cases against banks across Europe **106–9**
  compliance officers 117
  enforcement 105, 110, 112, 114–15, 117

violations/breaches 110–11, 113–15, 117
Anti-Money Laundering Directive 89–94, 96, 98
  Fifth 93–4
  Fourth 93–5, 113
  Second 92
  Sixth 93, 95, 111
  Third 93
antitrust rules, European Union (EU) 191
Arbour, L. 41
Argentina 6, 215, 242, 271, 279
Asia 45
atavistic criminals 276
  see also criminal(s)
Attorney General v Oldridge 230
Auchan Magyarország Kft. 198
Audretsch, D.B. 144–5
Australia 5, 208, 239, 271, 276
Austria 58
authoritarianism 293
Ayres, I. 22

B

Baer, M. 244
barristers 100n13
Barry, A. 298
Basel Committee on Banking Supervision Statement of Principles on the Prevention of Criminal Use of the Banking System for the Purpose of Money Laundering 90
Basic Payment Scheme 130
BAT Reference Document (BREF) 131
Bayle, E. 57, 61
BBC Newsnight 213
Becker, H. 152–3
Beijing Initiative for the Clean Silk Road 49–50
Belgium 104, 214, 280

Belitski, M. 144–5
Benson, K. 116
Benson, M.L. 193
Berger, P.L. 153
Berlin Wall 279
Bermuda 144
Bernat, I. 135–6
Bernhardsson, S. 169
Best Available Techniques
    (BAT) 131, 134
black labour market 164
BNP Paribas Fortis 104
Bonger, W. 1, 278–9
Born, G. 298
Braithwaite, J. 22–3, 25–6, 31
Brazil 279
breach of trust 226, 231
Brexit 4, 84, 127–8, 291
British East India Company 2
Bronitt, S. 247
Budai, G. 198
building socialism 151–2
Bulgaria 130, 191
Burdea, V. 58
Bureau of Justice Statistics (BJS) 222,
    224, 226–7
business-administrative groups
    (BAGs) 151
Business History 215

C
Cadwalladr, C. 213
Cambridge Analytica scandal 213
Campania 61
Campbell, L. 243
Canada 92, 98, 208, 239, 272
capitalism 199, 273, 275, 279, 280
    ecological disorganization 135
    embracing 151
    green 135
    neoliberal 129
    privatization of the Ukrainian
        mining 149
    transition to 149, 151–2, 280
capital markets 75, 79–80, 83–4
    see also market(s)
Caribbean 260
Carmichael Coal Mines 210
Caro, E. 168
cartels 10–11, 164, 187–91
    correlations of cases following change of
        regime 199–200
    criminological studies on 193, 196, 198
    without direct state intervention 196–8
cartelism 189, 193, 198–9
case study(ies)
    cartel from political gain (state-initiated
        cartelism) 198–9

cartels without direct state
    intervention 196–8
centred around time series 31
comparative 31–2
European welfare state 176
of farming industrialization 10, 127
local or national 4, 9, 56–7, 60–1,
    65, 170
market abuse 75–85
public-private relations 177
qualitative 67
qualitative and mixed-methods
    approaches 11
sale and servicing of cash registers in
    Hungary 193–6
CBA Commercial Ltd. 198
Celtejo 215
censorship backfire 212
Central America 260, 271–2
Central Europe 191–2
Central Statistics Office (CSO) 222, 226
Centre for Social and Labour Research
    (CSLR) 154
change(s)
    within (legal) context 181–2
    corporate governance 232
    in crime-prevention policy 31
    criminologists 31
    European construction industries 169
    institutional 146
    in labour code 156
    legislative 91, 194
    political 272
    social 134
    structural 135, 146–7
chilling effects 208, 212–13
China 153
Christöfl, A. 58
civil litigation against corporations 210
cognitive justice 275
Cohen, M. 244
Colombia 279
combating money laundering
    see anti-money laundering (AML)
Commission on Human Security 40
commitments 9, 192
    to equality 81
    European 75, 80, 285
    international 45
    moral 116
    normative 117
Committee for the Common
    Organisation of the Agricultural
    Markets (COM) 128–9
Committee to Protect Journalists 216
Common Agricultural Policy
    (CAP) 127, 130

common law
adversarialism 241
and civil law 11, 237–8, 241
consciousness of wrongdoing 82
corporate criminal liability 240
crimes 272
criminal lawyer 239
criminal processes 241
European discourse 76
offence 229–30
securities violations 79
standards 242
comparative research
criminal justice system 223
international 227
in Ireland and United States 221–33
standardized cross-national data 221
competition law
domestic 198–9
European Community 190, 192
European Union (EU) 188, 190, 198–9
Hungarian 188, 190, 192
compliance approaches 33n1
compliance officers 117
computer fraud 224, 226
conceptualizing corruption 62–4
see also corruption
conciliatory approach 29
construct validation 67
consumer demand 129
contingency approach 25
contrived randomness 21
cooperation
ad hoc efforts 179–80
between different national
agencies 184n2
formally structured efforts 178–9
in Netherlands 180–2
corporate and occupational crime 17–33
approaches **20**
defined 18
prevention 21–32
circumstances 27–9
combining approaches 21–4
in Europe 29–32
looking for 'right' combination 24–7
mapping variation in 18–21
research 258
Corporate Europe Observatory 133
corporate investigations market 180–1
corporate power *see* strategic lawsuits
against public participation (SLAPPs)
in Europe
Corporate Prosecution Registry 248n8
corruption
in Afghanistan 42
and bribery 41

and drug trafficking 147
entrepreneurial 146–53
fighting 157
and fraud 39
by government officials in Hungary 60
health-sector 43–4
and ostentation 43
political 145
prioritizing white-collar crime
and 42–3
scandal 57
and white-collar crime 42–3
corruption research in Europe 55–68
conceptualizing 62–4
learning 61–4
lines of inquiry 64–7
mapping research 56–61
national case studies 60
qualitative studies 59–60
specific cases of corruption 61
surveys and experiments 57–9
Council of Europe (CoE) 2–3, 68n1,
209, 214
Council of Europe Convention on
Laundering, Search, Seizure and
Confiscation of the Proceeds from
Crime and on the Financing of
Terrorism 95
COVID-19 pandemic 39, 46, 143,
264n2, 281
corruption during 44
crisis 171n1
epidemic 155
credible deterrence 82, 84
criminal(s) 92
atavistic 276
opportunities for 147
organized 152, 156
procedure 23, 226, 238, 241–2
property 95, 100n17
prosecution 17, 23, 237, 244–5,
274, 279
see also organized crime
criminalization 29, 278, 281
ambiguity around 292
minimum 77, 82–3
and prevention of money
laundering 91–2
criminal justice 210
decision makers 231
investigations 178
model 241
procedure/process 178, 223
statistics 224
system 76, 176–7, 180–1, 183, 223,
226, 242, 277
traditional 153

Criminal Justice (Theft and Fraud) Act 2001 229
criminal law 278
  modern 278
  prosecution under 191
  sanction of last resort 223
  settlements 238–40
criminological scholarship 285–99
  orientation to scholarship 291–5
  unit of analysis 287–91
criminology 271, 274, 276, 280
  academic 279
  corporate 10, 163–4, 166, 169, 171
  critical traditions in 126
  European 1
  green 272
  North American 1
  positivist 278
  socio-legal approach 126
Croall, H. 32, 125, 130
Croatia 214
cross-cultural theory 64
cross-sectional quantitative studies 31–2
Cumbers, A. 131
customer due diligence 92
cybercrime 39, 46–7, 257
Cyprus
  AML cases **108–9**
  monetary penalties 110
  sanctions 111, **112**
Czech Republic 191

D
Dakota Access Pipeline 208
Damaska 243
Danske Bank 2, 114
David–Barrett, E. 59
Davies, J. 153
deception 224, 229
de-colonial studies 275
defamation lawsuits/law 209–13, 216–17
Defence Aerospace 246
Deferred Prosecution Agreements (DPAs) 105, 238–40, 242–7
de Haan, W. 215
deliberative methods and corruption 66–7
  see also corruption
Delphi method 65–6, 68n2
Denmark 132, 134
de Oliveira Guterres, A.M. 43
De Rosa, M. 61
de Souza Santos, B. 275
deterrence approaches 19–20, 33n1
Deutsche Bank 114
Dickel, P. 58
Directive on Criminal Sanctions for Market Abuse (CSMAD) 77, 80, 82–3, 85n1–2

District Court of North Dakota 208
domestic competition law 199
  see also competition law
Dongriah Kondh 297–8
Dos Santos, I. 57
double jeopardy 246
Douglas, M. 20
Dudin, V. 156
Duke University School of Law 248n8
Dutch East India Company 2
Dutch Public Prosecution Office 178
Dutch Public Prosecution Service 175

E
E51 Deposit Company 194
Earthsight 146, 150–1, 156–7
economic violence 42, 50
  see also violence
egalitarianism 20, 24, 28, 81, 83
Egan, M. 133
Electronic Crimes Task Force (ECTF) 178
elite fraud 13n1
  see also fraud
Ellman, M. 151
embracing capitalism 151
  see also capitalism
empirical research 26, 30, 56, 62–3, 128, 261
Energy Transfer 208
Engels, F. 278
England 97, 239, 241, 244, 247
entrepreneurial corruption 146–53
  see also corruption
equal pay principle 169
Estonia 191
Estonian law 59
ethics
  business 19
  management 18–27, 29, 33n1
  morality and 63
  organizational 19–20
ethics management 19–22, 24–7, 29
  literature 23, 33n1
EU Anti-Money Laundering Directives 89–94, 96, 98
EU Farm Structure Survey 129
EU Market Abuse Regulation 190
Europe 1–7, 18, 44–5, 47, 98, 274–7
  about Great Britain 79–80
  construction industry see labour exploitation
  economic prosperity and societal cohesion 45
  essence or diversity 277–80
  identity 83–5
  prevention of corporate and occupational crime in 29–32

provocation 273–4
scholars 261–2
security agendas and policies 40
European Agenda on Security 39, 46–8
European Banking Authority (EBA) 113
European Central Bank 114
European Centre for Press and Media
   Freedom (ECPMF) 216
European Commission (EC) 2, 48, 55,
   76, 80, 113, 154, 188
European Common Market 128
European Community 188, 190, 192
European Competition Network
   (ECN) 190, 198
European Construction Monitor 166
European Convention of Human Rights
   (ECHR) 211, 214–15, 242
European Court of Justice 2, 188, 196–7
European Internal Security Strategy 46
European IPPC Bureau 131
European Labour Authority
   (ELA) 163, 170
Europeanness 75–85, 89, 98
   financial crime 75–80
   macro complexity 80–1
   market abuse 75–85
   micro complexity 80–1
   white-collar crime 75–81
European Parliament 2, 99n10–12,
   100n14–15
European Security Strategy 2003 46
European Single Market 80
European Society of Criminology 2, 5
European Sourcebook of Crime and Criminal
   Justice Statistics (Aebi) 221, 226–8
European Trade Union Confederation
   (ETUC) 163
European Union (EU) 2–3, 7, 18, 30–1,
   55, 68, 89, 111, 145, 154–7, 166–7,
   169–70, 238, 272
   agriculture and farming 127
   antitrust rules 191
   Brexit on food production 128
   competition law 188, 198–9
   instability 39
   institutions 76, 298
   integration 43
   internal and external security 45, 48–50
   international policy and 210
   meat production
      goals and opportunities in 128–31
      regulation in 131–3
      technological innovation 133–5
   member states 81, 211
   regulation 4
   security policy 41

European Working Group on
   Organisational Crime (EUROC)
   5–6, 263
EU Security Agenda 50
exclusion 41, 44, 243
exploitation see labour exploitation

F
Failure to Disclose: Regulated Sector 95
false universalism 59, 65
farming industrialization 135
fatalism 21, 24, 28
Fenergo 114
FIFA (Federation Internationale de
   Football Association) 57, 61
financial abuse 77
Financial Action Task Force (FATF)
   89–92, 272
Financial Conduct Authority 78
financial crime 75–80
Financial Services and Markets Act
   (FSMA) 78, 83
Finland 167
food production harms in European
   Union 125–36
   meat production 128–35
   technological innovation 133–5
   see also European Union (EU)
fragmentation 110–12, 118, 134
France 31, 98, 113, 133, 240, 242
fraud
   computer 224, 226
   deception and related offences 224
   elite 13n1
   food 125
   tax 105, 233n2
freedom of expression 209
Friedrichs, D.O. 195
Fundamental Rights Agency (FRA) 165

G
G7 Summit in Paris 90
Gaddafi, M. 104
Galizia, D.C. 208, 213–14
Garrett, B. 232
Gazprom 144, 191–2
Geis, G. 193
General Anti-Abuse Rule (GAAR) 85n5
General Data Protection Regulation
   (GDPR) 181–2
Generali-Providencia Biztosító 196
Georgia 148
Germany 58–9, 113, 131, 133–4, 167,
   242, 273, 278
Geshov, H. 214
Gill, M. 116
Gladkova, E. 261

Global Economic Crime and Fraud
  Survey 227
global financial crisis (2008-09) 81, 281
globalization/globalisation 45
  on business expansion 276
  international agenda and 273
  jurisdictions outside Europe 222
  and privatization 131
  role in economic growth 41
  threats linked to (political) white-collar
    and organized crime 46
glocalisation 93-7
Gordon v Marrone 212
Gorsira, M. 58, 60
governing through crime 47
Government Pension Fund of Norway 297
Graeff, P. 58
Gray, A. 126
Greece 166
green capitalism 135
  see also capitalism
Greenpeace 207-8
grey economy 164
grid, defined 20
grid-group cultural theory 19-20,
  24, 27-9
gross domestic product (GDP) 154
group, defined 20
Guardian, The 208, 213
Guernsey 144
Gunningham, N. 19, 22, 25
Güralp 245

H
Handbook of Food Crime, A (Gray and
  Hinch) 126
haphazard pursuit 81
hard core cartels 190
  see also cartels
Harrendorf, S. 228
healthcare after COVID-19 43-5
health-sector corruption 43-4
  see also corruption
Healy, D. 224, 292
Hebberecht, P. 279
Hinch, R. 126
HM Revenue & Customs 85n5
Hoban, M. 83
Holtfreter, K. 258
Hood, C. 20
Houtzager, M.J. 164
Hudson, B. 47-8
Huisman, W. 19, 116, 255
human security 40-1
human trafficking 164
Hungarian Association of Automotive
  Dealers (GÉMOSZ) 196-7
Hungarian Competition Act 189-91

Hungarian Competition Authority
  (HCA) 188, 190-9
Hungarian Melon Association 198
Hungarian Opel Sales Brokers 196
Hungarian Peugeot Dealers Insurance
  Brokers 196
Hungarian Supreme Court 196-7
Hungarian Tax and Financial Control
  Office (APEH) 194-5
Hungarian Vegetable-Fruit
  Intergovernmental Organization and
  Product Board 198
Hungary 60, 187-201, 294
  cartels 189-90, 199-200
  state-corporate crime 188

I
independent legal professional 96
in-depth approach 59
Indian Supreme Court 298
individualism 20, 24, 28
inductive-deductive-adaptive
  reasoning 63
industrial farming 136n1
industrialization 127-30, 135-6
informed morality 64
ING Group NV 1, 103-4, 114, 116,
  175, 248n4
insider dealing 75, 78-80, 84, 85n2
institutional changes 146
  see also change(s)
institutional viability 27
insurance market 196-8
Integrated Data Series 222
Integrated Pollution Prevention and
  Control (IPPC) Directive 131, 134
Intensive Rearing of Poultry and Pigs 131
intergovernmental organizations 68n1
  see also non-governmental
  organizations (NGOs)
International Competition Network 189
International Criminal Court 49
International Criminal Victimisation
  Survey (ICVS) 227
Internationale Kriminalistische
  Vereinigung (IKV) 278
International Labour Organisation
  (ILO) 154-5
International Monetary Fund 77
International Organization of Securities
  Commissioners (IOSCO) 81
international standards 94-6
Inter-Professional Law 198
Irish High Court 229
Irish Law Reform Commission 229, 240
Irish Supreme Court 230
Italy 60, 98, 164, 214, 240, 242, 273, 280
Ivory Coast 213

J

Jakarta Statement on Principles for
    Anti-Corruption Agencies 49
Jancsics, D. 60
Jaspers, J.D. 193
Jehova's Witnesses 215
Jordanoska, A. 255
Judeo-Christian 5
judicial reform 42

K

Kankaanranta, T. 164
Kazakhstan 148
Kharkiv 145
King, C. 240
kitchen sink approach 25
K-Monitor (Hungarian watchdog
    organization) 60
Knooppunt FINEC 180
Kosmarskii, V. 149
Kovacs, J.M. 152
Kuciak, J. 214
Kupatadze, A. 147–8, 152
Kuta Kondh 297–8

L

labour exploitation 163–71
  posted workers in European
    construction 167–70
  in Ukraine 154–6
  white-collar and corporate
    crimes 164–6
Latin America 271–2, 275, 279
Latvia 113, 191
law enforcement 59, 114, 145, 148,
    176–7, 179–82, 192, 260, 296
Law Reform Commission 229–30
Law Society 97
Lazarenko, P. 144–5
Leeson, N. 30
legal profession and AML in
    Europe 89–98
  framework 91–3
  global context 90–1
  glocality 93–7
  see also anti-money laundering (AML)
legal reforms 272–4, 281
legislative changes 91, 194
  see also change(s)
Lenin, V.I. 153
Leveson, B. 246
Levi, M. 17, 23, 33n1, 46, 144, 255
libel tourism 211, 216
Lidl Magyarország Kereskedelmi Bt. 198
Liechtenstein 144
Lithuania 144, 191
local contextualities 94
Lodge, M. 20

Lord, N. 17, 23, 33n1, 231, 240, 255
Lotspeich, R. 148
Luanda Leaks 57
Lynch, G. 242
Lynch, M.J. 263n1

M

macro complexity 80–1
Maesschalck, J. 20, 33n2, 294
Maesschalck, K. 261
Maidan (or Euromaidan) protests 145
Manne, H. G. 78
mapping variation, corporate and
    occupational crime 18–21
market(s)
  abuse 4, 9, 75–85, 292
  barriers for 193
  behaviour 79
  black labour 164
  capital 75, 79–80, 83–4
  and cartelists 193
  competition in 11
  competitive Western European gas 192
  corporate investigations 180–1
  economies 176, 183
  egalitarianism 81, 83
  EU common 128–31
  European policies 9
  exploitation of labour 288
  fair and free trade 4, 40, 48
  financial misconduct 78
  freer 131
  global food 130
  insurance 196–8
  integrity 80
  liberalization 131
  licit and illicit 64
  local 130
  manipulation 9, 78, 81, 84, 85n2
  national labour 168–70
  pan-European labour 166
  public goods 135
  regulated 128, 131, 136
  (de)regulation of 10
  Ukrainian labour 157
  unfair and restrictive practices 188,
    200
Market Abuse Directive 2003 (MAD
    2003) 82
Market Abuse Regulation 2014
    (MAR) 77
market-driven approach 133
Markovska, A. 149–50
Marx, K. 153, 278
McDonalds 208, 214
McEwan, J. 242
McGrath, J. 224, 232, 292
McGurrin, D. 263n1

meat production in European
  Union 128–35
  goals and opportunities in 128–31
  regulation in 131–3
  technological innovation 133–5
Mediterranean 277–8
Meerts, C.A. 185n8
Memoranda of Understanding 184n2
mens rea requirements 82
Mexico 271
micro complexity 80–1
Middle East 45
migrant labour exploitation 165
  see also labour exploitation
migration
  controlled 168
  of European capital markets 80
  and healthcare 9
  incentive for 46
  labour 166, 168, 171n2
  mass 4
  patterns 166, 168
  prioritizing white-collar crime and 45–7
  seasonal 168
  temporary 163, 167
  of workers 163, 167
Mikrosystem 194
Minister for Rural Development 199
Ministry of Finance 194
Ministry of Rural Development 198
misconduct in financial markets 80
modern slavery 164
money laundering 79, 226
  across Europe 9
  combating/fighting 99n12, 147
  corruption and 214
  data 228
  environmental pollution and 5
  in Europe 103–18
    aggressive enforcement
      paradigm 113–15
    cases against banks 105–10, **106–9**
    fragmentation 110–12
    risk 115–17
  within European discourse 79
  offence of 90, 96, 226, 260
  and organized crime 42
  risk 95
  role of financial institutions in 91
  role of lawyers in facilitating 98
  and terrorism/terrorist financing 89,
    94, 96, 99n9, 100n14, 272
  in UK 96
  see also anti-money laundering (AML)
Money Laundering and Counter-Terrorist
  Financing (Prevention) Act (AML/
  CTF Act) 103–4

moonlighting 185n6
moral entrepreneurs 64
morality see informed morality
Morris, D. 208, 214
Mosher, C.J. 227
multilateralization 183–4
multiple case studies design 30–1
Mungiu-Pippidi, A. 147
Muttilainen, V. 164
mutual evaluation process 91
mutuality approach 20
Mutual Legal Assistance Treaties 184n2
Myles v Sreenan 229–30

N
National Anti-Corruption Bureau
  (NABU) 145
National Bank of Belgium 104
national case studies 60
National Cash Register and Taxameter
  Technical Committee 194
negative feedback 27
negotiated justice 240, 247
Nelken, D. 33
neoliberal capitalism 129
  see also capitalism
nepotism/cronyism 62
Netherlands 57–8, 61, 98, 103, 111, 113,
  132–4, 167, 175–84, 240
  cooperation 180–2
  public-private relationships 178–80
Netherlands Public Prosecution Service
  (NPPS) 103–4
News of the World, The 61
New York Central & Hudson River
  Railroad Co. v United States 212 U.S.
  481 (1909) 245
New York Supreme Court 212
New Zealand 276
non-adversarial justice 240
non-governmental organizations
  (NGOs) 46, 127, 208–11, 293
non-judicial mechanisms (NJMs) 296
non-prosecution agreements (NPAs) 244
non-systemic banks 114
non-trial resolutions (NTRs) 238,
  240, 246
Nordea 114
normative commitments 117
North America 209, 260, 271–2
  authors **259**, 259–61
  criminology 1
  dominance 4
  scholars 261–2
North Atlantic Treaty Organization
  (NATO) Summit Declarations 42
Northern District of California 207

Northern Ireland 97, 127–9, 131–2, 134–6

O

occupational crimes 2, 18, 20–1, 24, 26–32, 295
Odisha, India 297
OECD Anti-Bribery Convention 240
OECD Foreign Bribery Report 240
Office for Professional Body Anti-Money Laundering Supervision (OPBAS) 97
oligarchs 214
Ontario Supreme Court 208
Organisation for Economic Co-operation and Development (OECD) 85n6, 189, 238, 242, 247, 272, 298
organizational crime 2, 18, **56**, 176
organizational ethics 19–20
    see also ethics
organized crime 39, 42–3, 46–9, 60–1, 146, 148, 164, 213, 260
organized criminals/criminality 148, 152, 156
    see also criminal(s)
Oslo Outcome Statement on Corruption 49

P

Pakes, F. 228
Paris Agreement 48–9
Passas, N. 126, 128
patteggiamento 248n5
PEN International 216
Perri 6 27
phantomization of firms 201n1
Pilatus Bank 114
Platform to Promote the Protection of Journalism and Safety of Journalists 214
Podgor, E. 229
Poland 191, 214
politics/political
    ambiguous legislation 157
    business-centric 195
    campaigning 63
    changes 272
    collusion 145–53, 156
    competitiveness 148
    conditionality 152
    corruption 145, 147, 156, 214
    crisis of 2014 145
    and cultural environment 30
    and cultural human rights 41
    decision-makers 64
    destructive entrepreneurs 149–51
    dysfunction and social disunity 43
    economies and 12, 63–5, 67, 129, 136, 187, 199, 274, 287–8

elites 1, 9, 63, 144, 152–3, 200, 209–10
    exploitation of labour in Ukraine 152–3
    gain (state-initiated cartelism) 198–9
    governmental policy and 195, 196
    influence and protection 150
    leadership 146
    and legal entrepreneurship 145, 148, 152–3, 157
    legitimate businesses and 157
    Maltese 213
    and media advocacy groups 216
    motivated corrupt entrepreneurship 144
    motivated entrepreneurship 10, 146
    national policies and 118
    nature of opportunities 148
    neoliberal capitalism 129, 222
    and non-governmental organization 127
    organizational funding 63
    pluralism 187
    power 148, 199
    processes 134
    rights and free speech 211
    risks 85
    and social reform 147
    and sociological fascination 60
Porsche Biztosítási Alkusz 196
Portugal 57, 166
positive feedback 27
post-Brexit Britain 84–5
postcolonial studies 275
Posted Workers Directive 164, 168–9, 171
post-soviet development 146–53
poverty 41, 44–5, 155, 295
Prins, A. 278
prioritizing white-collar crime 39–50
    corruption and 42–3
    EU internal and external security 48–50
    healthcare after COVID-19 and 43–5
    migration and 45–7
    proceeding with 47–8
    security 40–1
privatization 149, 151, 157, 177–8, 183
Probo Koala scandal 213
pro-Brexit Leave.EU campaign 213
Proceeds of Crime Act (POCA) 94–5
Progress 149
Prohibition of Unfair and Restrictive Market Practices 190
provocation 273–4
public-private relationships (PPPs) 176, 178–81
Punch, M. 30
Pusch, N. 258

Q

qualitative research 177, 223, 233, 258, 261–3

qualitative studies 56, 59–60
quantitative research 228, 262
Quinney, R. 44
quintessential white-collar offence 224

R

Racketeer Influenced and Corrupt
  Organizations (RICO) Act 207
radicalization 27, 39, 49
Rakké, J.T. 116
Ramos-Horta Report 43
Rayner, H. 57, 61
realist evaluation 27, 31, 33n3
Recommendations 46–7 49
regulatory enforcement pyramid 114
Rein, M. 25–6, 30
reparation 248n6
Reporters Without Borders 216
Resolute Forest Products 207–8
respondeat superior 245
responsibilization 183
  of legal professionals 116
  and multilateralization 178, 183–4
  private and public failure 177
  privatization and 176, 183
responsive regulation 22–3
  regulatory pyramid 25
  restorative justice approach to 26
  and social systems theory 261
  'tit-for-tat' approach 26
restorative justice approach 26
risk(s)
  assessment 96
  based approach 93
  based regulation 25
  businesses 168
  capital 294
  of collusion 28
  de-risking clients and services 117
  egalitarianism 28
  of employee theft 28
  and excesses 28
  falsely particular 60
  of generalization 12
  labour migration 166
  to lawyers 92
  match fixing 59
  minimization 193
  money laundering 92, 100n13, 115–17
  monitoring system 104
  of moral ambiguity 33
  non-compliance 25
  operational 145
  propensity to bribery (passive and
    active) 58
  of shirking 21
  social and economic 76
  transfer of knowledge 180

of vigilante justice 210
rivalry and competition 21
Rodriguez-Garavito, C.A. 296
Roermond scandal 61
Rohingya people 46
Rolls-Royce 2, 243, 245–6
Romania 130, 150
Roosevelt, F. 41
Routledge Handbook of White-Collar
  and Corporate Crime in Europe, The
  (Croall) 32, 125–6
Routledge Handbook of White-Collar and
  Corporate Crime in Europe, The (van
  Erp) 215
Ruhl, J. 136n1
rules and deterrence approach 19, 22
rules-based approaches 19–20, 22,
  24–5, 33n1
rural development 127, 136n2
Rural Development Programme 130
Russia 148, 153

S

Salama, O. 210
Salman v United States 84
sanctions levied on banks **112**
Sarclad 245
Savona, E.U. 164
Schimmelfennig, F. 152
Schwägerl, C. 132
Schweighofer 150
Scotland 97
Second World War 279
Securities and Exchange Commission 239
securities law 80
security
  biosecurity 44, 48
  human 9, 40–1, 43, 47, 50
  in-house 177
  internal and external 8, 40,
    44–5, 47–50
  international peace and 39
  narrative of 42
  over justice 47
  peace and 292
  policies 41, 47, 178
  prioritizing white-collar crime 40–1
  public-private 176, 183
  social 155
  threats 42, 44, 46–8, 50
  types 40
  urban 68n2
segregation 168
Serco Geografix Ltd 245
Serious Fraud Office 247
settling with corporations in
    Europe 237–48
  criminal procedure 241–2

deferred prosecution agreements
(DPAs) 238–40, 242–7
Shearing, C.D. 183
Simester, A.P. 116
Simpson, S.S. 193, 258
Singapore 239
Single Resolution Board (SRB) 113
Sipos, G. 193–5
situated knowledge 276, 280
situated production 63
Slingerland, W. 61
Slovakia 191
Slovenia 44
smart regulation 23
smorgasbordism 25
social changes 134
 see also change(s)
social harms 128, 130, 165, 292
social injustice 275
socialism 151–2
social policy 201n2
social reform 135, 147
sociocultural viability see grid-group
 cultural theory
solicitors 100n13
Solicitors Regulation Authority
 (SRA) 97
South America 5, 260, 271–2, 276
Soviet Union 143, 145–6, 148–9,
 280
Spain 113, 167, 273, 280–1
Spapens, T. 130
SPAR Magyarország Kereskedelmi
 Ltd. 198
SPEAK FREE Act 2015 216
stabilization 146
Stanbic Bank Tanzania 244
Standard Bank (SB) 244
Stand.earth 207
Standing, A. 130
State Authority for Geology and Subsoil
 (Ukraine) 151
state-corporate crime 42, 188, 195
state-facilitated corporate crime 195
state-initiated cartelism 198–9
Steel, H. 208, 214
strategic lawsuits against public
 participation (SLAPPs) in
 Europe 207–17, 293
 chilling effects 212–13
 defamation lawsuits 209–13
 examples 213–15
 public watchdogs 209–12
 Streisand effects 212–13
strategic litigation 211
Streisand, B. 212
Streisand effects 212–13

structural changes 135, 146–7
 see also change(s)
superinjunction 213
Supreme Court of Canada 99n8
surveys and experiments 57–9
Sustainable Development Goals
 (SDGs) 41
Sutherland, E. 44, 77–8, 215
Swedbank 114
Sweden 167, 169
Switzerland 144, 240

T
tax(es)
 abuse 79, 292
 advisers 92
 aggressive planning 85n6
 agreements 272
 avoidance/evasion 2–3, 79, 85n6, 155,
  224, 292
 and customs offences 226
 fraud 105, 225, 233n2
 French authorities 110
 HM Revenue & Customs guidance
  on 85n5
 non-payment of 292
 offences 224
Taylor, G. 116
technological innovation 133–5
Tejo (Tagus) River 215
Temporary Labour Migration
 Programmes (TLMPs) 167, 171n3
TESCO-GLOBAL Department Stores.
 Ltd. 198
Thacher, D. 25–6, 30
theft-prevention policy 28
theory of convergence 242
Thörnqvist, C. 169
tit-for-tat approach 26
top-down approach 111
Trabalzi, F. 61
transitional justice 279
Transparency International 63–4, 260
Treaty of Rome 168
Treaty on the Functioning of the
 European Union (TFEU) 189

U
UK Conservative Party 83
UK Ministry of Justice 245
Ukraine 45, 145, 148
Ukrainian Liaison Office 157
Ukrainian Parliament 150, 154–6
UN Commission on Human Security 40
UN Convention Against Corruption 49
Unfair Market Competition Act 195
UN Independent International Fact-
 Finding Mission on Myanmar 46

United Energy International Limited 144
United Kingdom 31, 44, 57, 59, 61, 111,
    167, 208, 238, 275, 280, 298
  case study 75–80
  criminal offences in 94–6
  domestic law 78
  European about 79–80
  Financial Services and Markets Act
    (FSMA) 78
  lawyers 100n13
  Money Laundering Regulations 94–6
  regulatory/supervisory
    environment 96–7
United Nations (UN) 43, 63, 272
United Nations Convention Against
    Illicit Traffic in Narcotic Drugs and
    Psychotropic Substances 90
United Nations Development Programme
    (UNDP) 40
United Nations General Assembly 41
United Nations Office on Drugs and
    Crime (UNODC) 260
United Nations Security Council 39
United States 3, 5, 113–14, 157, 207,
    227–8, 237, 271–2
  foreign aid 145
  purchase of COVID-19 drug
    Remdesivir 44
  social sciences 275
  white-collar crime 76, 258
Universal Declaration of Human
    Rights 40
University of Virginia School of
    Law 248n8
US Congress 216
US Constitution 216
US Department of Justice 239
US Model Penal Code 229
US Supreme Court 245
Utrecht University 215

V

values-based approaches 19, 22, 24–5, 27
van de Bunt, H. 164
van der Linden, T. 293
van Duyne, P.C. 164
van Erp, J. 19, 23, 215, 255, 293
Van Hamel, G. 278
van Rooij, B. 255
van Wingerde, K. 255
Vast Quantities of Assets (VQA) 49
Vaughan, B. 29
Vedanta 297–8
Versobank AS 114
vertical integration 132
vexatious litigation 211–12
victimization 227
victimless 76, 227, 287

Vietnam 153
violence
  economic 42, 50
  monopoly 183
  physical 47
  systemic 41
violent terrorism 49
vital freedoms 40
Volkswagen 2
voluntary compliance 33n1
von Hirsch, A. 116
Von Liszt, F. 278

W

Wales 97, 239, 241, 244, 247
Warsaw Convention *see* Council of
    Europe Convention on Laundering,
    Search, Seizure and Confiscation of
    the Proceeds from Crime and on the
    Financing of Terrorism
watchdogs
  and defamation lawsuits 209–12
  Estonian financial 114
  K-Monitor (Hungarian
    organization) 60
  public 208–12
Watergate scandal 274
Western Balkans (WB) 42
White, R. 135, 210
White Collar Crime (Sutherland) 215
white-collar crime
  and corporate crime 2–4, 17, 67,
    104–5, 111, 164–6, 170, 176, 233,
    238, 272, 277, 279, 286
  and corruption 42–3
  crime theories 4
  criminologists 45, 50
  in Europe 1–3, 7, 17, 125–6, 130,
    133–4, 136, 164–6
  Europeanness in 76, 80–1, 83–5
  food crime scholarship 133
  fraud and 175
  and healthcare after COVID-19 43–5
  in Hungary 187
  investigation 215
  and market abuse 77–9
  and migration 45–7
  and organized crime 46–7
  political 45, 156
  prevention 19
  quintessential 224
  regulated market and 131
  research 19, 47–50, 215, 222, 280, 289
  scholars 46
  scholarship 255–63
    and corporate crime research 258
    criminological 285–99

European authors/researchers/
  scholars **259**, 259–62
North American authors/researchers/
  scholars **259**, 259–62
orientation to 291–5
in Ukraine 143–58
  early 1990s 148–52
  entrepreneurial corruption 146–53
  labour exploitation 154–6
  political exploitation of labour 152–3
  post-soviet development 146–53
in United States and Ireland 222, 227,
  230, 232

Whyte, D. 136
Williams, C. 130
World Bank 272
World Trade Organization (WTO) 272

Y
Yakovlev, V. 149
Yale Studies on White Collar Crime 224

Z
Zabyelina, J. 149–50